THINKING THROUGH
REVELATION

THINKING THROUGH
REVELATION

Islamic, Jewish, and Christian Philosophy
in the Middle Ages

ROBERT J. DOBIE

The Catholic University of America Press
Washington, D.C.

Coniugi carissimae meae, Aurorae
et Albino Yvetteque, meis dilectissimis liberis,
qui sunt "animae dimidium meae"

CONTENTS

ACKNOWLEDGMENTS

The work of a scholar is never accomplished in isolation. He or she needs the support of a myriad of institutions but, most importantly, the love and friendship of others in order to bring his or her work to fruition. I am no exception.

I wish first of all to thank La Salle University, where I am employed as an associate professor of philosophy. Even when resources were tight, the administrators at La Salle always strove to make financial support available to faculty pursuing worthy scholarly projects. I want to thank in particular the provost, Dr. Brian Goldstein, and the assistant provost, Br. John McGoldrick, for their constant support. Equally important has been the warm support and encouragement of the deans of the School of Arts and Sciences, former dean Dr. Thomas Keagy, and the current interim dean, Dr. Lynne Texter.

I also want to thank the members of the philosophy department at La Salle, Dr. Cornelia Tsakiridou, Dr. Joel Garver, Dr. Joseph Volpe, Dr. Frederick van Fleteren, Dr. Whitney Howell, and Dr. John Hymers, for their warm collegiality. For me, La Salle's philosophy department is more like a home than a workplace, with all of us joined in a truly harmonious and genuine love of wisdom and of the tradition that has passed that wisdom down to us. And I want to thank in particular Dr. Marc Moreau who, when chair of the philosophy department, always gave me crucial support, both moral and bureaucratic, in pursuit of my work and who, as former chair, has given me much needed help in my first years as departmental chair myself, saving me from situations where I was clearly in over my head and giving sage advice when it was sorely needed. He has been more than a chair and colleague, but also a mentor and friend.

I should also dare not forget to thank the librarians at La Salle's

Connelly Library. In many ways the library is the beating heart of the university, for it provides the lifeblood for any student or scholar: books, learned journals, access to scholarly materials, and, above all, the high expertise of the professional librarian in locating often hard to find scholarly work. Specifically, interlibrary loan is a life-line for any scholar working at a university today, and I would like to thank in particular the librarian in charge of interlibrary loan at La Salle, Gerald Reagan, for his patience and determination in trying to find sometimes very obscure and difficult to procure publications.

Most of all, the scholar is ultimately not sustained only by books and institutions, but also by the love and companionship of family and friends. In particular, I would like to thank my dear friend Dr. Gregory Moule for his friendship. Our weekly meetings are a source of continual scholarly stimulation as well as simple pleasure. A published scholar himself, with a doctorate in medieval intellectual history, his questions and critiques have always attempted to keep this often flighty philosopher grounded in historical reality. Whether he has succeeded in doing so, the reader may judge.

Above all, I want to thank my family: first, my parents, Robert Aubin and Margaret Rose Dobie, whose continual love and support throughout my life have made any success I might have attained possible.

I also want to thank my dear wife, Aurora, without whose love, companionship, and aid I would not, I am convinced, been able to secure a teaching position, attain tenure, and survive the first years of being department chair; and my children, Aubin and Yvette, whose unfolding personalities, intelligence, and most of all, affection and love, fill me with continual wonder. This book is dedicated to them.

> Every best gift, and every perfect gift, is from above, coming down from the Father of lights, with whom there is no change, nor shadow of alteration. For of his own will hath he begotten us by the word of truth, that we might be some beginning of his creature. (Jas 1:17–18)

ABBREVIATIONS

De ver. Thomas Aquinas, *Quaestiones Disputatae de Veritate*
         ("Disputed Questions on Truth")

DT   Averroes, *The Decisive Treatise*

DUI   Thomas Aquinas, *De unitate intellectus contra Averroistas*
         ("On the Unity of the Intellect against the Averroists")

In Ioan. Thomas Aquinas, *Super Evangelium S. Ioannis Lectura*
          ("Commentary on John")

SCG   Thomas Aquinas, *Summa contra Gentiles*

S. Th. Thomas Aquinas, *Summa theologiae*

THINKING THROUGH
REVELATION

REASON AND REVELATION
IN THE MIDDLE AGES

MEANING AND VALUE

Medieval thought is born of the confrontation between the claims of a divine revelation and of human reason to truth. I take this assertion to be uncontroversial. It is a topic that has been explored in countless books, articles, and monographs. But what has not been explored, I believe, is a comparative study of how this relation is understood across the three most prominent religious traditions of the Middle Ages: Islam, Judaism, and Christianity.[1] When the theme of the relation between faith and reason or (in a slightly different key) between theology and philosophy in the Middle Ages is discussed, it is usually assumed that we are thinking of *Christian* revelation and its relation to philosophy and rational reflection. In other words, that it is a specifically Christian revelation that philosophical thinking confronts in this period often goes unsaid (unless, of course, one is specifically talking about Jewish or Islamic philosophy). In this study, I want to think what is usually unthought: how the specificity of a particular revelation, and even more fundamentally, the *mode* in which a particular tradition claims that revelation comes to us (that is, the nature of revelation itself), affects, alters,

---

1. There have, of course, been comparative studies on other aspects of medieval Muslim, Jewish, and Christian thought, the most exemplary being David Burrell, *Freedom and Creation in Three Traditions* (Notre Dame, Ind.: University of Notre Dame Press, 1993).

and transforms the understanding of the proper relationship between the claims of philosophy and of revelation to truth.

In looking at the way that philosophical thought was received in Muslim, Jewish, and Christian societies, the French scholar of medieval thought, Remi Brague, makes a very helpful distinction between the "meaning" (*sens*) of philosophy or revelation in these traditions and their "value" (*valeur*). Something may have the same *sense* in two different contexts but not the same *value*. To use Brague's own example (itself borrowed from Ferdinand de Saussure), "sheep" in English and "mouton" in French have the same "sense" or meaning; but the French word "mouton" will sometimes be translated into English as "mutton" and not "sheep," as the words have different values or connotations in the two languages. Thus, we cannot study a Christian, Jewish, or Muslim philosopher without studying not just the meaning, but also the *value* that both revelation and philosophical reflection have within these traditions. To give more precision to this distinction, Brague uses a term coined by Michel Foucault: that of the *episteme*. This term refers to the entire network of related and interlocking assumptions, principles, and understandings that underlie how people in a particular place, time, and culture think about themselves, the world, and their place in it.[2] To take one example, the *episteme* of classical Greek and Roman antiquity—all of its fundamental assumptions about God, humanity, and the world—was fundamentally altered in the Middle Ages by what was absent in antiquity: namely, the emergence of revealed religions.[3] In particular, the revealed doctrine of creation *ex nihilo* challenged the old assumption that the world always is, was, and will be. Whereas for ancient philosophers the order and intelligibility of the cosmos were the foremost philosophical problems, for medieval thinkers, the very *existence* of the world becomes a problem, precisely because the world is now seen as created.

What I propose to do in this study is to take this idea further: not only differences in revealed doctrine but, most importantly, *differences*

2. Remi Brague, *Au moyen du moyen âge: Philosophies médiévales en chrétienté, judaïsme et islam* (Paris: Flammarion, 2006), 81.
3. Ibid., 93.

in how revelation in understood to come to us establish in Christianity, Judaism, and Islam very different *epistemes* which determine, often decisively, not only how thinkers in these traditions understand the relation between revelation and philosophical reflection, but also the degree to which they are able to arrive at an adequate solution to the often seemingly contradictory claims of both. What revelation is and, in particular, the mode in which revelation is understood to come to us is often the unspoken and yet fundamental horizon in which Christian, Jewish, and Muslims thinkers thought and came to a solution, adequate or not, to key philosophical problems of their time (and all time).

MEANING AND VALUE, REASON AND REVELATION, IN ISLAM, JUDAISM, AND CHRISTIANITY

The three major religious traditions of the Middle Ages differ quite fundamentally from each other with regard to the *manner* or *mode* in which they understand how revelation comes to us. Thus, Brague takes issue with the phrase that has become very common today, which characterizes the three "monotheisms" of Christianity, Judaism, and Islam as "religions of the book." Quite apart from the problematic term, "monotheism,"[4] saying that Christianity and Judaism are "religions of the book" is, in fact, a very Islamic (and misleading) way of looking at them. For the Christian, God reveals himself in a *person*, Jesus Christ, not in a "book." The Gospels and the other documents in the New Testament are simply a testimony of the revelation embodied (literally) in the person of Christ and in his personal relationship with his believers. Nor is Judaism a "religion of the book": the Torah is a testimony of the covenantal relationship made by God with the Jewish people through Moses on Mount Sinai. It is this covenantal relationship, through Moses, of the Israelite people with God that constitutes revelation. The writings of the prophets have as their goal the keeping or restoration of this covenantal

---

4. The term "monotheism" is a nineteenth-century coinage and would have sounded strange to medieval theologians.

relationship. Only for Islam is the revelation the *book itself*, the Quran. There is no *personal* relationship with God per se in Islam;[5] there is only a relationship with the holy book enacted by fulfilling its commands. Hence, Brague can claim that "the only religion of the book is Islam!"[6]

Why is it so important to make this point? Well, as Brague explains:

> The very manner in which God speaks, even the style of his *logos*, determines the manner in which the latter will be elaborated. If the divine word is a law, one must explain and apply it with the maximum of precision. But it says nothing about the one who promulgates it. If this word is a person and if, in reverse, this person is a word who is *the very one who speaks*, this leads to a very particular knowledge [*connaissance*] of God.[7]

Islam, at least from the second century of its existence, was very self-consciously the religion "of a book." "To every prophet a Book, therefore Muhammad must have a Book" is how prominent scholar of Islam and Semitic languages Arthur Jeffery put the early Muslim attitude.[8] "Without Scripture there can be no true religion."[9] So for Islam, revelation is nothing other than the book itself and not the one who "sends it down."[10] The point here is that, while the Jewish and Christian scriptures developed out of conflict and debate over a long and slow process whereby believers came to the conclusion that certain works were inspired and, hence, authoritative, because they expressed especially clearly or fully the *relationship* of people with their God, the Quran was

5. I emphasize "personal" here because, as we shall see, there is a relationship with God in Islamic thought, but it is not personal in any significant sense.

6. Brague, *Au moyen du moyen âge*, 20. Also, A. J. Arberry, *Revelation and Reason in Islam (The Forwood Lectures for 1956 Delivered in the University of Liverpool)* (London: George Allen and Unwin, 1957), 10–11.

7. Brague, *Au moyen du moyen âge*, 20.

8. Arthur Jeffery, *The Qur'an as Scripture* (New York: Russel F. Moore Co., 1952), 27. For the rather long and torturous route by which the Quran was produced as we have it today, see the excellent little book by Alfred-Louis de Prémare, *Aux Origines du Coran: questions d'hier, approches d'aujourd'hui* (Paris: Téraèdre, 2004).

9. Jeffery, *The Qur'an as Scripture*, 28.

10. In fact, the word in Arabic that is used in the Quran to describe the mode of revelation is *nazala*, "to send down." Thus, "revelation" is assimilated to a sort of impersonal "emanation."

conceived as a book that would be *prior* to all development and, hence, put an end to all conflict and debate.[11] As a result of this historical and, thus, inter-generational and inter-personal development, the Jewish and Christian understanding of revelation by contrast is one of *testimony*: one that sees as inherent to revelation inter-personal communication, not just with respect to its human transmission but especially with respect to its divine transmission. Thus, this understanding relies on the testimony of many people over long stretches of time (at least for the Old Testament or Hebrew Scriptures—and indirectly for the Christian Scriptures insofar as Christ is seen as the fulfillment of Old Testament prophecies).[12] As Brague puts it quite concisely: "The religion of Israel is a history that results in a book, Christianity is a history that is recounted in a book, Islam is a book that results in a history."[13] What is important here is that it is the *mode* in which revelation is understood to come to humanity that affects decisively also the content of that revelation: "For Islam, God does not manifest himself, but only dictates his will in giving out commandments. It is out of the question that he enter into human history by concluding a covenant with humanity."[14] *How* God reveals himself says much, maybe everything, about *who* God is.

---

11. Indeed, the whole goal of Muhammad's missions seem to have been to give a book or "scripture" to the Arab peoples. This goal, however, was not fulfilled in his lifetime— indeed, it would not be fulfilled until over a century after his death. And the reason for this particular goal—to provide his people with a scripture—was to remove all "doubts" and "disputes" about the "Scriptures." This goal, needless to say, remained elusive even, as we shall see, to the time of Averroes, for whom, as he asserts at the end of the *Decisive Treatise*, it was *philosophy* that was to put an end to all disputes about the Quran! See Jeffery, *The Qur'an as Scripture*, 74. Jeffery notes that Muhammad's claim that the purpose of his mission was to put an end to all disputes about the scripture, was one made before by Mani, the founder of Manicheanism, and, indeed, seemed to have been the primary impetus for his prophetic mission (79). Indeed, one of the primary attractions of Manicheanism seemed to have been its claim to overcome the divisions and sects of the Christians. And as both Jeffery and de Prémare note, a key feature of early Muslim polemic both against Christians and, ironically, among themselves was that Islam was a religion devoid of such schisms and divisions.

12. Although we should note that, ultimately, the whole account of revelation in Islam relies entirely on testimony, but on the testimony of just one man, Muhammad.

13. Rémi Brague, *Du dieu des chrétiens et d'un ou deux autres* (Paris: Flammarion, 2008), 38.

14. Ibid., 44.

If God never manifests himself, then there is no possibility of knowing God, at least not in a personal way.

"INCLUSION" VERSUS "DIGESTION"

Remi Brague also remarks about a fact that should, indeed, strike us as remarkable, namely, that the Christian Bible includes within itself the scripture of a whole other religion. In fact, the Jewish Scriptures or "Tanakh," known to Christians as the Old Testament, makes up the vast bulk of the Bible. This is a phenomenon unique in the history of religions.[15]

The fact that the Christian revelation sees itself as the fulfillment and completion of an older one is the hallmark of what Brague calls an *episteme* of "inclusion." That is, the newer revelation does not erase or render null the older one; rather, it gives it a new meaning and value. To be sure, this new meaning and value are ones that followers of the older revelation will not recognize as valid. Nevertheless, for the Christian, the old covenant with Moses is a genuine revelation and the old law is of divine origin (though fulfilled in Christ). But, Brague argues, we can see the same relationship that Christianity has with its Judaic past hold for its relation to its Greco-Roman past, especially with ancient, pagan Greco-Roman philosophy. Christian thinkers were content to let the ancient philosophers stand on their own and speak in their own voice. The task of the Christian theologian and philosopher was to interpret these texts in a new light, the light of the Gospel. Hence, the commentary becomes the favored medium in and through which Christians appropriated the wisdom of the past and reconciled it to their faith.

By contrast, the Islamic *episteme* is one of "digestion." That is to say, Islam tends to absorb completely its religious and cultural antecedents and transform them into a form that is entirely Islamic. This starts with the Quran, which claims to supersede completely all previous scrip-

---

15. "C'est un fait unique dans l'histoire des religions que le livre sacré d'une religion contienne à côté de soi celui d'une religion précédente. Et le second livre, le Nouveau Testament, constitue comme une commentaire du premier." Brague, *Au moyen du moyen âge*, 283.

tures.[16] Indeed, to this day, traditional Muslim exegetes ignore the Bible completely in trying to explain passages of the Quran (even when they do not make sense without understanding the biblical references).[17] This is why there are not three "testaments" in Islam like in Mormonism. The Quran absorbs or "digests" all that has gone before it.[18] In the same way, Brague argues, Islamic philosophy is a philosophy of digestion. It not only took ancient philosophy and transformed it into a form all its own (thus Avicenna, although an Aristotelian, wrote a whole new "metaphysics" as did al-Farabi before him, which "absorbed" and rendered, in their view, superfluous the works of Aristotle themselves), but it even does the same with Islamic revelation and theology. In a word, the inherent drive of Islamic thought was either to absorb philosophy into the religious law (as theosophy, to take one development)[19] or to absorb the religious law into philosophy (as we find in Avicenna and, most thoroughly, in Averroes).[20] Indeed, the Mu'tazilites, an early school of

16. Although the Quran itself is not quite consistent on this point, alternately asserting the divine inspiration of the Torah and Gospels, while at the same time claiming that they are corrupted.

17. "Le Coran est ainsi comme une paraphrase de l'Ancien et du Nouveau Testaments. On pourrait même aller jusqu'à parler d'un *paratexte*: dans le Coran, les récits bibliques son présupposés." Brague, *Au moyen du moyen âge*, 282.

18. Indeed, the Quran itself and its language show many antecedents. Christoph Luxenberg, in his book, *The Syro-Aramaic Reading of the Koran: A Contribution to the Decoding of the Language of the Koran* (Berlin: Verlag Schiler, 2007), argues that many of the grammatical and lexicographical oddities in the Quran can be resolved by positing under the Arabic text a Syro-Aramaic subtext, much of it derived from Syriac Christian lectionaries (*Quryans*). In fact, Luxenberg posits that the strangeness of the Arabic found in the Quran is due not to any tribal dialect (*Quraysh*), but to an Arabic-Aramaic hybrid that was spoken in Mecca, since there is some evidence that Mecca had Aramaic origins. As a result, due to several factors—faulty transcription of the original Syro-Aramaic script, the defective nature of early Arabic script, and the breaking of the oral tradition—by the time a definitive edition of the Quran was produced early in the eighth century, much of the meaning of the original text had been lost or hopelessly garbled. But, in a sense, this shows how thoroughly Islam is a culture of digestion: transforming into its own form past influences, while forgetting that past as such.

19. Most notably in the writings of Abu Hamid al-Ghazali, Suhrawardi, Mulla Sadra, and, most extensively, in Ibn al-'Arabi's massive *futuḥāt al-makkīyya*. See my *Logos and Revelation: Ibn 'Arabi, Meister Eckhart and Mystical Hermeneutics* (Washington, D.C.: The Catholic University of America Press, 2010).

20. That Averroes wrote extensive commentaries on Aristotle is a case of the exception

Islamic theology or *kalām*, posed the following dilemma: either prophecy is in accord with reason or it is not. In the first case, prophecy is superfluous; in the second, it must be rejected.[21] The great French scholar
of Islamic thought Henry Corbin contrasts this situation with what he
calls the "laicisation métaphysique" that came about in Christendom,
whereby philosophy and theology, knowledge and belief were first made
distinct and then (tragically in his view) separated.[22]

   Thus, while the study of philosophy became an important and integral part of Christian university education (indeed, the arts degree was
in essence simply a course in Aristotelian philosophy and an essential
prerequisite for the study of theology, medicine, and law), the study of
philosophy always remained a completely private pastime in the Islamic world (Averroes worked as a physician and judge, Maimonides also
as a physician and judge of the Jewish community). As a result, when
philosophical thought was pursued in the Islamic world, it was pursued
in a particularly "pure" form—"pure" in the sense that it was *seemingly*[23]
done quite free from theological or scriptural concerns.[24] By contrast,
the institutionalization of philosophy as a preparation for theology (or

---

proving the rule. While we can say that Averroes's work is a counter-example of "inclusion"
rather than "digestion" in Islam, it must be pointed out that Averroes had absolutely no
followers or imitators in the Islamic world. His influence, by contrast, among Christian and
Jewish philosophers and theologians was immense, no doubt due to the "inclusive" nature
of these traditions which found in Averroes a congenial spirit.

   21. Henry Corbin, *Histoire de la philosophie islamique* (Paris: Gallimard, 1986), 71.

   22. Ibid., 26–27. This also led, according to Corbin, to the doctrine of the double truth
insofar as Christian philosophers almost reflexively interpreted the teachings of Averroes in
a manner conformable to this Christian distinction between what we can know by reason
and what we can know by revelation.

   23. I emphasize this word because, as we shall see through this book, the understanding of revelation to which a philosopher subscribed at least implicitly affected quite decisively how he did philosophy.

   24. Thus, Peter Abelard, in his *Dialogue between a Philosopher, a Jew and a Christian*,
hints that the "philosopher" who, although he believes in God, follows only the "natural
law" and not any religious law, is, nevertheless, a Muslim or, at the very least, someone from
an Islamic society. Indeed, Abelard specifically refers to him has a "pagan." Peter Abelard,
Dialogus inter Philosophum, Iudeaum et Christianum, ed. Rudolf Thomas (Stuttgart-Bad
Cannstatt: Friedrich Frommann Verlag, 1970); translated by Paul Vincent Spade as *Ethical
Writings: Ethics and Dialogue between a Philosopher, a Jew, and a Christian* (Indianapolis:
Hackett Publishing, 1995).

medicine or law) is the contrary of digestion: theological truth builds upon philosophical truth, but does not negate it. In the Islamic world, however, philosophical thought was either digested into theosophical Sufism or, as in the case of Muslim philosophers like Averroes, religious law was digested into philosophy, to such an extent that Brague can claim, "it would be false to say that the graft of philosophy onto Muslim culture failed. One can say ironically that it succeeded all too well!"[25] That is to say, the tendency in Islamic thought is for religious law to absorb philosophy, or the inverse, for philosophy to "digest" revelation.

INCLUSION, DIGESTION, AND THE FALLENNESS OF THE INTELLECT

Nowhere does this contrast between an *episteme* of inclusion and that of digestion become more salient than in the medieval doctrines concerning the intellect. Besides our main thesis that the mode of revelation in a tradition conditions the reception and resolution of philosophical problems, it is a further contention of this book that an *episteme* of digestion will conceive the relation of the intellect to human beings very differently than an *episteme* of inclusion. A religion "of the book," which understands revelation primarily as the "sending down" of written commands will necessarily assimilate this understanding of revelation to its understanding of the intellect, namely as a separate and unitary reality, to which the human individual is united as something "other" and extraneous.[26] An *episteme* of inclusion, by contrast, which sees revelation as actualized not by a book but by and through a personal or quasi-personal encounter, cannot understand revelation as the impersonal emanation of a "book" cum "intellect" from "on high": rather, revelation comes to us as a fulfillment and completion of the created order, which orients the believer to its Creator, God, who is outside this order. On this account, revelation perfects the natural order, even the incarnate nature of the

---

25. Brague, *Au moyen du moyen âge*, 104.

26. As we shall see, some Muslim philosophers, in particular, Averroes, strove mightily to avoid characterizing the intellect as "other" and "extraneous" to the individual human being—but unsuccessfully as we shall show.

human intellect, and, by doing so, does not negate what is outside the natural order, but orients the human intellect to a super-eminent, transcendent, super-intelligent being who freely established that order. To deny the goodness and perfection of the natural order created by God is to *fall* from communion with the intellect and will that established that order.

Curious, however, for its absence in the Muslim tradition is any discussion of the intellect insofar as it is *fallen*. Such a discussion is absent because, of course, it is absent from the Quran. But this should not surprise us. If revelation is understood as an impersonal handing down of a book, then this presumes that the human intellect is *not* fallen: there is no inter-personal relationship to repair but simply commands or guidance to follow. This presumes a couple of things: first, that it is not essential that the human intellect be individuated according to the body—as a purely passive recipient of revealed impersonal truths, it is not necessary that the intellect be many; it is sufficient that it be one. Second, it follows that the human intellect can follow divine commands all on its own by its own understanding and own effort. But this opens up a problem in medieval Islamic thought: if the human intellect can follow these commands all on its own, then is not philosophy enough? What need does the unfallen intellect have for revelation? Alternatively, if the revealed book *is* all the guidance that humanity needs, then what need is there for philosophy or human reason at all? In other words, does not the one separate intellect "digest" the revealed book into itself or, inversely, does not the revealed book become in effect the "separate intellect" for all believers?

The Christian tradition, by contrast, has a very different understanding of the relation of revelation to the human intellect. It does agree with the Islamic tradition that revelation is basically intellectual in that it perfects the human intellect. But what does it mean to perfect the human intellect? Is the human intellect perfected as separate and universal only or is it perfected as the incarnate form of the individual human being? The Fall, however, for the Christian, is the rupture of a relationship between an "I" and a "thou," of *this* person with *that* person.

But what individuates the human intellect is the body, the *flesh*.[27] Understanding the human intellect as individuated and, in particular, as *embodied*,[28] in turn, leads not just to differing philosophical arguments of how we understand, but also to a differing understanding of what constitutes divine revelation.

But what is the intellect by nature and by operation? We can understand the term "intellect" or *intellectus* in contrast to the term "reason" or *ratio*: "Often *ratio* is used to refer specifically to thinking through an issue discursively (that is, in step-by-step fashion), and in this usage it stands in contrast to *intellectus*, which is the term that tends to be used in the sense of intellectual insight or intuition, that is, the grasp of some point without any apparent mental process."[29] While reason moves from concept to concept in order to arrive at a conclusion, intellect or the act of intellection grasps the truth of the matter in one act.[30] Thus, we can say, with Etienne Gilson, that "Reason, then, is to intellection what

27. This assertion, it must be said, was the subject of much debate and controversy among Christian theologians in the Middle Ages. There long lingered in medieval thought (and well thereafter) the notion taken from pagan antiquity (and expressed most clearly by Aristotle) that only what is universal or immaterial can be intelligible. Matter or the individual as such is unintelligible. That the human person constitutes a unique intelligible reality as such was never fully grasped, I think, even by the best of thinkers and even though this insight is most powerfully expressed in Christian revelation. Perhaps Duns Scotus's doctrine of *haecceitas* was an attempt to come to grips with this problem; but Scotus seems to introduce this concept precisely to avoid the implication that human beings are individuated by something so lowly and unintelligible as the flesh.

28. At the heart of the relation of the human intellect to the world is its embodied nature, the fact that it can know things only in and through the *flesh*. Thus, "comprendre est le fait de l'individu." Brague, *Au moyen du moyen âge*, 194–95. And as individuals in the flesh, we human beings can only have knowledge of anything insofar as it is mediated through what Brague calls a "social flesh," that is to say, through inter-personal communication and testimony: "La connaissance est médiatisée à travers une chair sociale. La connaissance de soi n'est possible que par la médiation de l'ami." Ibid., 196.

29. Joseph W. Koterski, SJ, *An Introduction to Medieval Philosophy: Basic Concepts* (Chichester, UK: Wiley-Blackwell, 2009), 11.

30. There is an ambiguity in the Latin term *intellectus* insofar as it can refer to the *act itself* of intellection and to the *faculty* by which this act is performed. Indeed, it can also refer, thirdly, to a *spiritual being* whose entire essence is this faculty of intellection; hence, medieval philosophers refer to the separate *intellects*. For the purpose of this introduction, however, I will not make too much of this distinction.

movement is to repose or acquisition to possession."[31] In this sense, the act of intellection is not an act of abstraction; it does not deal in the formation, judging, and relating of abstract concepts. To the contrary, it is an act which grasps the thing in its concrete and unique truth; it is, to use a word coined by Rousselot, an act of "intusspection" ("*intussuscep-tion*")—of "looking in" to the essence of the thing in all of its concrete relations.[32] In this way, intellect completes the movement of reason and allows it to rest in the truth of the thing (or of things). It connects the mind not with ideas but with the things themselves.

Intellect, therefore, is not only the completion and perfection of the movement within reason itself, but it also can serve as the principal starting point for a new movement of reason. That is, reason not only leads *to* intellect, but can also lead *from* it, as the intuition of fundamental principles that serve as the first principles of another science. Thus, intellection is the basis for a sort of "philosophical faith," that is, the recognition that many sciences must assume the principles of other sciences. Optics, for instance, depends on physics for its first principles, and physics in turn depends on metaphysics for its first principles. But the first principles of the first sciences are in themselves indemonstrable; they can only be intuited or intellected.[33] In this way, the very nature of intellect and intellection implies or leads to a way of knowing that we can only characterize as *faith*: as the "trusting" of one science in the principles of a "higher" or more fundamental science, which can only be "revealed" to the lower by one intellecting those principles in oneself. Hence, Aquinas notes, the rational nature of human beings, as rational, participates in the divine nature "in as much as it apprehends the universal notion of good and being" so that it may thereby be "immediately related to the universal principle of being." Consequently:

31. Etienne Gilson, *The Christian Philosophy of St. Thomas Aquinas*, trans. L. K. Shook, CSB (New York: Random House, 1956), 211.

32. "Nous pouvons donc conclure en disant que, dans ce système, loin qu'il faille caractériser l'intelligence comme faculté de l'abstraction, il faut la dire, au contraire, faculté de totale intussusception." Pierre Rousselot, *L'Intellectualisme de Saint Thomas* (Paris: Félix Arcan, 1908), 20.

33. Koterski, *Introduction to Medieval Philosophy*, 28.

The perfection of the rational creature consists not only in that which is suitable to it according to its nature but also in that which may be attributed to it by a certain supernatural participation in the divine goodness. Whence it was said above (S.Th. I-II, 3, 8) that the final blessedness of man consists in a certain supernatural vision of God. To which vision man is unable to come unless by way of being taught by God as a teacher: thus according to John 6:45: "Everyone who has heard of the Father and has learned, comes to me." Man does not participate in this teaching all at once but gradually according to the mode of his nature. It is necessary then that everyone who learns in this way must believe in order that he may arrive at perfect knowledge; thus even the Philosopher (De soph. elench., i, 2) says that it is necessary for the learner to believe.

Thomas concludes: "Hence, in order that man may come to the perfect vision of beatitude, it is incumbent that he believe God as a pupil believes the master teaching him."[34] Believing trustworthy testimony, then, is not contrary to reason. Indeed, it is constitutive of reason itself insofar as it leads reason back to its first principles, to intellect: that is why the physician must rely on the testimony of the biochemist and the biochemist on that of the physicist. As Aquinas says specifically in the passage above, the human intellect knows God only to the degree that it participates in God's knowledge of himself, just as the practitioner of a "lower" science can acquire knowledge only by participating in the principles or "mind" of a "higher" science. In other words, intellection is a supremely communitive activity, one that establishes and builds on relations not primarily of intellect to *things*, but of intellect to intellect. Hence, as Aquinas implies above, human beings can participate in God's knowledge of himself only to the degree that God enables that participation by participating in human nature himself (for human beings learn only *according to the mode of their nature*).

Hence, for the Christian tradition, the distinction between rational (knowledge) and faith is best understood as a distinction between two different *kinds* of knowledge, namely, between things known by *scien-*

---

34. S. Thomae Aquinatis *Summa Theologiae*, ed. Peter Caramello (Turin: Marietti, 1962), II-II, q. 2, a. 3. All translations from the Latin are the author's unless otherwise noted.

tia (and adjacent modes of cognition) and things known by testimony from God.[35] As Etienne Gilson, in an now old, but still very valuable, study of the relation between reason and revelation in the Middle Ages, helpfully puts it: "I know by reason that something is true because I *see* that it is true; but I believe that something is true because *God has said it*. In those two cases the cause of my assent is specifically different, consequently science and faith should be held as two specifically different kinds of assent."[36] A moment's reflection on how we come to know things, he argues, will confirm this:

> For instance, I cannot possibly ask you to believe that I am here; you cannot believe it, because you see it. On the other hand, I cannot cause you to see that I am now interpreting for you the fifth article of the second section of the second part of the *Summa Theologica* of Saint Thomas Aquinas. I can only ask you to believe it. Later on, if you check up my reference, you will see whether I was right or wrong in quoting it, but it will become impossible for you to believe it. Now the same distinction should apply to the problem of reason and revelation. According to its very definition, faith implies assent of the intellect to that which the intellect does not see to be true, either as one of the first principles, or as one of their necessary conclusions. Consequently, an act of faith cannot be caused by a rational evidence, but entails an intervention of the will. On the contrary, in scientific knowledge, my assent is sufficiently and completely determined by its very object.... In short, one and the same thing cannot be at one and the same time both an object of science and an object of faith.[37]

This is a distinction that is so simple and elementary that it can be easily overlooked. But it is crucial for the thesis of this book, because the claim that I will make is that the meaning and value of revelation and reason shift dramatically depending on whether this distinction *is* made and understood. As Aquinas notes in his *Summa contra Gentiles*: "The divine substance is thus not beyond the faculty of the created intellect

35. Mats Wahlberg, *Revelation as Testimony: A Philosophical-Theological Study* (Grand Rapids, Mich.: Eerdmans, 2014), 8.

36. Etienne Gilson, *Reason and Revelation in the Middle Ages* (New York: Charles Scribner's Sons, 1948), 72–73.

37. Ibid., 732–74.

as something totally extraneous to it [*extraneum ab ipso*], as is sound to vision or an immaterial substance to the senses; … but it is beyond the faculty of the created intellect insofar as it exceeds its power [*sicut excedens virtutem eius*], as the excellence of sensible things are beyond the faculty of the senses."[38] As made "according to the image of God" (*ad imaginem dei*), the human being, especially *qua* intellect, shares in the divine already, but as a finite and fallen being, the human intellect cannot know God on its own. Indeed, it is this inability on the part of the human intellect to know the Truth in itself, God, in the only manner in which it can be known that *gives rise* to reason itself: *Neccessitas rationis est ex defectu intellectus* (the necessity of reason is from the "defect" [or "fall"] of the intellect). Reason, therefore, is the product of the fall from intellectual insight, and insight that has as its essence the very self-disclosure of the source of all truth and being itself to the intellect.[39] Only God's self-disclosure through his *Word* as the source of existence, goodness, and truth itself can restore intellectual insight, because not any created thing or created intellect, but only the uncreated Intellect itself can restore the human intellect to an unfallen condition, communion of intellect to intellect with God.

The case of the relation of philosophy to revelation within medieval Judaism, particularly in the thought of Moses Maimonides, by contrast, will provide us with an interesting and illuminating *tertium quid* in our exploration of Brague's thesis and our application of it to the most important and original thinkers of the High Middle Ages. On the surface, Maimonides takes over the Muslim understanding of the relation of revelation to the intellect, whereby there is little or no distinction between prophecy and the purely "natural" process of intellection.[40] And

---

38. Thomas Aquinas, *Liber de Veritate Catholicae Fidei contra errores Infidelium seu "Summa Contra Gentiles,"* ed. Ceslaus Pera (Turin: Marietti, 1961), III, 54.

39. Which is why Fr. Rousselot can claim that at the center of St. Thomas's intellectualism is not an axiom but a person. Rousselot, *L'Intellectualisme de Saint Thomas*, 118.

40. See the chapter on "Prophecy" in Daniel Rynhold, *An Introduction to Medieval Jewish Philosophy* (London: I. B. Taurus, 2009), 122. See also Barry S. Kogan, "Understanding Prophecy: Four Traditions," in *The Cambridge History of Jewish Philosophy: From Antiquity through the Seventeenth Century*, ed. Steven Nadler and T. M. Rudavsky (New York: Cambridge University Press, 2009), 481–523.

yet, as we shall also see, Maimonides is very uneasy with this position, especially in light of the fallenness of the human intellect, which for him is the hermeneutical key for reading and understanding the language of Scripture in the *Guide of the Perplexed*. Thus, the Jewish law, while not personal in any sense, nevertheless establishes a relationship between God and the human intellect that perfects the latter and restores it to its proper relationship with God, which Maimonides characterizes as "intellectual love." Likewise, in discussing prophecy, Maimonides implies, like his Muslim predecessors al-Farabi and Avicenna, that prophecy is indistinguishable from the natural perfection of the intellect. Yet he asserts rather strangely that God can refuse revelation to any such intellect, no matter how perfect it may be, if he so wills it—he can "veto," so to speak, his own self-disclosure to anyone. In this way, Maimonides modifies significantly the tradition of *falsafa* that he inherited, adapting it to the exigencies of the Jewish understanding of what revelation is and what its proper mode is. And this modification is built upon an understanding of the relation of creation to its Creator that also breaks in significant ways from the Muslim tradition of *falsafa*, one that is reflective of the covenantal nature of revelation as the Jews understand it. His understanding of creation also opens up a sense in which the Jewish tradition is fundamentally "inclusive" (in Brague's sense), at least *in potentia*. In this way, the thought of Maimonides, perhaps most clearly of the three, opens up the problems and lays bare the assumptions that affect any understanding of how the claims of revelation and those of reason to truth are to be reconciled at all.

WHY AVERROES, MAIMONIDES, AND AQUINAS?

In undertaking this study, I decided to concentrate on the work of three important figures of medieval thought, Averroes, Maimonides, and Aquinas (with more than a passing glance at al-Ghazali in my chapters on Averroes). Why? The simplest and most obvious answer is that of all the thinkers of the Middle Ages, whether Muslim, Jewish, or Christian, almost everyone recognizes that the works of Averroes, Maimonides, and Aquinas are outstanding with regard to their inherent richness, originality, and subsequent influence. A second reason is more mundane: I had to concentrate on only three (or three and a half) thinkers for the simple reason of intellectual economy. This author has neither the time nor expertise to cover every significant medieval Christian, Jewish, and Muslim thinker.

But I will also assert that I do need to do so in order to demonstrate my thesis: looking at thinkers of such depth, importance, and influence as Averroes, Maimonides, and Aquinas is enough to do so. I am well aware of possible objections to this approach: Averroes, it will be said, and, *mutatis mutandis*, Maimonides and Aquinas are hardly typical medieval thinkers. Averroes's position on the relation of the religious law to philosophy never found any followers in the Islamic world.[41] Maimonides's rationalist interpretation of the purpose and content of the Jewish law, among his other positions, was deeply and bitterly contested among rabbis and Jewish thinkers well into the modern period. Aquinas's adoption of Aristotle as a philosophical guide as well as his positions on many theological and philosophical controversies (such as the unity of the substantial form) made him deeply suspect to many Christian theologians and ecclesiastics for decades after his death, notwithstanding his subsequent canonization and high reputation.[42]

In reply, I would argue first, that there is no such thing as a "typical" medieval thinker in Christianity, Judaism, or Islam. If research over the last half-century has shown anything, it is the vast and surprising variety of thought in all three traditions during the Middle Ages.[43] It is there-

---

41. See the last chapter ("An Ambiguous Audience") of Dominque Urvoy, *Ibn Rushd (Averroes)*, trans. Olivia Stewart (London: Routledge, 1991).

42. Indeed, some of Thomas's philosophical and theological positions were condemned by the archbishop of Paris, Etienne Tempier, in 1277. See various articles in *Nach der Verurteilung von 1277. Philosophie und Theologie an der Universität von Paris im letzten Viertel des 13. Jahrhunderts*, eds. J. Aertsen, K. Emery Jr., and A. Speer (Berlin: Walter de Gruyter, 2000); A. Zimmermann, *Ontologie oder Metaphysik? Die Diskussion über den Gegenstand der Metaphysik im 13. Und 14. Jahrhundert* (Leiden: E. J. Brill, 1965); and L. Honnefelder, "Die zweite Anfang der Metaphysik. Voraussetzungen, Ansätze und Folgen der Wiederbegründung der Metaphysik im 13./14. Jahrhundert," in *Philosophie im Mittelalter, Entwicklungslinien und Paradigmen* (Hamburg: Felix Meiner, 1987).

43. Including even atheist or quasi-atheist thinkers such as Razes in Islam or David of

fore vain to try to find a "typical" thinker from this period. But I would argue, second, that often it is in the works of the most unusual and original thinkers in any period that essential themes and hidden or unstated assumptions of the age come to light. This is precisely because it is the mark of a deep and influential thinker to uncover such assumptions by thinking things through to their logical conclusions. I think that it will become clear to the reader, as he or she reads through this study, that Averroes, Maimonides, and Aquinas are such thinkers. Third, original as all three were as thinkers, it should become clear that the religious traditions to which they belonged and to which they were committed deeply and decisively marked their thought (while at the same time it should be evident that they were more than able to take a critical stance towards their own traditions). One cannot imagine a work such as the *Guide of the Perplexed* being written by a Muslim or Christian nor, *mutatis mutandis*, the works of Averroes or Aquinas being written by someone outside their particular religious traditions. All three, therefore, reflect well the philosophical possibilities made available by these three traditions' understandings of revelation and therefore demonstrate how the specifically different understandings of revelation in the Muslim, Jewish, and Christian traditions shaped the horizon within which they attempted to reconcile the claims of reason and divine revelation to truth.

Dinant in Christianity. For an overview of the astonishing philosophical range of medieval thinkers, even verging on the extremes of "free thought," see Alain de Libera, *Penser au moyen âge* (Paris: Editions du Seuil, 1991).

CHAPTER 1

WHAT IS "DECISIVE" ABOUT
AVERROES'S *DECISIVE*
TREATISE?

The *Decisive Treatise* or *kitāb faṣl al maqāl wa taqrīr ma bayna al-sharīʿah wa al-ḥikma min al-itiṣāl*, is a *fatwa* or determinative legal ruling.[1] While primarily known in the West as a philosopher, and the "Commentator" *par excellence* of the works of Aristotle, Averroes was also an Islamic jurist, or *qadi*—indeed, this was his primary and principal occupation his whole adult life. We cannot, therefore, understand the philosophical thought of Averroes without understanding his thinking as a Muslim jurist and the nature of law in Islam.[2] And indeed, this is the question that Averroes's *Decisive Treatise* asks: what is the nature of the "relation" (*itiṣāl*) between the "law" (*sharīʿah*) and "wisdom" (*ḥikma*) or philosophy.[3] A *fatwa* determines the legitimacy of a certain practice using the

1. "Le *Faṣl al-maqāl* est une *fatwa*. C'est un avis légal—les Latins diraient un *responsum*," Averroes, *Le Livre du discours décisif*, trans. Marc Geoffory (Paris: Flammarion, 1996), 11. "Le *Faṣl* est un discours de la méthode," Averroes, *L'Islam et la raison: Anthologie de textes juridiques, théologiques et polémiques*, trans. Marc Geoffroy (Paris: Flammarion, 2000), 17.

2. See Abdel Magid Turki, "La Place d'Averroès juriste dans l'histoire du Malikisme et de l'Espagne musulmane," in *Multiple Averroès: Actes du colloque international organisé à l'occasion du 850e anniversaire de la naissance d'Averroès, Paris 20–23 septembre 1976*, ed. Jean Jolivet (Paris: Les Belles Lettres, 1978), 33–41. See also Richard Taylor, "Averroes," in *The Cambridge Companion to Arabic Philosophy*, ed. Peter Adamson (Cambridge: Cambridge University Press, 2005), 180–200.

3. In making his ruling, Averroes was guided to a great extent by the writings of Ibn Tumart, the spiritual founder of the Almohad dynasty then ruling Spain. A rather obscure

criteria of Islamic law or *sharia*. In brief, Averroes is bringing philosophy before the tribunal of Islamic law in order to determine its legitimacy for the Muslim. And of course, Averroes's answer is an unequivocal, "yes, philosophical reflection is in perfect conformity with the religious law."

But there is more here that can easily be overlooked. Averroes's procedure is actually the exact inverse of that of Thomas Aquinas who, in the first question of his *Summa theologiae*, asks whether any science other than philosophy is necessary. In other words, Aquinas brings theology before the tribunal of philosophy in order to determine its legitimacy. Hidden in this seemingly trivial observation, are quite different if not opposed understandings of the relation of faith and reason, revelation and philosophical thought. The intent of Aquinas was "to reconstruct philosophy in such a way that its accord with theology would appear as a consequence of the demands of reason itself and not as the accidental result of a simple desire of conciliation."[4] The attitude of Averroes, by

---

imam from the Atlas Mountains of Morocco, Ibn Tumart gathered around him a group of warrior-followers who followed a very simple Islamic creed, or *'Aqīda*, which he himself formulated. These followers then went on under his successors to cross the Straits of Gibraltar and to conquer the already teetering Almoravid dynasty. Ibn Tumart's *'Aqīda* was a curious blend of literalist elements—since he exhorted Muslims to have no recourse to arguments outside the text of the Quran but to derive them from the text itself—with rationalist ones—since he then goes on to make purely rational arguments for the existence and attributes of God based on these texts. We shall see how Averroes himself reproduces this curious blend of literalism and rationalism in his own *Decisive Treatise*, mainly with a view to destroying the opposition both to philosophy and to the Almohad regime by dialectical theologians, the most prominent of whom were the Ash'arites (on whom more later). See Marc Geoffroy, "L'Almohadisme théologique d'Averroès (Ibn Rushd)," *Archives d'histoire doctrinale et littéraire du moyen âge* 66, no. 1 (1999): 23. Indeed, it was most probably from Ibn Tumart that Averroes took as his central idea: "If there is a revealed religious truth, it is necessarily in complete accord with rational truth." This is also a strong indication that, contrary to what we find in the literature going back to the famous book of Ernst Renan published in 1854 on Averroes, Averroes was not a free-thinker, let alone an atheist, but a sincere Muslim seeking to bring the demands of Islamic law and the wisdom of philosophy into a close and fruitful relationship and collaboration. Indeed, it was most probably from Ibn Tumart that Averroes took as his central idea: "If there is a revealed religious truth, it is necessarily in complete accord with rational truth." Roger Arnaldez, *Averroes: A Rationalist in Islam*, trans. David Streight (Notre Dame, Ind.: University of Notre Dame Press, 2000), 3; and George F. Hourani, "Averroès Musulman," in Jolivet, *Multiple Averroès*, 21–30.

4. "It is in taking account of these radical differences, that it is necessary to inquire into the relationship between philosophy and theology in Ibn Rushd and Thomas

contrast, is opposite and yet symmetrical: his goal is to reconstruct the religious law in such a way that its accord with philosophy would appear as a natural consequence of the demands of the law itself.[5] For Aquinas, philosophy, when pushed to its conceptual limits, shows the need for divine grace, that is, revelation. Averroes, however, claims that the religious law, when properly understood, legitimizes the perfection of the intellect through philosophy. It is the revealed "book" that forms the supreme template for all philosophical thinking, while it is philosophical thinking that reveals the "true" meaning of the holy book.

THE RELATION BETWEEN THE
LAW AND PHILOSOPHY

As a *fatwa* the *Decisive Treatise* is also a sort of "discourse on method." Averroes's method will be primarily one that is drawn from legal reasoning: given that the law commands such and such a practice, what inferences can we draw from these commands? And, indeed, cannot the very act of legal reasoning—from commands to logical inferences from these commands—be an integral part of what the law commands? Averroes's strategy is, therefore, twofold: it is to demonstrate that the law commands the cultivation of the philosophical sciences, and it is to show how the law itself makes use of logical reasoning in applying its commands to the variegated circumstances of human life.

　　As is traditional in the format of any ruling in Islamic law, Averroes begins his argument by asking whether the pursuit of the philosophical sciences falls under one of the five categories of activity as outlined by

---

Aquinas. Comparing only what is comparable, we can hazard the following formula: if, as Gilson wrote, 'the entire secret of Thomism lies in an immense effort of intellectual honesty *to reconstruct philosophy* such that *its accord with theology* appears as a result of *the exigencies of reason itself* and not as the accidental result of a simple desire for harmonization,' the attitude of Ibn Rushd can be characterized in the opposite, yet symmetrical way." De Libera, introduction to Averroes, *L'Islam et la raison*, 36.

　　5. "One can in effect claim, inverting the formula of Gilson, that 'the entire secret of Averroism is an immense effort of intellectual honesty *to reconstruct theology* in such a way that *its accord with philosophy* appears as *a consequence of the exigencies of revelation itself* and not as the accidental result of a simple desire for harmonization." Ibid.

Islamic law: (1) the obligatory, (2) the recommended, (3) the permissible, (4) the distasteful, and (5) the forbidden. In all schools of Islamic law, any human activity must fall under one of these categories. Thus Averroes asserts: "Now, the goal of this statement is for us to investigate from the perspective of law-based reflection, whether reflection upon philosophy and the sciences of logic is permitted, prohibited, or commanded—and this as a recommendation or as an obligation—by the law."[6] Averroes's answer as a jurist is that the activity of philosophy is obligatory or, at the very least, recommended:

> If the activity of philosophy is nothing more than reflection upon existing things and consideration of them insofar as they are an indication of the Artisan [*sani'*]—I mean insofar as they are artifacts [*maṣnūʿāt*], for existing things indicate the Artisan only through cognizance of the art in them, and the more complete that cognizance of the art in them is, the more complete is cognizance of the Artisan—and if the law has recommended and urged consideration of existing things, then it is evident that what this name indicates is either obligatory or recommended by the law.[7]

Averroes here puts forth a particular understanding of what philosophy means: it is "reflection upon existing things" insofar as they display the intelligent activity of an "artisan." Thus, philosophy is the consideration of existent things insofar as they display indication of having been made (*maṣnūʿa*).[8] In this vein, the Quran itself commands that we use syllogistic or logical reasoning in considering how things are intelligently made and, from that, inferring to the existence and perfection of a Maker: "There is His statement (may He be exalted), 'Consider, you who

---

6. Averroes, *Decisive Treatise* (hereafter, *DT*), in *Decisive Treatise and Epistle Dedicatory*, trans. Charles E. Butterworth (Provo, Utah: Brigham Young University Press, 2001), no. 1.

7. Ibid., no. 2.

8. In this way, as we shall see, Averroes wishes to counter the position of al-Ghazali, who argues in the third discussion of his *Incoherence of the Philosophers*, that the philosophers cannot demonstrate that God is a supreme Artisan who makes all things in accordance with a rational pattern or idea. Al-Ghazali argues that God is rather an agent of pure will, who is not bound to make anything that resembles an "artifact" or anything rational at all. See Averroes, *Le Livre du discours décisif*, 177n3.

have sight' [59:2]; this is a text for the obligation of using both intellectual and law-based syllogistic reasoning [*al-qīyās shār'ī*]. And there is
His statement (may He be exalted), 'Have they not reflected upon the
kingdom of the heavens and the earth and what things God has created?' [7:185]."[9] In defining philosophy as the study of the order or purpose
in the world, Averroes subtly alters the understanding of philosophy
that his supreme master, Aristotle, held. For Aristotle, God is the first
cause of everything insofar as he is the *goal* or *final cause* of the motion
of changeable or natural beings.[10] There is no sense in Aristotle of God
as the "maker," let alone "creator," of beings. As we shall see, Averroes
sees no discrepancy here: even if Aristotle did not talk about God as a
supreme Artisan, the whole thrust of his philosophy, Averroes argues,
moves in the direction of affirming such a being.[11] More to the point
here is that Averroes, in making this ruling, has uppermost in mind his
opponents within Islam, the adherents to a school of speculative or dialectical theology (*kalām*) called Ash'arism. While for Averroes, creation
exhibits "art" or rational order that proves the existence of the deity,
for the Ash'arites, the dominant school of Islamic *kalām* or dialectical
theology, represented most forcefully by the great al-Ghazali, all events
and beings in the world are manifestations of God's absolute power and
therefore do not have to "obey" anything—including any rational order—outside the divine will. All beings and events cannot exist even for
a moment on their own without being created anew by God; nor does
any created thing cause or affect anything else, for that would arrogate to
the creature what only God can do: God simply creates the effect after
creating the cause, with no necessary or inherent relation between them.
For Averroes, this position abolishes any sort of art or rational order
in the world in favor of a capricious god. As Averroes says in a slightly
later work detailing his objections to Ash'arite theology, the *Exposition*

9. *DT*, no. 2.

10. It is notable that Averroes always refers to God as the "Artisan" or "Maker" (*sāni'*)
rather than as the "Creator" (*khāliq*), perhaps in an effort to get us to understand God as an
intelligent and not purely willful agent.

11. See Avital Wohlman, *Al-Ghazali, Averroes and the Interpretation of the Qur'an: Common Sense and Philosophy in Islam* (London: Routledge, 2010), 19.

of Methods: "It abolishes wisdom, because wisdom is nothing more than the knowledge of the causes of existing things, and if there are no necessary causes which necessitate the existence of these things, in the form in which those of their kind exist, then there is no knowledge here that distinguishes the Wise Creator from any other."[12] Thus, if the Ash'arite arguments were true, then it would be useless and vain for the Quran to command all Muslims to reflect upon the wise order of creation.

Averroes, however, must deal with the fact that the Quran is not a philosophical text or, at least most of it is not philosophical in nature. But, it is a significant part of Averroes's argument that this is as it should be. In approaching a sacred text like the Quran, we need to distinguish between "demonstration" (*burhān*) and both "dialectical reasoning" (*qiyās jadalī*) and "rhetorical reasoning" (*qiyās khuṭabī*).[13] In demonstrative reasoning, the mind proceeds from premises evidently true in themselves through a valid syllogism resulting in a true conclusion concerning something not known before. And in such a syllogism, the middle term should reveal the *cause* of why the conclusion is true. As mentioned above, a crucial aspect of Averroes's argument is that, even if the Quran itself does not command such syllogistic, demonstrative reasoning, the very application of the law which the Quran reveals does so implicitly:

> For just as the jurist infers from the command to obtain juridical understanding of the statutes the obligation to become cognizant of the kinds of juridical syllogistic reasoning and which of them is syllogistic reasoning and which not, so, too, is it obligatory for the one cognizant [of God] [*al-'ārif*] to infer from the command to reflect upon the beings the obligation to become cognizant of intellectual syllogistic reasoning and its kinds. Nay, it is even more fitting that he do so; for if the jurist infers from His statement (may He be exalted), "Consider, you who have sight" [59:2], the obligation to become cognizant of juridical syllogistic

12. *Al-Kashf 'an Manāhij al-'Adilla fī 'Aqā'id al-Milla*, ed. Muhammad Abd Al-Jabri (Beirut: Markāz Dirasāt al-Waḥda al-'Arabī, 1998), 113 (English trans., 28).

13. This classification of arguments goes back to the Peripatetic commentators of late antiquity and was picked up quite enthusiastically by Muslim and Arabic language philosophers. See I. Madkour, *L'Organon d'Aristote dans le monde arabe*, 2nd ed. (Paris: Vrin, 1969), 10–19.

reasoning, then how much more fitting is it that the one cognizant of God infer from that the obligation to become cognizant of intellectual syllogistic reasoning.[14]

Far from being a "heretical innovation" (*bidā'*), the use of syllogistic reasoning is embedded within the concept and application of Islamic law itself. Nor does it matter whether the ancient philosophers were Muslims or not—sound syllogistic reasoning is sound regardless of who does the reasoning. Whatever is correct in the books of the ancients, we are bound to accept; whatever is not correct, we are bound to reject, since all that is true is consonant with God's Law.[15]

This appeal to the validity of truth no matter where it is found—in non-Muslims as well as in Muslims—is embedded in a larger claim that all the first principles of all arts and sciences are in fact eternal. As we shall see, this larger claim is central to Averroes's thinking not just about creation but also about the nature of the intellect and the relation of both to the individual and to the revealed law. Of course, all developments in the arts and sciences are built upon the insights and discoveries of those who plied these arts and sciences before: "It is evident, moreover, that this goal is completed for us with respect to existing things only when they are investigated successively by one person after another and when, in doing so, the one coming after makes use of the one having preceded—along the lines of what occurs in the mathematical sciences."[16] But even more to the point, Averroes argues that if a man were to engage in the sciences alone and without the aid of a long tradition and the knowledge and principles it has built up, such a man would not be capable of discovering adequately the truth about things, *unless it were by a sort of revelation*:

> For if we were to assume the art of geometry and, likewise, the art of astronomy to be nonexistent in this time of ours, and if a single man

14. *DT*, no. 4. The term that Averroes uses here, *al-'ārif*, has a strong mystical connotation. Given, however, that Averroes had a strong aversion to mysticism of any stripe, it most likely indicates here the philosopher whose goal is genuine knowledge of God and the happiness that comes from that knowledge. See Averroes, *Le Livre du discours décisif*, 181n14.

15. *DT*, nos. 4–7.

16. Ibid., no. 8.

wished to discern on his own the sizes of the heavenly bodies, their shapes, and their distances from one another, that would not be possible for him—for example, to become cognizant of the size of the sun with respect to the earth and of other things about the sizes of the planets—not even if he were by nature the most intelligent person, *unless it were by means of revelation or something resembling revelation.* Indeed, if it were said to him that the sun is about 150 or 160 times greater than the earth, he would count this statement as madness on the part of the one who makes it. And this is something for which a demonstration has been brought forth in astronomy and which no one adept in that science doubts.[17]

Just as the message of the Quran is an eternal one calling men from our forgetfulness, so does it command believers who are intellectually capable and prepared to cultivate the arts and sciences, which have been cultivated by men from time immemorial; only they have, through decadence and forgetfulness, fallen into oblivion and disuse: "From this it has become evident that reflection upon the books of the Ancients is obligatory according to the law, for their aim and intention in their books is the very intention to which the law urges us." Thus it is contrary to the Law to bar "people [who are qualified] from the door through which the law calls them to cognizance of God—namely, the door of reflection leading to true cognizance of Him."[18] But what seems to be the most important point of this passage is the claim that revelation for Averroes is an aid to human reason *in the absence* of a developed philosophical and scientific tradition. In other words, the revealed religious law allows a people or religious community (*milla*) to "skip over" laborious developments in intellectual life so that it can get immediately down to the business of philosophical reflection. In doing so, the religious law is simply a part of the providential order of creation. Conversely, the knowledge given in philosophical reflection is generically no different than that given in revelation, differing from revelation only in *how* it is attained: that is, not commanded from without by a revealed book, but realized conceptually by the perfection of the intellect from within.

17. Ibid., no. 8, emphasis added.
18. Ibid., no. 10.

So, just because philosophers such as al-Farabi and Avicenna fell into some serious errors, Averroes argues, this does not invalidate the pursuit of philosophy as such. What the opponents of philosophy (or, more accurately, the sort of Neoplatonic Aristotelian philosophy popularly known in the Islamic world by its Arabic cognate, *falsafa*) do not acknowledge is that both philosophy and the religious law differentiate which sorts of arguments are suitable to the natures of which sorts of people. It is the unique task of the religious law to call all Muslims to a supreme happiness, which lies in the knowledge of God.[19] But the religious Law calls them in a way suitable to their nature: "Since all of this has been determined and we, the Muslim community, believe that this divine law of ours is true and is the one alerting us to and calling for this happiness [*sa'ada*]—which is cognizance of God (Mighty and Magnificent) and of His creation—therefore, that is determined for every Muslim in accordance with the method of assent his temperament and nature require."[20] Some Muslims are capable of recognizing the truth of arguments laid out in a syllogistic, demonstrable form; others are incapable of understanding such arguments and must therefore rely on dialectical arguments (arguments based on verses from the Quran or on prophetic traditions—*hadith*) or rhetorical arguments (arresting poetic images that appeal to our emotions or our desire for pleasure and our aversion to pain): "That is because people's natures vary in excellence with respect to assent [*taṣdīq*]. Thus, some assent by means of demonstration; some assent by means of dialectical statements in the same way the one adhering to demonstration assents by means of demonstration, there being nothing greater in their natures; and some assent by means of rhetorical statements, just as the one adhering to demonstration assents by means of demonstrative statements."[21] For Averroes, as for his eponymous grandfather, also a prominent Malakite jurist, the Quran is complete only in a *formal* sense: that is, it provides a complete set of

---

19. Ibid., no. 11.

20. Ibid.

21. Ibid. See Arthur Hyman, "Les types d'arguments dans les écrits théologico-politiques et polémiques d'Averroès," in *Penser avec Aristote*, ed. Muhammad Allal Sinaceaur (Toulouse: Erès, 1991), 657–58.

principles for both speculative and practical knowledge. It is not, however, complete in a *material* sense; that is, the formal principles laid out
in the Quran must be completed by philosophical and scientific investigation on the part of believers. In other words, the religious law is
incomplete only accidentally, not essentially, namely, only insofar as it
does not address every contingency explicitly. Be that as it may, Averroes's ultimate goals are practical: they are to bring about conditions in
which individual human beings and human society as a whole have the
virtues requisite for pursuing philosophical knowledge or wisdom, just
as it is a goal of the religious law to bring about virtue and of medicine
to bring about health.[22]

Important for understanding what Averroes is doing in the *Decisive
Treatise* is the recognition that he is operating with the assumption of
a "greater organon" or a much wider notion of what constitutes "logic." Thus, "logic" includes not just rules for the validity of syllogisms,
but includes poetry and rhetoric as well. This expansive definition of
logic Averroes inherited from late antiquity. It includes the notion that
crucial to logic is not just the truth or falsity of propositions or the
validity and invalidity of syllogisms, but also the effectiveness or inef-
fectiveness of communication and of instilling truth in the soul.[23] In
other words, essential to philosophical reflection is reflection on how it
may be transmitted and received. For al-Farabi, for example, a perfect
philosophy does not just comprehend the truth but communicates that
truth to others and orders society along its lines.[24] By bringing about
the proper conditions within which philosophy may flourish, the religious law, far from contradicting philosophical truth, confirms it and
upholds it: "Since this law is true and calls to the reflection leading to
cognizance of the truth, we, the Muslim community, know firmly that

22. Thus, in a sense, it was for Averroes the legal sciences, on the one hand, and medical
science, on the other, that provided the paradigms of reasoning—not philosophy. See Ali
Benmakhlouf, *Averroès* (Paris: Les Belles Lettres, 2000), 20. And yet, as we shall see, the
goals of the law (like those of health) are for the sake of philosophical reflection, not the
other way around.

23. Ibid., 99. See also Salim Kemal, *The Philosophical Poetics of Alfarabi, Avicenna and
Averroes: The Aristotelian Reception* (London: Routledge, 2003).

24. Benmakhlouf, *Averroès*, 102.

demonstrative reflection does not lead to differing with what is set down in the law. For truth does not oppose truth; rather, it agrees with and bears witness to it."[25] The last sentence of this passage is particularly well known, since it constitutes a sort of epigrammatic summation of Averroes's entire argument.

The notion that "truth does not oppose truth" and that it "agrees with and bears witness to it" has, as Richard Taylor has shown, its origins in the logical works of Aristotle and, therefore, did not have an obvious implication for conflicts between philosophy and religious law.[26] Nevertheless, it is for this purpose that Averroes uses this ancient Aristotelian maxim. The religious law agrees with and bears witness to philosophy in commanding Muslims to study the intelligible order in nature and in creating the conditions of virtue in individuals and good order in society in which philosophical science may flourish. Philosophy, in turn, provides the conceptual tools by which ambiguous passages in the law may be properly interpreted. Even here, however, Averroes puts down narrow limits: if there is no contradiction between the law and philosophical reflection about a matter of demonstration, then there is no need for philosophy. If the law is not silent, but is in agreement with demonstration, then there is again no conflict nor need for philosophical reflection. Only if there is a conflict is there then a need for interpretation (*ta'wil*). "The meaning of interpretation is: drawing out the figurative significance of an utterance from its true significance without violating the custom of the Arabic language with respect to figurative speech in doing so."[27]

Extending the use of the legal concept of "witnessing" further, Averroes claims that, even if individual passages from Scripture may, in their

---

25. *DT*, no. 12.

26. "What Averroes is asserting here is that the primary approach to the understanding of reality and interpreting religious law is to be found with the Aristotelian method of philosophical demonstration and that all other methodologies are secondary to this. This is the deeper import of the principle of the unity of truth, a principle whose source in Aristotle Averroes chose to conceal in his *Faṣl al-Maqāl* with what was surely the full and complete intention of concealment." Richard Taylor, "'Truth Does Not Contradict Truth': Averroes and the Unity of Truth." *Topoi* 19, no. 1 (2000): 10–11.

27. *DT*, no. 13.

apparent sense, contradict demonstrative reasoning, if we look at the law in its totality, then we shall inevitably find a passage whose apparent sense bears out the demonstrative or philosophical truth: "Indeed, we say that whenever the apparent sense of a pronouncement about something in the law differs from what demonstration leads to, if the law is considered and all of its parts scrutinized, there will invariably be found in the utterances of the law something whose apparent sense bears witness, or comes close to bearing witness, to that interpretation."[28] And indeed, Averroes, as we shall see, goes on to give several examples of this, bringing in textual support for this bold claim.

There is, of course, among the Muslim 'ulema disagreement as to which verses are to be taken in their apparent sense and which not.[29] The Quran is frequently unclear as to whether a verse is to be taken literally or figuratively. Indeed, one can easily find verses that seem to be in contradiction to one another. But for Averroes, far from being a defect, this ambiguity and the seeming contradictions are manifestations of a deeper wisdom in Scripture:

> The reason an apparent and an inner sense are set down in the law is the difference in people's innate dispositions and the variance in their innate capacities for assent. The reason contradictory apparent senses are set down is to alert "those well-grounded in science" to the interpretation that reconciles them. This idea is pointed to in His statement (may He be exalted), "He it is who has sent down to you the Book; in it, there are fixed verses..." on to His statement, "and those well-grounded in science" [3:7].[30]

Ambiguities and apparent contradictions in Scripture and in the divine law are pointers for those capable of sustained philosophical thought and comprehension to a deeper truth, one in accordance with the very mind and intention of the Creator himself. Thus, as Dominique Urvoy remarks, if Averroes is a rationalist, he is a very particular sort of ra-

---

28. Ibid., no. 14.

29. "The Ash'arites, for example, interpret the verse about God's directing Himself [2:29] and the Tradition about His descent, whereas the Hanbalites take them in their apparent sense." Ibid., no. 14.

30. Ibid., no. 14.

tionalist in that he manifests a complete faith that the Quran and the religious law can and do embrace a rational understanding of creation.[31] Indeed, the "book" is conceived as being "sent down" (*nuzila*) as a repository of all science.

This still leaves Averroes, however, with the problem of which verses are to be taken in their apparent sense and which are to be interpreted, for to determine which verses are to be taken in their apparent sense or are to be interpreted itself presupposes demonstration. For we cannot interpret a verse as figurative unless we first know it contradicts the findings of philosophical thought or scientific research. Averroes admits that there can probably never be a consensus on this issue; and, again, he claims that, far from being a problem, this is a mark of the wisdom of the divine law: "So how is it possible to conceive of consensus about a single theoretical question being transmitted to us when we firmly know that no single epoch has escaped having learned men who are of the opinion that there are things in the law not all of the people ought to know in their true sense?"[32] Consensus over which passages in Scripture are to be taken in their apparent sense and which in their "true" sense shifts depending on what the wise think the masses should know and should not know.[33] This is because it is an essential property of wisdom

31. "There is no doubt that Ibn Rushd belonged to that *madhab al-fikr* 'doctrine of the Logos' of Almohadism denounced by the traditionalists. He is not a rationalist in the reductive sense of a thinker like Renan, but rather in the sense that applied to his contemporaries, even non-Muslims such as Saint Anselm. Certainly, there is a degree of this in the latter, Ibn Rushd's thought being 'less a *fides quaerens intellectum* than a perfect faith which embraces rational knowledge' (Arnaldez, *Encyclopédie de l'Islam*)." Urvoy, *Ibn Rushd*, 81. Also there is this remark from Richard Taylor: "While this entire approach founded on the principle of the unity of truth puts demonstrative philosophy in a position of priority and judgment in some cases, it does not claim that philosophy contains in actuality all truth and that philosophy is thereby in actual possession of the right to judge the truth of all scriptural interpretation. Rather, divine revelation is a fit guide for all human beings in all their differing classes, rhetorical, dialectical, or demonstrative, into which Divine Wisdom has placed them." Richard Taylor, "Averroes," in *A Companion to Philosophy in the Middle Ages*, ed. Jorge Gracia and Timothy Noone (London: Blackwell Publishing, 2003), 186. Philosophy is unfit as a guide for *all* people, and thus, in this sense, the law takes priority over philosophy. Nevertheless, on key point of doctrine—creation and divine knowledge—it is philosophy that takes priority over the law.

32. *DT*, no. 15.

33. This is a serious issue, since one of the major "sources" (*uṣūl*) of Islamic law is the

to know how truth will be grasped and applied by which types of people, just as it is essential to a wise physician to tell his patient only as much as he or she needs to know in order to get well.

In sum, revelation for Averroes is supernatural; but it is supernatural only in the sense that it makes available to the masses what is known naturally by the philosopher. And by making the perfectly natural wisdom of the philosopher supernaturally available to the average believer, revelation makes possible the fullest development of philosophical thought, since the religious law completes and perfects the society in which philosophy must develop. But is the truth, whether of nature, of man, or of God, grasped as truth only in philosophical thought? Are the philosophers alone in possession of the true meaning of revelation? And are not the philosophers guilty of manifest unbelief?

ARE THE PHILOSOPHERS GUILTY OF UNBELIEF? TWO CASES

The argument that Averroes presents to the reader in the first third or so of the *Decisive Treatise* is all very well and good, one might say. But an educated Muslim reader of Averroes's time would no doubt raise the question: do not the philosophers teach manifest heresy and unbelief in asserting that the world is eternal and was not created in time and that God does not know particular things, least of all particular human beings such as you and me, and cannot, therefore, reward good and punish evil? It is fine to say that the divine law commands and establishes the conditions for philosophical reflection, but what are we to say when that reflection ends up seeming to contradict and undermine that law itself in the eyes of the people? In this case, philosophical thought leads not to truth but to error. The only sure guide to knowledge of God is his holy book.

But the holy book itself is full of ambiguity. All speech demands interpretation and the speech of the Quran is no exception. Even those claims of the Quran which are clear and need no interpretation (or so

---

consensus of the community (*umma*). Thus, a hadith reports Muhammad to have said, "My community will never come into accord on an error." Averroes, *Le Livre du discours décisif*, 193n58.

it seems) need to be distinguished from those which are not, and this demands interpretation:

> Those faithful not adept in science are people whose faith in them is not based on demonstration. So, if this faith by which God has described the learned is particular to them, then it is obligatory that it come about by means of demonstration. And if it is by means of demonstration, then it comes about only along with the science of interpretation. For God (may He be exalted) has already announced that there is an interpretation of them that is the truth, and demonstration is only of the truth. Since that is the case, it is not possible for an exhaustive consensus to be determined with respect to the interpretation by which God particularly characterized the learned. This is self-evident to anyone who is fair-minded.[34]

For every ambiguous passage in the Quran, there is a true meaning that is known to God and, Averroes implies here and clearly asserts later, is also known to the learned by philosophical demonstration. That this is, however, "self-evident to anyone who is fair-minded" is an important qualification, because, as we shall see, this was not "self-evident" to the Muslim *'ulema*, hence, Averroes's crucial qualification of "fair-minded" (*'and min 'ānṣaf*). Two of these ambiguities are, as mentioned above, the creation of the world *de novo* and *ex nihilo* and God's knowledge of particulars. In addressing these two problems, Averroes's goal is to establish that the "book" *is* philosophical intellection in concrete form, leading the believer to a deeper conformity to God's providential order in creation.

The doctrine of creation *ex nihilo* or *de novo* is actually not clearly expressed in the Quran.[35] To be sure, the Quran asserts that all things other than God are utterly dependent upon God for their being and existence. Nothing can exist without God's creative power. Still, it is not clearly stated that God created and still creates all things out of nothing or that creation had a definite beginning in time. For al-Ghazali and the orthodox schools of *kalām*, such as the Ash'arite, creation *ex nihilo* and *de novo* are clearly implied in the teaching of the Quran and the Had-

---

34. *DT*, no. 16.

35. "Il faut l'y mettre pour la trouver." Roger Arnaldez, "La doctrine de la création dans le 'Tahafut,'" *Studia Islamica* 7 (1957): 101.

ith. Hence, al-Ghazali and other dialectical theologians aimed a battery of arguments against the notion of an "eternal creation" in which God without beginning or end creates beings out of a pre-existing matter. This notion of "eternal creation" was the solution put forth by al-Farabi and Avicenna who strove to reconcile the apparent teaching of Aristotle that the world is eternal with the Quranic doctrine of creation. Indeed, for these philosophers the world *must* be eternal if God is to be pure actuality, for otherwise, there would be a "time" when God did not act, which is absurd; moreover, if creation were not eternal, then the species of things would not have intelligible forms, because the essence of intelligibility is that it be rooted in something unchanging and eternal. Yes, they argued, God creates, but in the same way that the sun continually creates new life through the actualizing power of its light and warmth. For al-Ghazali, however, this argument limits God's freedom and power and, even more importantly, reduces God to a mere natural substance like the sun or fire, which cannot but shine or burn whether it "will" to do so or not, which he argues is clearly contrary to Quranic teaching.

In a similar fashion, the Quran clearly teaches that God knows even an "atom's weight" of a creature and thus, presumably, knows every creature down to the most particular detail.[36] And yet, according to Aristotle and the best of the Greek philosophers, genuine knowledge is only of universals—of genera and species—which alone are truly intelligible. The individual as such, in its particularity, is unintelligible and accidental, giving us no genuine universal and necessary scientific knowledge. Al-Farabi and Avicenna again try to square the circle by arguing that, yes, God only knows universals, not merely because universals alone are truly intelligible, but also because they are unchanging and God is unchanging. If God knew particulars, then God's knowledge and God himself, since God's knowledge and essence are one and the same, would change. Thus, God can know particulars, but only as inferences deduced from God's universal knowledge of things (so that God, according to an example used by Avicenna, can deduce a particular eclipse from his perfect knowledge of the general movements of the heavens; neverthe-

---

36. *Quran* 2:255, 19:64.

less, God would still not know the particular eclipse as such). Again, al-Ghazali argues that this would mean that God's knowledge is actually more limited than ours, which is absurd. And in any case, it would make the notion of individual rewards and punishments in the afterlife also utterly absurd, since God would not know whom to reward or punish!

It is into this long-standing debate that Averroes steps. Now it would be a mistake to assume immediately that Averroes unreservedly takes the side of the philosophers in these controversies. In fact, he is often as harsh in his criticisms of al-Farabi and Avicenna as al-Ghazali is, and, in turn, he often has to admit, somewhat grudgingly, that many of al-Ghazali's criticisms of the philosophers are just. So, with regard to God's knowledge, Averroes claims that both the philosophers and the dialectical theologians make the same error. They assume God's knowledge is more or less like ours, when in truth it is radically different:

> So, whoever likens the two kinds of knowledge to one another sets down two opposite essences and their particular characteristics as being one, that is the extreme of ignorance. If the name "knowledge" is said of knowledge that is generated and of knowledge that is eternal, it is said purely as a name that is shared, just as many names are said of opposite things—for example, *al-jalāl*, said of great and small, and *al-ṣarīm*, said of light and darkness. Thus, there is no definition embracing both kinds of knowledge, as the dialectical theologians of our time fancy.[37]

To predicate "knowledge" of God in the sense that we understand from our own experience is futile. "Knowledge" as applied to God and "knowledge" as applied to us becomes an equivocal term. With regard to the nature of God's creation, Averroes takes a somewhat different tack: whereas in the question of divine knowledge, the philosophers and the *mutakallimun* use the same term for two different realities, in the case of creation it is the reverse: they use different terms for the same reality. The rigorous application of philosophical reasoning to the nature of what creative activity is will reveal that what the religious law and what philosophy say amount to the same thing.[38]

37. *DT*, no. 17.

38. The *Decisive Treatise* is not the only work in which Averroes makes this argu-

Averroes's argument in a nutshell is this: what we mean by God
creating the world is that every finite thing in which there is the least
degree of potentiality (even in the immaterial intellects insofar as they
are in potentiality to receiving intelligible forms) depends utterly for its
actuality on God, who is pure actuality. There is nothing in what we
mean by "creation" that allows us to infer that it began at a certain finite
time in the past or that it drew beings out of nothing.[39] Averroes argues
that any contradiction between philosophical reflection and Scripture
disappears if we explain what we mean by "creation." We can identify
two "extremes" when we talk about the world and its "creation."[40] At one
extreme, there are things that exist from something other than themselves by something else, that is, they have an efficient and material
cause. Therefore, a certain time precedes their existence. The Ancients
(that is, the Greek philosophers) and Ash'arites both name such exis-

---

ment. He, in fact, wrote an opuscule that addresses directly and in more detail this problem and tries to offer a solution. See Barry Kogan, "Eternity and Origination: Averroes'
Discourse on the Manner of the World's Existence," in *Islamic Theology and Philosophy: Studies
in Honor of George F. Hourani*, ed. Michael E. Marmura (Albany, N.Y.: State University of
New York Press, 1984), 203–35. Averroes here argues that we must conceive of the nature of
time as cyclical and not linear; hence, as in a cycle, time has no *absolute* beginning or end—
though it may have a *relative* beginning and end. In this way, Averroes tries to reconcile the
claims of the philosophers and those of the mutakallimun.

39. Nevertheless, as Majid Fakhry makes clear, this explanation would have struck
Averroes's opponents as unsatisfactory: "What gives the problem of the eternity of the
world its entire acuteness is the circumstance that it introduces a necessary determinism
into the initial genesis of the cosmic order, occasioned by its conception of an entity (such
as the World, Matter, or Movement) co-eternal with God. For in this conception there
lurks a positive limitation of God's creative power, insofar as He is not conceived as Agent
in an absolute sense; but rather as the Agent of becoming or mutation only, whose activity
consists merely in bringing forth into a state of actuality the virtual possibilities latent in
Prime Matter, which is alleged to be co-eternal with Him." Majid Fakhry, *Islamic Occasionalism and its Critique by Averroes and Aquinas* (London: George Allen and Unwin, 1958),
118. We shall have to wait and see whether Averroes is successful in meeting these objections to an "eternal creation" and, indeed, whether he is successful in making a coherent
case for an understanding of creation that meets rigorous Aristotelian conceptual demands
while also remaining faithful to the text of the Quran. Suffice it to say here that Averroes's
tack is to argue that all important differences between the law and philosophy are problems
of language and can be resolved through proper logical reasoning (a line of argument later
very congenial to Christian Scholastics).

40. *DT*, no. 18.

tents "things generated." At the other extreme is something that has not come into existence from something else or by something else. Time does not precede its existence. This is God.

So far, so good: neither the philosophers nor orthodox theologians such as the Ash'arites would disagree. Between these two extremes, however, there is, Averroes argues, a "middle term" or, better, "middle existent"—the world as a whole (*al-ʿalam baʾsra*): "The sort of being between these two extremes is an existent thing that has not come into existence from something and that time does not precede, but that does come into existence by something—I mean, by an agent. This is the world as a whole."[41] The world as whole, Averroes claims, is created insofar as it is generated from another, being composed of finite, generated beings; and yet, it is eternal insofar as no time precedes it and at no time could it have been in pure potentiality to its own existence. Hence, whether we call the world "generated" or "eternal" depends, Averroes argues, on which term we emphasize:

> So it is evident that this latter existent thing has been taken as resembling the existing thing that truly comes into being and the eternally existing thing. Those overwhelmed by its resemblance to the eternal rather than to what is generated name it "eternal," and those overwhelmed by its resemblance to what is generated name it "generated." But, in truth, it is not truly generated, nor is it truly eternal. For what is truly generated is necessarily corruptible, and what is truly eternal has no cause. Among them are those who name it "everlastingly generated"—namely, Plato and his sect, because time according to them is finite with respect to the past.[42]

Here, Averroes attempts to stake out a middle position: the world is truly created because it cannot be the cause of itself—it must be caused by another; but it is, in a sense, eternal, because that there is "no time" when

41. Ibid.

42. Ibid., no. 19. By implying that the debate on the "eternity" of the world goes back to Plato and Aristotle, Averroes is setting the reader up for his own conclusion: that there is no real fundamental difference between the two views and that, far from being in opposition to Islam, philosophy contains within itself the resolution to this problem. See Averroes, *Le Livre du discours décisif*, 200n80.

God began causing the world. In other words, Averroes, in trying to establish this "middle" position, has to make use of terminology reminiscent of eternal "emanation" as employed by the Neoplatonists, although, as we shall see, Averroes rejected emanation in any strict sense.[43] And yet, Averroes reminds the reader, the terms "eternal" and "generated" do not, strictly speaking, apply here: if by "eternal" we mean, "without a cause," then it does not apply to the world and, if by "generated" we also mean "corruptible," then it does not apply to the world either, because the world, as a whole, is both caused and incorruptible (and even in part, if we consider the celestial bodies, which are incorruptible by their very natures). So the world is some third thing, whose meaning is partially captured by "eternal" and "generated," but only partially.

Not forgetting that he is a *qāḍī* and jurist making a ruling on a point of Islamic law, Averroes also argues that he has scriptural warrant for this middle position. As he states:

> For if the apparent sense of the law is scrutinized, it will become apparent from the verses comprising a communication about the coming into existence of the world that, in truth, its form is generated, whereas being itself and time extend continuously at both extremes—I mean, without interruption. That is because His statement (may He be exalted), "And He is the one Who created the heavens and the earth in six days, and His throne was on the water" [11:7], requires, in its apparent sense, an existence before this existence—namely, the throne and water—and a time before this time, I mean, the one joined to the form of this existence, which is the number of the movement of the heavenly sphere.[44]

Far from the philosophers violating the clear and apparent meaning of Scripture, it is the dialectical theologians who do not take the Quran in its apparent sense but interpret it, since there is no statement in it to

43. Early in his career, Averroes seemed to have subscribed to the theories of emanation as found in the writings of Avicenna and al-Farabi. But he then changed his mind. Kogan argues that this was not primarily because of a deeper reading of Aristotle, but rather due to the devastating critique of the principle of emanation by al-Ghazali. See Barry Kogan, "Averroes and the Theory of Emanation," *Medieval Studies* 43 (1981): 384–404.

44. *DT*, no. 21. For the Aristotelian definition of "time" given at the end of this passage, see *Aristotelis Physica*, ed. W. D. Ross (Oxford: Oxford University Press, 1950), IV, 11, 220a24–26.

the effect that God created things out of nothing or with a beginning in time.[45] And indeed, as was mentioned before, the Quran itself nowhere states explicitly that God created *de novo* and *ex nihilo*.

However reasonable Averroes thought his proposed solution to the problem, it certainly appears forced. Averroes assumes for the sake of his argument that we can treat the whole world as a single substance. But this assumption is dubious on the very Aristotelian grounds that Averroes was dedicated to defending: for Aristotle, what is primary are individual substances; we cannot treat the world as a whole as an individual substance, which would be committing the fallacy of composition. Nor would this solution satisfy objections on theological grounds, such as al-Ghazali's claim that the philosophers reduce God's creative agency to that of a merely natural, material, mindless, will-less substance such as earth or fire. Nothing in Averroes's proposed solution answers this objection. Nevertheless, Averroes apparently sees his position as definitely refuting the charge that the philosophers are "associating" (*yashrikūn*) the universe with God or making it "co-equal" with him, which would be idolatry. That God's creative agency is not like a mindless, material, natural substance, he takes up in his solution to the second problem—that of divine knowledge and agency.

The problem of God's knowledge and what we mean by "knowledge" when applied to God is treated in some detail in a document, called the *Damimah* or "appendix," that was attached to the *Decisive Treatise* at a quite early date. Far from being an afterthought, however, as the name "appendix" implies, most modern scholars now think that this short work in epistolary form was composed as an introduction to the subject matter of the *Decisive Treatise*.[46] Hence, it has been translated into English as "Epistle Dedicatory" and should be read as an exploratory essay setting up some of the main conceptual distinctions and arguments of the *Decisive Treatise*. In this epistle, Averroes explains with admirable clarity the problem in ascribing the predicate "knowledge" to God based on our understanding of our own acts of knowledge:

45. *DT*, no. 22.

46. See the explanatory introduction by Charles Butterworth in Averroes, *Decisive Treatise and Epistle Dedicatory*, xxxix–xl.

The doubt is inevitably like this: If all of these [things] are in God's knowledge (may He be glorified) before they come about, are they in His knowledge the same before their coming about, or are they in His knowledge at the moment of their existence other than the way they are in His knowledge before they exist? If we say that they are in God's knowledge at the moment of their existence other than the way they are in His knowledge before they exist, it results that eternal knowledge changes and that when they emerge from nonexistence to existence additional knowledge is generated. That is preposterous for eternal knowledge.[47]

If God knows particulars that come to be and pass away in time, does that not introduce some sort of change in God, since God would have to know them in time? But God, in Aristotelian terms, is pure act without any potentiality and cannot change. Therefore, it seems that God cannot know particulars as particulars: "Therefore, one of two matters is obligatory: either eternal knowledge differs in itself, or generated things are not known to it. Both matters are preposterous for it (may He be glorified)."[48]

One way of resolving this difficulty is to say that that the temporal accident of the particular thing's existence does not matter for the knowledge of it. What truly matters is the relation of knower and the thing known, which is eternal on the side of the knower, God. And yet, Averroes does not see this solution as satisfactory: the time during which something exists is indeed a necessary property of its particularity. It makes no sense to say God knows this particular thing without also knowing *when* it exists: "In sum, it is difficult to conceive that knowledge of something before it exists and knowledge of it after it exists is the very same knowledge."[49] It is, in short, a very different thing to say that I have knowledge of what a "chair" is in its ideal form before it comes to exist *in rerum natura*, and what *this chair* that exists before me now is after it comes to exist. To assume that God is not cognizant of this difference is to take something away from God's knowledge, not to explain it.

The key mistake, as Averroes sees it, is to think of God's cognition

47. Averroes, "Epistle Dedicatory," in *Decisive Treatise and Epistle Dedicatory*, no. 3.
48. Ibid., no. 3.
49. Ibid., no. 5.

of created things in a way analogous to the way we human beings know things, when, in fact, divine cognition and human cognition are radically different. Again, the mistake is to describe with one term two different realities. Averroes sums up the difference thusly:

> What resolves this doubt for us is to become cognizant that the case for eternal knowledge with respect to existence is different from the case for generated knowledge with respect to existence. That is because existence is the cause and reason of our knowledge, while eternal knowledge is the cause and reason of existence. If additional knowledge comes to be generated in eternal knowledge when existence exists after having not existed, as that is generated in generated knowledge, it results that eternal knowledge would be caused by existence—not be a cause for it. Thus, in that instance there must be no change generated such as is generated with respect to generated knowledge.[50]

Our knowledge of things is caused by the things known—the actual chair is the cause of my coming to known the chair. Our intellect is only actualized as intellect when it comes to know particular things. It is otherwise with God—God's cognition of "this chair" is what actualizes or brings into existence "this chair." God's intellect is fully actualized, since it is simply a necessary attribute of his purely actual existence. Therefore, it is God's fully actualized knowledge of all things, even in their particularity, that actualizes the existence of these things *in rerum natura*:

> Therefore, eternal knowledge is connected with existence as an attribute other than the one by which generated knowledge is connected with it. It is not that it is not at all connected, as it was related that the philosophers said concerning this doubt, namely, that He (may He be glorified) does not know particulars. The matter is not as was fancied with respect to them. Rather, they are of the opinion that He does not know particulars by means of generated knowledge—a stipulation of which is that it is generated as they are generated—since He is a cause of them and not caused by them, as is the case with generated knowledge. This is the ultimate in removing imperfections [from God] that is obligatory to acknowledge.[51]

50. Ibid., no. 7.
51. Ibid., no. 9.

Despite these explanations, it still remains elusive what Averroes really means by divine cognition. Like in the problem of the eternity of the world, Averroes suggests that God's knowledge of things is in between two extremes: on the one hand, God knows particulars insofar as he causes them to exist; and yet, God, as an immaterial being, cannot know matter as such—he can only actualize the immaterial form that is potentially in the matter. God can only know universals, since he only actualizes universal forms in particular matter; and yet, Averroes argues, universals in the human intellect are only potential insofar as they need to be realized in knowing particular substances, and the divine intellect must be free of all potentiality. So God's knowledge of things is both universal and particular, and yet can be neither universal nor particular. Nor does Averroes explain clearly or coherently how God's knowledge is the cause of creatures. He seems to argue that God's knowledge is the formal and final cause of the existence of creatures, in the sense that his knowledge draws their actuality out of the pre-eternity of the potentiality of matter.[52] Averroes knows that he has no scriptural warrant for this. But this is, perhaps, besides the point. Just as al-Ghazali's goal, in his *Incoherence of the Philosophers*, was not to prove the philosophers wrong on God's ignorance of particulars, but simply to show that they did not and could not prove such a thing on their own principles, Averroes's goal here seems to be that the theologians cannot prove that the philosophers deny to God knowledge of particulars. In other words, Averroes's goal here seems to be primarily dialectical, that is, to show that the charges against the philosophers are inconclusive.

But there is, it seems, another, more demonstrative, goal. Precisely because it is impossible for the human intellect to grasp the essence of divine knowledge, we must content ourselves with understanding the intelligible order in creation of which divine knowledge is the cause. That creation is an eternal yet generated order should be sufficient to lead

---

52. Barry Kogan, *Averroes and the Metaphysics of Causation* (Albany, N.Y.: State University of New York Press, 1985), 230–31. "God is thus identified with the hierarchy of existents, not in all respects, as a pantheist would suppose, but in cognition alone. More specifically, He is the totality of their forms but only because He, unlike the world, has no material dimension." Ibid., 235.

those qualified to a knowledge of God—being eternal, the world shares in the eternal and timeless nature of intelligible forms and thus of divine knowledge; being generated, it manifests the handiwork of the divine Craftsman. So Averroes's response to the second problem, whereby he argues that we must understand that we must use the word, "knowledge," in an equivocal sense when applied to God and to human beings, supports his response to the first problem: we can know God through his generated yet eternal handiwork. This knowledge comes about primarily through philosophical reflection on both the universe and on the nature and place of the human intellect within the universe. For only by understanding the nature and scope of the human intellect and its place in the cosmic order can we understand how, to what degree, and for whom the religious law is necessary for coming to a knowledge of God and, by the same token, to whom philosophical reflection is to be restricted.

The purpose of the divine law, then, is to command the study of the order in creation in order to come to a greater and surer knowledge of its Creator. This purpose is not nugatory: without such a law, human society would be bereft of right guidance and most people would be ignorant of what sorts of actions lead to happiness and a good society in which philosophical activity is cultivated. This is why the law also limits to a select few those who are able to interpret the demonstrative truth behind the ambiguities of the law: "Now what judge is greater than the one who makes judgments about existence, as to whether it is thus or not thus? These judges are the learned ones whom God has selected for interpretation, and this error that is forgiven according to the law is only the error occasioned by learned men when they reflect upon the recondite things that the law makes them responsible for reflecting upon."[53] For the law to complete and fulfill its purpose, it itself commands those who are learned in the philosophical sciences to "make an effort" (*ijtihād*) in laying bare the demonstrative truths taught by the law.[54] These demonstrative truths then become the vehicle by which the intellects at least of a few are perfected and attain to supreme happiness.

53. *DT*, no. 23.
54. Ibid., no. 24.

This does not mean that these "learned few" will not make mistakes in reasoning. But this does not mean either, Averroes argues, that philosophical reasoning is opposed to the law or undermines it. The philosopher in the truest and fullest sense is one who recognizes that the "genius" of the religious law is in adapting the philosophical truths about God to the various abilities and disposition of people in society. And since all philosophizing must take place in society (unlike what Averroes's older contemporary Ibn Tufayl supposed),[55] the religious law performs an absolutely necessary function:

> Concerning the things that are known only by demonstration due to their being hidden, God has been gracious to His servants for whom there is no path by means of demonstration—either due to their innate dispositions, their habits, or their lack of facilities for education—by coining for them likenesses and similarities of these [hidden things] and calling them to assent by means of those likenesses, since it is possible for assent to those likenesses to come about by means of the indications shared by all—I mean, the dialectical and rhetorical. That is the reason for the law being divided into an apparent sense and an inner sense. For the apparent sense is those likenesses coined for those meanings, and the inner sense is those meanings that reveal themselves only to those adept in demonstration. These [likenesses and meanings] are the four or five sorts of existing things that Abu Hamid [al-Ghazali] mentioned in the book *The Distinction*.[56]

Precisely for fulfilling its purpose of leading all men to a knowledge of God suited to their characters and abilities, the religious law stipulates that there is an apparent sense for which it is unbelief to interpret. On

---

55. Such as in his work *Hayy ibn Yaqdhan* ("The Living One Son of the Awakened").

56. *DT*, no. 27. For the five "degrees" of existence in al-Ghazali, see the discussion by Avital Wohlman in her book, *Al-Ghazali, Averroes and the Interpretation of the Qur'an*, 38ff. The first degree is that of the objective domain of the real, on which depend all the other degrees, which are (2) the subjective existence of things as experienced in the human mind, (3) the perduring representations of things in the human mind, (4) the meanings of things independent of their existence in the human mind, and (5) an analogous or metaphorical mode of existence which, technically, is not a separate degree but a mode in which one degree of existence is related to another. Hence, al-Ghazali is unclear on whether the number is four or five, and Averroes follows him in his indecision. See Averroes, *Le Livre du discours décisif*, 202n96.

the other hand, there is an apparent sense for which it is unbelief *not* to interpret for those adept in demonstration. Examples of these are verses referring to God as being in a "place" or as having a body. There are, however, verses for which there lacks a consensus as to whether the apparent sense is to be left standing or if it is to be interpreted—an example of such verses are those that raise the question of the nature of the afterlife:

> For anyone not adept in science, it is obligatory to take them [the descriptions of the next life] in their apparent sense; for him, it is unbelief to interpret them because it leads to unbelief. That is why we are of the opinion that, for anyone among the people whose duty it is to have faith in the apparent sense, interpretation is unbelief because it leads to unbelief. Anyone adept in interpretation who divulges that to him calls him to unbelief; and the one who calls to unbelief is an unbeliever.[57]

Demonstrative reasoning leads to the conclusion that there is an afterlife only in the sense that one intellect for all human beings survives the death of the body; the religious law, by contrast, encourages ordinary Muslims to believe that there is a personal immortality and resurrection of the body. For Averroes, the religious law teaches Muslims to believe this for a very good reason: ordinary people will cultivate virtue and avoid vice only if they think they will be individually rewarded for the former and individually punished for the latter. The philosopher, by contrast, realizes that knowledge of God and the perfection of the intellect and the actualization of virtue that follows from that knowledge are their own rewards. Nevertheless, the philosopher must keep such knowledge to himself, and Averroes even criticizes al-Ghazali for divulging to the unlearned things that should be kept only among the learned, as well as being inconsistent with his own principles, since he was a "philosopher among philosophers, an Ash'arite among Ash'arites, and a Sufi among Sufis."[58]

For Averroes, then, there is nothing given to us by the best use of human reason that does not agree with what is in the religious law. Un-

57. *DT*, no. 34.
58. Ibid., no. 35.

like a Christian theologian like Aquinas, however, Averroes argues that all that is found in the religious law is, in principle, accessible to and demonstrable by human reason.[59] Alain de Libera thus asserts: "Averroes does not consider the possibility of a contradiction between philosophical *truth* and religious *truth*. There are only two fundamental possibilities: contradiction between philosophical error and philosophical truth; contradiction between theological error and revealed Truth."[60] Hence, Averroes tries to show that the two key problems at issue between the law and philosophy—whether the world is eternal or created in time and whether God knows particulars—find their resolution in philosophy itself (as exemplified in the supposed debate between Plato and Aristotle on whether the world is created). What the religious law does is to get men and women to act in accordance with this philosophical truth, whatever it may be; but it itself does not resolve the issue or perfect our knowledge of God. But this view of revelation is precisely what we would expect if revelation is conceived of as an impersonal emanation in the form of a book. Its truth lies not in the relationship it establishes between the human and the divine, but in the content of that revelation. And if it is only the content that matters, then it is something that is accessible, in principle, to philosophical speculation (or Sufi ecstasy, as in al-Ghazali).

THE INTENTION OF THE LAW
CONTRA AL-GHAZALI

According to Averroes, the highest intention of the law is to give men of wisdom (philosophers) knowledge about God and about divine truths. And yet, the primary intention of the law is to make these truths accessible to all men, even those of the lowest intellectual ability and of

---

59. "If he claims that he is at least sure that nothing in human reason is contrary to the truth of the faith, Thomas, in contrast to Ibn Rushd, takes care to maintain that reason does not suffice in being able to comprehend the integral content of revelation. At the same time, he brings back, as he should, philosophical *certainty* to the evidences of the first principles of what we know by nature, without reducing this certainty to them." De Libera, introduction to *L'Islam et la raison*, 63.

60. Ibid., 67.

the most sluggish virtue. There is in the religious law, then, a tension between revealing divine truths that, comprehensible as they may be to the learned, will destroy the faith of the simple and concealing those truths from the simple, so that a socio-religious order may be preserved in which all men are pointed to right action and happiness:

> You ought to know that what is intended by the law is only to teach true science and true practice. True science is cognizance of God (may He be blessed and exalted) and of all the existing things as they are, especially the venerable ones among them; and cognizance of happiness in the hereafter and of misery in the hereafter. True practice is to follow the actions that promote happiness and to avoid the actions that promote misery; and cognizance of these actions is what is called "practical science."[61]

As this passage indicates and as Roger Arnaldez argues, the primary intention of the religious law for Averroes is practical: it is to raise up the ordinary man of limited intelligence and occupied with the task of earning a living to higher goals and more refined thoughts; and in turn, the religious law commands the man of philosophical science and demonstration to employ his wisdom for the good of his community and of the Muslim *umma*. Thus, the very form of the *Decisive Treatise* as a *fatwa* commands both the mass of men and the learned elite to actualize philosophical wisdom to the degree that is appropriate to their intellectual ability and station in life.[62]

The purpose of the religious law is, therefore, not very different from "law" as Plato envisioned it: a setting up a rational organization of

---

61. *DT*, no. 38. See Muhsin Mahdi, "Remarks on Averroes' *Decisive Treatise*," in *Islamic Theology and Philosophy*, 201.

62. "As for the unity of the law, it shows the unity of man in body and soul: he should not be content with the material observance of what the law prescribes, neither should he turn away from the world of the senses to be absorbed in a purely contemplative life. Thus, through law, the man of flesh is raised up toward the spirit, and the spiritual man is called back to his duties in the world. We would not be surprised if this concept were the deep conviction of Averroes, the jurist and the philosopher." Arnaldez, *Averroes*, 24–25. Hence, Averroes is in accord with the general view of Islam by Muslims as the "happy medium" between the religious "laws" of the Jews and that of the Christians, whereby the former is seen as too "carnal" and the latter as too "spiritual" and, therefore, not as suitable to human life as is Islamic law.

society whereby philosophical contemplation may be more easily realized, at least by the few both able and willing to realize it. And like Plato, Averroes sees the religious law as regulating not just outward, bodily or moral actions, but also the inner disposition of the soul: "These
[actions commanded by the law] are divided into two divisions. One
is the apparent, bodily actions. The science of these is what is called
'jurisprudence.' The second division is actions of the soul—like grati-
tude, patience, and other moral habits that the law calls to or bans. And
the science of these is what is called 'asceticism' [*al-zahd*] and 'the sciences of the hereafter' [*'ulūm al-ākhira*]."[63] Averroes mentions al-Ghazali's
Revival of the Religious Sciences (*Ihya' 'ulūm al-dīn*) in connection with
the second type of actions. In this magisterial work, al-Ghazali attempts
to explain the "inner meaning" of the law's prescriptions, showing that
they lead both to happiness and to knowledge of God. Averroes seems
to be saying very much the same thing. Nevertheless, there is at least one
crucial difference: for al-Ghazali, at least in those matters that Averroes
mentions above of moral science, asceticism (leading, according to the
Sufis at least, to knowledge of God) and in what concerns the hereafter,
the religious law *dispenses with* philosophical knowledge. While the philosophical sciences are useful and even necessary when we are doing logic
or mathematics, or practicing medicine or astronomy, when it comes to
knowledge of God and human happiness, philosophical knowledge is
not only useless but harmful. The main concern of al-Ghazali's mystical
writings is "the apprehension of realities." "Direct experience of them
involves mystical vision. It is this mystical vision that yields certainty."[64]
Philosophical reasoning about divine things only yields confusion, "incoherence," and uncertainty. The goal of the religious law, therefore, is
to make this direct experience or mystical vision possible.[65] Revela-

---

63. *DT*, no. 38.

64. Michael E. Marmura, "Al-Ghazali," in Adamson, *Cambridge Companion to Arabic
Philosophy*, 152.

65. "The way of putting reason at the service of faith, then, has been set. It will be a
way of practice and interiorization. Not the task of transforming speculative reason so that
philosophy itself might serve as a vehicle of insight into matters divine, but rather to har-
ness the discerning powers of reason to the inner task of becoming the sort of person I am
called to become. The operative power in that activity will be the heart, for it is natural to

tion gives us by direct unveiling what the philosophers claim to give us by syllogistic reasoning. But unlike the reasoning of the philosophers, unveiling gives the believer a direct "taste" (*dhawq*) or "witnessing" (*mushāhida*) of divine realities.

So, there is a strange sense in which al-Ghazali is not really opposed to the cognition or knowledge that philosophy claims to give us about God (something which we shall demonstrate in some detail in the next chapter); he is opposed, rather, to the claim that philosophy can establish or give this knowledge *independent* of revelation.[66] In short, al-Ghazali wanted to deprive philosophy of its power to *establish* the claims of religion (or the *shari'a*) on its own. Even if it goes too far to call al-Ghazali's *Incoherence of the Philosophers* a "pseudo-refutation,"[67]—for al-Ghazali clearly appears to think that philosophy is unable to establish *any* of its claims about divine things using reason—it is still clear for the "proof of Islam" that the religious law *usurps* philosophical knowledge and replaces it with direct cognition and mystical experience.[68] This is why al-Ghazali trains all his considerable argumentative power on trying to show the utter contingency of all finite things and the

---

the heart to respond to God's command (*'amr*). The goal of understanding God and God's world is clearly subordinated to the practical aim of aligning one's entire self to the response of an untrammeled heart. Yet the subordination is a tactical one, for with that alignment will come an understanding far surpassing the necessary truths it is native to intellect to know. What is revealed to the pure of heart, whose intellectual efforts are bent on detecting and detaching the veils of concern from their hearts, are the mysteries of the *malakūt*: the spiritual world, quite invisible to intellect (*'aql*) alone." David Burrell, "The Unknowability of God in al-Ghazali," *Religious Studies* 23, no. 2 (1987): 175.

66. See Alexander Treiger, *Inspired Knowledge in Islamic Thought: Al-Ghazali's Theory of Mystical Cognition and Its Avicennian Foundation* (London: Routledge, 2012), 94.

67. This is the claim of Treiger. See ibid., 104. Thus, al-Ghazali's attacks on the self-subsistent and therefore immortal nature of the human soul does not mean that he denies the immortality of the soul or even its immaterial nature; it only means that he argues that philosophy cannot establish these truths with any certainty and that only revelation can do so. See also Timothy J. Gianotti, *Al-Ghazali's Unspeakable Doctrine of the Soul: Unveiling the Esoteric Psychology and Eschatology of the "Ihya"* (Leiden: E. J. Brill, 2001), 95.

68. Hence subsequent Sufis like Ibn al-'Arabi will argue that revelation contains within itself a wisdom (*ḥikma*) that unveils itself directly to the believer who is prepared intellectually, morally, and ascetically to receive these unveilings. Not only is reason unnecessary for *ḥikma*, but reason as embodied in *falsafa* is a particularly stubborn obstacle to the reception of this wisdom. See my book, *Logos and Revelation*, chap. 5.

fallacy of any supposed necessary causal connection between them, for if every particular thing and every event is utterly contingent, then human reason is powerless to infer anything about God other than what the divine book itself reveals. This is also why al-Ghazali argues that God is not, strictly speaking, the *cause* of the universe, first or otherwise, but a "personal agent who freely chooses and who precedes His creation."[69] "If God becomes no more than the necessary correlative of a necessary world, divine activity is drastically curtailed; the world's ontological status, extravagantly enlarged. God is the ground of being, but nothing more; the world remains 'dependent' on God, but hangs only by the most tenuous metaphysical thread, vaguely characterized as 'ontological dependence.'"[70] For al-Ghazali such a view is heresy: philosophy gives us only vain reasonings, while the religious law directly unveils divine truths only to those who abandon such vain reasonings.

Needless to say, Averroes argues strenuously against this notion of the purpose of the divine law. Not only does al-Ghazali's notion of the divine law's purpose claim that the religious law, when properly realized by the enlightened Sufi, renders philosophy utterly superfluous, but it also, according to Averroes, causes immense damage to the general run of Muslims by leading them into spiritual and intellectual waters beyond their ken. Given that the goal of the law for Averroes is to teach true science and true practice, it can teach these things in two ways: by forming concepts or by bringing about assent. And it can do these two things in the three ways discussed above—by demonstration, by dialectical reasoning, or by rhetoric. Indeed, it is obligatory according to the law to use these three methods, whereas al-Ghazali, from Averroes's perspective, makes no such proper distinctions in his explications of the true meaning of the religious law. For the Muslim, Averroes asserts, faith is above all a form of *practice*. "There is no opposition between the two [religion and philosophy], but neither is any communication possible between the symbolic language intended for the former [the masses]

69. Frank Griffel, *Al-Ghazali's Philosophical Theology* (Oxford: Oxford University Press, 2009), 280.

70. Lenn E. Goodman, "Ghazali's Argument from Creation," *International Journal of Middle East Studies* 2, no. 1 (1971): 77.

and the demonstrative language of the latter [the philosophers]."[71] The symbolic language of the Quran is not some veil hiding a deeper "mystical" truth; it is, rather, simply a rational technique for bringing correct belief and right conduct to the masses. The Quran is not, then, a vehicle for higher philosophical truths except insofar as it *brings them down* to the ordinary people, as opposed to being a vehicle for the supposed *ascent* of the Sufi to higher cognition.

Thus, we have the law's provision for the three types of people found in any polity: it provides for no interpretations for the multitude (*al-jumhūr*) even in dialectical or rhetorical books:

> For this kind [of people], it is obligatory to declare and to say, with respect to the apparent sense—when it is such that the doubt as to whether it is an apparent sense is in itself apparent to everyone, without cognizance of its interpretation being possible for them—that it is one of those [verses] that resemble one another [whose interpretation is] not known, except to God, and that it is obligatory for the stop in His saying (may He be exalted) to be placed here: "None knows their interpretation but God" [3:7]. In the same way is the answer to come forth with respect to a question about obscure matters for whose understanding no path exists for the multitude—as with His saying (may He be exalted), "And they will ask you about the spirit, say: 'The spirit is by the command of my Lord; and of knowledge you have been given only a little.'" [17:85].[72]

So, for the ordinary Muslim, the learned must cite verse 3:7 of the Quran to the effect that "None knows their [the ambiguous verses' interpretation] but God," putting the "stop" or period after "God." But, as has been pointed out, Averroes is being disingenuous here, since there is no consensus on where verse 3:7 ends, for the verse continues, "and those firmly grounded in knowledge, who say, 'We believe in it; it is all from the Lord.'" Among the *'ulema* in Averroes's time, there was—and still is—a good deal of controversy as to where one puts the period in verse 3:7 of the Quran "*Wa mā ya'alamu ta'wīlahu illā illahu* [period?]/*wa-r-rasikhūna*

71. Urvoy, *Ibn Rushd*, 79.
72. *DT*, no. 46.

fi l-'ilmi.[73] Thus we have a choice between two conflicting theses: (1) God alone knows the meaning of the ambiguous verses, or (2) God and "those firmly grounded in knowledge" (that is, the philosophers) know this meaning. Averroes implies that the "learned" will put the period after "and those firmly grounded in knowledge…." Truth is "double" in the sense that the masses must hold the apparent meaning of every verse in the Quran as true so that they do not fall into doubt and unbelief, while the philosophers, on the other hand, know the true meaning of various difficult verses of the Quran, which they cannot communicate to the masses. In this way, the conflict between the thesis that only God knows the interpretation of the verse—a thesis reserved for the common people among the Muslims—and that both God and the learned know the interpretation—reserved for the philosophers—is resolved:

> For we have witnessed some groups who suppose they are philosophizing and have, by means of their astounding wisdom, apprehended things that disagree with the law in every manner—I mean [things] not admitting of interpretation. And [they suppose] that it is obligatory to declare these things to the multitude. By declaring those corrupt beliefs to the multitude, they have become the reason for the multitude's and their own perdition in this world and in the hereafter.[74]

There is a sense, then, in which Averroes tries "to turn the tables" on theologians like al-Ghazali by charging *them*, and not the philosophers, for trying to spread esoteric interpretations of the Quran that lead the common run of people to become confused and ultimately fall into unbelief.

In short, the mistake of theologians like al-Ghazali, Averroes seems to be saying, is that they do not understand the true purpose of the religious law. The purpose of the religious law is not to "veil" deep phil-

---

73. Friedrich Niewöhner, "Zum Ursprung der Lehre von der doppelten Wahrheit: eine Koran-Interpretation des Averroes," in *Averroismus im Mittelalter und in der Renaissance*, ed. Friedrich Niewöhner and Loris Sturlese (Zurich: Spur Verlag, 1994), 32. As Niewöhner remarks, even contemporary translations of the Quran into modern European languages are split as to where to place the period in this verse. The recent translation of the Quran by M. A. S. Abdel Haleem (Oxford: Oxford University Press, 2004) tries to finesse the issue by the liberal use of dashes.

74. *DT*, no. 47.

osophical truths so that they may be "unveiled" in experiential, mystical cognition; the purpose of the religious law is simply to instill true belief in the mass of humankind so that the mass of humankind is led to a sort of "spiritual health," which in turn leads to happiness. Averroes draws an analogy between the religious law and medicine, and between the Lawgiver and the physician:

> Now this illustration is certain and not poetical, as someone might say. It is a sound linking between the one and the other. That is because the link between the physician and the health of bodies is [the same as] the link between the Lawgiver and the health of souls—I mean, the physician is the one who seeks to preserve the health of bodies when it exists and to bring it back when it has disappeared, while the Lawgiver is the one who aspires to this with respect to the health of souls.[75]

"This health is what is called 'piety' [*taqwā*]."[76] Hence piety is attained by means of law-based actions and not by theoretical cognition of divine truths. "It can be seen that the problem raised is that of the interior balance of concrete men, and not the conciliation of abstract concepts like reason and faith."[77] The religious law is like a medicine that is administered by the learned to the common people for the sake of their spiritual health and happiness; but only the learned know the demonstrative truth of why this law is healthful and the principles that make the law effective and beneficial. In this way, the religious law can be assimilated almost completely into secular learning.

By healing division and strife in the interpretation of the religious law, philosophy fulfills the highest purpose and intention of the religious law which is knowledge of God. By using dialectical arguments to destroy the legitimacy of philosophy to interpret difficult verses of the Quran, the theologians have only brought the literal and apparent meaning of the Quran into doubt and disrepute:

> If it were said, "If these methods followed by the Ash'arites and other adepts in reflection are not the shared methods by which the Lawgiver

75. Ibid., no. 50.
76. Ibid.
77. Arnaldez, *Averroes*, 82.

intended to teach the multitude and by which alone it is possible to teach them, then which ones are these methods in this law of ours?" we would say: "They are the methods that are established in the precious Book alone. For if the precious Book is examined, the three methods existing for all the people will be found in it; and these are the shared methods for teaching the majority of the people and [the method for teaching] the select. And if the matter is examined with respect to them, it will become apparent that no better shared methods for teaching the multitude are to be encountered than the methods mentioned in it."[78]

It is, therefore, the philosophers and not the theologians who have greater respect for the apparent sense of the Quran insofar as they keep their interpretations to the ranks of the learned.[79] If it is philosophy that gives knowledge and not mere belief, then it is philosophy that is in greater accord with the intentions of the law and with the text of the Quran than is dialectical theology in general, and Ash'arism, its most important school, in particular.[80] This is because the intention of the religious law is both to establish the conditions within which philosophy may flourish as well as direct all men of whatever ability or interest to right beliefs and right conduct. The religious law does this by making philosophical principles pervade all of society, consciously or unconsciously.

Thus, Averroes does not plead against the law or against theology (*kalām*); nor does he plead against the masses in favor of philosophy; rather, he pleads for *both* the masses *and* for philosophy: a double pleading that has as its target the masses *and* the elite against the various legal and theological sects in Islam.[81] And this is precisely the program that the Almohads, the "triumphant rule" referred to at the end of the *Decisive Treatise*, have brought to fruition in Andalusia:

78. *DT*, no. 55.
79. Ibid., no. 57. "Ce sont donc les ash'arites qui, sur la question du monde, *interprétant indûment* le Texte révélé, tandis que les péripatéticiens, mais pas les platoniciens, soutiennent une doctrine conforme au sens obvie du Coran." De Libera, *L'Islam et la raison*, 70. Thus, Averroes argues that the Ash'arites cannot appeal to *ijma'* or consensus because there is a class of Muslims, the philosophers, who do not accept that consensus. Hence, if the *'ulema* is to establish a consensus, they must do so with the philosophers. De Libera, introduction to *Le Livre du discours décisif*, 39.
80. Geoffroy, "L'Almohadisme théologique," 40.
81. De Libera, introduction to *Le Livre du discours décisif*, 55–56, 68.

God has removed many of these evils, ignorant occurrences, and mis-
guided paths by means of this triumphant rule. By means of it, He has
brought many good things closer, especially for that sort who follow
the path of reflection and yearn for cognizance of the truth. That is,
this rule calls the multitude to a middle method for being cognizant of
God (glorious is He), raised above the low level of the traditionalists
yet below the turbulence of the dialectical theologians, and alerts the
select to the obligation for complete reflection on the root of the law.[82]

And indeed, in the last part of the *Decisive Treatise*, after a long cata-
logue of the various sects and divisions in Islam, Averroes argues that it
will be the *philosophers*, not the *'ulema*, who will resolve these divisions
and unite the *umma* against the infidels, because they will know and
apply the true meaning of the divine book.

This does not mean that Averroes fails to distinguish between the
spheres of philosophy and theology; still less, that the law is coterminous with philosophy in scope and, therefore, thrusts the law "out of
the domain of the rational altogether," because it supplies nothing that
philosophy does not supply already.[83] The religious law is distinct from
philosophy insofar as it encompasses within itself all sorts of arguments,
from rhetorical to demonstrative such that all men may be directed to
the truth and happiness. It is rational insofar as it communicates effec-
tively a rational end to all. Nevertheless, when it comes to the "highest
goal" of the religious law, that can only be obtained within the domain
of philosophy: only philosophy gives a true cognition, which is to say a
conceptual grasp through demonstration, of divine things. So, while the
divine law is perfect in its sphere—that of communicating right belief
and right conduct leading to happiness for the multitude—so philos-

82. *DT*, no. 60.

83. Such is Majid Fakhry's argument, at least early in his career, writing on the conceptual alternatives available to early Muslim thinkers: "Yet such is the wages of the failure
to distinguish between the two separate spheres of theology and philosophy: theology is
either pronounced coterminous with philosophy in scope, or its claims are dismissed as
groundless. In both cases the validity of its positive claims is impaired and its authority and
validity endangered. In the former case, because it is inevitably subordinated to the authority of reason and reduced to sheer rational dialectic; in the latter, because it is thrust out of
the domain of the rational altogether." Fakhry, *Islamic Occasionalism*, 115.

ophy is perfect in its own sphere—that of grasping conceptually what happiness is and the truths that cause happiness. The two—divine law and philosophical reflection—work hand in hand, but each is complete and perfect in its own sphere. What each does in its own way is to perfect the human being as a rational—and potentially fully intellectual—being: "The determination of the connection between the divine law and human wisdom must ultimately be based on understanding the nature of one of God's creations, man, which the divine law and human wisdom mean to perfect in their respective ways."[84] This is why questions connected with the nature of the intellect and its perfection and relation to the individual human soul come to play such an important role in Averroes's thought.

The purpose of the religious law, then, according to Averroes, is not to impede philosophy, banish philosophy, nor suppress philosophy; far from it. But neither is the purpose of the religious law to perfect philosophy, by correcting any errors or by revealing the supreme Artisan himself.[85] Rather, the purpose of the religious law is to create the conditions in which philosophical perfection may be realized, a perfection that lies in the perfection of the human being *qua* intellect or intelligence. In order to do this, the religious law must have, however, an absolute character: it must be able to command philosophical reflection on its own authority and, therefore, does not need philosophy to establish its own legitimacy. The law's legitimacy comes from the providential and rational order of creation itself. So, while both philosophy and the religious law both, in their own way, perfect man as man, they do not and cannot complete or perfect each other. Philosophy becomes the judge of the religious law, but only for the learned few. The religious law legitimizes philosophy, but only in the eyes of the multitude.

84. Mahdi, "Remarks," 201.

85. De Libera, introduction to *Le Livre du discours décisif*, 67. Thus, as Jacques Attali notes "Science et foi sont pour lui [Averroes] autonomes." *Raison et foi: Averroès, Maïmonide, Thomas d'Aquin* (Paris: Bibliothèque nationale de France, 2004), 24. While Attali is not a scholar of medieval philosophy but an economist and *homme politique*, he is surely right on this point, even if this author disagrees with much of his analysis of these three figures elsewhere in his short book.

CONCLUSION

It is a fair question to ask, however, how decisive is this decision? Could anyone, the masses, the religious scholars or *'ulema*, or a philosopher be content with such a ruling? Putting aside the masses, who would probably not even understand the ruling, the religious scholars would certainly not be inclined to view philosophy, mere human reasoning, as the judge of a divine and hence absolutely authoritative law. And they would naturally be skeptical, even hostile, for reasons well beyond corporative interest. For in what sense can the religious law have an absolute and binding character if intellectual perfection lies outside its purview? If the religious law is a truly perfect and comprehensive blueprint for society—and Averroes basically says as much—then why cannot the religious law perfect the intellect without recourse to philosophy at all? Averroes's argument, in effect, seems to be circular: it is using the law to legitimize an activity that essentially lies outside the law and even judges the true or inner meaning of the religious law.

This is precisely the claim, *avant la lettre*, of al-Ghazali, against whose arguments the *Decisive Treatise* is not so subtly aimed. The entire work of al-Ghazali—and particularly his *Iḥya' 'ulūm ad-dīn*—is basically an attempt to demonstrate that the religious law can not only perfect the intellect, but do so in a way superior to philosophy.[86] In this sense, al-Ghazali is much more decisive than Averroes: the perfection of the intellect comes about either through following and contemplating the religious law or through philosophical reasoning and contemplation; it cannot be both. There is no sense in al-Ghazali that philosophical reasoning can itself be perfected by divine grace and corrected and elevated by divine revelation; rather it must be annihilated quite literally in *fana'*, the annihilation of the individual intellect in the effulgence of the divine Light. There is, in short, no notion of grace perfecting nature as we find in Aquinas. But neither do we find this notion in Averroes: philosophy needs no perfection, since it is the highest perfection of the human being as human being, nor does the divine law need perfection,

---

86. Marmura, "Al-Ghazali," 152.

since it is an integral part of the divine order of the world established by the supreme Artisan. In short, what we have in Averroes is an epitome of what Brague calls an *episteme* of digestion: philosophy understands revelation insofar as revelation is swallowed up into the cosmic order.

It is evident from what we have seen in this chapter, that the nature, operation, and place in the cosmic order of the human intellect is of critical importance for Averroes (and al-Ghazali) in understanding the proper nature and function of revelation. What the nature and role of the human intellect is, according to these prominent Muslim thinkers, will tell us much about how Islam understands (or fails to understand) the nature and role of reason vis-à-vis revelation, which will be topic of our next chapter.

CHAPTER 2

IS REVELATION REALLY
NECESSARY?

Revelation and the Intellect in
Averroes and al-Ghazali

As we saw in the last chapter, Averroes argues that philosophy and the religious law accord in leading to the perfection of the human intellect, which is the proper end of philosophy and the highest goal of the religious law. Hence, problems concerning the nature of the intellect and its perfection are central to Averroes's philosophical and religious thought. Indeed, his doctrine of the intellect would be what most medieval Christian and Jewish philosophers and theologians thought of when they heard the name "Averroes."[1]

---

1. As Remi Brague reminds us, the *Decisive Treatise* constitutes an almost infinitesimal portion of Averroes's *oeuvre* and a rather unrepresentative portion at that. His main preoccupation is with philosophical truth, which means, of course, the philosophy of Aristotle. Key to the realization of the truth, however, is the perfection of the intellect, a project for which Aristotle gives very little guidance, and what little guidance he gives is cryptic and obscure. See Brague, *Au moyen du moyen âge*, "Averroès est-il un gentil?" 397–412. Averroes, therefore, had to strike out on his own, whether he realized it or not. And the relation of the religious law to the perfection of the intellect will play, again whether he realized it or not, an important role in his development of Aristotle's thought on the intellect. Indeed, his teaching on the intellect would be constitutive of "Averroism," a school of philosophical thought taking its inspiration from Averroes's commentaries on Aristotle and popular among medieval and early modern Christian and Jewish thinkers (though absent in the Islamic world).

But the nature, power, and ontological status of the intellect is not just central for Averroes but also for the entire Islamic philosophical tradition—al-Ghazali included. Indeed, the perfection of the intellect through revelation is a central theme in almost all of al-Ghazali's works. This assertion may seem strange, since al-Ghazali has the reputation of being the enemy—the "destroyer"—of philosophy. And there is a sense in which this is correct, as we shall see. But central to al-Ghazali's thought, as we shall detail below, is the purification of the intellect through detachment from worldly concerns below and illumination from God's revealed book from above. In essence, al-Ghazali's vision of the purified or perfected intellect has much in common with the Platonic vision as found, for example, in the *Phaedo* of Plato or in the *Enneads* of Plotinus. Revelation, of course, is necessary for this purification, since the human intellect lacks the proper illumination to perceive divine realities, an illumination that only the divine realities themselves can supply. But it is purely philosophical in that this illumination is utterly *impersonal* and the human being is only purified *qua* intellect, not *qua* individual human being. Now, to be sure, al-Ghazali claims that revelation is quite clear in asserting a bodily resurrection and individual rewards and punishments in the hereafter; and these assertions must be believed by any Muslim. But still, he has very little basis in his own development of the relation between the intellect and revelation for asserting how this is philosophically possible.

In other words, Averroes and al-Ghazali have much more in common that at first meets the eye. They also fall into the same impasses. For Averroes, it is philosophical reflection that perfects the intellect by conjoining it to the separate agent intellect. In this conjunction there is no room for the perfection of the human being as such, as this individual. So what are we to make of the revealed law and its claims? They simply make possible the matrix in which philosophical reflection can be perfected by an intellectual elite. But this means that revelation does not perfect the intellect as such; in short, revelation has little to do with the apprehension of *truth*—at least, not directly. Of course, someone like al-Ghazali (had he been a contemporary of Averroes) could find this answer unacceptable; for in this case, revelation would be not strictly necessary for knowing the truth of things. So, in order to preserve the claim that revelation *alone* can illumine the human intellect about divine things, philosophy itself—or at least its metaphysical and theological claims—must be destroyed. We can never reason ourselves to divine illumination; all depends upon God.

So, what we shall examine in this chapter are these two diametrically opposite impasses into which Averroes and al-Ghazali fall in trying to think through the relation of the human intellect to divine revelation. The question then becomes, does the way in which Islam conceives revelation, its mode or nature and how it comes to us, make it such that these impasses are inevitable?

REVELATION AND THE INTELLECT
ACCORDING TO AL-GHAZALI

If we look at the doctrine of the intellect in the thought of al-Ghazali, we find an account of the intellect that is ultimately not appreciably different from what we find in Averroes or even in Greek philosophy (especially Platonism or Neoplatonism). For al-Ghazali argues that not only is the human intellect unfallen, but that all it needs is a purification from all earthly thoughts and concerns in order for the intellect to be fully realized as such. To be sure, it is the Quran and its doctrine of *tawḥīd* or the absolute unity and uniqueness of God that allows such a purification. This purification should result in a direct apprehension or "taste" (*dhawq*) of "realities" in an experience that we have come to call "mystical" and which alone yields certainty.[2] But this experience is philosophical insofar as the certainty it yields is philosophical; only it does so without all the vain reasonings of the philosophers. Thus, as Jules Janssens has pointed out: "One sometimes gets the impression that al-Ghazzali is convinced that Ibn Sina's philosophy, including its metaphysics, when

2. "In *The Niche of Lights*, al-Ghazali elucidates what was always known in Islam: that purification of the heart, sincerity, and attaining closeness to God are the inevitable interdependent human results of realizing *tawhid*." Al-Ghazali, *The Niche of Lights* (*mishkāt al-anwār*), parallel English-Arabic text, trans. David Buchman (Provo, Utah: Brigham Young University Press, 1998), xxxi.

'adapted' into the right 'framework,' is acceptable."[3] Al-Ghazali differs from the philosophers, not in the goal, which is knowledge of divine realities, but in the *means* to that goal.

But what are we to make of the reputation of al-Ghazali as the scourge of the philosophers, as the one who "killed" *falsafa* in the Islamic world? In response, one can only say that one has to be careful in receiving standard narratives of the history of philosophy. Certainly al-Ghazali attacked the doctrines of the philosophers in his *Incoherence of the Philosophers* (*tahāfut al-filāsifa*). But a careful reading of the text should make clear that al-Ghazali was not opposed to philosophy as such: logic, natural philosophy, and astronomy, for example, are fine for Muslims to pursue. Nor does he find problematic *per se* the teachings of the philosophers on God and divine things (*illahiyyāt*). Rather, the mistake of the philosophers is twofold: that of *taqlīd* or blind imitation in following the "ancients" and that of overconfidence in demonstration which leaves no room for direct mystical experience or revelation (understood as *unveiling*).[4] The realization of the intellect cannot come about through reasoning or demonstration, al-Ghazali argues, but only through the word of God as revealed in the Quran. To this end, al-Ghazali seeks to demonstrate that all attempts to find a necessary relationship between cause and effect are vain; and if such attempts are vain, then all human reasonings, insofar as they are based on this necessary relationship, are vain.[5] In a world that is utterly contingent and in which every event is brought about by the inscrutable will of God, the "necessitarianism" (whereby the world is the result of an absolutely

3. Jules Janssens, "Al-Ghazzali's *Tahafut*: Is It Really a Rejection of Ibn Sina's Philosophy?" *Journal of Islamic Studies* 12, no. 1 (2001): 15. Although al-Ghazali wishes to rid himself of philosophy through his critiques, he must confront the fact that the two experiences, philosophical and mystical, are *solidaires*. See Mohammed Chaouki Zine, "L'interprétation symbolique du verset de la lumière chez Ibn Sina, Ghazali et Ibn 'Arabi et ses implications doctrinales," *Arabica* 56, no. 6 (2009): 543–95.

4. Janssens, "Al-Ghazzali's *Tahafut*," 15–16.

5. "Against Avicenna and with his Ash'arite tradition, al-Ghazali empties the concept of the natures of created things; things in their different kinds are generally depicted as empty receptacles of God's action, determinantly limiting conditions of what can be received and so of what God can do." Richard Frank, "Al-Ghazali's Use of Avicenna's Philosophy," *Revue des études islamiques* 55–57 (1987–89): 278.

necessary chain of causes proceeding necessarily from the First Cause) of Avicenna and the other *falasifa* is broken.[6] What is left is what is, for al-Ghazali, a purely "Islamic noetic" whereby the Quran is assimilated to a Neoplatonic model of purification and illumination of the intellect and vice-versa.[7]

Indeed, in the most succinct account of this "Islamic noetic" among his many works, *The Niche of Lights* (*mishkāt al-anwār*), al-Ghazali identifies the intelligible light of the (neo)Platonists with the Quran itself:

> The greatest wisdom is the speech of God. Among [those things that] He has spoken is the Quran specifically. For the eye of the rational faculty, the Quran's verses take the place that is occupied by the sun's light for the outward eye, since seeing occurs through it. Hence, it is appropriate for the Quran to be named "light," just as the light of the sun is named "light." The Quran is like the light of the sun, while the rational faculty is like the light of the eye. In this way, we should understand the meaning of His words, "Therefore, have faith in God and His messenger and in the light which We have sent down" [64:8] and His words, "A proof has now come to you from your Lord. We have sent it down to you as a clear light" [4:174].[8]

Al-Ghazali quite explicitly assimilates revelation to an impersonal intelligible light that illuminates the human intellect. As Cornelia Tsakiridou puts it, in al-Ghazali's works "the encounter with the divine Word is principally gnosiological."[9] That is to say, revelation is conceived by al-Ghazali as perfective of the intellect as a purely impersonal "emanation" from God. There is nothing "personal" in this encounter nor does it engage the human being except as pure intellect. To be sure, al-Ghazali

---

6. Griffel, *Al-Ghazali's Philosophical Theology*, 173.

7. "What the scheme represents is nothing less than a systematic organization of common Muslim religious and theological terms so as to conform to a neo-Platonic model and one which, as is evident in the texts, derives principally from Avicenna." Richard Frank, "Al-Ghazali's Use," 279.

8. Al-Ghazali, *Niche of Lights*, I, no. 25, 10.

9. Cornelia Tsakiridou, "Theophany and Humanity in St. Symeon the New Theologian and in Abu Hamid Al-Ghazali," *International Journal of Orthodox Theology* 2, no. 3 (2011): 179. Farther on in the *Niche of Lights*, al-Ghazali even likens the Quran to an "inner sun" (I, no. 26, 11).

argues that the soul must be purified through pious actions done with pure intention in complete conformity to Islamic law. But these acts are only preparatory to what is essential to revelation: inner illumination.

Even more, al-Ghazali claims that the Quran has within itself the similitudes of all that is here "below." The visible world is but a shadow of the "world of dominion." Again, using imagery very reminiscent of Neoplatonism, al-Ghazali argues that the devout Muslim can come to know the exemplary "world of dominion" through a deep and meditative practice of the law, *not* through reasoning from effect to cause:

> For when someone is in the world of dominion, he is with God, "and with Him are the keys to the unseen" [6:59]. In other words, from God the secondary causes [*al-asbāb*] of existent things descend into the visible world, while the visible world is one of the effects of the world of dominion. The visible world comes forth from the world of dominion just as the shadow comes forth [*mujarī al-ẓil biliḍāfa*—"by annexation or attribution"] from the thing that throws it, the fruit comes forth [*biliḍāfa*] from the tree, and the effect comes forth [*biliḍāfa*] from the secondary cause [*sabab*]. The keys to knowledge of effects are found only in their secondary causes. Hence, the visible world is a similitude of the world of dominion—as will be mentioned in the clarification of the niche, the lamp, and the tree. This is because the effect cannot fail to parallel its secondary cause or to have some kind of resemblance with it, whether near or far. But this needs deep investigation. He who gains knowledge of the innermost reality of this discussion will easily have unveiled for himself the realities of the similitudes of the Quran.[10]

While al-Ghazali mentions in this passage that "the keys to knowledge of effects are found only in their secondary causes," it must be mentioned that the translation here of *asbāb* as "secondary causes" is misleading. *Asbāb* simply means "causes," and it is unclear whether al-Ghazali is referring to a "secondary" or "primary" (that is, the divine) cause. The total sense of the passage should incline the reader to the second: that the only real cause is God, the Primary Cause, of anything, and that all that is in the visible world is but a shadow of the divine realities. This reading is also more consistent with al-Ghazali's claims in his other works, partic-

10. Al-Ghazali, *Niche of Lights*, I, no. 31, 12.

ularly his *Incoherence of the Philosophers*. The entire thrust of al-Ghazali's argument is to establish that God's will is totally free and unhindered by any necessity in cause and effect and that, therefore, it is vain for the philosophers to think that they can know anything about God through reasoning from effect to cause.[11] Thus when he describes the relation of effect to cause he uses the fourth aspect of the Arabic root *ḍāfa* (*biliḍ āfa*), which means, among many meanings, "to annex to," "to connect," "to bring into relation." In other words, it is God, not the created thing that relates the effect to the cause, there is nothing in the created thing itself that does so.

Thus, al-Ghazali argues that all that is other than God and the "world of dominion" is in a sense non-existent. The only true or unconditioned existent is God; all else is "annihilated" in his presence.[12] Or, more accurately, things have existence only insofar as they are turned toward God, who is existence itself: "Each thing has two faces: a face towards itself, and a face toward its Lord. Viewed in terms of the face of itself, it is nonexistent; but viewed in terms of the face of God, it exists."[13] As al-Ghazali explains a paragraph earlier: "when the essence of anything other than He is considered in respect of its own essence, it is sheer non-existence. But when it is viewed in respect of the 'face' to which existence flows forth from the First, the Real, then it is seen as existing not in itself but through the face adjacent to its Giver of Existence. Hence, the only existent is the Face of God."[14] It is clear in this passage that al-Ghazali is making use of the Avicennian distinction between essence, quiddity (*mahiyya*) and existence (*anniyya*). As Avicenna argued, the essence of any finite or caused thing is nothing in itself; its existence must be caused

11. "If God becomes no more than the necessary correlative of a necessary world, divine activity is drastically curtailed; the world's ontological status, extravagantly enlarged. God is the ground of being, but nothing more; the world remains 'dependent' on God, but hangs only by the most tenuous metaphysical thread, vaguely characterized as 'ontological dependence.'" Goodman, "Ghazali's Argument from Creation," 77. See also R. E. A. Shanab, "Ghazali and Aquinas on Causation," *Monist: An International Quarterly Journal of General Philosophical Inquiry* 58, no. 1 (1974): 140–50; and Lenn E. Goodman, "Did Al-Ghazali Deny Causality?" *Studia Islamica* 47 (1978): 83–120.

12. Al-Ghazali, *Niche of Lights*, I, no. 42, 16.

13. Ibid., no. 43, 17.

14. Ibid., no. 42, 16.

by something else.[15] Any finite or caused essence cannot exist in and of itself; it must be caused by something that has existence necessarily, as its very essence. This is God. But, as is his wont, al-Ghazali translates this distinction into Quranic language, using the term "face" to refer to Avicenna's idea of essence or quiddity. Thus, the "face" of the creature in itself is nothing; but insofar as the creature "faces" God, who exists necessarily, it "is": "nothing other than He possesses the level of 'with-ness' [ma'iyya]; everything possesses the level of following. Indeed, everything other than God exists only with respect to the face adjacent to Him. The only existent thing is his Face."[16]

Indeed, so absolute is God's existence for al-Ghazali, and so other from the essence of any finite and created being, that God is above all relation or comparison: "the meaning of 'God is most great' is to say that God is too great from any relation or comparison. He is too great for anyone other than He—whether it be prophet or angel—to perceive the innermost meaning of His magnificence. Rather, none knows God with innermost knowledge save God."[17] Creatures can exist and know God only to the degree that they are "faced" toward him, that is, only insofar as their existence is identified with the divine existence (something which only intellectual creatures, like prophets and angels, can do). And yet, what God is in himself, in his existence, can only be known to God himself, for only God exists in and through himself. Thus, not even a prophet or angel can know "the innermost meaning" of God's existence. Only to the degree that the intellectual creature knows, lives, and acts out of God's existence, and not out of its essence, does it come to know God in any way. That is, only insofar as it "extinguishes" in fana' (extinction or annihilation) any sense of existing on its own does it comes to know God through God's own existence. This "extinction" or "annihilation" is not, of course, the extinction or annihilation of anything real,

---

15. Avicenna, *Metaphysics of the Healing*, ed. and trans. Michael E. Marmura (Provo, Utah: Brigham Young University Press, 2006), 1.8. See also the account of Frank Griffel on al-Ghazali's *Niche of Lights*, in *Al-Ghazali's Philosophical Theology*, 245–64. See also Gerald Smith, SJ, "Avicenna and the Possibles," *New Scholasticism* 17, no. 4 (1943): 340–57.

16. Al-Ghazali, *Niche of Lights*, I, no. 44, 17.

17. Ibid., no. 44, 17.

since the creature only exists in and through God in the first place.[18] Accordingly, al-Ghazali asserts that the Sufi must be "extinct from extinction."[19] That is, the annihilation of any sense of his or her own existence is really an affirmation of the divine existence as the only existential act.

Extended to the human action, this principle means that the human being only "exists" insofar as he or she is turned toward God and, even more importantly, "emptied" of all desires and reasonings that would obstruct the divine presence. The human intellect must become a "mirror" in which the divine reality can be reflected. That is the sense, al-Ghazali claims, in which we can understand the hadith which states, "one knows one's Lord by knowing oneself."[20] This is the theme that al-Ghazali develops in some detail in book twenty-one of his magisterial *Revival of the Religious Sciences*. Here he describes the "heart" of the realized knower or "gnostic" (*'ārif*) as being not the physical organ but the seat of the intellect. It is a mirror that can be more or less polished and thus more or less "reflective" of divine realities:

> Know that the seat [*maḥall*] of knowledge ['*ilm*] is the heart, by which I mean the subtle, tenuous substance [*laṭīfa*] that rules all the parts of the body and is obeyed and served by all its members. In its relationship to

18. Hence, Alexander Treiger identifies two moments or aspects of al-Ghazali's speculative Sufism: a monistic moment in which God is realized as the only real existent in relation to him, and to him only do creatures have any existence at all; and a monotheistic moment, in which one realizes that the *essences* or *quiddities* of creatures are not like God in any way. Therefore, God is utterly distinct from creatures. Thus, philosophical knowledge, which deals only with essences, cannot come to a genuine knowledge of God; yet, it is through the polishing of the intellect in pure "philosophical" contemplation that the monistic perspective is realized. That is why Treiger can assert that, compared to statements of earlier Sufis like Hallaj and Bistami, al-Ghazali's Sufism "remained philosophical through and through." Alexander Treiger, "Monism and Monotheism in al-Ghazali's *Mishkat al-anwar*," *Journal of Qur'anic Studies* 9, no. 1 (2007): 16.

19. Al-Ghazali, *Niche of Lights*, I, no. 48, 18.

20. Ibid., II, nos. 32–33, 31. For the intimate connection between al-Ghazali's cosmology and the "realization" of the intellect—a connection that interestingly brings him closer than the tradition would have one believe to the thought of al-Farabi and Avicenna, see Arent Jan Wensinck, "On the Relationship between al-Ghazali's Cosmology and His Mysticism," *Mededeelingen der Koninkijke Akademie van Wettenschappen, Afdeeling Letterkunde*, Deel 75, Serie A (1933): 183–209. As Wensinck notes, for al-Ghazali, Adam's "sin" was to turn his essence away from God and toward other, external essential causes (205–6).

the real nature of intelligible [ma'lūmāt], it is like a mirror in its relationship to the forms [ṣuwar] of changing appearances [mutalawwināt]. For even as that which changes has a form, and the image [mithāl] of that form is reflected in the mirror and represented therein, so also every intelligible has its specific nature, and this specific nature has a form that is reflected and made manifest in the mirror of the heart. Even as the mirror is one thing, the forms of individuals another, and the representation of their image in the mirror another, being thus three things in all, so here, too, there are three things: the heart, the specific natures of things, and the representation and presence of these in the heart. The "intellect" [al-'ālim] is an expression for the heart in which there exists the image of the specific natures of things. The "intelligible" [al-ma'lūm] is an expression for the specific natures of things. "Intelligence" [al-'ilm] is an expression for the representation of the image in the mirror.[21]

The heart of the Sufi is one that is completely polished and thus utterly reflective of divine realities. Thus, the intellect, for al-Ghazali, is "reflective" in the primary and original sense of mirroring the specific natures of things in God. Only in a derivative sense can we apply "reflective" to the reasonings of the philosophers, whose knowledge comes from observing supposed necessary relationships between causes and effects:

> So this is the difference between the knowledge of the prophets and saints and that of the learned and the philosophers [ḥukuma']: the knowledge of the former comes from within the heart through the door that is opened toward the world of spirits, whereas the knowledge of the philosophers comes through the doors of the senses that open to the material world. The wonders of the world of the heart and its wavering between the visible and invisible worlds cannot be fully dealt with in a [study of the] knowledge of proper conduct.[22]

This "labor" of gathering knowledge through the senses and then using reasoning from cause and effect to know the natures of things is completely bypassed by the Sufi, who simply polishes his heart through

---

21. Al-Ghazali, Kitāb sharḥ 'ajā'ib al-qalb: The Marvels of the Heart, Book 21 of the Ihya' 'ulūm al-dīn: The Revival of the Religious Sciences, trans. Walter James Skellie (Louisville, Ky.: Fons Vitae, 2010), 35/III, 16.

22. Ibid., 61/III, 28.

the scrupulous practice of the religious law and meditation on the Quran: "The learned work to acquire knowledge itself and gather it into
the heart, but the saints among the Sufis labor only [with the goal of]
polishing, cleansing, clarifying, and brightening the heart."[23]

To illustrate the difference between knowledge of the philosopher
and that of the Sufi, al-Ghazali recounts, in this same chapter of the
Revival of the Religious Sciences, the fable of the caliph who invited two
groups of painters to decorate a room in his place—one group from Chi-
na and the other from the Byzantine Empire (Rum). So that each group
could not see what the other was doing, the caliph had a curtain hung
down the middle of the room. The Byzantine painters labored mightily to decorate their wall with elaborate mosaics in rich and bold colors
and elaborate designs, whereas the Chinese seemed to do nothing. The
mystery was revealed when the curtain went down: the Chinese simply
put up a finely polished mirror on the other end of the hall, reflecting
the elaborate image put up by the Byzantine artists. The point of this
fable is clear: "The care of the saints in cleansing, polishing, purifying, and
clarifying the heart until the true nature of the Real shines forth clearly
therein with utmost illumination [nihāyat al-ishrāq] is like the work of
the Chinese. The care of the learned and the philosophers in acquiring
and adorning knowledge [naqish al-'ulūm], and the representation of
this adornment in the heart, is like the work of the Byzantines."[24] In one
sense, this fable or parable is a way of illustrating how philosophy and
Sufism are equal ways to comprehend the divine.[25] After all, the philosophers *do* represent the truth of things, which is why al-Ghazali has no
compunction in using philosophical categories, particularly from Avicenna, to articulate the Sufi path or explain the meaning of the Quran. But
in another sense, it is an illustration of how *useless* philosophy is if the
Sufi is able to come to the same knowledge through the mere polishing
of the heart through the ascetic practices of the religious law. The Quran
and Islam are the way to truth without dangerous presumption that human beings can *reason* their way to the truth without the religious law.

23. Ibid.
24. Ibid., 63/III, 28.
25. Griffel, *Al-Ghazali's Philosophical Theology*, 264.

Indeed, the point of this parable seems to be, at the basic level, that only the one who has abandoned reasoning and has allowed his heart to be polished by the Quran and the religious law has intellect in the true sense—not the philosopher. After all, to be intellect is essentially to be reflective. And for the intellect to be reflective, it must be devoid of any personal supposit; the intellect must become completely *impersonal*. As Professor Tsakiridou notes:

> The purified heart will reflect reality because there is nothing left in it of the particular man or women to whom it belongs to obstruct the divine transmission. In this respect, it is not really somebody's heart anymore but an impersonal primordial mirror in which God can project the original creative act, the inscription of the Preserved Tablet—here concentrated and released in bursts or flashes of knowledge of the divine. The Sufi's heart is a tablet on which God paints and writes. When the heart is opened to the divine reality, it is imprinted with the divine archetypes which it then contemplates in "dream-visions" [*rū-ya*]. But it is not thoroughly transfigured, as we see in Symeon. God does not embrace the heart. He imprints it.[26]

As she remarks a little later: "It is not persons that encounter the deity but intellects."[27]

So, although al-Ghazali attacks the presumptions of the philosophers to sure knowledge of the divine, and while he argues for the clear superiority of the Sufi way over vain philosophical reasonings, his ideal of the polishing, perfection, and purification of the intellect is purely philosophical. Most importantly, towards the end of the *Niche of Lights*, al-Ghazali argues that knowledge is "higher" than faith: "Knowledge is above faith, and tasting is above knowledge; [this] because tasting is a finding [*wajdān*], but knowing is a drawing of analogies [*qīyās*], and having faith is a mere acceptance through imitation [*taqlīd*]"[28] Since

---

26. Tsakiridou, "Theophany and Humanity," 182.

27. Ibid., 183. See also "Although he never goes so far as to say that the heart is above *all* essential association with the material world, his mystical cosmology, when considered in the light of his esoteric psychology, seems to leave no room for any other possibility." Gianotti, *Al-Ghazali's Unspeakable Doctrine of the Soul*, 166.

28. Al-Ghazali, *Niche of Lights*, II, no. 53, 38.

there is no notion in al-Ghazali—or in Islam for that matter—of faith grounded in a personal relationship of love and trust, "faith" for him can be nothing other than blind assent or imitation.[29] The highest level of the spiritual life is actually the "extinction" (fana') of the believer in the all-encompassing existence of God. Al-Ghazali describes such people thusly: "In their essences they are effaced and annihilated. They become extinct from themselves [anfusihum l-fanai'him 'an anfusihim], so that they cease observing themselves. Nothing remains save the One, the Real [al-wāḥid al-ḥaqq]."[30] Again, as was noted above, this does not mean that the individual Sufi or "gnostic" ceases to exist as such; rather, it means that he or she realizes that he or she had no individual act of existence to begin with, but always only existed in and through God. So, in the end, revelation in general and the Quran in particular are not supplements or aids to our knowledge of the world—they are not a "grace perfecting nature"—but rather they *replace* all natural knowledge and render it superfluous, because we all exist in and through God—we exist only insofar as our "faces" are turned toward him—from the very beginning. Philosophy by itself cannot explain our original "relation"[31] to God nor effect our return to him. Again, the end or goal of philosophical reflection is indeed the highest goal or end of the human being; but it is revelation and, most particularly, the holy book that effects this goal, not the vain reasonings of the philosophers.

In turning to Averroes again, we shall have the occasion to ask: is he not doing only the inverse of al-Ghazali in making the intellection of the philosopher generically the same as the illumination that the Sufi attains through the sacred book?

---

29. "Without the assumption of human nature, God remains distant and impersonal and therefore amenable to philosophical and metaphysical speculation as an abstraction." Tsakiridou, "Theophany and Humanity," 186.

30. Al-Ghazali, *Niche of Lights*, III, no. 33, 52.

31. I put "relation" in scare-quotes because, ultimately, for al-Ghazali, there is no relation as such between the creature and God, since the essence or the quiddity of the creature is nothing outside the divine existence itself.

THE INTELLECT AND METAPHYSICS
ACCORDING TO AVERROES

The intellect, for Averroes, plays a crucial role in completing what he understands to be Aristotle's metaphysical thought.[32] Metaphysics, as we saw in the last chapter, is for Averroes the investigation of the intelligible order and providential purpose of creation. Separate, self-subsistent intelligences must be an integral part of this order, not just to explain the movements of the celestial spheres but also because, according to the very principles of Aristotelian metaphysics, what is actual is prior to what is potential. Hence, actualized intelligence, subsistent intellects, must be prior to what is intelligible or what is intellect in potency. Therefore, Averroes needs to demonstrate that such intellects exist and that they are many and differ by degree of actualization. And Averroes tries to demonstrate that at least one such intellect, the separate agent and possible intellect that is one for all human beings, exists. As Richard Taylor explains:

> In his metaphysical explanations Averroes required support on several principles from psychology [understood here literally as "science of the soul" or "intellect"]: (1) proof is required that the immaterial separate forms asserted as immaterial movers by physics are, in fact, intellects; (2) grounds are required for the assertion of some similarity at least of an analogical kind between the human activity of knowing and the activity of separate substances (including God) which is denominated knowing; and (3) proof is required that a potency as the basis for a hierarchy could exist somehow in these separate substances.[33]

32. The whole project of Averroes was to "purify" the thought of Aristotle from its Neoplatonic accretions as found in the works of many of the Muslim Peripatetics such as al-Farabi and Avicenna. On the whole Averroes succeeded in his project—except on the matter of the nature of the material and agent intellects. Curiously, on this issue, Averroes moved very far away from what the contemporary scholarly consensus agrees to be the authentic thought of the Stagirite. Herbert A. Davidson, *Alfarabi, Avicenna, and Averroes on Intellect: Their Cosmologies, Theories of the Active Intellect, and Theories of Human Intellect* (Oxford: Oxford University Press, 1992), 257.

33. Taylor, "Averroes," 190. See also Richard Taylor, "Averroes on Psychology and the Principles of Metaphysics," *Journal of the History of Philosophy* 36, no. 4 (1998): 507–23.

The human intellect provides the "link" between the principles of changing natural being "here below" and the immaterial, eternal principles of metaphysics "up above," in a way that it does not do so in Aristotle. For Averroes, then, the perfection of the intellect conceived as the "conjunction" (*itiṣāl*) of the individual human being with the one, transcendent human intellect also completes the divine order in creation. Since all intellects other than the divine intellect have something *analogous* to potency in them ("analogous" because such intellects are immaterial), they are distinct from God and from each other, depending on their degree of potency (with the human intellect having the most potency).[34] Nevertheless, by conjoining with the separate agent and material intellects, the human intellect not only comes to full knowledge of the divine order and, by doing so, comes to knowledge of God, but also the divine order in creation is completed and, in effect, "revealed."

How, then, can we think through the relation of the individual thinking human being and his or her intellect? This intellect, Averroes argues, conjoins with the thoughts of the individual human being as form conjoins with and actualizes matter in the composite substance. In this way, the propositions we make about things in the world are the "matter," whereas whatever universal truths those propositions may signify are the work of the agent intellect:

> For with respect to every activity which has come to be from the compound of two different things, it is necessarily the case that one of those two be as it were matter and instrument and the other be as it were form or agent. The intellect in us, therefore, is composed of the intellect which is in a positive disposition and the agent intellect, either in such a way that the propositions are as it were matter and the agent intellect is as it were form, or in such a way that the propositions are as it were the

---

34. Between a God on whom the whole universe depends and whose wisdom and power rules all below, and the zone "below" where human beings dwell, are the various intellects or subsistent intelligences that serve as intermediaries between the two realms. The positing of intelligences co-eternal with God is, of course, irreconcilable with the Quran, but it is philosophy that must judge the truth of the matter for Averroes. See Jean Jolivet, "Divergences entre les métaphysiques d'Ibn Rushd et d'Aristote," *Arabica* 29, no. 3 (1982): 240.

instrument and the agent intellect is as it were the efficient [cause]. For the disposition is similar in this case.[35]

So when I form the proposition "fire burns," materially I am affirming a contingent state of affairs—that fire does burn; but I am also stating a universal truth, that it is of the essence of fire to burn. The form of this universal truth cannot come from the individual human being but from our agent intellect, since the human being *qua* material and individual is changing and contingent. And it is in the "material" or possible intellect that these intelligible truths are received as in a subject in the proper sense, while being received *in* a derivative or secondary sense in the individual human being. It is evident that with this solution Averroes thinks that he is now able to extend the principles of Aristotle's metaphysics "across the board," so that the workings of the intellect become not an exception to metaphysical principles but both their prime instantiation and that through which these principles are primarily known:

> When this conjoining in us between the agent intellect and the material intellect has been established, we will be able to find out the way in which we say that the agent intellect is similar to form and that the intellect which is in a positive disposition is similar to matter. For in regard to any two things of which one is the subject and the second is more actual than the other, it is necessary that the relation of the more actual to the less actual be as the relation of form to matter. With this intention we say that the proportion of the first actuality of the imaginative power to the first actuality of the common sense is as the proportion of form to matter.[36]

Here we have a statement of Averroes's doctrine of "conjunction" (*conjunctio—itiṣāl*) of the material intellect with the agent intellect and, through the material intellect, of the human being (*qua* "acquired" or theoretical intellect) with both.[37] Two things are worth noting in the

---

35. *Averroes (Ibn Rushd) of Cordoba: Long Commentary on the "De Anima" of Aristotle,* trans. Richard C. Taylor (New Haven, Conn.: Yale University Press, 2009), 397. This is an English translation of the Latin translation of Averroes's commentary, the original Arabic text is no longer extant.

36. Averroes, *Long Commentary on the "De Anima,"* 398.

37. "If it were legitimate to speak of dogmas in Averroes, the possibility of conjunction

passage above; (1) Averroes specifically states (or, at least, the Latin translation) that the conjoining is "in us," and (2) that the agent intellect with the material intellect and, in turn, both with the human being are as form to matter. In other words, although the intellect is separate from and one for all human beings, it nevertheless is, in some way, immanent to the human being. The intellect moves the human being to think not as a mover moves something movable, but as fire imparts its form to the red-hot iron. Hence we can explain why the intellect is conjoined to us at the end and not at the beginning: "For because that in virtue of which something carries out its proper activity is the form, while we carry out our proper activity in virtue of the agent intellect, it is necessary that the agent intellect be form in us."[38] Thus, Averroes attempts to answer the objection that, if both the material and agent intellects of man are separate, then how can they be, in any sense, the final actuality or perfection of the human being *qua* rational and intellectual being?

Averroes argues that both the material (or potential) intellect and agent intellect are the final form of the human being, although separate and transcendent.[39] Insofar as the human being engages in thought, he or she does it through the separate material and agent intellects, which, once our perishable acquired intellect is perfected, is conjoined to them "in all ways":

> It is evident that when that motion is complete, immediately that intellect will be conjoined with us in all ways. Then it is evident that its relation to us in that disposition is as the relation of the intellect which is in a positive disposition in relation to us. Since it is so, it is necessary that a human being understand all the intelligibles through the intellect

with the active intellect would rank high on the list." Davidson, *Alfarabi, Avicenna, and Averroes on Intellect*, 323. In fact, it is the notion of "conjunction" of the human intellect with the agent intellect that united the Latin Averroists (and not necessarily the eternity of the world or the unity of the intellect). Maurice-Ruben Hayoun and Alain de Libera, *Averroès et l'averroisme* (Paris: Presses Universitaires de France, 1991), 106.

38. Averroes, *Long Commentary on the "De Anima,"* 399.

39. Whether the "potential" intellect constitutes the form of man or not became a matter of confusion in subsequent interpretations of Averroes. Certainly, many Latin Averroists and their opponents, such as Thomas Aquinas, certainly understood Averroes to deny that the potential intellect is the form of man, although this is never formally stated in the *Long Commentary*. Davidson, *Alfarabi, Avicenna, and Averroes on Intellect*, 302.

proper to him and that he carry out the activity proper to him in regard to all beings, just as he understands by his proper intellection all the beings through the intellect which is in a positive disposition when it has been conjoined with forms of the imagination.[40]

Each human being is disposed differently to the transcendent intellect, hence the differences in intellectual abilities among men. Nevertheless, those differences disappear once the human being is perfectly disposed to the intellect and conjoined with it. Then, the human being becomes like God, not by conjoining to God himself, which is impossible, but by being conjoined to our intellect in a manner analogous to the way in which God knows himself and all intelligibles: "In this way, therefore, human beings, as Themistius says, are made like unto God in that he is all beings in a way and one who knows these in a way, for beings are nothing but his knowledge and the cause of beings is nothing but his knowledge. How marvelous is that order and how mysterious is that mode of being!"[41]

To the degree that there is any "mystical element" in Averroes's thought, this is the closest to which it comes. And yet, conjunction with the intellect really has very little to do with the sort of direct experience or "taste" (dhawq) of divine realties that Sufis such as al-Ghazali or Ibn al-'Arabi describe. For these speculative Sufis, the final stage of wisdom is the abandonment of all rational thought and categories, whereas for Averroes, this conjunction is the final and perfect affirmation of all rational principles and intelligibles.[42] Indeed, Averroes seems to deny, in

40. Averroes, *Long Commentary on the "De Anima,"* 399. Thus the agent intellect plays no role in the generation and corruption of men; only the intelligibles are engendered in man by means of the agent intellect, because such intelligibles are separate from matter. Charles Touati, "Les Problèmes de la génération et le rôle de l'intellect agent chez Averroès," in Jolivet, *Multiple Averroès,* 157–64.

41. Averroes, *Long Commentary on the "De Anima,"* 399.

42. "This is the state [conjunction] to which the Sufis aspire. It is evident that they do not reach it, since one cannot reach it except through speculative knowledge, which they have given up, just as they cast off the senses and the other faculties of the soul. This is how their state appears to them to be a divine perfection. On this point Averroes is in agreement with Avempace in his criticism of the mystics. It is only through homonymy that one can speak of a faculty open to natural perfection and a faculty open to divine perfection. When the faculty for natural perfection exists in actuality, there is entelechy in its

his *Long Commentary*, that conjunction with the intellect even means the direct knowledge of the agent intellect itself; all that is implied by "conjunction" is that the intellect, so perfected, has a perfect grasp of intelligibles in the sensible world as well as of the essential properties of intellectual substance.[43] Once this happens, such a person will have a full and perfect grasp of the rational order of creation, as made and ordained by God, and will, therefore, enjoy supreme happiness.[44] But

---

relationship to what it perfects. According to this relationship, the active intellect is called acquired. In other words, the active intellect is not for man a separate perfection that he would reach in knowledge of the pure object of intellect in itself, by breaking with all that precedes it in the soul, but it is an act that gives to human knowledge the final perfection of an acquired intellect." Arnaldez, *Averroes*, 76–77. "Averroes was obviously concerned in this connection to vindicate the essential efficacy of the intellect, against the Neoplatonists and the mystics (Sufis), who tended to conceive of it as passive, and accordingly dependent on some external source of 'illumination' (*ishrāq*), such as the Active Intellect, or God." Majid Fakhry, *Averroes (Ibn Rushd): His Life, Works and Influence* (Oxford: One World Publications, 2001), 68.

43. "The *Long Commentary* accordingly does not, as far as I could discover, ever hint at a direct human thought of the active intellect." Davidson, *Alfarabi, Avicenna, and Averroes on Intellect*, 339. There is no support for the view that our active intellect is a detached part of the divine intellect. "Nor does Ibn Rushd mention any kind of *unio mystica* in the pages of his commentary. All he is saying is that the highest happiness resides in the intellectual apprehension of the intelligible. This is God's permanent state, whereas we can only attain it for a short period because our intellect is still tied down to matter and potentiality. When we reach that state, however, we become like God in that we think ourselves, or our own essence (1617, 4–10); but this 'like' indicates a mere comparison: there is no identification, no union." Charles Genequand, introduction to *Ibn Rushd's Metaphysics: A Translation with Introduction of Ibn Rushd's Commentary on Aristotle's Metaphysics, Book Lam* (Leiden: E. J. Brill, 1986), 51.

44. In his earlier work, Averroes seems to hold to an emanationist metaphysics whereby natural forms are constituted by emanations from the active intellect (the sphere of the moon), whereas he gives a very naturalistic interpretation of the nature, origin, and function of the human intellect. In his later writings, however, he moves in the opposite direction: giving a more naturalistic interpretation of the origins and causes of natural things, but making the intellect into a transcendent entity. Davidson, *Alfarabi, Avicenna, and Averroes on Intellect*, 298. Thus, Averroes's interpretation of Aristotle is not a fusion of Aristotelianism and Neoplatonism; rather it is the work of a mind infused with many Neoplatonic ideas, assumptions, and terminology trying to work itself back to a "pure" Aristotle, which, of course, always remained elusive. Genequand, introduction to *Ibn Rushd's Metaphysics*, 57–58. For a good statement of this connection between intellectual perfection and human happiness, see Averroes, *La Béatitude de l'âme*, ed. Marc Geoffroy and Carlos Steel (Paris: Vrin, 2001). This text is a meld of two "Averroist" texts stitched together by a later Christian editor. Nevertheless, it is valuable as an example of how Averroes's thought on the intellect was appropriated by Latin Christian thinkers.

this can, and does, come about perfectly naturally, without the need for divine revelation (but which, in a sense, *is* revelation, as we shall see).

This perhaps explains why Averroes's *Long Commentary on the Metaphysics* leaves the ontological status of the agent intellect ambiguous.[45] In his *Long Commentary on the Metaphysics*, Averroes asserts that there is a parallel between how the first mover moves the cosmos, by being the object of desire of separate intelligences which are also movers of the heavens, and the way that the active intellect "moves" lower things, such as us human beings, to think:

> It clearly appears from that that Aristotle thinks that happiness for men *qua* men consists in this contact with the intellect which has been shown in the *De Anima* to be principle, mover, and agent for us. The separate intellects *qua* separate must be principle of that of which they are principle in both senses, I mean as movers and as ends. The active intellect, insofar as it is separate and principle for us, must move us in the same way as the beloved moves the lover; and if every motion must be in contact with the thing which produces it as end, we must ultimately be in contact with this separate intellect, so that we depend on such a principle, on which the heaven depends, as Aristotle says, although this happens to us for a short time.[46]

There is an analogy, therefore, between the macrocosm where the First Mover actualizes all natural (and intelligent) beings, and the microcosm and how the agent intellect actualizes thought in individual human beings. In this way, an investigation of the nature of the intellect and how we become conjoined to it becomes the key to unlocking how all of being is related to its first mover. The germ of this idea is already present in Averroes earlier "epitome" of Aristotle's *Metaphysics*:

> Since the human intellect in actuality is nothing else than the conceptualization of the order and system present in this world and in each of its

45. "Let it be said at once that they [relevant passages from Averroes commentary on book Lambda of Aristotle's *Metaphysics*] offer no clue as to the cosmological status of the Active Intellect, which remains as obscure as ever. There is certainly nothing, neither here nor in the *De Anima* commentary, to support Gauthier's (*Ibn Rochd*, 245, 253) description of it as'émané de la sphere de la lune.'" Genequand, introduction to *Ibn Rushd's Metaphysics*, 49.

46. Averroes, *Ibn Rushd's Metaphysics*, 157; Averroes, *Tafsīr mā baʿd aṭ-ṭabiʿāt* (Beirut: Imprimerie catholique, 1948), 1612–13.

parts and the knowledge of all that is in this [world] through its remote and proximate causes up to a complete [knowledge of] the world, it follows necessarily that the quiddity of the intellect which brings about this human intellect is not distinct from the conceptualization of these things. For that reason one says that the active intellect thinks the things of the present world. However, its thinking of these things must take place in a nobler way [than ours], for otherwise there would be no difference between us and this [intellect], and how could that be? As has already become clear, our intellect in actuality is subject to coming-to-be and corruption due to its connection to matter, whereas its intelligible [object] is eternal [and] immaterial. Due to its insufficiency the human intellect depends in its thinking on the senses. This is why, if we are deprived of one of the senses, we have no intellection of its [objects]. Similarly, if the perception of a certain thing is difficult for us, we fail to grasp its intelligible and cannot establish it other than by general assumptions. Accordingly, there might be things in the present world whose causes are unknowable to us, but present in the essence of the agent intellect (this may be a viable account of the causes of dreams and other such forebodings). In any case this insufficiency of our [intellect] is a consequence of matter.[47]

Since, in the epitome, Averroes is still more strongly under the influence of a Neoplatonizing interpretation of Aristotle, he conceives of the agent intellect as containing within itself, *qua* intelligibles, the rational order of creation. Hence, the agent intellect can "know" things inaccessible to us. As we saw above, however, Averroes came to reject this and argue that the agent and material intellects cannot know anything without experiencing things in and through individual human beings. Nevertheless, Averroes never seems to reject the basic idea that it is the human being and, in particular, the human intellect that serves as the link between the realm of sense and nature and the realm of intelligibility and pure intelligence:

As for forms realized after the blending and composition of the elements such as the forms of plants, animals, and man, their existence as such is only for the sake of the rational soul, while the existence of the

47. Averroes, *On Aristotle's "Metaphysics": An Annotated Translation of the So-called "Epitome,"* ed. Rütiger Arnzen (Berlin: De Gruyter, 2010), 159–60.

rational soul is for the sake of the best [disposition], as is the case with the celestial bodies. For that reason we hold that man is that which comes closest in rank to the celestial bodies in this world, and [that] he is a sort of intermediate between eternal beings and that which is subject to coming-to-be and corruption. [Thus] the existence of the rational soul in matter is likewise due to necessity. Furthermore, the rational soul is related in the present world to the forms inferior to it as the rational [forms] are related to the acquired intellect; and the sensitive [soul] is related to the rational [soul] like matter [to form]. The same applies to the relation between nutritive and sensitive [souls]; and matter to form. [Finally,] this very [relation] is how the forms of homeomeric [bodies] are related to the elements of the human [body]. Man is thus the link which connects sensible being and intelligible be-ing, which is why God perfected through this [intelligible being] that [former] being which is afflicted with deficiency due to its remoteness from [God].[48]

Throughout nature, then, there is a relation of matter to form, of poten-tiality to actuality, of what is "below" to what is "above." In this manner, all created beings are linked together in a seamless whole of which the human intellect plays a critical part, bridging material being with im-material, intelligible being. Thus, Averroes concludes his epitome of the *Metaphysics* by arguing that this order manifests the working of divine providence, where the superior is not for the sake of the inferior, but rather the inferior is for the sake of the superior; and all evils are due to the insufficiency of matter. All that is contingent and defective in ma-terial being is ultimately ordered to the eternal perfection of intelligible being. It is the better part of human wisdom, therefore, to insert oneself into this order by preparing oneself for conjoining with the material and agent intellects.

The implication of all this for Averroes is that, while the human being as material individual is corruptible and perishable, insofar as he or she thinks in and through the separate material and agent intellects, he or she participates in what is eternal. There is here a strong parallel with what Averroes says in the *Decisive Treatise* about the eternity of the

---

48. Ibid., 175–76.

world: while individual substances may be corruptible and perishable, the world as a whole is not, being continuously created or, better, "actualized" by the divine Artisan (ṣāni'). In like manner, individual men come and go, and yet human thought and the sciences that are the products of human thought never cease:

> One might say that the final knowledge the understanding can reach will seem to the common man at first sight something absurd. And this happens not only in the theoretical sciences but in the practical sciences as well. Therefore, the assumption that one of the sciences should vanish and then come into existence again, at first sight would seem to be impossible. For this reason many have thought that those sciences are of supernatural origin ["achievements or mental faculties not of human origin"—mudārak laisat b-insānīyya] and some attribute them to the jinn, others to the prophets, so that Ibn Hazm goes so far as to affirm that the strongest proof of the existence of prophecy is the existence of these sciences.[49]

What is remarkable about this passage from Averroes's *Tahāfut al-tahāfut* or *The Incoherence of the Incoherence* is how he equates the eternal, intelligible principles of all the sciences with the content of revelation. As he says, these sciences were thought by many in ancient times to be of "not of human origin" and that some, like his fellow Andalusian, Ibn Hazm, thought their existence a "proof" of prophecy. As for Averroes himself, there seems not to be much of a difference between the sciences as they exist in the intellect *qua* intelligibles and revelation except that the latter is acquired (probably through the design of divine providence) by someone ignorant and unlettered and, therefore, expressed in a way so that these intelligibles and the sciences they make possible may be understood by all men according to their capacity for understanding. This, as we saw in the last chapter, is a central and repeated assertion of Averroes. The perfection of the intellect comes not so much in knowing God as such, but in knowing the intelligible order that God has ordained and elicited

---

49. Averroes, *Tahāfot at-Tahāfot* (*The Incoherence of the Incoherence*), trans. Simon Van Den Bergh (Cambridge: Gibb Memorial Trust, 1978), 1:125; Averroes, *Tahāfot at-Tahāfot*, ed. Maurice Bouyges, SJ (Beirut: Imprimerie Catholique, 1930), 208.

in the universe.[50] And by knowing this order, the human being inserts
him- or herself into the very cosmic order he or she knows by conjoining
with the intellect that is the linchpin of this order.

This brings Averroes back to the central concern of this particular
discussion: that by making God into a quasi-human agent, whose "power" and "freedom" are indistinguishable from chance and caprice, the
Ash'arite theologians remove any possibility of knowing anything in the
universe and, therefore, of knowing God. For by making any event an
arbitrary act of divine will, they remove any causal stability in nature
and, indeed, remove any essential natures by which we may know and
even name things:

> The argument by which they [the Ash'arites] tried to show that there
> is in the universe something like this principle was that they compared
> natural acts of will and said that every act, insofar as it is an act, de-
> mands this [occasionalism]; and they tried to prove the truth of this by
> arguing that what is not living is inorganic and dead, and, since from the
> dead there cannot proceed any act, there does not proceed any act from
> what is not alive. Thus they denied the acts which proceed from natural
> things, and moreover they refused to admit that the living beings which
> we see in the empirical world have acts; they said that these acts *seem*
> connected with the living in the empirical world [*al-shahīd*], but their
> agent is only the living God in the divine world [*al-ghā'ib*—the "hid-
> den"]. But the logical conclusion for them would be that there is in the
> empirical world no life at all, for life is inferred from things in the em-
> pirical world, because of their acts; and, further, it would be interesting
> to know how they arrived as this judgment about the divine world.[51]

Even worse, if we carry out the Ash'arite position to its logical conclusion, then *even revelation and prophecy become impossible*, because if all
events are due to divine caprice, then there is no *law* or rational order
that could be revealed. In effect, there is no difference between the

---

50. Roger Arnaldez, "La théorie de Dieu dans le 'Tahafut,'" *Studia Islamica* 8 (1957): 16.
Hence, Averroes is in agreement with al-Ghazali (and *contra* Avicenna) that it makes no
sense to talk of God as a "necessary being" apart from his relation to creatures, because we
can know God only from his relation to creatures (21).

51. Averroes, *The Incoherence of the Incoherence*, 1:131; Averroes, *Tahāfot at-Tahāfot*, 220.

Ash'arite position and that of the atheist who asserts that all that exists is due to chance or accident. For Averroes, indeed, revelation is, in a fundamental sense, nothing but the rational order of creation as "handed down" through the agent and material intellects:

> The act which proceeds from that quality through which the prophet is called prophet, that is the act of making known the mysterious and establishing religious laws which are in accordance with the truth and which bring about acts that will determine the happiness of the totality of mankind. I do not know anyone but Avicenna who has held the theory about dreams Ghazali mentions. The ancient philosophers assert about revelation and dreams only that they proceed from God through the intermediation of a spiritual incorporeal being which is according to them the bestower of the human intellect, and which is called by the best authors the active intellect and in the Holy Law angel.[52]

As Averroes here remarks, only Avicenna, among the philosophers, suggested that revelation is otherwise than the intellectual apprehension of the rational order of creation. And Averroes here rejects Avicenna's assertion (though Averroes's dismissal is not categorical).[53] What makes a prophet a prophet is that such a person is able, through no special learning of their own, to intuit through the separate intellects laws that will lead all people "in accordance with the truth" and, thus, lead them to happiness.

So there is a sense in which Averroes rejects "revelation" as anything miraculous or added to nature. It is simply an aspect of the intelligible order of nature itself which the prophet has the gift of drawing out and formulating laws for all types of people. In other words, there is, in

---

52. Averroes, *The Incoherence of the Incoherence*, 1:315–16; Averroes, *Tahāfot at-Tahāfot*, 516.

53. In his epitome of the *Parva Naturalia*, Averroes argues that phenomena such as true dreams, clairvoyance, and revelation (*waḥi*) do not give us any knowledge that reason and philosophical science do not give us; if they did, then their function would be "superfluous, since man also attains theoretical knowledge through his [mental tools]." Later on, however, in his *Tahāfut at-tahāfut* and in the *Kashf al-Manāhij*, Averroes seems to contradict himself, arguing that the prophet and the phenomenon of revelation do teach theoretical matters to the common people in figures and images appropriate to their (low) intellectual abilities. Two solutions seem to offer themselves: either Averroes changed his mind, or he is using terms like "prophet" and "revelation" in a very different, even equivocal, sense. Davidson, *Alfarabi, Avicenna, and Averroes on Intellect*, 343, 350–51.

Averroes's thought, nothing miraculous about revelation. Just as there is an analogous relation between God's thought and knowledge and our conjunction with the separate intellects, so there is an analogous relation between the conjunction of the philosopher with the separate intellects and that of the prophet with the divine law. Only in the conjunction of the prophet with the divine law, the conjunction in-forms not just the prophet, but also the whole religious community (*mila*).

This position, of course, puts Averroes at clear loggerheads with al-Ghazali, for whom not only revelation but all created things and events are, in effect, miraculous. Thus, al-Ghazali devotes the seventeenth discussion of his *Incoherence of the Philosophers* to refuting any assertion that there might be any necessary connection between cause and effect. Al-Ghazali seems to think that refuting the causal relationship in *all* of nature is necessary in order to affirm the possibility of the miraculous nature of revelation in general and of the Quran in particular.[54] Averroes, by contrast, is convinced that, far from establishing the divine nature of revelation and of the Quran, al-Ghazali's arguments destroy any basis for affirming God as a wise and providential creator and therefore of any possibility of knowing God as the supreme Artisan and thus of knowing whether there is a god at all—chiefly because, on al-Ghazali's principles, one could not extend the causal relationship to that between God and creation itself, a relationship which al-Ghazali seems to admit and, indeed, require. Without things having inherent natures or essences behaving in regular and determinate ways, and without

54. "The contention over the first [theory—that of a necessary connection between cause and effect] is necessary, inasmuch as [on its refutation] rests the affirmation of miracles that disrupt [the] habitual [course of nature], such as the changing of the staff into a serpent, revival of the dead, and the splitting of the moon. Whoever renders the habitual courses [of nature] a necessary constant makes all these [miracles] impossible. [The philosophers] have thus interpreted what is said in the Quran about the revivification of the dead metaphorically, saying that what is meant by it is the cessation of the death of ignorance through the life of knowledge. And they interpreted the staff devouring the magic of the magicians as the refutation by the divine proof, manifest at the hand of Moses, of the doubts of those who deny [the one God]. As regards the splitting of the moon, they often deny the existence [of this occurrence] and claim that there has been no soundly transmitted, indubitable reporting of it." Al-Ghazali, *The Incoherence of the Philosophers*, trans. Michael E. Marmura (Provo, Utah: Brigham Young University Press, 2000), 163.

regular causal relationships that flow from these natures and essences, then, Averroes argues, all knowledge, not only of the natural word, but of God and his existence, becomes impossible.[55]

GREEK METAPHYSICS AND
ISLAMIC REVELATION

The question that remains is what all this means for Averroes's understanding of the relation between philosophy, the intellect, and the nature and purpose of revelation or the religious law, and what would someone like al-Ghazali make of this. Averroes expended much effort in trying to show that philosophy gives the "true sense" of the law. Thus, the religious law contains nothing that is not contained in philosophical reflection as engaged in by the perfected intellect.[56] In other words, revelation of a religious law is analogous to the conjunction of the human being with the separate intellects. The revealed law functions as a sort of "separate intellect" for the masses. This means that, for Averroes, there is nothing miraculous about revelation, save, perhaps, for the revelation of the sacred book itself.[57] That a man as rude and unlettered as the Muhammad was able to encapsulate within a sacred book the highest truths of

---

55. In the *Incoherence of the Incoherence*, Averroes reminds the reader that the true philosopher will take pains not to question the miraculous character of revelation for the good of the community, but inculcate in the masses the notion that the origins of the principles of religion surpass human reasoning: "The learned among the philosophers do not permit discussion or disputation about the principles of religion, and he who does such a thing needs, according to them, a severe lesson. For whereas every science has its principles, and every student of this science must concede its principles and may not interfere with them by denying them, this is still more obligatory in the practical science of religion, for to walk on the path of the religious virtues is necessary for man's existence, according to them, not in so far as he is a man, but in so far as he has knowledge; and therefore it is necessary for every man to concede the principles of religion and invest with authority the man who lays them down. The denial and discussion of these principles denies human existence, and therefore heretics must be killed. Of religious principles it must be said that they are divine things which surpass human understanding, but must be acknowledged although their causes are unknown." Averroes, *The Incoherence of the Incoherence*, 322; Averroes, *Tahāfot at-Tahāfot*, 527.

56. Benmakhlouf, *Averroès*, 188.

57. Ibid., 191.

philosophy could be seen as a miracle; but there is nothing miraculous about the truths themselves. This is because, for Averroes, nature does not reduplicate knowledge with other, inferior, means; truth is one and, in principle, accessible to all who are learned in the philosophical sciences and thus does not stand in need of any "supplement." This is perhaps why, according to Davidson's suggestion, it is significant that Averroes calls the author of Scripture a "lawgiver" rather than a "prophet." "Lawgiver" implies someone who simply applies higher, theoretical truths to the contingent and messy affairs of men, while "prophet" implies someone who has access to a "higher knowledge" inaccessible to philosophical reflection. Such knowledge, however, is for Averroes an oxymoron and, therefore, would not be knowledge at all.

Averroes deals directly with the nature of revelation, the religious law, and prophecy in his work, *Al-Kashf ʿan Manāhij al-ʾAdilla fī ʿAqāʾid al-Milla* or the "Exposition of Methods of Proof." This work, along with the *Decisive Treatise* and *The Incoherence of the Incoherence*, completes a trilogy of works written on the relation of the religious law to philosophy and in what Averroes calls the "dialectical mode," whereby he eschews strict demonstrations in favor of arguments designed to show the probability of his views and the contradictory or incoherent nature of the arguments of his opponents. One of the points of contention among the various schools of *kalām* or dialectical theology that Averroes addresses in this work was the nature of God's attributes: in what sense can we predicate unity, knowledge, willing, seeing, hearing, and speaking to God? Among these, one of the more important attributes was that of speaking, precisely because the revelation of God, the Quran, is claimed to be the direct speech of God to men. How can we attribute speech to God when God has no bodily organ nor is he like us in any way? Averroes answers by arguing that audible speech, using a bodily organ as its instrument, is not essential to speech as such; we can call "speech" any disclosure of meaning from one mind to another:

> Revelation, then, is the creation of that meaning in the soul of the person receiving it without the intermediary of utterances created by [Him] [*bi-ghaīr wāsṭa lafẓ*], or the disclosure of that meaning [of the

utterance] to [him] through some action He performs in the soul of the addressed person; as the Almighty says: "Coming thus within two bows' length or closer. Then He revealed to His servant what He revealed" [53:9–10]. And "from behind a veil" refers to the speech that takes place through utterances created by [God] in the soul of the one He favors with His speech. This is the real speech, and it is the one that God favored Moses with. For this reason, the Almighty says: "Allah spoke to Moses directly" [4:164]. As for His saying: "Otherwise, He sends forth a messenger," it is the third way that occurs through the intermediary of an angel. God's speech might also include that which He imparts to the learned who are the heirs of the prophets through the intermediary of demonstrations [b-wāsat al-burāhīn]. From this perspective, it is established among the learned that the Quran is God's speech.[58]

Significant for our purposes here is how Averroes includes the philosophers, "who are heirs of the prophets through the intermediary of demonstrations," among those who receive directly God's "speech" in the form of the direct communication of meaning from one mind to another. What then, is the nature of this direct communication? It seems to be nothing other than the intelligible order of creation and providential arrangement of nature that communicates this "revelation" (including the activity of the separate and unique agent/passive intellect). For, much of the first part of the *Exposition of Methods* is taken up with his argument for God's existence and nature from the rational order of creation and the providential arrangement of things in nature for man's use and enjoyment.

Hence, for Averroes, the *meaning* of the Quran, as God's "speech," is eternal and unchanging and coincides with the eternal truths uncovered by philosophy. But, if we take the words of the Quran in their material manifestation—as audible words in the Arabic language or signs written on a page—then the Quran is created. In this way, Averroes seeks to find a middle way through a controversy that roiled Islam in its third and fourth centuries, with the Hanbalites or Traditionalists arguing that the Quran, down to the audible and written words, is eternal and the

58. Averroes, *Exposition of Methods*, in *Faith and Reason in Islam*, 48–49 (Al-Jabri, 131–32).

Mu'tazilites, to the contrary, arguing that the Quran is created.[59] As this passage makes clear, Averroes thinks both are right and both are wrong once we distinguish the proper sense of "speech":

> It will thus have become evident to you that the Quran, which is the speech of God, is eternal, but that the words denoting [*lafz al-dāl 'aleyhi*] it are created by God Almighty, not by men. In this respect the words of the Quran differ from the words used elsewhere other than in the Quran; I mean, the latter words are our own work with God's permission, whereas the words of the Quran are created by God.... Now whoever looks at words apart from meaning and does not distinguish the two, would maintain that the Quran is created; but those who look at the meaning of the words would say that the [Quran] is not created. The truth, however, consists in combining the two views.[60]

All that we wish to note here is how Averroes's position on this specific controversy—the eternity of the Quran—is consistent with his overall view of the relation of philosophy to revelation or, more accurately, to the religious law. The "meaning" or "essence" of the religious law is the same as what the best philosophy (that is, that of Aristotle) teaches; the law, by contrast, is the communication of that meaning among all men.

When, therefore, the orthodox theology of Islam, Ash'arism, denies any inherent nature or essence to things and, by extension, any causal power to them, it denies that the Quran or revelation has any coherence or wisdom, for this revelation enfolds within itself the wisdom of philosophy. But more importantly for Averroes, by denying the wisdom of God and the inherent intelligibility of nature, Islamic theology denies any possibility for *grace*, because "grace"—and particularly the "grace" of revelation—only makes sense when man and all natural things have natures upon which a free gift over and above their nature could be bestowed:

> For were it possible, as they claim, for all the existing entities to be other than what they are, just as easily as they actually are, then there would

---

59. For an account of this controversy, see Corbin, *Histoire de la philosophie islamique*, 170ff.

60. *Exposition of Methods*, 49 (Al-Jabri, 132).

be no correspondence between mankind and the existing things, with whose creation God has favored man and commanded him to thank Him for. What this opinion entails is that the possibility of His creating man as part of this world is equivalent to the possibility of creating him, for instance, in the void, which they believe exists. Indeed for them [the Ash'arites] it is possible for man to be a different shape and a different constitution, and still act like a human being! It is also possible, in their view, that he may be part of another world entirely different from this world in definition and detail, in which case there would be no grace [na'ma] for which man should be thankful. For that which is not necessary or is not the most fitting for man's existence, man can certainly dispense with, and that which man can dispense with does not count as a grace he is favored with [fa-laysa wujūduhu bi-'anām 'alayhi]. All this is contrary to human nature.[61]

Indeed, Averroes argues that if you take the extreme occasionalism of the Ash'arites, whereby every event is a direct act of God and every creature is a new, instantaneous creation, to its logical conclusion, it asserts that all is a product of chance, which is indistinguishable from an atheism that asserts that all that is is purely a product of blind chance.[62] In such a scheme of things, prophecy and revelation make no sense: if everything is an act of God or a communication from God, then nothing is an act of or communication from God. Otherwise, Averroes notes, there would be "no grace for which man should be thankful," that is, the providential order of created and stable natures.

Averroes speculates as to why the Ash'arites would defend a position that, in his eyes is so destructive of both reason and revelation. It seems that their chief fear was to admit of any free, creative agent in the world other than God.[63] Their other fear, Averroes surmises, is that admitting

---

61. *Exposition of Methods*, 84 (Al-Jabri, 166–67).

62. "In general whenever we repudiate the causes and their effects, there remains nothing whereby the advocates of chance can be rebutted (by which I mean those who claim that there is no Maker [of this world], but that everything that happens in it is due to material causes). It is more appropriate that one of two possibilities might occur by chance, than from a willing agent." *Exposition of Methods*, 85 (Al-Jabri, 167).

63. "What led the Ash'arite theologians to adhere to this position was the desire to escape from recognizing the action of natural faculties which God has implanted in existing

the existence and efficacy of natural causes must lead to asserting that
the world has a natural cause, without understanding that, by destroying
natural causality, they also destroy the sole means of proving that the
universe has a Maker (ṣāniʿ).[64] They also destroy the sole means of
determining whether something is a revealed truth, or, more accurately,
a revealed law or not, for it is only insofar as that law is reflective of
the rational order of the world that it can be asserted to be a divine or
religious law.

There is, in short, nothing miraculous or even "supernatural" about
a genuine religious law, except, perhaps, accidentally (insofar as miracles
may—or may not—accompany its promulgation). Miracles are, then,
not an essential attribute of prophecy: "If this is the case, then, the extraordinary thing with which he, God's blessing and peace be upon him,
challenged people and offered as evidence for his truthfulness regarding
the message he proclaimed is the Precious Book."[65] This is important
for Averroes to assert, because, as all the Muslim sources and sirāt (biog-
raphies) of Muhammad frankly admit, the Prophet performed no miracles. So, for Averroes—and, I think he would argue, for any Muslim—
one cannot resort to miracles as "proof" of Muhammad's divine mission.
At most, one can assert the "miraculous nature" of the Quran. But even
here doubts arise: miracles are, according to Averroes, no doubt possible,
but only in the sense that they are events that are indistinguishable from
what Aristotle described as natural but chance events, that is, events that

---

entities, endowing some with souls and other efficacious causes. They avoided admitting
the existence of causes for fear of admitting that there are [in this world] active agents other
than God. How can there be any other agent than God, when He is the Inventor of Causes
and their causal efficacy is by His leave and His preserving them in existence?" *Exposition
of Methods*, 87 (Al-Jabri, 169–70).

64. "Furthermore, they refrained from admitting natural causes for fear that they
would have to admit that the world is the product of a natural cause. However, if they
know that nature is created and that there is no more conclusive proof [of the existence] of
the Maker than the existence of a being so well-made, then they would have known that
whoever denies nature rejects a great part of the grounds of the proof of the existence of the
Maker of the world, by repudiating the existence of a part of God's creation. For, whoever
repudiates one kind of existing creation denies in fact one of God's actions, which is close
to denying one of His attributes." *Exposition of Methods*, 87–88 (Al-Jabri, 170).

65. *Exposition of Methods*, 97 (Al-Jabri, 179).

are indeed caused and caused by purely natural causes, but whose effects are other than what nature does "for the most part." God, however, can use the *perception* among men that they are miracles to affect a certain result, such as the revelation of a law conducive to intellectual perfection and happiness for men. If a man acquires this miraculous revelation, however, then we can only call him a "man" equivocally,[66] because such an activity belongs more to the nature of a separate intelligence or even just to the workings of divine providence operating through the natural order than to that of a man. Thus, while Averroes admits, as we saw above, the need for revelation as a kind of *grace* (*na'ma*) over and above human nature, it cannot be a grace that perfects the human being *qua* human being; it can only perfect man indirectly by creating the social conditions for the cultivation of philosophy, which is what perfects the human being as such.[67]

So, while Averroes admits, as we saw above, the need for revelation to be a *sort* of grace added to and perfecting nature, he, in the end, refused to consider revelation as a grace. To be sure, for a communication to count as revelation it must fulfill two criteria: (1) the communication must not come through human learning, and (2) it must lay down a religious law. But any miracles that may accompany revelation are extraneous to the revelation itself and cannot constitute a definitive proof of it:

> For what is extraordinary, when it exceeds [the kind] of knowledge involved in laying down religious laws, proves that this action is not the product of instruction, but revelation from God, and this is what is called prophethood. However, the extraordinary that does not consist in laying down religious laws, such as the splitting of the sea and the like, does not necessarily prove the property called prophethood; but only if it is conjoined to the former type of evidence. By itself this characteristic is not evidence [of prophethood]. That is why [this characteristic] does not indicate in the case of the saints [*al-awlya'*] this notion

66. See Kogan, *Averroes and the Metaphysics of Causation*, 82–83.

67. This is a typical strategy of Averroes, which is to transform an epistemological issue into a political problem. Oliver Leaman, *Averroes and His Philosophy* (Oxford: Oxford University Press, 1988), 53. For al-Ghazali the real problem is that the philosophers do not allow for miracles, whereas for Averroes, the true problem is what miracles are *for*, and what their proper context is (53–54).

[of prophethood], even if they have it. In this way, then, you should understand how the miraculous is proof of prophecy. The miraculous, both in knowledge and in action, is the only definitive proof of the attribute of prophethood, but the miraculous in other actions is merely a warrant and strong proof thereof.[68]

But, as we also saw above, even the miraculous nature of the Quran is, for Averroes, not really miraculous, insofar as its communication can be seen as in accordance with the workings of God's rational order in the universe. Thus, the gifts of the Prophet are "miraculous" only in the same sense as those of someone who has a "knack" or "gift" of healing while having no formal medical training. His or her knack or gift is simply something ordained by divine providence:

> If someone were to ask, "But how does the Quran prove that it is itself extraordinary and miraculous and of the type of miracle which indubitably proves the attribute of prophethood (extraordinary in the sense that it is intrinsic to the act of prophethood and is evidence for it, just as the act of healing is evidence for the attribute of medicine that is identical with the function of medicine)?" our answer would be that this can be learned in many ways: (1) the laws contained in [the Quran] regarding action and knowledge cannot be acquired through instruction, but only through revelation; (2) the information it contains regarding the future; and (3) its style, which differs from the style which is the product of reflection and deliberation.[69]

The only features which distinguish the religious law from conjunction with the separate intellects, then, is that the law is given "without instruction," gives information concerning the future, and is in a style that appeals to all men. These features, however, are accidental to intellectual apprehension itself, whether it occur through philosophy or by the law. In itself, the law simply renders possible the conditions favorable for philosophical perfection.

In this sense, then, the essence of revelation, and a "proof" of genuine prophecy, is that the revelation lay down a law. This is why, as men-

---

68. *Exposition of Methods*, 100 (Al-Jabri, 181).
69. *Exposition of Methods*, 100–101 (Al-Jabri, 181).

tioned above, Averroes is careful to call Muhammad a "lawgiver" (*shāri'*) rather than a "prophet" (*nabī*)—just as he prefers to refer to God as the supreme "artisan" (*ṣāni'*) rather than "creator" (*khāliq*). For the function of prophecy is simply to make known to the mass of men the rational order of creation and to guide men's actions in accordance with that rational order. The end result of this is human happiness.[70] Thus, for Averroes, what makes a religious law divine and superior to any other is that it brings human belief and conduct into harmony with the rational order of things, just as the "proof" that someone is a physician is that he heals his patients and operates in accordance with the principles of health, no matter whether he has medical training or not. So, if we have two physicians, one of whom said, "The proof of my being a physician is that I can walk on water" and the other, "The proof of my being a physician is that I can heal the sick," our believing the first rests on conviction whereas our belief in the second rests on demonstration. The first is the better and superior way of conviction only in the sense that it persuades and convinces most people. The second way is what is sure and rational.[71]

CONCLUSION

In the thought of Averroes, therefore, revelation or prophecy in general, and the Quranic revelation in particular, is a religious law, given in a book, that brings philosophical wisdom to the masses in such a way that it creates the conditions for the perfection of that wisdom by an intellec-

---

70. Therefore, in a discussion in the following section of the *Exposition of Methods*, which deals with the "divine decree" (*al-quda'*) and "predestination" (*al-qadr*), Averroes argues that God's decree and predestination of events does not conflict with human freedom, for the reason that God orders creation in such a way that it includes within its order the free acts of human beings. Thus, it is false to compare God's agency and human agency to that of a writer and his pen, as al-Ghazali does: Averroes claims that "agency" in the pen is used equivocally of "agency" in the writer. Human agents lack the absolute power and knowledge that God has; nevertheless, human beings have an agency and freedom within the rational order ordained by God. In fact, we cannot even predicate "agency" of God (as the only Agent, as the Ash'arites do), unless we have experience of real agency in human subjects.

71. *Exposition of Methods*, 104–5 (Al-Jabri, 185).

tual elite. If revelation, in other words, is conceived of or understood to be basically a *book* or *law* handed down from God as part of the providential order of things, then that book or law must either negate human reasoning and natural causes or it must simply confirm and coincide with human reasoning and natural causes. It cannot in itself perfect or add a new relationship to human reasoning or nature. Al-Ghazali, and orthodox Islamic theology in general, draws the first conclusion: all revelation is essentially miraculous, and if miraculous, then the Quran must be miraculous. And if the Quran is miraculous and is the eternal speech by which God creates all things, then every thing and every event in nature must be a miraculous manifestation of God's absolute power. As we saw above, Averroes vigorously rejects this line of reasoning; in fact, he argues that the nature of revelation as *law* is much more in accordance both with what Muslims understand to be the essential nature of the Quran and with what the philosophers assert to be the subject-matter of philosophical reflection. But in doing so, Averroes must give up the notion that the Quran and the prophetic career of Muhammad are in any real and true sense miraculous. He must argue that they are simply manifestations of the divine rational order in creation and nothing more. In other words, while for al-Ghazali, all is grace at the expense of nature, for Averroes, all is nature at the expense of grace.

But there is a sense in which Averroes and al-Ghazali are in deep agreement with each other and, it goes without saying, with the whole Muslim tradition: revelation, that is, the handing down of a holy book to a prophet and his subsequent giving of a religious law to a people, is conceived of in a way analogous to how the separate intellect makes thinking among individual human beings possible. Indeed, for al-Ghazali, the Quran is the *lawḥ mafuḍh*, or the "Preserved Tablet" which is separate, eternal, and one for all men like the agent and material intellects of Aristotle and the Neoplatonists. If anything, al-Ghazali is more consistent than Averroes insofar as he seems to argue that the separate and eternal "Tablet" or Quran makes the positing of separate intellects and thus the philosophical life superfluous. He at least does not "multiply entities beyond necessity." In reading Averroes, it is unclear what the *ontological* relationship is between the separate intellect and the religious law. For

Averroes, the religious law seems to be simply part of the providential order of creation, creating the conditions in society for the pursuit of philosophical contemplation of the truth. As such, it is part of the same providential order as the separate intellect itself, but it cannot be identified with this intellect as such. This lack of clarity about the ontological and epistemological status of the Quran (does the Quran really give us "truth" or is not that the preserve of philosophy?) is what, I think, proved fatal to Averroes's philosophical *oeuvre* in the Muslim world.

For al-Ghazali, by contrast, all is revelation at the expense of philosophical reflection. Or, more accurately, revelation *is* philosophical reflection itself, whose agent, however, is not the individual human being *qua* individual human being but God himself. As such, any reasoning from nature to God must be undermined and destroyed, for this would imply that there is an agent of philosophical reflection other than God; and God can be the only real agent in al-Ghazali's understanding of Islam. In any case, like Averroes, al-Ghazali sees the perfection of the human intellect as a sort of impersonal *gnosis* that, to be sure, leads to individual rewards, but not to a personal knowledge of God as such. In this sense, al-Ghazali can claim that *faith* (*imān*) is actually much lower in perfection than knowledge. Both Averroes and al-Ghazali can only conceive knowledge as impersonal and destructive of the individual as individual. In this conception, "faith" can only be belief without "demonstration" for one and belief without "taste" for the other.

In other words, Averroes and al-Ghazali, coming at the same problem from different ends and with different conclusions, manifest the same impasse that confronts Muslims in reconciling the demands of faith and those of reason. If revelation is an impersonal "sending down" of a book or law, then it is very difficult to determine in what way it can relate to philosophical wisdom, which is also, in a way, an impersonal "sending down" of knowledge. More precisely, such a conception of revelation *reinforces* or *entrenches* an understanding of philosophical knowledge (or any knowledge) as a sort of "conjunction" with an impersonal, unitary separate agent (be it intellect or revealed book). The Muslim philosopher is therefore confronted with a dilemma: assimilate revelation to philosophical wisdom in such a way that revelation loses any claim to truth or to the miraculous (the way of Averroes); or assimilate philosophical reflection to the revealed book, making all philosophical reasoning superfluous or even dangerous (the way of al-Ghazali). In either case, a true reconciliation of the claims of revelation and the claims of human reason to truth that recognizes the unique integrity of both becomes exceedingly difficult.

CHAPTER 3

LAW, COVENANT, AND INTELLECT IN MOSES MAIMONIDES'S *GUIDE OF THE PERPLEXED*

Turning from Averroes to Maimonides, it would seem that we are on familiar territory: Maimonides's great philosophico-theological work, the *Guide of the Perplexed*, was written in Judeo-Arabic and makes copious use of concepts common to the Islamo-Arabic Peripatetic tradition. Indeed, both Maimonides and Averroes came from the same city in Muslim Spain—Cordoba—and were roughly contemporaries, so they would have had almost the same cultural and philosophical influences and references.[1] Furthermore, it would seem that Maimonides's treatment of the relation of the religious law to philosophical reflection would be similar to that of Averroes. Both Islam and Judaism are "re-

---

1. "When at a mature age he wrote the *Guide*, he was, in the domain of philosophy and philosophical theology, still almost exclusively involved with the problems with which he must have been familiar in his youth in Spain and the Maghrib." Shlomo Pines, "Translator's Introduction: The Philosophic Sources of *The Guide of the Perplexed*," in *The Guide of the Perplexed*, vol. 1, trans. Shlomo Pines (Chicago: University of Chicago Press, 1963), cix. In addition, Maimonides was aware of the work of Averroes and may have read some of the commentaries late in life. For a good account of the life, times, and cultural background of Maimonides, see Joel L. Kramer, *Maimonides: The Life and World of One of Civilization's Greatest Minds* (New York: Doubleday, 2008); and Aviezer Ravitsky, "On the Study of Medieval Jewish Philosophy," in *History and Faith: Studies in Jewish Philosophy* (Amsterdam: J. C. Gieben, 1996), 9n12.

ligions of the Law." We would then expect Maimonides to articulate
an understanding of the relation of the religious law to philosophical
reflection similar to that articulated by Averroes: the law needs philosophy to draw out all of its material consequences, and philosophy needs
the law in order to create a society in which philosophical thought can
be pursued in peace, but neither contribute to the formal completion or
perfection of the other. In other words, the religious law orders society
in such a way that the perfection of the philosophical life becomes possible, while it is philosophy and the philosophical life itself that actually
perfects the human being with regard to the intellect and the intellection of truth.

But this is not what Maimonides argues. In this chapter we shall
investigate how Maimonides articulates a very different understanding
of the relation of religious law to philosophical thought than one might
expect given his cultural and intellectual background and that this understanding is rooted in the very different and peculiar understanding
that the Jews had of their religious law (halakah) and the nature and
content of divine revelation itself.

In the first place, Jews, unlike Muslims, must deal with the fact that
their religious law is addressed not to humanity as a whole—as in Islam—but to a very particular people. Indeed, as Maimonides makes
clear, one of the purposes of the Jewish law is to set the Jewish people
apart. This creates a problem, because, from its very beginning, philosophical thought always has claimed that its principles, arguments, and
conclusions are open to every rational being; in other words, philosophy makes a claim to universal validity. So the Jewish philosopher must
make sense somehow of this tension between the universal claims of
philosophy and the very particular claims and applicability of the Mosaic Law.[2] The question, therefore, that Maimonides has before himself
is this: is the Mosaic Law not only rational in what it demands, but does
it also, in some way, actually *perfect* or *complete* human reason in ways
other religious "laws" do not? In other words, is the Jewish law particular not in the sense of opposed to the universality of reason but in the

2. Ravitsky, "On the Study of Medieval Jewish Philosophy," 5. See also Rynhold, *An Introduction to Medieval Jewish Philosophy*.

sense of completing or perfecting it? I shall argue that this is indeed how Maimonides understands the relationship between philosophy and the revealed law. This means that religious law and reason perfect and complete each other: philosophical reflection uncovers the true and universal sense of Scripture.[3] But, in turn, revelation or the religious law perfects the human intellect by lifting it out of its fallen state and purifying it of all material—and which, strangely for us, include primarily "ethical"—concerns so that it may engage in the intellectual contemplation of God, which is nothing less than pure love of God.[4] And since philosophical, primarily understood as ethical, thinking is a consequence of the Fall, philosophy in itself cannot perfect the intellect to the degree that the religious law can.

The key, I shall argue, to understanding how Maimonides attempts to reconcile the universal claims of human reason and the particular claims of the Torah and Jewish tradition is hinted at above when I mentioned the intellect's fallen state. That the human intellect is fallen, a key teaching of the Torah itself, is also the key to understanding the relation between reason and faith, philosophy and revelation in Maimonides. In the state of innocence, Adam and Eve enjoyed a pure and immediate intellectual contemplation of God; they had, as a result, no need for a religious law or revelation nor did they have a need for philosophical reasoning. But once they disobeyed God and fell, they no longer enjoyed this intellectual contemplation. Instead, their minds were darkened by matter and material concerns. They could no longer think of God except in bodily or corporeal terms and thus fell into idolatry, the worship of material creatures instead of the immaterial God who created them. Later, when philosophers such as Aristotle developed the science of physics and metaphysics, these sciences were still infected with materialist thinking, even though human reason was able to come to some

3. "The notion that there is a body of truth discovered independently of the accepted religious tradition provides the foundation for the philosophical interpretation of scripture." Howard Kreisel, "Philosophical Interpretations of the Bible," in Nadler and Rudavsky, *Cambridge History*, 94.

4. The goal of the Torah is the love of God, a goal that Maimonides thinks can only be reached if the law is interpreted through the lens of philosophy. David Hartman, *Maimonides: Torah and Philosophic Quest* (Philadelphia: Jewish Publication Society, 1976), 84.

important truths about God and creation through them, since human reason, for Maimonides, is not completely corrupt. Nevertheless, God in his grace gave, through Moses, the law by which our fallen intellect might be repaired. Thus, for Maimonides, the law contains within it all the higher principles of physics and metaphysics, but expressed in such a way as to be conformable to the fallen intellect.[5] Maimonides confronts this problem of two sources of truth—revelation and philosophical reflection—by responding in a twofold manner: on the one hand "purifying" our concept of God with regard to revelation and, on the other hand, submitting philosophy—and not only Kalam but Aristotle as well—to a critique in which he notes when and how philosophy can and does go beyond what it can assert with any authority.[6] In other words, Maimonides always has in mind what reason can affirm *de jure*, that is, by its own inherent power and perfection, and what it can assert *de facto*, that is, what it can know in its fallen state. So, yes, philosophy is universal in its claims; but it cannot demonstrate its highest claims due to the fallen state of the human intellect. The Jewish law is, indeed, particular, but it is particular in the sense of that which perfects what is universal, just as a particular form perfects universal matter.

In light of this distinction, we are now in a position to understand the structure of the *Guide*, which to the first-time reader may appear, well, "perplexing." The *Guide* is divided into three parts. The first part is, in a sense, a propaedeutic; that is, its purpose is to eliminate false conceptions of God and defective philosophical and theological approaches to God. Thus, consequent to the fall of the intellect, human beings were unable to grasp anything, most importantly God, except in a material way. So the first part of the *Guide* has as its aim to reinterpret all corporeal images and predicates of God in the Bible immaterially and intellectually. This task culminates in a rigorous analysis of the names and predicates that we habitually attach to God whereby Maimonides

5. Maimonides's choice of audience is crucial to the structure and plan of the *Guide*. See Leo Strauss, "How to Begin to Study the Guide of the Perplexed," in Maimonides, *The Guide of the Perplexed*, 1:xx.

6. Georges Vajda, "La pensée religieuse de Moise Maimonide: unité ou dualité?" *Cahiers de civilisation médiévale* 33, no. 1 (1966): 41.

argues that only negative terms can properly be predicated of God, since positive terms always imply some sort of corporeality. Maimonides then finishes with a critique of the Islamic Kalam theology, the importance of which we shall address in its proper place.

The second and third parts treat, respectively, of the "Account of the Beginning" (*ma'aseh bereshith*), which Maimonides identifies with "natural science" or physics; and the "Account of the Chariot" (*ma'aseh merkabah*), which he identifies with "divine science" or metaphysics. This identification of the Genesis account of Creation with physics and the prophet Ezekiel's account of his vision of the divine chariot with metaphysics may strike the contemporary reader as odd and fanciful. But there is no reason not to take Maimonides at his word when he says that the second part treats of physics and the third of metaphysics.[7] For Maimonides as for most medieval Jewish and Christian exegetes, divine revelation conceals within itself the highest truths of both physics and metaphysics. If there is any truth in physics and metaphysics, so runs the argument, it must also be found in Scripture, since God is the source of all truth and Scripture is the Word of God.[8] Nevertheless, as we shall see, Maimonides does not see a simple one-to-one correspondence between the truths of philosophy and those of revelation. Revelation, in fact, radically alters our understanding of the philosophical sciences. The doctrine of creation out of nothing, for example, alters fundamentally how we understand physics since it underscores the radically contingent nature of the intelligible order of nature and its very existence. Likewise, Scripture elevates metaphysics and, by extension, the human intellect to perfection insofar as it resituates metaphysical knowledge within an understanding of divine providence and the providential giving of the divine law, which

7. Joseph A. Buijs, "The Philosophical Character of Maimonides' *Guide*: A Critique of Strauss' Interpretation," in *Maimonides: A Collection of Critical Essays*, ed. Joseph A. Buijs (Notre Dame, Ind.: University of Notre Dame Press, 1988), 66.

8. "What he means by identifying the core of philosophy (natural science and divine science) with the highest secrets of the Law (the Account of the Beginning and the Account of the Chariot) and therewith by somehow identifying the subject matter of speculation with the subject matter of exegesis may be said to be the secret par excellence of the *Guide*." Strauss, "How to Begin to Study," xvi–xvii. This, however, would have been an "open secret" for medieval biblical exegetes.

leads to the perfection of the intellect and the pure (that is, intellectual) love of God, who is the proper subject-matter of metaphysics.

Thus, Maimonides often takes seemingly opposed positions on crucial issues not because he is a muddled thinker or because of some "esoteric" doctrine, but because he seeks to bring together two extremes.[9] An example of such extremes is the assertion by Kalam theologians that nothing happens except by the capricious and inscrutable will of Allah and the opposing assertion of the Peripatetics that nothing happens except by the absolute necessity of the thing's nature. Maimonides rejects both claims, mainly because, as we shall see, they both reject or ignore what Maimonides sees as key to understanding the proper relationship between the Creator and the creature. Maimonides asserts that only the reader in whom "our Law has become established in his soul" will understand the purpose of the Guide:

> For the purpose of this Treatise and of all those like it is the science of Law in its true sense. Or rather its purpose is to give indications to a religious man for whom the validity of our Law has become established in his soul and has become actual in his belief—such a man being perfect in his religion and character, and having studied the sciences of the philosophers and come to know what they signify. The human intellect having drawn him on and led him to dwell within its province, he must have felt distressed by the externals of the Law and by the meanings of the above-mentioned equivocal, derivative, or amphibolous terms, as he continued to understand them by himself or was made to understand them by others.[10]

Only the reader who has actually felt and lived the tension between the law and philosophy can be prepared to understand how each completes and perfects the other essentially, because only such a reader can actually experience intellectually this completion and perfection.

9. Marvin Fox, *Interpreting Maimonides: Studies in Methodology, Metaphysics, and Moral Philosophy* (Chicago: University of Chicago Press, 1990), 22.

10. Maimonides, *The Guide of the Perplexed*, trans. Shlomo Pines (Chicago: University of Chicago Press, 1963), intro., 5; *Dalalāt al ḥa'irīn*, Judeo-Arabic text established by S. Munk, ed. Isshachar Joel (Jerusalem: J. Junovitch, 1930–31), 3a. Hereafter *Guide*. Citations will refer to the part and chapter of the *Guide*, followed by the page number of the Pines translation and the page number of the critical edition by S. Munk.

Now, Maimonides himself states explicitly that nothing in the *Guide*
was written at random: "For the diction of this treatise has not been
chosen at haphazard, but with great exactness and exceeding precision,
and with care to avoid failing to explain any obscure point. And nothing
has been mentioned out of its place, save with a view to explaining some
matter in its proper place."[11] Moreover, Maimonides states that there
will be, to the reader, what will in many places seem like "contradictions"
(or, perhaps better, "divergences").[12] This has given rise to many speculative theories about the supposed "esoteric" nature of the *Guide* and
its "true" message.[13] Many of these theories, though often supported
with great erudition, usually lead down any number of rabbit holes in
which we are to intuit "finally" the "true" message of Maimonides. In
such a hermeneutical universe the interpreter can have Maimonides say
anything he or she wishes.[14] We shall thus, for our purposes, stick to
the more wholesome hermeneutical "prejudice" that Maimonides means
more or less what he says. This is not to say that Maimonides is always
open and plain about his meaning: "For my purpose is that the truths
be glimpsed and then again be concealed, so as not to oppose that divine
purpose which one cannot possibly oppose and which has concealed

11. *Guide*, intro. (Pines, 15; Munk, 9a).

12. As Marvin Fox points out, many of what the translations of Maimonides refer to
as "contradictions" are not contradictions in the strict Aristotelian sense (that is, statements
that cannot be both true *and* false at the same time and in the same respect). Rather, many
of these statements are, at best *contraries* (that is, statements that cannot both be true at the
same time and in the same respect, but can both be false) or mere "divergences" (*ikhtilāf*—
which is, in fact, the term that Maimonides uses). Fox, *Interpreting Maimonides*, 72.

13. See the following essays and articles in which these various theories are critical-
ly discussed: Aviezar Ravitzky, "Samuel Ibn Tibbon and the Esoteric Character of the
Guide of the Perplexed," in his *History and Faith: Studies in Jewish Philosophy* (Amsterdam:
J. C. Gieben, 1996), 205–45; Ravitzky, "The Secrets of Maimonides: Between the Thir-
teenth and Twentieth Centuries," in *History and Faith*, 248–56; Strauss, "How to Begin
to Study," xi–lvi; Herbert Davidson, "Maimonides' Secret Position on Creation," in *Studies in Medieval Jewish History and Literature*, ed. I. Twersky (Cambridge, Mass.: Harvard
University Press, 1979), 16–40; Warren Zev Harvey, "A Third Approach to Maimonides'
Cosmogony-Prophetology Puzzle," *Harvard Theological Review* 74, no. 3 (1981): 287–301; and
Jonathan Malino, "Aristotle on Eternity: Does Maimonides Have a Reply?" in *Maimonides
and Philosophy*, ed. S. Pines and Y. Yovel (Dordrecht: Martinus Nijhoff, 1986), 52–64.

14. Indeed, for Leo Strauss, the "true" position of Maimonides on any contested issue
must be the one that he supports *the least* in his text!

from the vulgar among the people those truths especially requisite for His apprehension."[15] He clearly thinks that there are arguments in the *Guide* that could be easily misunderstood by the "vulgar," and so he uses language that purposely obscures his position.[16] Nevertheless, to the educated and attentive reader, Maimonides always makes clear not only where he stands but also that the "hidden" truths which he discovers in Scripture are not destructive of Jewish piety but, to the contrary, are perfective of it.

THE FALLEN INTELLECT AND THE INCORPOREALITY OF GOD

The perplexed reader whom Maimonides wishes to guide is perplexed because he does not understand how the figurative language of the Bible can square with the precise concepts of philosophy; the two modes of expression seem not only to conflict but to lead their reader to opposing conclusions on such crucial questions as the creation or eternity of the world and God's providential care for his creation. According to Maimonides, the solution to this dilemma is not to privilege one mode of expression over the other, nor to isolate the one from the other, arguing that revelation and philosophy are completely separate and autonomous avenues to divine truth. Rather he sees the solution in understanding each as essential to the perfection of the other. Within Scripture lie hidden the highest (and deepest) truths of philosophy, which must be uncovered by philosophical reflection, but which, like the doctrine of

---

15. *Guide*, intro. (Pines, 6–7; Munk, 4a).

16. Maimonides lists seven types of apparent contradiction that could trouble the new or unprepared reader. Most are rather anodyne, and their solutions obvious to the educated and attentive reader (such as taking biblical parables in the inner as opposed to outer sense). Indeed, for Maimonides, only two apparent contradictions are relevant to the reader, the fifth and the seventh. The fifth is where the teacher may have to introduce a concept or example that may be in itself wrong or misleading, but is stated in order later to establish a deeper or more difficult truth that modifies or denies the first premise or example. So, for example, a teacher may try to explain Einstein's general theory of relativity by assuming that physical space has only two dimensions, when, of course, we all know that it really has three. The seventh cause of apparent contradiction has already been stated above: to hide certain truths from the vulgar.

creation out of nothing, would have been inaccessible to philosophical reflection alone. These truths of revelation Maimonides compares to an apple of gold that, however, is covered in filigree of silver (that is, in figures and parables):

> "The Sage has said: 'A word fitly spoken is like apples of gold in settings [mashiyyoth] of silver.'" The parables of the prophets, peace be on them, are similar. Their external meaning contains wisdom that is useful in many respects, among which is the welfare of human societies, as is shown by the external meaning of *Proverbs* and of similar sayings. Their internal meaning, on the other hand, contains wisdom that is useful for beliefs concerned with the truth as it is.[17]

To go beyond the "silver traceries" to perceive the golden apple is the task of the philosopher. "The sacred texts stand for Maimonides as starting points, just as *ta endoxa* stand as starting points for Aristotle."[18] This does not mean that Maimonides does not pay very close attention to the context in which a Scripture passage appears, nor does he ignore the evident intention of the author of the biblical book in which it is found (although the ultimate "author" is, of course, God).[19] And compared to many other medieval biblical exegetes, Maimonides is actually very restrained in his use of allegory and, when he does use it, applies it only in a general sense.[20]

The biblical "parable" which Maimonides considers perhaps the most important is that of the Fall, which occurs in the third chapter of Genesis. This parable is important precisely because it explains how Scripture itself is to be read and also makes clear how the power and scope of the human intellect are to be understood. In part one, Maimonides takes as his task an explanation of several terms from the Bible that imply or seem to imply corporeality in God. And the first he un-

17. *Guide*, intro. (Pines, 12; Munk, 7b).

18. Daniel H. Frank, "Divine Law and Human Practices," in Nadler and Rudavsky, *Cambridge History*, 795.

19. Frank Talmage, "Apples of Gold: The Inner Meaning of Sacred Texts in Medieval Judaism," in *Jewish Spirituality: From the Bible through the Middle Ages*, ed. Arthur Green (New York: Crossroad, 1986), 328.

20. Ibid., 332.

dertakes to explain is the term "image" or *ṣelem*, because Genesis itself states that man was "created in the image and likeness of God." Now does this imply that God has a corporeal, human form? No, it does not, for "the term 'image' [*ṣelem*] … is applied to the natural form, I mean to the notion in virtue of which a thing is constituted as a substance and becomes what it is. It is the true reality of the thing insofar as the latter is that particular being."[21] The term "image" is used in contrast to "likeness" [*demuth*]. "Likeness" refers to similarity in terms of notion (such as elevation and sublimity), but not in terms of form or species. "It was because of this something, I mean because of the divine intellect conjoined with man, that it is said of the latter that he is *in the image of God and in His likeness*, not that God, may He be exalted, is a body and possesses a shape."[22] So the terms "image" and "likeness" refer purely to the intellectual nature and not to a bodily form or likeness.

But if this is so, why does any clear and unequivocal knowledge of God elude us? This is because of the Fall; for, by eating of the Tree of the Knowledge of Good and Evil, Adam and Eve ruptured the intimate and immediate contact that the human intellect had with the divine intellect. As a result, they reduced the human intellect to mere reasoning about means and ends among finite, material creatures.

Now Scripture's account of the Fall, while clear in its general meaning, is not unproblematic in detail. As Maimonides himself relates, a certain "objector" made to him the following argument: what distinguishes man from the beast and, indeed, ennobles him is precisely his ability to distinguish good from bad and right from wrong. And yet, by eating of the Tree of the Knowledge of Good and Evil, this apparently distinguishing and ennobling power was conferred on human beings. So, was not the Fall really an "elevation"? Maimonides's answer is "no." The problem with the objection, he argues, is that it assumes that the ability to distinguish good and evil is the highest or most distinguishing feature of the human being. Rather, the noblest and most distinguishing faculty of the human being is the intellect, and the intellect, as Maimonides asserts, has as its proper object not good or evil but truth:

21. *Guide*, I, 1 (Pines, 22; Munk, 13a).
22. *Guide*, I, 1 (Pines, 23; Munk, 13b).

For the intellect that God made overflow unto man and that is the latter's ultimate perfection, was that which *Adam* had been provided with
before he disobeyed.... For commandments are not given to beasts and
beings devoid of intellect. Through the intellect one distinguished between truth and falsehood, and that was found in [Adam] in its perfection and integrity. Fine and bad, on the other hand, belong to things
generally accepted as known [*al-mashhūrāt*, such as *endoxa*], not to
those cognized by the intellect.[23]

Adam enjoyed full and unobstructed intellectual contemplation of
God. In this contemplation, considerations of good or evil had no part,
for to consider finite creatures in themselves is to consider whether they achieve their proper ends or not (when they do, they achieve
their "good"; and when they do not, they fall into "evil"). But according to Maimonides, Adam considered creatures *already* in their highest
and perfect end, God, and thus had no need to consider either "good"
or "evil." By disobeying the command not to eat of the fruit of the Tree
of the Knowledge of Good and Evil, Adam disobeyed his intellectual
nature, and "became absorbed in judging things to be bad or fine."[24] As
a result of the Fall, man was reduced to the level of a beast, calculating
good and evil.[25] Thus, far from an elevation, the ability to discern between good and evil is, indeed, for Maimonides a "fall."

This reading of the Fall is certainly, for the contemporary reader at
least, rather strange and unusual. But such a reading would not have
struck Maimonides's contemporaries so. In this sense, all religion (or
at least pagan religion, a crucial qualification here for Maimonides) is
a "fall" from purely philosophical reflection.[26] Indeed, one can argue

23. *Guide*, I, 2 (Pines, 24; Munk, 14a–b).

24. *Guide*, I, 2 (Pines, 25; Munk, 14b).

25. Indeed, according to the "faculty psychology" of many Peripatetics in the Islamo-
Arabic tradition, one of the "faculties" (or "powers") of the soul common to both human beings and beasts is the *estimative faculty*, by which a sheep, say, discerns that a wolf is harmful
or "bad" and therefore to be fled from, while seeing its own kind as harmless or "good" and
therefore to be pursued. This sort of faculty psychology, and especially the estimative faculty,
was developed in particular detail by Avicenna.

26. A notion that Maimonides most probably took from al-Farabi, a philosopher
whom he greatly admired. Lawrence V. Berman, "Maimonides on the Fall of Man," *AJS
Review* 5 (1980): 13–14.

that this view of the relation between theoretical reason, which contemplates being as true or false, and practical reason, which understands being as good or bad, goes back to Aristotle himself. Truth applies to theoretical thinking in a more fundamental sense than it does to practical thinking in Aristotle due to the fact that the truth of something is only aimed at accidentally in practical reasoning.[27] But it is in the Islamo-Arabic Peripatetic tradition, represented most fully by al-Farabi, that this is elevated to a sort of principle: "the volitional good is what is conducive to intellectual perfection. Its antithesis, the volitional evil (*al-sharr al-irādi*), also called that which is bad (*qubiḥ*), comes about whenever the rational faculty has an erroneous conception of happiness and is helped by other psychic faculties in the attempt to achieve this false ideal."[28] It follows from this that it is immaterial, for Maimonides or the Jewish tradition as whole, that the Fall must have been a real historical event. As Jeffrey Bernstein remarks:

> What Christianity construes as "original sin," Judaism sees as a legal transgression. Put differently, there is no theological necessity in Judaism for viewing the exile from the Garden of Eden as an historical event, a fall from perfection which brings about a condition that gets transmitted through generations. It is, at most, an exile that explains the human processes of giving birth, working, and dying. In sharp contrast, the reality of the Fall (for Christianity) is what necessitates the Incarnation as the gratuitous event that manifests divine grace and love.[29]

The upshot is that for Maimonides, the intellect *qua* intellect is wholly oriented to contemplation of God, who is Truth in itself; and the human being cannot know what is truly good for him or for anything else

---

27. Shlomo Pines, "Truth and Falsehood versus Good and Evil: A Study in Jewish and General Philosophy in Connection with the *Guide of the Perplexed*," in *Studies in Maimonides*, ed. Isadore Twersky (Cambridge, Mass.: Harvard University Press, 1990), 106.

28. Ibid., 117. Nevertheless, Maimonides differs from the Islamo-Arab Peripatetic tradition in at least two respects: (1) there is no suggestion that the differentiation between good and evil devolves upon a distinct "practical intellect," and (2) the *telos* of the good and that of the true are not merely different but may be incompatible with each other. Ibid., 127.

29. Jeffrey A. Berstein, "Righteousness and Divine Love: Maimonides and Thomas on Charity," in *Questions on Love and Charity: "Summa Theologiae, Secunda Secundae," Questions 23–46*, ed. Robert Miner (New Haven: Yale University Press, 2016), 344.

without this Truth, because he or she is in exile from immediate and intimate intellectual contemplation of God.

That the human being is basically a fallen intellect has important implications for how Maimonides both reads Scripture and understands philosophy. We should, by nature, be able to contemplate God fully and immediately; but, *de facto*, we cannot, because our intellect is immersed in matter or, more accurately, material concerns. Human reason, therefore, is in dire need of healing; it needs revelation from God himself in order to know God. In other words, "revealed knowledge, like the Torah, 'although it is not natural, enters into what is natural.'"[30] Investigation of the limits of reason is not just desirable but absolutely necessary for the theologian, for only such an investigation exposes to us the need for revealed knowledge. Hence, philosophy is integral to the theological project.[31] And it is in this assertion that Maimonides and the Jewish tradition he represents departs clearly from the Islamic Peripatetic tradition.

Philosophy is perhaps most integral to the theological project in that it is essential to purifying our language about God.[32] Since our intellect is fallen, we cannot think or talk about God without using predicates that refer to material or corporeal attributes. The goal, therefore, of the first part of the *Guide* is to purify our intellect of any corporeal language about God so that our intellect, fallen though it is, may be made ready to receive God's revelation of himself in truth: "The purpose of everyone endowed with intellect should be wholly directed to rejecting corporeality with respect to God, may He be exalted, and to considering all these

30. Idit Dobbs-Weinstein, *Maimonides and St. Thomas on the Limits of Reason* (Albany, N.Y.: State University of New York Press, 1995), 29.

31. Ibid., 32: "According to both Maimonides and Aquinas, it is knowledge which guards against intellectual pride, a wisdom (*sapientia*) possessed by those who acknowledge the natural limitations of human reason (*scientia*) and which manifests man's provident participation in divine providence and government." See also her essay "Medieval Biblical Commentary and Philosophical Inquiry as Exemplified in the Thought of Moses Maimonides and St. Thomas Aquinas," in *Moses Maimonides and His Time*, ed. Eric L. Ormsby (Washington, D.C.: The Catholic University of America Press, 1989): 120.

32. See Arthur Hyman, "Maimonides on Religious Language," in *Perspectives on Maimonides: Philosophical and Historical Studies*, ed. Joel L. Kraemer (Oxford: Oxford University Press, 1991), 175–91.

apprehensions as intellectual, not sensory. Understand this and reflect on it."[33] In doing this, philosophical reflection brings to light the very limitations of human reason and, therefore, its need for revelation if it is to know anything of God: "Know that the human intellect has objects of apprehension that it is within its power and according to its nature to apprehend," but there are other objects that are by nature beyond the apprehension of the human intellect. "This difference in capacity [between individuals of the species] is likewise not infinite, for man's intellect indubitably has a limit at which it stops. There are therefore things regarding which it has become clear to man that it is impossible to apprehend."[34] Maimonides is at pains to stress that this conclusion is not dictated by the religious law or any religious concerns; it is a conclusion of reason itself reflecting upon its own nature and powers:

> Do not think that what we have said with regard to the insufficiency of the human intellect and its having a limit at which it stops is a statement made in order to conform to Law. For it is something that has already been said and truly grasped by the philosophers without their having concern for a particular doctrine or opinion. And it is a true thing that cannot be doubted except by an individual ignorant of what has already been demonstrated. We have put this chapter before others only with a view to its serving as an introduction to that which shall come after it.[35]

The fact that human reason is limited by its very nature means that beginning a study of the "divine science," that is, the study of God or metaphysics, without this sort of purification of our language and concepts about God is very harmful.[36] That the human intellect is further corrupted by the effects of the Fall also means that the cultivation of the moral virtues is essential for the acquisition of rational virtues.[37] All this goes to show, for Maimonides, that philosophical thought, far

---

33. *Guide*, I, 28 (Pines, 61; Munk, 32b).

34. *Guide*, I, 31 (Pines, 65; Munk, 34b).

35. *Guide*, I, 31 (Pines, 67; Munk, 35b).

36. "Know that to begin with this science is very harmful, I mean the divine science." *Guide*, I, 33 (Pines, 70; Munk, 37a.)

37. *Guide*, I, 34 (Pines, 76–77; Munk, 40b).

from being alien to the Torah or corrupting our understanding of it, is actually essential if our understanding of the *Torah itself* is *not* to be corrupted or distorted.

The chief virtue of philosophical thought at its best is, therefore, that it enables the believer to think of God incorporeally or as pure spirit. This is important because, for Maimonides, belief in the corporeality of God is worse even than idolatry, for this distorts the image we have of God himself.[38] The idolater may simply understand the idol as a *means* to communicate with the god he or she is worshipping or praying to; but to think that God himself is material or has a body is to distort and blaspheme the very idea we have of God himself. So in reading Scripture, we must rigorously reinterpret any bodily or sensible attributes predicated of God in purely spiritual or intellectual terms:

> To sum up all this: God, may He be exalted above every deficiency, has had bodily organs figuratively ascribed to Him in order that His acts should be indicated by this means. And those particular acts are figuratively ascribed to Him in order to indicate a certain perfection, which is not identical with the particular act mentioned. For instance, an eye, an ear, a hand, a mouth, a tongue, have been figuratively ascribed to Him so that by this means, sight, hearing, action, and speech should be indicated. But sight and hearing have been figuratively ascribed to Him with a view to indicating apprehension in general. For this reason you will find that the Hebrew language substitutes the apprehension made by one sense for that made by another. Thus Scripture says: "See the word of the Lord"; which is like *hear*, for the intended meaning is: apprehend the meaning of His speech.[39]

Indeed, Maimonides spends much of the first part of the *Guide* going through dozens of terms one by one, reinterpreting each in the manner mentioned above. In each case, Maimonides "ambiguates" the term, showing that it has multiple meanings; he them "disambiguates" it by selecting at least one term that can be applied unproblematically to the deity. He wishes to show that there is in the term some noncorporeal,

38. *Guide*, I, 36 (Pines, 84–85; Munk, 44b).
39. *Guide*, I, 46 (Pines, 99; Munk, 51a–b).

nonanthropomorphic sense that can be applied to God.[40] Ultimately, the goal of this analysis is make the term or the name correspond ever more closely with the reality of the living God, for to think of God otherwise than what he is is not to know or communicate with God at all:

> For there is no belief except after a representation; belief is the affirmation that what has been represented is outside the mind just as it has been represented in the mind. If, together with this belief, one realizes that a belief different from it is in no way possible and that no starting point can be found in the mind for a rejection of this belief or for the supposition that a different belief is possible, there is certainty. When you shall have cast off desires and habits, shall have been endowed with understanding, and shall reflect on what I shall say in the following chapters, which shall treat of the negation of attributes, you shall necessarily achieve certain knowledge of it. Then you shall be one of those who represent to themselves *the unity of the Name* and not one of those who merely proclaim it with their mouth without representing to themselves that it has a meaning.[41]

As this passage indicates, a "reformation" of language of God alone is not enough to know God: we must also cast off corrupt "desires and habits" in order to think and talk about God in a way that is true and meaningful. As we shall see, the religious law is crucial for affecting this "casting off" of corrupt desires and habits. But philosophy is just as necessary if our language about God is to be truly meaningful, that is, it puts us in intellectual contact with the true and living God.

REVELATION, NEGATIVE THEOLOGY, AND THE FALLEN INTELLECT

To know God, therefore, we must know his image and likeness. But there can be no material or bodily image and likeness of a being who is incorporeal, immaterial, and purely spiritual. We can only find that image and likeness in what is spiritual and incorporeal. But where can

---

40. Josef Stern, "Meaning and Language," in Nadler and Rudavsky, *Cambridge History*, 259.

41. *Guide*, I, 50 (Pines, 111–12; Munk, 57b).

we find such an image and likeness? In the human being, of course, for the Torah states explicitly that man is made in the image and likeness of God. This, however, only accentuates the problem, since human beings are not only not pure intellect, being corporeal beings as well, but also fallen beings whose intellects are now turned almost wholly to bodily objects and material concerns. We, therefore, can only have anything like a clear and faithful image and likeness of God when the human intellect has been purified of all that is bodily and is transformed in love, contemplation, and worship of "the invisible and hidden God alone."[42]

What all this means is that the human intellect, in its present state, cannot know God like any other object in the material universe. As Maimonides bluntly states, "God cannot be defined."[43] There can be no relation between God and creature, for God "has a necessary existence while that which is other than He has a possible existence."[44] Just as there cannot be a relation between intellect and color, so there cannot be any relation between the pure and infinite being which is God and the changing, finite being which is the human being. We can only predicate attributes of God by "absolute equivocation." "There is, in truth, no relation in any respect between Him and any of His creatures." As Creator of all, God cannot be in any way similar to any one creature, nor can he be similar to any one attribute that all creatures may have in common (such as being, oneness, or goodness) because such a common attribute in creatures would be finite and thus totally unlike what it would be in God. "There is accordingly no way of escape offering the possibility of affirming that He has an attribute, not even with regard to relation, if one has knowledge of true reality."[45]

The logical consequence of this view is that any language about God becomes impossible or at least exceedingly difficult. If we are to attach

42. "Only if God is incorporeal is it absurd to make images of God and to worship such images. Only under this condition can it become manifest to everyone that the only image of God is man, living and thinking man, and that man acts as the image of God only through worshipping the invisible or hidden God alone. Not idolatry but the belief in God's corporeality is a fundamental sin." Strauss, "How to Begin to Study," xxii.
43. *Guide*, I, 52 (Pines, 115; Munk, 59b).
44. *Guide*, I, 52 (Pines, 117; Munk, 61a).
45. *Guide*, I, 52 (Pines, 118; Munk, 61b).

attributes to the divine, we must do so in such a way that they refer not to his essence but to the things God has created. The problem is that, if we did so, we would, according to Maimonides, be implying that within God is a notion or essence distinct and even separate from his one divine essence. But God does not create by means of a notion separate or superadded to his essence. "His essence is, on the contrary, one and simple, having no notion that is superadded to it in any respect."[46] And so, for example, to say that God is good is to imply that there is an essence, "goodness," that is distinct and even separate from the divine essence, since we "super-add" goodness onto the divine essence by saying, "God is good."

What we can do, Maimonides argues, is predicate attributes of "action" to God, since they say nothing about God's essence but only about his actions in the world: "The proof of the assertion that the thing, the apprehension of which was promised to him, was the actions of God, may He be exalted, is the fact that what was made known to him were simply pure attributes of action: *merciful and gracious, long-suffering.*"[47] In other words, what we can say about God is that his *actions* in the world may be like or comparable to actions we observe either in human activity or in the activity of natural things. So God is "merciful" and "gracious" and "long-suffering" insofar as his actions in the world resemble such qualities in human beings. But these attributes say nothing, Maimonides claims, about God's essence: "The meaning here is not that He possesses moral qualities, but that He performs actions resembling the actions that in us proceed from moral qualities."[48] So although God's actions in the world are like those of a merciful human being, this says nothing about *what* God is—anymore than it says anything about what a human being is either (since any rational being, such as an angel, can be merciful as well). Nevertheless, according to Maimonides, attributes that tell us something of the character of God's actions do also give us some knowledge of the character of God himself.[49]

46. *Guide*, I, 53 (Pines, 122; Munk, 64a).
47. *Guide*, I, 54 (Pines, 124; Munk, 64b).
48. *Guide*, I, 54 (Pines, 124; Munk, 65a).
49. Attributes of character such as "merciful" and "gracious" "invoke an image of God

Besides attributes of action, Maimonides also discusses attributes of negation, that is, those which say what God is not (for example, incorporeal, undivided, etc.). Attributes of negation are similar to attributes of affirmation insofar as they bring about some particularization of the object to be known, but they differ from attributes of affirmation insofar as they give us no knowledge of the essence of the object aimed at. "It has thus become clear to you that every attribute that we predicate of Him is an attribute of action or, if the attribute is intended for the apprehension of His essence and not of His action, it signifies the negation of the privation of the attribute in question."[50] In the end, we do not know what or even who God is; our minds and wills are only directed to "someone" who has created us and who addresses us through the law and prophets and to whom our proper response should be obedience and love.[51] The radical difference between Creator and creature leads Maimonides to the conclusion that the only thing that we can say of God is what he is *not*. In other words, Maimonides, in the second half of part one of the *Guide*, argues that only a thoroughly "negative" theology is adequate to the reality that is God and that is the relationship between God and creatures. The goal of this negative theology is to remove all corporeal representations we may have in our minds about God; its goal is to purify our minds as much as or even more than our language about God.[52]

Nevertheless, as many have noted, a purely negative theology is not as straightforward as it sounds.[53] In order for our negations of God to be meaningful, Maimonides argues that we need to keep in mind

---

as a moral person worthy of imitation." Ehud Z. Benor, "Meaning and Reference in Maimonides' Negative Theology," *Harvard Theological Review* 88, no. 3 (1995): 341.

50. *Guide*, I, 58 (Pines, 136; Munk, 72a).

51. Thus, as Ehud Benor argues, for Maimonides negative theology is about determining the reference of the word "God"; but it leaves the word itself devoid of meaning. It is about how we are to *direct* our minds to God. Benor, "Meaning and Reference," 350.

52. "I believe it is significant that Maimonides's famous statement that belief is not a matter of utterance or proclamation, but rather of representation in the mind, opens his exposition of negative theology [at I. 50]." Benor, "Meaning and Reference," 348.

53. See the classic article by Harry A. Wolfson, "Maimonides on Negative Attributes," in *Studies in the History of Philosophy and Religion*, vol. 2, ed. Isadore Twersky and George H. Williams (Cambridge, Mass.: Harvard University Press, 1977), 195–230.

one key principle: that God is one. This is not a "positive" attribute: to be "one" is simply to negate all division essentially. Any attribute that we predicate of God that implies division or multiplicity must be negated of God. If predication is understood in this sense, then for Maimonides it does give us some knowledge of God.[54] Thus for Maimonides to attribute only predicates of action to God is to say that we cannot predicate anything of God *tertium adiacens* but only *secundum adiacens*.[55] An example of a predication *tertium adiacens* is something like, "Socrates is bald." In such a proposition, the verb "is" is only a copula that asserts nothing about the existence of Socrates or of baldness but of their connection in one subject, Socrates. Here, the attributes are understood to be separate in some way from the particular subject (though not from any subject). It does not matter whether Socrates exists or not for it to be true. In a proposition *secundum adiacens*, such as "Socrates is" or "exists," the verb "is" "lies second" to the subject and is predicated of the subject itself. It says something about the existence of the subject itself (although nothing about his essence). The problem, as Maimonides sees it, of predicating anything of God is that all attributes that we attach to God can only be predicated *secundum adiacens*.[56] In saying, "God is," we must mean that "is" or "exists" belongs to the very essence of God, because in order for God to be God he must be absolutely one:

> Accordingly, His existence is identical with His essence and His true reality, and His essence is His existence. Thus His essence does not have an accident attaching to it when it exists, in which case its exis-

54. A common mistake among the interpreters of Maimonides, both Jewish and Christian, was to claim that Maimonides "allowed attributes to be positively affirmed of God when such attributes are interpreted causally: 'God is wise insofar as He causes wisdom in creatures.'" Aquinas, of course, quickly exposed the incoherence of such a position: if God is the cause of bodies, should not he also be a body? But, Professor Feldman argues, Maimonides himself never made such a claim. Maimonides rigorously denies that we can say anything positive about the divine essence, even as cause. The cause of this mistake most probably was due to the inability to differentiate sufficiently between relational and actional attributes in Maimonides's own discussion of these attributes. See Seymour Feldman, "A Scholastic Misinterpretation of Maimonides' Doctrine of Divine Attributes," in Buijs, *Maimonides*, 268.

55. Wolfson, "Maimonides on Negative Attributes," 196.

56. *Guide*, I, 56 (Pines, 130; Munk, 68a ff).

tence would be a notion that is superadded to it. For His existence is necessary always; it is not something that may come suddenly to Him nor an accident that may attain Him. Consequently He exists, but not through an existence other than His essence; and similarly He lives, but not through life; He is powerful, but not through power; He knows, but not through knowledge. For all these attributes refer back to one notion in which there is no idea of multiplicity, as will be made clear.[57]

God is existence in all its concrete plenitude; we cannot, therefore, predicate any abstract terms of God as if they were other than his existence. Nothing in God can be accidental to his existence but all that we say truly of God must be, if God is to be purely one and absolutely incorporeal, absolutely necessary to his existence.[58] Existence is, however, "accidental" to the essence of the creature, which implies that some will wills it into existence.[59] We can predicate various attributes of creatures unambiguously because the essence of a creature is not identical to its existence: we can say "The tree is living" because "tree," "is," and "living" are three different essences or realities that come together accidentally in this particular tree. But in God the subject, predicate, and copula are all one reality, which makes any statement about what God is problematic. Even to say simply that "God is" is unhelpful insofar as "God" and "is" or "exists" are thought of as separate essences or realities.

It is clear, however, from the development of Maimonides's discussion of negative theology that it does not interest him for its own sake, as a theological or philosophical problem. Maimonides clearly sees that the goal and end of negative theology is to make the believer like unto God himself: "For the utmost virtue of man is to become like unto Him, may He be exalted, as far as he is able; which means that we should make our actions like unto His, as the Sages made clear when interpreting the verse, 'Ye shall be holy.' They said: 'He is gracious, so be you also gracious; He is merciful, so be you also merciful.'"[60] And we become

57. *Guide*, I, 57 (Pines, 132; Munk, 69b).

58. "In the case of God, existence is not merely actual but necessary." Alexander Altmann, "Essence and Existence in Maimonides," in Buijs, *Maimonides*, 153.

59. "Existence is thus from yet another angle accidental to essence. But its accidental nature is now seen to derive from the Will of God." Ibid., 154.

60. *Guide*, I, 54 (Pines, 128; Munk, 67a).

like unto God insofar as we become pure intellect, which is to say, intellect devoid of all thought of corporeal things and free of all material concerns. In other words, the goal of negative theology is, paradoxically, to *incapacitate the intellect*, at least with regard to its fallen condition and raise it to a sort of "holy ignorance": "Glory then to Him who is such that when the intellects contemplate His essence, their apprehension turns into incapacity; and when they contemplate the proceeding of His actions from His will, their knowledge turns into ignorance; and when the tongues aspire to magnify Him by means of attributive qualifications, all eloquence turns into weariness and incapacity!"[61] This sort of holy or "learned ignorance" (to borrow a term from Nicholas of Cusa) is higher than all other human knowledge precisely because it is a knowledge and awareness of the incapacity of the human intellect to attain apprehension of the divine: "Apprehension of Him consists in the inability to attain the ultimate term in apprehending Him." Thus, the psalm says "Silence is to praise Thee" (Ps. 65:2).[62] In this sense, the use of language about God is not referential—pointing out or describing to the intellect an essence for its gaze and contemplation—but heuristic—pointing the intellect to an encounter with a mystery that goes beyond its ability to comprehend or conceptualize.[63] As Kenneth Seeskin notes: "That is why the best response is silence. Like Plotinus, Maimonides believes there are contexts in which silence actually contains more truth than speech."[64] This is perhaps why Maimonides prefers the attributes of action: they focus on what God *does* and not on what God *is*, and therefore aid the human intellect in actually *being* like the divine intellect rather than in thinking *about* it.[65] In other words, the proper

61. *Guide*, I, 58 (Pines, 137; Munk, 72b).

62. *Guide*, I, 59 (Pines, 139; Munk, 73b).

63. Kenneth Seeskin, "Sanctity and Silence: The Religious Significance of Maimonides' Negative Theology," *American Catholic Philosophical Quarterly* 76, no. 1 (2002): 9.

64. Ibid., 15.

65. "In practice, he [Maimonides] continually returns to the language of action—perhaps as a pedagogical tool to help the student understand negative statements about the divine. Perhaps, then, we should understand his description of God as intellect not as a positive attribute, but as an attribute of action. Knowing may describe not what God is, but what God does, an effect of God's activity, rather than God's essential nature." Diana Lobel, "'Silence Is Praise to You': Maimonides on Negative Theology, Looseness of

end of Maimonides's negative theology is not more accurate descriptions of the essence of God, which is impossible and foolhardy, but a love and awe of God rooted in a "true ignorance" of God that introduces no corporeality or multiplicity into our notion of who God is.[66]

Maimonides is well known (in the Thomistic literature at least) for arguing then that all attributes we predicate of God must be predicated equivocally: when we say that God is "wise" and that a man is "wise" the senses of the term "wise" in this case have as much in common as the word "bank" does when we say "the duck is sitting on the bank" and "I have money in the bank." The only thing the senses of the term have in common is the same word or sound. This is also the case, Maimonides also asserts, of such terms as "speaking" and "saying" when applied to God.[67] God cannot be understood to "speak" to us in any way that is common with human speech. The most we can say is that God's *actions* in history, especially with regard to the prophets, are like human speech. Indeed, Maimonides repeats frequently the rabbinic dictum that "God addresses us in the language of men." But this does not mean that anything like language belongs to God in his essence. What it does mean, however, is that God can use language to purify the human intellect from language, so that it can be fully actualized as intellect in silent love and contemplation. And then the image and likeness of the human being to God becomes complete.

It is appropriate, therefore, that Maimonides spends much of the latter part of part one of the *Guide* discussing the nature of the intellect. Following Aristotle, Maimonides argues that the human being starts off as intellect only potentially: we need to sense and to cognize objects in

---

Expression, and Religious Experience," *American Catholic Philosophical Quarterly* 76, no. 1 (2002): 36.

66. "Negative theology and positive worship can indeed go hand and hand. Negative theology ensures that the being we worship is truly God. Negative theology brings correct knowledge of God—knowledge through negation—which inspires love and awe." Ibid., 49.

67. *Guide*, I, 65 (Pines, 158; Munk, 84b): "The purpose of this chapter is to set forth that the words *speaking* and *saying* are equivocal, applied both to utterance by the tongue—as when it says, 'Moses spoke'; and 'Pharaoh said'—and to notions represented by the intellect without being uttered—as when it says, 'Then said I in my heart'; 'Then I spoke in my heart'; and 'thy heart shall speak,'" etc.

order to become intellect in actuality.[68] Maimonides also asserts with Aristotle that in cognition, the intellect becomes the thing known, at least with respect to its immaterial form (if not with respect to its individuating matter): "Intellect realized *in actu* is the pure abstract form, which is in his mind, of the piece of wood. For intellect is nothing but the thing that is intellectually cognized."[69] Thus, intellect and cognition, apprehension and what is apprehended, or, more generally, activity and substantial being are one activity or two sides of the same coin: "You should not then think that the intellect *in actu* is a certain thing existing by itself apart from apprehension and that apprehension is something else subsisting in that intellect. For the very being and true reality of the intellect is apprehension" or as Maimonides puts even more pithily a little further in the text: "Now its act is identical with its essence."[70] So, taken in its essence, intellect and intellection are one and the same act or actuality. If, however, we take apprehension and intellect potentially, such as in the human being or any other intellectual creature, then the intellect and the thing apprehended are two separate things. But this is only accidental to the intellect of the creature, for the unity of essence and activity hold only for the intellect *per se*: "It is accordingly also clear that the numerical unity of the intellect, the intellectually cognizing subject, and the intellectually cognized object, does not hold good with reference to the Creator only, but also with reference to every intellect."[71] What this suggests is that for Maimonides it is the nature and activity of the intellect as such that can bridge the gap between what we can say about God's actions and what we can say about his essence. As the intellect becomes actualized, to that degree its activity fulfills its essence; and given that the human being is made in the image and likeness of God with respect to his will and intellect, to the degree that the human intellect ascends to the purity of intellect, to that degree it comes to know God's essence.[72] In this, the position of Maimonides lies very close to that of Averroes, discussed in the previous chapter.

68. "Know that before a man intellectually cognizes a thing, he is potentially the intellectually cognizing subject." *Guide*, I, 68 (Pines, 163; Munk, 87a).

69. *Guide*, I, 68 (Pines, 164; Munk, 87a–b).

70. *Guide*, I, 68 (Pines, 164; Munk, 87b).

71. *Guide*, I, 68 (Pines, 165; Munk, 88a–b).

72. "This suggests that for Maimonides the God of the *via negativa* is the same as the

Maimonides's position here, however, seems to be in tension if not overt contradiction with his negative theology. If all that we can say of God can only be said of him equivocally, then, to be consistent, we must also include the attributes "intellect" or "intellectual" in these terms.[73] But one can ask whether there really is a contradiction or even a tension. If God is incorporeal, then he is pure form—pure intellect. Indeed, if the intellect is the "form of forms," we can say nothing positive about God.[74] Such a concept of God is purely formal, that is, devoid of positive content. In this sense, then, the human intellect is an image and likeness of God, but, again, in a purely formal way. We can therefore come to know God by knowing the intellect in itself. Hence, philosophical reflection is necessary if we are to purify our intellects of all that is bodily. But Scripture or revelation is necessary in this purification because our intellects are fallen and, if they relied on philosophy alone, would reduce God to the measure of what the fallen intellect can conceive of God, that is, as a will-less purely logical concept. Here, Maimonides differs radically from Averroes.

But before Maimonides can discuss the proper roles of revelation and philosophy in coming to a knowledge of God, he must offer a critique of the Islamic Kalam, which claimed to offer a rational defense of (Quranic) revelation that also "destroyed" (see al-Ghazali) the claims of the philosophers. As we saw in the chapters on Averroes, the most prominent school of *Kalām* was the Ash'arite school and their chief assertion was that there is no necessity in created things or in nature as a whole but all things and all events come about simply due to the sheer will of God. That a match causes fire is simply due to God's willing it—there is no power within the nature of the match or even of fire to

---

God conceived as *Nous*." Carlos Fraenkel, "God's Existence and Attributes," in Nadler and Rudavsky, *Cambridge History*, 587.

73. Hannah Kasher, "Self-Cognizing Intellect and Negative Attributes in Maimonides' Theology," *Harvard Theological Review* 87, no. 4 (1994): 461–72. Kasher argues that it is not Maimonides's intention in I.68 to argue that God *is* intellect but rather that intellect, subject, and object must form one notion in God. But such a minimal claim seems to go against the general argument of this section of the *Guide* (see ibid., 465).

74. Barry S. Kogan, "'What Can We Know and When Can We Know It?' Maimonides on the Active Intelligence and Human Cognition," in Ormsby, *Moses Maimonides and His Time*, 132.

cause fire in something else. If God willed it, the match would cause paper to freeze or smell of lilacs. Now, for the benefit of us humans, God wills that things follow a rough regularity, but this is only (divine) "custom": "For the foundation of everything is that no consideration is due to how that which exists is, for it is merely a custom; and from the point of view of the intellect, it could well be different. Furthermore, in many places they follow the imagination and call it intellect."[75] That is, according to Maimonides, the *mutakallimun* claim that if we can *imagine* something to be otherwise, then not only *can* God make it otherwise but it is not otherwise only because God *actually* chooses for it not to be otherwise. But if this is the case, Maimonides argues, then there can be no rational discussion at all, not only about the world but also about God. For, according to the doctrine of the *Kalām*, our knowledge does not have to conform to the way things are because the "way things are" is completely arbitrary and it is just as "logical" to imagine them to be otherwise (which is, in fact, to destroy any logic or reason in nature): "To sum up: I shall say to you that the matter is as Themistius puts it: that which exists does not conform to the various opinions, but rather the correct opinions conform to that which exists."[76] If all is due to divine caprice, then not only can we not say anything about God from any rational order in creation, but we cannot attribute to God any meaningful revelation of himself through Scripture or the prophets, because there could be no distinction in such a world between what is natural and what is supernatural.

Now the presumed aim of the *mutakallimun* was to try to demonstrate that the world is created *de novo* or at a specific time in the past. If no creature can cause anything else except by the divine will, then it is easy to assert that nothing would exist except by the divine will and that he made all things to begin at a certain time in the past. But for Maimonides, the premises of the *mutakallimun* are deeply flawed. They assume that if we can *imagine* that the world has a beginning in time, then it *must* have had a beginning in time. To prove that there is a First Cause, God, then becomes easy—too easy. We must rely instead

75. *Guide*, I, 71 (Pines, 179; Munk, 96a).
76. *Guide*, I, 71 (Pines, 179; Munk, 96a).

on the firmer and demonstrable principles of the philosophers if we are to establish the possibility of creation *de novo*.[77] This is because the philosophers establish the existence of God by assuming the eternity of the world, an assumption that, while no more self-evidently true than creation in time, does not beg the question of a first cause, as the Kalam arguments do.

Maimonides does concede that the *mutakallimun* were right in one limited sense: that God creates freely. The philosophers, by contrast, argue that God must do everything by necessity, in strict accordance with his divine nature.[78] Thus even philosophers (like Averroes) who admitted that God creates, argued that God does so by necessity and therefore eternally (not *de novo*). For Maimonides this is just as damaging to a true concept of the deity as the ascription of pure will to God of the *mutakallimun*. In sum, the philosophers see, if only dimly, that by virtue of our intellect we are made in the image and likeness of God. But because we are fallen from pure intellectual contemplation to calculating good and evil with regard to our will, they do not see that God wills freely and relates to us freely. It is for this reason that Maimonides, in the second part of the *Guide*, must sort out what creation truly means, how it is possible, and what are its implications for the possibility or even necessity of revealed knowledge of God.

CREATION AND PROPHECY

Part 2 of the *Guide*, if we take (rightly, I think) Maimonides at his word, constitutes Maimonides's physics, that is, the science of nature in light of both philosophical thought and divine revelation. But if part 2 is Maimonides's physics, it is to the contemporary reader a strange physics.

77. *Guide*, I, 71 (Pines, 180–81; Munk, 96b–97a).
78. "As Isaac Abrabanel has pointed out, the issue is not between creation and non-creation but between creation by will and design or creation by necessity. Creation by will and design as conceived by Kalam left no room for a realm of essence, and, vice versa, creation by necessity as conceived by the philosophers seemed to ignore the nature of existence.... Maimonides assumes an intermediate position. He does not share the rejection of the term 'Cause' for God (I, 69), and, at the same time, adopts the Kalam notion of *taḥṣīs*, which expresses the concept of will and design." Altmann, "Essence and Existence," 155.

This is not merely because by "physics" Maimonides means the science as understood by Aristotle and not as it is understood today since the time of Newton; it is also because for Maimonides any study of nature, *physis*, must necessarily be grounded in a discussion of the precondition of nature itself, creation.[79] Far from being an unproblematic given, the very existence of nature, as revealed in Scripture, becomes a problem—a problem that is paradoxically philosophical and yet incapable of philosophical solution. Hence, reflection on the possibility and nature of creation must lead to an exploration of the possibility and nature of prophecy. For any knowledge that goes beyond physics must come from God himself, not through the natural abilities of the philosopher alone, but through a supernatural "infusion" into the prophet.[80]

For Maimonides, the biblical doctrine of creation *ex nihilo* and *de novo* should alter radically how the believing Jew understands nature and how he is to pursue the science of nature or physics, insofar as that science is conceived as a self-sufficient explanation of reality.[81] While there is a rational and necessary order in creation, this rational order or necessity is not absolute. God could have made the order of the universe other than he did and any necessity in that order is purely conditional—*given* that God created things thus, then they must act in such and such a manner.[82] So, in a sense, Maimonides's interest in physics in this part of the *Guide* is only incidental to the larger discussion of the very conditions of nature itself. Thus, in his preface to part 2, Maimonides says:

79. "The only ontological distinction which matters from the theological point of view is the one between created and uncreated being. All created existence is caused, actualized from potentiality, and willed by God. The term 'being' is therefore used homonymously of God and the created beings." Altmann, "Essence and Existence," 162.

80. This distinction between "natural disposition" and "supernatural infusion" will have to be qualified much more heavily as our discussion proceeds.

81. If the universe is a product not of blind chance or caprice but is an expression of *hesed* or divine grace or graciousness, then Scripture introduces a dimension of personalism into nature and charges nature with moral and aesthetic meaning. See Alfred L. Ivry, "Maimonides on Creation," in *Creation and the End of Days: Judaism and Scientific Cosmology*, ed. David Novack and Norbert Samuelson (Lanham, Md.: University Press of America, 1986), 187–88.

82. "Before the world existed, he [Maimonides] acutely observes, there were none of the physical restrictions which obtain after creation, and thus God had a free hand to create what and how He wished." Ibid., 193.

My purpose in this Treatise, as I have informed you in its introduction is only to elucidate the difficult points of the Law and to make manifest the true realties of its hidden meanings, which the multitude cannot be made to understand because of these matters being too high for it.... I only intend to mention matters, the understanding of which may elucidate some difficulty of the Law; in fact, many knots will be unraveled through the knowledge of a notion of which I give an epitome.[83]

Essential to Maimonides's project in discussing the possibility of creation (and especially creation *de novo*, which we shall explain presently) is that establishing the possibility of creation *de novo* also establishes the possibility (maybe even necessity) of prophecy and, therefore, the foundations of the religious law. In this way Maimonides carries on the critique of philosophy made a century earlier by his co-religionist and fellow Andalusian, Judah Halevi, that: "The myth of philosophy is that we can know based on our native powers alone, and that God is a conclusion only reached at the end of inquiry. In reality, belief in God is a necessary presupposition for the very project of philosophy. For philosophers' trust in their ability to attain truth presupposes ungrounded faith in God who ordains a correspondence between sense perceptions and external reality."[84] It is this insight that Maimonides tries to develop throughout part 2. The natural world exhibits a rational order, but it is a rational order rooted in free will and, ultimately, a relationship with a free and therefore living Creator.

Thus, for Maimonides, everything hinges on what can be understood from the "Account of the Beginning" (part 2 of the *Guide*) and from the "Account of the Chariot" (part 3), which deal with the problems of prophecy and knowledge of the deity:

Accordingly in whatever chapter you find me discoursing with a view to explaining a matter already demonstrated in natural science, or a matter demonstrated in divine science, or an opinion that has been shown to be the one fittest to be believed in, or a matter attaching to what has been explained in mathematics—know that that particular matter nec-

83. *Guide*, II, 2 (Pines, 253; Munk, 12a).
84. Michah Gottlieb, "Mysticism and Philosophy," in Nadler and Rudavsky, *Cambridge History*, 130.

essarily must be a key to the understanding of something to be found in the books of prophecy, I mean to say of some of their parables and secrets. The reason why I mentioned, explained, and elucidated that matter would be found in the knowledge it procures us of the "Account of the Chariot" or of the "Account of the Beginning" or would be found in an explanation that it furnishes of some root regarding the notion of prophecy or would be found in the explanation of some root regarding the belief in a true opinion belonging to the beliefs of Law.[85]

Maimonides quite explicitly states here that in discussing physics or metaphysics his real intention is to lay bare the inner truth of Scripture, for it is in understanding Scripture more fully and more profoundly that the fallen human intellect is restored to something like its pre-fallen (that is, purely intellectual) condition and, only then, can secular sciences like physics and metaphysics be understood in their truth (who is God). Crucial to a genuine understanding of physics is understanding the true nature of creation as the precondition of the very existence of nature itself. By creation, Maimonides means creation *de novo* or creation that has a beginning in time. Now one can, like Maimonides's Muslim contemporary and fellow Aristotelian, Averroes, argue for a notion of creation that is eternal: all things are created directly by God, but God does this eternally without any temporal beginning. In arguing this, such philosophers believed they were preserving the unchanging and fully actual nature of the deity, attributes that philosophers argued must be predicated necessarily of the deity if our concept of the deity was to have any coherence. But, as we shall see, Maimonides sees this understanding of creation as destructive of revelation, the foundations of the law, and of biblical religion in general.[86] So, the question becomes, can we deduce by necessary reasoning the existence of the order of things from God, their First Cause? And, more importantly, could

---

85. *Guide*, II, 2 (Pines, 254; Munk, 12a–b).

86. "For Maimonides, it was not eternity, but rather the absolutely necessary character of the emanation of all things from a First Cause that destroys the foundations of biblical religion." William Dunphy, "Maimonides and Aquinas on Creation: A Critique of Their Historians," in *Graceful Reason: Essays in Ancient and Medieval Philosophy Presented to Joseph Owens, CSsR*, ed. Lloyd P. Gerson (Toronto: Pontifical Institute for Mediaeval Studies, 1983), 375.

only an unfallen intellect in no need of revelation or a religious law do so? And, even if such an intellect could do so, would that not already beg the question, presupposing a will-less, impersonal deity?

Thus, Maimonides finds good reasons for taking Genesis seriously: the idea of creation *de novo* in Genesis does not try to derive the diversity of the world from God's unity but rather does so in terms of both God's will and of his wisdom.[87] Whether the world is created or not, let alone created *de novo* or *ab aeterno*, cannot be decided by reason itself. Indeed, Maimonides strategy in part 2 is to sharpen, not lesson, the reader's impression that reason is helpless before this issue.[88] But this is done in order to destroy the pretensions of the (Aristotelian) philosophers that they can demonstrate by reason that the world is eternal. By destroying these pretensions, Maimonides is then able to propose creation *de novo* as not only rationally possible but even intellectually preferable given a full examination of the nature of the world.[89]

In making his argument, Maimonides begins by outlining three possible positions on the deity and its relation to the world: "There are three opinions of human beings, namely, of all those who believe that there is an existent deity, with regard to the eternity of the world or its

87. Lenn E. Goodman, "Creation and Emanation," in Nadler and Rudavsky, *Cambridge History*, 610.

88. William Dunphy, "Maimonides' Not-So-Secret Position on Creation," in Ormsby, *Moses Maimonides and His Time*, 171.

89. At the beginning of part 2, Maimonides does present, as a prelude to his argument for God's existence, twenty-five theses of the philosophers, which he claims have been demonstrated. Nevertheless, Maimonides says that he will add one more to this list, that of the eternity of the world, which, however, has *not* been demonstrated. But he will do so *for the sake of argument* only. "I shall add to the premises mentioned before, one further premise that affirms as necessary the eternity of the world. Aristotle deemed it to be correct and the most fitting to be believed. We shall grant him this premise by way of hypothesis in order that the clarification of that which we intended to make clear should be achieved" (*Guide*, II [Pines, 237; Munk, 5a]). This is because the alternative proposition—that the world was created with a beginning in time—and the arguments used by the *mutakallimun* to support it beg the question: they assume what they are trying to prove, which is the existence of a first cause or creator. So any demonstration of God's existence must assume for the sake of argument that the world had no beginning in time (an assumption that Aquinas follows Maimonides in making). But *after* demonstrating the existence of God and the contingency or created-ness of the world, *then* we can weigh the rationality and cogency of the claim that God created the world *de novo*.

production in time."[90] The first is that God created the world out of nothing and that this creation had a beginning in time. Maimonides identifies this view with "Moses our Master" and therefore as having absolute authority for any pious and believing Jew:

> The first opinion, which is the opinion of all who believe in the Law of *Moses our Master, peace be upon him*, is that the world as a whole—I mean to say, every existent other than God, may He be exalted—was brought into existence by God after having been purely and absolutely nonexistent, and that God, may He be exalted, had existed alone, and nothing else—neither an angel nor a sphere nor what subsists within the sphere. Afterwards, through His will and His volition, He brought into existence out of nothing all the beings as they are, time itself being one of the created things. For time is consequent upon motion, and motion is an accident in what is moved.[91]

There can be, therefore, no "time" before the creation of the world; If you assert a time "before" creation then you, in effect, affirm the eternity of the world, because time needs a "substratum" in which to exist. For Maimonides, this assertion of creation *de novo* is not some idle speculation on metaphysical matters but, after belief in the unity of God, one most basic to the religious law, because it establishes both the possibility and necessity of the law itself:

> This is one of the opinions [on creation]. And it is undoubtedly a basis of the Law of *Moses our Master*, peace be upon him. And it is second to the basis that is the belief in the unity [of God]. Nothing other than this should come to your mind. It was *Abraham our Father, peace be upon him*, who began to proclaim in public this opinion to which speculation had led him. For this reason, he made his proclamation "in the Name of the Lord, God of the world"; he had also explicitly stated this opinion in saying: "Maker of heaven and earth."[92]

---

90. *Guide*, II, 13 (Pines, 281; Munk, 27a). Maimonides also mentions positions such as those of the Epicureans for whom there is neither creation nor any deity as first cause. But Maimonides dismisses such philosophies as being so incompatible with revelation as not worth engaging.
91. *Guide*, II, 13 (Pines, 281; Munk, 27a).
92. *Guide*, II, 13 (Pines, 282; Munk, 28b).

For again, if everything were the product of a simple and eternal emanation from God, then God himself would be in principle knowable by
human reason unaided by divine revelation, simply by reasoning back
from effects to cause. This presupposes, in turn, that our intellect is unfallen and not in need of repair and redemption by a revealed law.

But Maimonides also outlines two other opinions on whether the
world is created or eternal: "The second opinion is that of all the philosophers of whom we have heard reports and whose discourses we have
seen.... They believe that there exists a certain matter that is eternal as
the deity is eternal; and that He does not exist without it, nor does it
exist without Him."[93] This, of course, is the teaching that goes back to
Plato's *Timaeus*, in which a "demiurge" or god, using the eternal, immaterial forms as models, molds a pre-existing eternal matter into the various
material substances of our experience. Plato's student Aristotle, however,
rejected this and asserted that the world of formed matter or material
substances is eternal both with respect to the past as well as with respect
to the future. While individual material substances, of course, come into
being and pass away, the material world as a whole does not:

> The third opinion is that of Aristotle, his followers, and the commenta-
> tors of his books. He asserts what also is asserted by the people of the
> sect that has just been mentioned [Platonists], namely, that something
> endowed with matter can by no means be brought into existence out of
> that which has no matter. He goes beyond this by saying that the heav-
> en is in no way subject to generation and passing-away. This opinion on
> this point may be summed up as follows. He thinks that this being as a
> whole, such as it is, has never ceased to be and will never do so; that the
> permanent thing not subject to generation and passing-away, namely,
> the heaven, likewise does not cease to be; that time and motion are per-
> petual and everlasting and not subject to generation and passing-away;
> and also that the thing subject to generation and passing-away, namely,
> that which is beneath the sphere of the moon, does not cease to be.[94]

As Maimonides states here, Aristotle simply extended the eternity of
matter to the heavens; that is, whereas Plato envisioned that the demi-

93. *Guide*, II, 13 (Pines, 282–83; Munk, 28b).
94. *Guide*, II, 13 (Pines, 284; Munk, 29a–b).

urge created the heavenly bodies out of a pre-existing matter, Aristotle asserted that these bodies are eternal and unchanging. Nevertheless, in the end, for Maimonides, there is no essential difference between the second and third opinions.[95] Both assert that there is something eternal apart from God himself, namely, matter and that, therefore, God does not so much *create* the world as *generate* it out of a pre-existing material.[96]

The problem, of course, for the pious Jew is that the (Peripatetic) philosophers claim that the truth of the eternity of the world is demonstrable. This means that to believe otherwise is not only to go against reason but also to claim that God and his revelation also go against reason. But, Maimonides argues, the philosophers have no such demonstration nor did their master, Aristotle, ever claim to have one about the world's eternity:

> My purpose ... is to make it clear that Aristotle possesses no demonstration for the world being eternal, as he understands this. Moreover he is not mistaken with regard to this. I mean to say that he himself knows that he possesses no demonstration with regard to this point, and that the arguments and the proofs that he sets forth are merely such as occur to the mind and to which the soul inclines.[97]

The philosophers cannot demonstrate that the world is eternal any more that the *mutakallimun* can demonstrate that the world has a temporal beginning. Nor can any demonstration of the existence of God, which Maimonides believes is possible, indeed, necessary, help us here.[98] For

95. *Guide*, II, 13 (Pines, 285; Munk, 30a).

96. Why Maimonides brings up the second or "Platonic" opinion if it is essentially no different from the Aristotelian position has fueled much speculation about Maimonides's intentions and the possibility of a "hidden" or "secret" position on creation that is at odds with Jewish orthodoxy. See note 5 above. I think such speculation is misplaced given that Maimonides's intention here is clear, which is to eliminate two opinions on creation or the eternity of the world that seem to conflict with "Moses, our Master." Maimonides brings up the "Platonic" option only because it was an option and one that might mislead believing Jews because it seemed to be an attractive "intermediate" position: "intermediate," that is, in that it asserted on the one hand a "creation" of sorts, thus satisfying Jewish religious sensibilities, but on the other hand denying creation from nothing, thus satisfying the supposed rational demands of the philosophers. It seems then that Maimonides brings it up only to make sure that he can refute it and eliminate it as an option for Jews.

97. *Guide*, II, 15 (Pines, 289; Munk, 32b).

98. "The question about temporal or eternal beginning of the Universe is irrelevant to

the existence of a God who is essentially one, completely actual, and immaterial is consistent with a creation that is eternal and one that has a beginning in time. We cannot deduce (as some philosophers, such as Avicenna and Averroes, tried to do) out of the existence and nature of God one position or the other. Therefore, Maimonides asserts, "It is preferable that a point for which there is no demonstration remain a problem or that one of the two contradictory propositions simply be accepted."[99] And the position to be accepted must be creation *de novo*. Not only is the truth of this position possible, but, even more tellingly, prophetic knowledge necessarily implies such a doctrine and such knowledge is acknowledged as not only possible but also real even by those who argue for the eternity of creation:

> What I myself desire to make clear is that the world's being created in time, according to the opinion of our Law—an opinion that I have already explained—is not impossible and that all those philosophic proofs from which it seems that the matter is different from what we have stated, all those arguments have a certain point through which they may be invalidated and the inference drawn from them against us shown to be incorrect. Now inasmuch as this is true in my opinion and inasmuch as this question—I mean to say that of the eternity of the world or its creation in time—becomes an open question, it should in my opinion be accepted without proof because of prophecy, which explains things to which it is not in the power of speculation to accede. For as we shall make clear, prophecy is not set at nought even in the opinion of those who believe in the eternity of the world.[100]

In other words, given that the two positions are indemonstrable, it is the reality of prophecy that should incline us positively to the doctrine of creation *de novo*, an argument we shall return to presently.

According to Maimonides, the chief objection of the philosophers

---

the demonstration of the existence of God." Mercedes Rubio, "Maimonides' Proofs for the Existence of God and Their Aristotelian Background in the 'Guide of the Perplexed,'" in *Was ist Philosophie im Mittelalter: Akten des X. Internationalen Kongresses für mittelalterische Philosophie der Societé Internationale pour l'étude de la Philosophie Médiévale 25, Bis 30, August 1997 in Erfurt*, ed. Jan A. Aertsen and Andreas Speer (Berlin: Walter de Gruyter, 1998), 921.

99. *Guide*, II, 16 (Pines, 293; Munk, 34b).

100. *Guide*, II, 16 (Pines, 293–94; Munk, 34b–35a).

to the doctrine of creation *de novo* is a philosophical principle as old as Parmenides who asserted that "nothing can come from nothing." All generation presupposes something from which generation can occur, so a human being can only be generated from another human being. Now Aristotle does state that man, *together with the sun*, generates man,[101] but by this Aristotle only means that the process of generation needs other causes for it to operate. Still, there can be no absolute beginning to generation as such. So while the doctrine of eternal creation might be consistent with this philosophical principle, since it posits an unending chain of "generators" going back to eternity, the doctrine of creation *de novo* is not.

But, Maimonides argues, a fallacy is hidden in this objection: it confuses what the Bible means by "creation" with what the philosophers call "generation." "Creation," in short, is not "generation." To confuse creation with generation is to presume that our experience of the world as it is now pertains also to its very coming into existence; it presupposes that the event of creation follows the same principles as the coming-to-be of an individual, material substance in the already-existing world of things. But it does not, because there is no "world" into which a "generation" can occur in the act of creation: "No inference can be drawn in any respect from the nature of a thing after it has been generated, has attained its final state, and has achieved stability in its most perfect state, to the state of that thing while it moved toward being generated." Maimonides continues with an example: "Assume, according to an example we have made, that a man of a most perfect natural disposition was born and that his mother died after she had suckled him for several months."[102] Then suppose that this boy had grown up completely apart from any experience of pregnancy and childbirth. Suppose further that the father had told his son that there was a time when he lived entirely in water without breathing and that he was nourished without drinking or eating. Without remembering or experiencing the process of gestation for himself, the boy would find the father's statements outlandish and contrary to both reason and experience. So it is with the doctrine

101. Aristotle, *Physica*, II, 2 (194b13).
102. *Guide*, II, 17 (Pines, 295; Munk, 35b–36a).

of creation: if we observe the world as it is, it seems impossible that it had been created with a beginning in time out of nothing; but this only serves to show both the limits of the human intellect and of human experience, and thus the limited and contingent nature of the truths of physics:

> Consider this example and reflect upon it, you who are engaged in speculation, and you shall find that this is exactly our position with regard to Aristotle. For we, the community of the followers of *Moses our Master and Abraham our Father*, may peace be on them, believe that the world was generated in such and such a manner and came to be in a certain state from another state, which came after another state. Aristotle, on the other hand, begins to contradict us and to bring forward against us proofs based on the nature of what exists, a nature that has attained stability, is perfect, and has achieved actuality. As for us, we declare against him that this nature, after it has achieved stability and perfection, does not resemble in anything the state it was in while in the state of being generated, and that it was brought into existence from absolute nonexistence. Now what argument from among all that he advances holds good against us? For these arguments necessarily concern only those who claim that the stable nature of that which exists, gives an indication of its having been created in time. I have already made it known to you that I do not claim this.[103]

Now this analogy that Maimonides draws is not perfect (no analogy is). While the biological process of gestation and birth takes time, creation occurs in an instant. And while time and the very principles of nature begin to exist at creation, they do not in gestation and birth.[104] But,

103. *Guide*, II, 17 (Pines, 296; Munk, 36a–b).

104. Jacob Haberman is particularly harsh in his criticism of Maimonides's analogy here: "The strange idea of God creating the world by *one* set of laws, and then keeping it going by an entirely *different* set degrades the idea of God to the level of a deceiving Cosmic Magician who uses a double standard to lead astray Aristotle and other humble seekers of truth in order to mock poor human reason into forming a conception of a changeless Deity.... Nor is Maimonides's drawn-out illustration from biology very illuminating. As if there is any valid comparison between the human organism at two stages of its life, with the attendant changes brought about by the natural processes of continuity and gradualness, and the instantaneous positing of the whole universe which is the heart of the supernatural notion of volitional creation *ex nihilo*." Jacob Haberman, *Maimonides and Aquinas:*

I think, Maimonides's example does establish his main assertion: "The essential point is, as we have mentioned, that a being's state of perfection and completion furnishes no indication of the state of that being preceding perfection."[105] In other words, nature in itself cannot tell us anything about how or why it exists, nor can it tell us with any necessity who or what the Creator of nature is in his essence. The existent world can, at most, tell us that a First Cause of its existence exists and that that Cause must be one and immaterial. But beyond that, nature tells us nothing nor can the human intellect, fallen or not, go beyond what nature gives it. Thus, the supposedly eternal movement of the celestial spheres is no demonstration of the eternity of the world; it only shows how our intellect fails, once the motion has begun, to imagine it having a beginning: "Similarly the assertion that circular motion has no beginning is correct. For after the spherical body endowed with circular motion has been brought into being, one cannot conceive that its motion should have a beginning."[106] This shows that the philosophers cannot demonstrate from the world itself that the world is eternal or that creation with a beginning in time is impossible.[107]

Maimonides's defense of the notion of creation *de novo* is, in many senses, an attempt to defend the notion that creation is free and yet not capricious but imbued with a rational order: "The world exists neither through chance, nor through inexorable necessity, but as the result of the

---

A Contemporary Appraisal (New York: Ktav Publishing House, 1979), 28–29. I think, however, that Haberman's criticism is directed at a straw man and therefore misses the point: Maimonides is not arguing that there are "two sets" of "laws"—one for the world and one for creation—but that creation is the very pre-condition for the "laws" of nature. And while, of course, the comparison with human biology is imperfect, it does get across the notion that the human intellect is limited by what it can know empirically from nature and, therefore, cannot know *on its own* (that is, *without the testimony of the father*) what lies beyond nature and its sensible experience of nature.

105. *Guide*, II, 17 (Pines, 297–98; Munk, 37a).

106. *Guide*, II, 17 (Pines, 297; Munk, 36b).

107. "For at present we do not want to establish as true that the world is created in time. But what we wish to establish is the possibility of its being created in time. Now this contention cannot be proved to be impossible by inferences drawn from the nature of what exists, which we do not set at nought. When the possibility of this contention has been established, as we have made clear, we shall go back and we shall make prevail the opinion asserting creation in time." *Guide*, II, 17 (Pines, 298; Munk, 37a).

purposive activity of an intelligent Creator."[108] Thus, the goal of almost all of Maimonides's discussion in part 2 of the *Guide*, where he discusses issues in physics and astronomy is, as he explicitly states, to show that, yes, creation exhibits a rational order, but this rational order is itself not necessary—God could have chosen a different, yet still perfectly coherent and rational, order. This is particularly the case with the heavens: while Maimonides asserts that what Aristotle says about the sublunar realm is "indubitably correct," what Aristotle says about the heavens and, particularly, the order of intelligences is "analogous to guessing and conjecture."[109] In other words, there is no way that the philosophers can show that the heavens *must* exhibit the order that they do. This necessarily infers for Maimonides that the order we find in the heavens is the result of some choice by a supreme will.

It follows that not only can the philosophers not demonstrate the eternity of the world, but there is a positive (though not demonstrable) evidence against it. He holds to this even though he states that one could, like Averroes, interpret all biblical passages asserting creation *de novo* in a figurative way, like all texts implying corporeality in God:

> For we can interpret them [biblical texts describing the creation of the world *de novo*] as figurative, as we have done when denying His corporeality. Perhaps this would even be much easier to do: we should be very well able to give a figurative interpretation of those texts and to affirm as true the eternity of the world, just as we have given a figurative interpretation of those other texts and have denied that He, may He be exalted, is a body.[110]

But Maimonides does not do this for two reasons: that the deity is not a body has been demonstrated and thus anything in Scripture inconsistent with this must be interpreted figuratively. But the eternity of the

---

108. *Guide*, II, 19 (Pines, 303; Munk, 40a). Cited by Fox, *Interpreting Maimonides*, 282.

109. *Guide*, II, 22 (Pines, 319–20; Munk, 50b).

110. *Guide*, II, 25 (Pines, 328; Munk, 55a). In other words, Maimonides could have made the same hermeneutical move as Averroes, interpreting references in Scripture to "creation" in an eternal sense (since neither the Quran nor the Bible is explicit in this). That he quite explicitly does not make such a move is strong proof, in my opinion, that Maimonides is both serious and sincere in defending the traditional belief that the world was created *de novo*.

world has not been demonstrated. "The second cause is as follows" and is, we would claim, far more important:

> Our belief that the deity is not a body destroys for us none of the foundations of the Law and does not give the lie to the claims of any prophet. The only objection to it is constituted by the fact that the ignorant think that this belief is contrary to the text; yet it is not contrary to it, as we have explained, but is intended by the text. On the other hand, belief in the eternity the way Aristotle sees it—that is, the belief according to which the world exists in virtue of necessity, that no nature changes at all, and that the customary course of events cannot be modified with regard to anything—destroys the Law in its principle, necessarily gives the lie to every miracle, and reduces to inanity all the hopes and threats that the Law has held out, unless—by God!—one interprets the miracles figuratively also, as was done by the Islamic internalists [ahl al-bāṭin]; this, however, would result in some sort of crazy imaginings.[111]

This is the crux of the matter. The world as the philosophers imagine it, taking their lead from Aristotle, is one in which all causes operate by necessity from one principle cause. This not only leaves no room for miracles, but it leaves no room for revelation. The First Cause would communicate itself entirely in its causal activity. There could be no way in which God could have an "inner life" that could be revealed freely to another in a covenantal communication, as God did with the prophets:

> Know that with a belief in the creation of the world in time, all the miracles become possible and the Law becomes possible, and all questions that may be asked on this subject, vanish. Thus it might be said: Why did God give prophetic revelation to this one and not to that? Why did God give this Law to this particular nation, and why did He not legislate before it or after? Why did He privilege the prophet with the miracles mentioned in relation to him and not with some others? What was God's aim in giving this Law? Why did He not, if such was His purpose, put the accomplishment of the commandments and the non-transgression of the prohibitions into nature? If this were said, the answer to all these questions would be that it would be said: He wanted it this way; or His wisdom required it this way. And just as He brought

111. *Guide*, II, 25 (Pines, 328; Munk, 55a–b).

the world into existence, having the form it has, when He wanted to, without our knowing His will with regard to this or in what respect there was wisdom in His particularizing the forms of the world and the time of its creation—in the same way we do not know His will or the exigency of His wisdom that caused all the matters, about which questions have been posed above, to be particularized. If, however, someone says that the world is as it is in virtue of necessity, it would be a necessary obligation to ask all those questions; and there would be no way out of them except through a recourse to unseemly answers in which there would be combined the giving the lie to, and the annulment of, all the external meanings of the Law with regard to which no intelligent man has any doubt that they are to be taken in their external meanings.[112]

This passage is worth quoting in length because it explains very clearly the essential link Maimonides sees between creation *de novo* and the foundations of the religious law. While the philosophers are right in seeing a rational order in the world, they are wrong to see this order as necessary or absolute in itself. Realization of this opens the human intellect to the possibility of prophecy and divine revelation, which is in many ways the center of Maimonides's concerns.[113]

As there are three different opinions on creation, so, Maimonides claims, there are three opinions on the nature of prophecy: "The opinions of people concerning prophecy are like their opinions concerning the eternity of the world or its creation in time. I mean by this that just as the people to whose mind the existence of the deity is firmly established, have, as we have set forth, three opinions concerning the eternity of the world or its creation in time, so are there also three opinions concerning prophecy."[114] The first opinion Maimonides attributes to both

112. *Guide*, II, 25 (Pines, 329–30; Munk, 55b–56a).

113. "The entire drama of Maimonides's intellectual enterprise unfolds in his discussion of prophecy." "Although philosophy and prophecy appear, on the surface, to be two rival modes of cognition, Maimonides makes great efforts to expose the philosophical dimensions of the latter." Ithamar Gruenwald, "Maimonides' Quest beyond Philosophy and Prophecy," in *Perspectives on Maimonides: Philosophical and Historical Studies*, ed. Joel L. Kraemer (Oxford: Oxford University Press, 1991), 148.

114. *Guide*, II, 32 (Pines, 360; Munk, 73a). This claim has also given rise to much controversy and speculation. Is Maimonides trying to link a particular position on creation to one on prophecy? And does this "reveal" something of the "true" position of Maimonides

the pagans and to the vulgar multitude of the Jewish people: "The first opinion—that of the multitude of those among the Pagans who considered prophecy as true and also believed by some of the common people professing our Law—is that God, may He be exalted, chooses whom He wishes from among men, turns him into a prophet, and sends him with a mission."[115] The divine sends prophetic messages on whomever it wills—what that man's state might be, intellectually, socially, or morally, is irrelevant. This is in direct contrast to the second opinion, that of the philosophers: "It affirms that prophecy is a certain perfection in the nature of man."[116] Prophecy is, in essence, no different from direct intellection of the divine realities that flow to a properly perfected intellect that is prepared to receive these emanations. In other words, there is no essential difference between prophecy and philosophical intellection or intuition of first principles. But Maimonides states that there is a third opinion on prophecy, distinct from the first two and which, moreover, represents the true teaching of the religious law: "The third opinion is the opinion of our Law and the foundation of our doctrine. It is identical with the philosophic opinion except in one thing. For we believe that it may happen that one who is fit for prophecy and prepared for it should not become a prophet, namely, on account of the divine will. To my mind this is like all the miracles and takes the same course as they."[117] True prophecy, therefore, is an intellection that flows

---

(which is, inevitably, in opposition to Jewish orthodoxy)? Many scholars have tried various permutations whereby they have attempted to link one opinion in creation to one opinion on prophecy. But all of these attempts have problems and none are convincing. I follow Kenneth Seeskin's position, which I believe is the most sensible and which the passage from Maimonides cited above seems to confirm: "The fact that no set of correspondences is compelling and that some are obviously forced suggests that Maimonides may not have intended a one-to-one linkup. Perhaps all he meant is that both sets of opinions sort themselves into three alternatives and make us decide between naturalism and belief in miracles. In both cases he rejects naturalism in its unqualified form but accepts it in a weakened version." Kenneth Seeskin, *Maimonides on the Origin of the World* (New York: Cambridge University Press, 2005), 178.

115. *Guide*, II, 32 (Pines, 360; Munk, 73a).
116. *Guide*, II, 32 (Pines, 361; Munk, 73b).
117. *Guide*, II, 32 (Pines, 361; Munk, 73b–74a). That is, if belief in the creation of the world in time makes belief in miracles possible, *a fortiori* it makes belief in prophecy possible. See Gruenwald, "Maimonides' Quest," 150.

upon the perfected human intellect from the divine, so in that sense it is identical to philosophical intellection. But there is a crucial difference from philosophy in what the law teaches, namely, that the divine will can withhold this emanation if it so desires. Hence, prophecy is similar to God's miraculous interventions in nature: although God has established a rational order both in nature and in philosophical intellection, nevertheless, he may prevent from time to time the natural working out of this order with a view to communicating a higher, "metaphysical" truth to his people.

This third position which Maimonides claims is the true position of the law on prophecy struck even his contemporaries as odd: does God exercise a sort of "veto" over prophecy? And if so, in what sense, if any, can we say that prophecy has any positive content that is different from that of philosophical intellection? It struck many and still strikes many today as an incoherent and deeply problematic compromise on Maimonides's part. How are we to square his stating that prophecy is a purely natural gift of the active intellect with his claim that God can withhold prophecy—especially if prophecy should be something that God "grants"?[118]

Maimonides's position on prophecy, however, becomes clearer and far more coherent and plausible if we look at it in the context of his doctrine on creation and of the importance of the fallenness of the human intellect. Prophecy is indeed an "overflow" from God onto the created intellect, but one that is not necessary or automatic:

> Know that the true reality and quiddity of prophecy consist in its being an overflow overflowing from God, may He be cherished and honored, through the intermediation of the Active Intellect, toward the rational

118. Lawrence Kaplan, "Maimonides on the Miraculous Element in Prophecy," *Harvard Theological Review* 70, no. 3/4 (1977): 244. "We may sum up Maimonides's views thus: The fundamental principle concerning prophecy is the philosophical principle that if one is to be a prophet, he must possess all the requisite perfections. This fundamental principle is supported by many biblical and rabbinic texts. The assertion that God can withhold prophecy from one who possesses the requisite perfections is neither a fundamental principle nor is it clearly supported by any biblical or rabbinic texts" (ibid., 247). Kaplan argues further that if Maimonides differs from the philosophers, it is in that he admits the possibility of miracles with regard to prophecy.

faculty in the first place and thereafter toward the imaginative faculty. This is the highest degree of man and the ultimate term of perfection for the imaginative faculty. This is something that cannot by any means exist in every man. And it is not something that may be attained solely through perfection in the speculative sciences and through improvement of moral habits, even if all of them have become as fine and good as can be. There still is needed in addition the highest possible degree of perfection of the imaginative faculty in respect of its original natural disposition.[119]

On the one hand, the action of the divine overflow is often so powerful upon the active intellect of the prophet that he cannot but proclaim the divine truth, even in the face of threats and punishment.[120] But on the other hand, certain intellectual and moral requirements are necessary (if not sufficient) for the reception or interpretation of prophecy. This notion of prophecy actually parallels Maimonides's position on creation quite neatly: as creation exhibits rational order, so prophecy is an emanation upon the intellect and is intellectual apprehension of divine reality; but as the rational order of creation is not necessary in itself but could be otherwise, so prophetic intellection is subject to what the divine will chooses to reveal. Just as the human intellect can understand the rational order in creation but not precisely why *this particular* order pertains, so the prophetic intellect may understand what God has revealed to him but not why God chose to reveal *this* rather than *that*. In other words, the prophet understands that it is not just some impersonal principle that emanates into his intellect but that he is being addressed by a being characterized by free will. In addition, the human intellect is a fallen intellect. As such it is tied to matter and to the imagination. The prophet therefore needs to have the highest perfection not just of the intellect but also of the imagination "in respect of its original [that is, pre-fallen] natural disposition." I take this to mean that, for genuine prophecy to occur, God must restore the imagination of the prophet to what it was before Adam fell, when it was a "handmaiden" of the intellect and not a "harlot" leading it astray. According to Maimonides, the only prophet whose imagination was thus restored was Moses.

119. *Guide*, II, 36 (Pines, 369; Munk, 78a–b).
120. *Guide*, II, 37 (Pines, 375; Munk, 82a).

Hence, for Maimonides, the prophecy of Moses is the linchpin upon which all other genuine prophecy depends. All such prophecy either prepares for Moses' prophecy (such as that of Abraham, Isaac, Jacob, and the other patriarchs) or it calls the people to return to and obey the Law of Moses (as with the latter prophets such as Isaiah, Ezekiel, Daniel, et al.).[121] Such is the importance of Moses for Maimonides that he asserts that it is unclear whether we should classify Moses as a prophet or even whether we should discuss the nature of his "prophecy."[122] For uniquely, according to Maimonides, Moses not only has an intellectual apprehension of divine realities but he was also perfect with regard to his imagination and was thus able to transmit that apprehension to the mass of the Jewish people in such a way that they would be providentially bound to God in a covenantal relationship. Indeed, one scholar has termed the unique nature of Moses' prophecy in Maimonides's account as a "super-prophecy."[123] What makes Moses superior to the other prophets, then, is not just intellectual apprehension of divine realties, something that is natural and therefore accessible to the philosophers. The philosopher apprehends divine realities as coming from an impersonal principle; all the prophets other than Moses would apprehend divine realities through a vision or dream.[124] But Moses apprehended divine realities "face to face" not as in a vision or dream nor as one apprehends a mathematical principle, but as coming from a supremely intellectual yet utterly free *will*, before which the only proper response besides intellection is *love*.

For Maimonides then, prophecy derives from a divine emanation

121. *Guide*, II, 39 (Pines, 378 ff.; Munk, 84a ff).

122. "As for the prophecy of *Moses our Master*, I shall not touch upon it in these chapters with even a single word, either in explicit fashion or in a flash. For to my mind the term 'prophet' used with reference to *Moses* and to the others is amphibolous." *Guide*, II, 35 (Pines, 367; Munk, 77a).

123. "Thus, we may say, Moses' super-prophecy unequivocally epitomizes Maimonides' quest beyond prophecy. And if there really are realms in which prophecy transcends the realms of philosophy, then Moses' prophecy transcends ordinary prophecy—to say nothing of philosophy." Gruenwald, "Maimonides' Quest," 156.

124. "Prophecy occurs only *in a vision* or *in a dream*, as we have already explained several times. Accordingly we shall not perpetually repeat this." *Guide*, II, 44 (Pines, 394; Munk, 92a).

from the divine intellect to the human intellect. As such it is supremely intellectual. As Alexander Altmann argues, Maimonides's theory of
prophecy presupposes an Avicennian ontology in which there is no
radical break between God and creation but rather a "continuum" in
which there is a flow of emanations from God through to the lowest
creatures. "This entire universe is a system of free-flowing grace as it
were, and does not require special acts of divine grace for special purposes. Here grace is abounding at all times, and its reception and efficacy
depend solely on the receptivity or disposition of the recipient."[125] And
yet, the "receptivity or disposition of the recipient" has been damaged
by the Fall. Hence, the need for the religious law which prepares the intellect for the reception of God's grace in intellectual emanation. While
the law itself is not natural but rather a miraculous aid, freely given to
humans by an act of the divine Will for their intellectual perfection,
it "enters into what is natural" in that it restores the human intellect to
what was its natural, prelapsarian condition: "Therefore I say that the
Law, although it is not natural, enters into what is natural. It is a part of
the wisdom of the deity with regard to the permanence of this species
of which He has willed the existence, that He put it into its nature that

125. Alexander Altmann, "Maimonides and Thomas Aquinas: Natural or Divine
Prophecy?" in *Essays in Jewish Intellectual History* (Hanover, N.H.: University Press of New
England, 1981), 81. This is what constitutes a radical difference between Maimonides's and
Thomas Aquinas's theories of prophecy, Altmann argues. This despite the fact that Aquinas
borrowed a great deal from Maimonides on this issue: "Thomas Aquinas, on the other
hand, breaks with the Avicennian ontological scheme that had dominated the Neoplatonic
phase of Latin Scholasticism, although he retains some of its Augustinian features. The
most radical step in this direction was the relocation of the Aristotelian active intellect
from the semidivine and transcendent position it had been assigned to in the Alexander
of Aphrodisias tradition down to Averroes. Thomas interpreted the active intellect as a
part of the human intellect. He adhered to the concept of Intelligences correlated to the
celestial bodies, but cancelled the emanationist theory and thereby did away with the notion of a divine continuum in which grace is a matter of free-flowing divine activity. In the
Augustinian-Avicennian tradition the boundaries of grace and nature had been blurred. All
cognition had been described as a seeing in the divine light. St. Thomas sharply differenti-
ated between nature and grace. *Gratia perficit naturam*, which means that the two are not
a single activity anymore." Ibid., 82–83. David Burrell also developed this difference in his
book, *Knowing the Unknowable God: Ibn Sina, Maimonides, Aquinas* (Notre Dame, Ind.:
University of Notre Dame Press, 1986).

individuals belonging to it should have the faculty of ruling."[126] The law restores the human intellect by giving such a precise and detailed set of commandments regarding good and evil that it allows the intellect to turn away from material concerns and focus on divine realties. Properly understood, it also restores the imagination to its proper place as adjunct to the intellect.

In this sense, then, the law comes through prophecy, but it is the law, in turn, that makes prophecy possible. This is not necessarily a vicious circle: prophetic intellection is in itself beyond time, though finding its fullest and definitive "incarnation" in the prophecy of Moses. But, as timeless intellection, prophecy is also pure metaphysics, which is why Maimonides turns to the subject matter of metaphysics in part 3 of the *Guide*.

LAW, GRACE, AND THE RESTORATION OF THE INTELLECT

The *Guide* culminates in the third part with a study of Ezekiel's "Account of the Chariot," which Maimonides identifies with metaphysics. The reader who has followed Maimonides through parts 1 and 2 should not be surprised: for since all truth comes from God, it should not be strange that God's revelation of himself should also contain the highest principles of being or existence itself. For Maimonides as well as for his contemporary and fellow Andalusian, Averroes (and, as we shall see, in contradistinction to Thomas Aquinas), the proper subject matter of metaphysics is not being *qua* being, but being in its purest and highest instance, the First Cause of being, God.[127] Whereas for Aquinas there

126. *Guide*, II, 40 (Pines, 382; Munk, 86a).

127. "But after this general agreement, their [Maimonides's and Aquinas's] conceptions of metaphysics diverge radically. Maimonides follows the tradition of Greek commentators on Aristotle, also adopted by Averroes, that metaphysics is primarily a study of God or immaterial being. Aquinas, like the majority of his Christian contemporaries, accepted the teaching of Avicenna, that the subject matter of metaphysics is not God but being qua being or being in general (*ens commune*). In this science God is studied, not *in se*, but as the first cause of being." Armand A. Maurer, "Maimonides and Aquinas on the Study of Metaphysics," in *A Straight Path: Studies in Medieval Philosophy and Culture; Essays in Honor*

is a distinction between a divine science that studies God *in se* and in terms of God's self-revelation to us (theology) and another that studies being in general and its cause(s) (metaphysics), there is no such distinction for Maimonides. Thus, as Armand Maurer explains:

> For the Jewish theologian, metaphysics, as rational speculation about God, is in continuity with the exegesis of, and inquiry about, the rabbinical scriptures. It culminates in the illumination and mysticism of prophecy. These appear to be no more than different ascending moments or phases of the same divine science. Thus Maimonides identifies divine science or metaphysics with the account of the chariot, which, as part of the secrets of the Torah, interprets the visions of the prophet Ezekiel. And who are the prophets but metaphysicians—believers who have achieved the perfection of demonstrative knowledge of the creator and, beyond this, have received the fullness of divine illumination and a place in the council of God.[128]

Thus, the notion that Maimonides's project is the "harmonization" of science and philosophy with Scripture is actually alien to his outlook: for him, philosophy and science are integral to the scriptural worldview.[129] Scripture *is* philosophy in its deepest and most comprehensive form, and the religious law *is* metaphysics insofar as it redeems and perfects the fallen human intellect.

Metaphysics is the science that studies being as such apart from any particular instantiation or kind of being. In particular, metaphysics studies being apart from matter, for it is matter that individuates being, while metaphysics seeks to know what being is universally or in itself. Matter or material being, therefore, is a hindrance to metaphysical

---

of *Arthur Hyman*, ed. Ruth Link-Salinger, Jeremiah Hackett, Michael Samuel Hyman, R. James Long, and Charles H. Manekin (Washington, D.C.: The Catholic University of America Press, 1988), 214.

128. Ibid., 215.

129. Herbert A. Davidson, *Moses Maimonides: The Man and His Works* (Oxford: Oxford University Press, 2005), 262. Hence, Maimonides's account of Ezekiel's image of the chariot reveals for him the deep meaning of Aristotle's metaphysics: namely, that the matter of the universe is not one. There is a celestial and a terrestrial matter. See Sarah Pessin, "Matter, Form, and the Corporeal World," in Nadler and Rudavsky, *Cambridge History*, 285.

knowledge. Matter is inherently unstable—according to Aristotle, it is pure potentiality for form—and thus always seeking some other form. Hence, Maimonides likens matter to a "married harlot": like a married woman matter is never found without being joined to or in-formed by some form, and yet like a harlot, matter is ever seeking a new form or "husband" to in-form it.[130] Maimonides insists that he is not saying that matter is bad or evil; matter is a divine gift. The key task is to know what matter is suitable and what is not suitable for any given form and to control matter and all material impulses that may cloud the intellect:

> As for [Solomon's] dictum, "A woman of virtue who can find?" and this whole parable, it is clear. For if it so happens that the matter of a man is excellent, and suitable, neither dominating him nor corrupting his constitution, that matter is a divine gift. To sum up: it is easy, as we have mentioned, to control suitable matter. If it is unsuitable, it is not impossible for someone trained to quell it. For this reason *Solomon*—both he and others—inculcated all these exhortations. Also the commandments and prohibitions of the Law are only intended to quell all the impulses of matter. It behooves him who prefers to be a human being in truth, not a beast having the shape and configuration of a human being, to endeavor to diminish all the impulses of matter.[131]

Since it is the goal of the religious law to quell material impulses that may cloud our intellect, the goal of the religious law is the same as metaphysics.

A necessary presupposition of actually carrying the science of metaphysics to fruition is, therefore, the perfection of the intellect, because only an intellect free from material concerns or cognition is able to contemplate being *qua* being, that is, God. "The apprehension of His true realty is impossible for us because of the dark matter that encompasses us and not Him, may He be exalted; for He, may He be exalted, is not

130. "For matter is in no way found without form and is consequently always like a *married woman* who is never separated from a *man* and is never *free*. However, notwithstanding her being a *married woman*, she never ceases to seek for another man to substitute for her husband, and she deceives and draws him on in every way until he obtains from her what her husband used to obtain. This is the state of matter. For whatever form is found in it, does but prepare it to receive another form." *Guide*, III, 8 (Pines, 431; Munk, 12a).

131. *Guide*, III, 8 (Pines, 433; Munk, 13b).

a body."[132] Indeed, as we shall see, part 3 of the *Guide* is a metaphysics only in the sense that it functions as a sort of *purification* of the intellect for metaphysics. Indeed, the perfection of the intellect for and in its contemplation of divine truths is the ultimate goal of both Scripture and metaphysics. As Herbert Davidson so aptly describes it:

> If medieval writers gave their books subtitles, Maimonides might have given his the subtitle: *In Praise of Intellect*. Scripture, he insists, must be read with "the true nature of the intellect, and after [one has attained] perfection in the demonstrative sciences and knowledge of the secrets of prophecy." Scriptural exegesis must, in other words, rest on a scientific picture of the universe and on propositions demonstrated by the intellect such as the propositions that God is an incorporeal and wholly unitary being; that God can be properly described only in negative terms; that the prophet prophesies by tapping into an emanation emitted by the active intellect; that prophetic experiences are visions and not perceptions of anything outside the prophet's soul.[133]

There is actually very little discussion of being or God himself in part 3 (this should not be surprising if we take into account Maimonides's negative theology outlined in part 1, whereby we cannot say anything positive about God). Rather, part 3 is mostly taken up with the divine law and how it has been sent providentially to purify and perfect the human intellect for the contemplative love of God, who is being or existence in itself. In this sense, part 3 is less a metaphysics as it is a *praeparatio metaphysicae* or treatise on the perfection of the intellect.

Maimonides begins his discussion of metaphysics with a detailed discussion of divine providence. The reason for this seems to be that Maimonides thinks he must address the material nature of the universe and all the evils that seem to flow from the mutability and instability of matter. How can we say that God is the all-good and all-powerful Creator of a world so full of evils? In response to such a question, Maimonides argues that we must first take hold of the first and most fundamental insight that "All evils are privations."[134] Evil is nothing positive

132. *Guide*, III, 9 (Pines, 437; Munk, 16a).
133. Davidson, *Moses Maimonides*, 386.
134. *Guide*, III, 10 (Pines, 439; Munk, 17a).

in itself; it is not a "being" or "thing" but rather the privation of being in a thing that should by its nature have it. Moreover, human beings inflict evil upon one another due to the privation of knowledge of God and his divine Law. Hence, like blind men stumbling due to lack of sight, so human beings inflict harm upon one another due to a lack of the truth, to an intellect that has fallen from the pure contemplation of divine Truth to considering material things and means and ends to those things.[135]

There are, therefore, three types of evil: there are those evils which come from the nature of coming-to-be and passing-away among finite and created beings; there are those evils that men inflict upon one another; and there are those that we inflict upon ourselves.[136] Now, with regard to these three evils, Maimonides outlines five different opinions on whether there is a providential order in them. There are: (1) the opinion of Epicurus, who argued that there is no providence and that all is chance; (2) that of Aristotle, for whom certain things, such as the heavens, are governed by providence, and others, namely those beings in the terrestrial realm, are left to chance; (3) that of the Ash'arites, who argued that everything is governed by divine will alone; (4) that of the Mu'tazilites for whom absolutely everything, no matter how insignificant, is governed by divine wisdom; (5) that of "our Law," that is, the Law of Moses, which declares that man has free will and that God has willed this from his eternal volition "that all animals should move in virtue of their will and that man should have the ability to do whatever he wills or chooses among the things concerning which he has the ability to act."[137] Maimonides summarizes these positions on providence a little later in this way: "I have summed up these opinions for you as follows: All the various circumstances of the individuals among the Adamites are considered by Aristotle as due to pure chance, by the Ash'arite as consequent on will alone, by the Mu'tazila as consequent on wisdom, and by us as consequent on the individual's deserts, according to his actions."[138] In other words, only the (true) Jewish conception of provi-

---

135. *Guide*, III, 11 (Pines, 440–41; Munk, 18a).
136. *Guide*, III, 12 (Munk 20b).
137. *Guide*, III, 17 (Pines, 469; Munk, 35a).
138. *Guide*, III, 17 (Pines, 469; Munk, 35b).

dence attempts to understand it as being able to "use" or "guide" the free actions of individual human beings in such a way that they contribute to the overall rational order of creation, an order in which God's supreme goodness triumphs:

> As for us, we believe that all the human circumstances are according to deserts, that He is exalted above injustice, and that among us only those deserving punishment are punished. This is what is stated literally in the *Torah of Moses our Master*, namely, that everything is consequent upon the deserts; and the multitude of our scholars also speak in accordance with this opinion. For you will find them saying explicitly: "There is no death without sin, and no sufferings without transgression."[139]

Aristotle has no notion of the individual created in the image and likeness of God and thus could not conceive of how providence could extend below the eternal and regular movements of the heavens. Now, Maimonides does mention that Aristotle is right with regard to *non-human* beings in the terrestrial realm—*qua* individuals they are governed more or less by chance. But this is not the case for the human being precisely because of his or her special intellectual status: "divine providence watches only over the individuals belonging to the human species and that in this species alone all the circumstances of the individuals and the good and evil that befall them are consequent upon deserts, just as it says: "For all His ways are judgment." But regarding all the other animals and, all the more, the plants and other things, my opinion is that of Aristotle."[140] The two main schools of Islamic theology, Ash'arism and Mu'tazilism, are equally erroneous: one, the Ash'arite, denies human freedom and merits, while the other, the Mu'tazilite, sees divine providence as so all-pervasive that it erases the distinction between the human being and the rest of creation.[141]

For Maimonides, divine providence has as its entire purpose and end the restoration of the human intellect from its fallen state to a loving contemplative union with the divine Intellect. Once the intellect is purified of all material concerns and cognition, it rises to the level of the

---

139. *Guide*, III, 17 (Pines, 470; Munk, 35b).

140. *Guide*, III, 17 (Pines, 471; Munk, 36b).

141. As for the Epicurean opinion, Maimonides does not consider it worthy of serious consideration, as it explicitly denies the existence of any sort of providence.

active intellect, which makes it then receptive to the divine "overflow."[142] Thus to the extent that an individual is united to the active intellect, to that degree divine providence will watch more carefully over that individual than over others. "Accordingly, divine providence does not watch in an equal manner over all the individuals of the human species, but providence is graded as their human perfection is graded.... For it is this measure of the overflow of the divine intellect that makes the prophets speak, guides the actions of righteous men, and perfects the knowledge of excellent men with regard to what they know."[143] This, that the human intellect comes within the "orbit" of divine providence to the degree that it is intellectual is, Maimonides states, one of the fundamental principles of the law. But correlative to this principle is that it is the law that completes and perfects divine providence with regard to the human intellect.[144] As Idit Dobbs-Weinstein puts it:

> The Torah was given to human beings so that through it, if they so choose, they may gain real knowledge and be able to participate in divine providence and avoid "evil." Since, by definition, that is, literally as guidance, the Torah must play an essential cognitive role in human perfection, failure to be instructed by it manifests the freely willed human rejection of the divine gift or, conversely, the human choice of evil.[145]

Moreover, the revelation of the law restores the intellect from its fallen condition. To quote Dobbs-Weinstein again, in the Fall, "the immediate hierarchically ordered relation between reason and will was severed and their interaction impaired in a manner such that reason no longer can determine immediately the fittingness of a particular end desired by the

142. "This being known, it is also known that the divine overflow that exists united to the human species, I mean the human intellect, is merely what exists as individual intellects." *Guide*, III, 18 (Pines, 474; Munk, 38b). Maimonides holds to the then-dominant opinion among Peripatetic philosophers (like Averroes) that there can be essentially only one intellect for all men, but once the active intellect "overflows" into human subjects, it is individuated according to the number of material substrata in which it inheres as an accident.

143. *Guide*, III, 18 (Pines, 474–75; Munk, 38b).

144. "Maimonides's and Aquinas's commentaries [on Job] seem to suggest that it is highly doubtful that provident wisdom ever can be attained without revelation. At the same time, however, they seem to indicate that revelation without intellectual knowledge does not suffice for human perfection." Dobbs-Weinstein, *Maimonides and St. Thomas*, 59.

145. Ibid., 102.

will to the ultimate end.... Thus understood, the role of divine law in human perfection is, first and foremost, cognitive and only secondarily moral."[146] To understand divine providence is therefore *not* to "justify God's ways to man" but rather to liberate the human intellect from the vanity of the material world. In short, understanding what divine providence *is* is the purification of the intellect.

The aim of the law is to command moral and ritual actions not for their own sake but in order to free the human being for intellectual contemplation. This is impossible through the study of philosophy alone.[147] As God knows all things with one single knowledge, no "new" knowledge comes to Him.[148] "How then can they [the philosophers] think that they can apprehend His knowledge, seeing that His knowledge is not a thing that is outside of His essence?"[149] As such, a purely natural knowledge of God is impossible. Between our fallen intellect and the divine intellect there can be no comparison:

> And just as there is a necessarily existent essence from which—according to their opinion—every existent derives of necessity, or that—according to our opinion—produces all the things that are other than itself after they have been nonexistent—so do we say that this essence apprehends all that is other from it; and that between our knowledge and His knowledge there is nothing in common, as there is nothing in common between our essence and His essence. With regard to this point, only the equivocality of the term "knowledge" occasions the error; for there is a community only in the terms, whereas in the true reality of the things there is a difference. It is from this that incongruities follow necessarily, as we imagine that things that obligatorily pertain to our knowledge pertain also to His knowledge.[150]

146. Ibid., 110–11.

147. "One point to emphasize here is that revelation guarantees accessibility and authoritativeness, in a way for which there is no counterpart in Aristotle. The Maimonidean agent achieves ethical understanding through knowledge of the Law and knowledge of God. Thus, the need for Aristotelian practical wisdom in ethical life is met in a different way." Jonathan Jacobs, "Aristotle and Maimonides: The Ethics of Perfection and the Perfection of Ethics," *American Catholic Philosophical Quarterly* 76, no. 1 (2002): 151.

148. *Guide*, III, 20 (Pines, 480–81; Munk, 42a).

149. *Guide*, III (Pines, 20, 482; Munk, 42b).

150. *Guide*, III, 20 (Pines, 482; Munk, 42b).

Since, as we have seen Averroes also argue, God's knowledge does not come from the things, but rather things follow upon his knowledge, we cannot predicate "knowledge" of God and man in any sense that is common to both.[151] Unlike Averroes, however, Maimonides argues that we cannot know God from the rational order of the universe alone. What this means for Maimonides is that revelation is necessary for us to know anything of God and what God wants of us. It is therefore the religious law that bridges the gap between God and man.

More immediately, the aim of the law is twofold: "The Law as a whole aims at two things: the welfare of the soul and the welfare of the body. As for the welfare of the soul, it consists in the multitude's acquiring correct opinions corresponding to their respective capacity."[152] Maimonides adds that it is the second aim that is the more certain one and more fundamental one. In attempting to explain how the law fulfills this second function, Maimonides is going to try, again, to avoid two extremes. On the one hand, he argues that in order to fulfill its aim, the law cannot be irrational or capricious: if we look closely enough we will see that every commandment either has an evident rational aim or, if this aim is not evident, it is possible to posit one.[153] On the other hand, Maimonides wants to avoid any notion that we can "deduce" through necessary inferences the content of the law through natural reason alone. That God gave the Jewish people *this* law and not *that* is due to the pure free will of God. In other words, God could have given the Jewish people a wholly different—though equally rational—set of laws.[154] So, again, the religious law, while not natural is not contrary to nature.

151. *Guide*, III, 21 (Pines, 485; Munk, 44b).

152. *Guide*, III, 27 (Pines, 510; Munk, 60a).

153. "Although we cannot speak literally and accurately about God's will, it is clear that for Maimonides it is never permissible to identify any aspect of divine behavior with the arbitrary or the capricious. The point is illuminated in a later discussion [to that of creation], where he is setting the background for his exposition of the reasons for the commandments. Maimonides confronts there an analogous problem." Fox, *Interpreting Maimonides*, 284–85.

154. Maimonides's work therefore, according to Menachem Kellner, combated the tendency among some Jews of his time to "ontologize" or give mystical qualities to the Jewish law, to the Hebrew language, and even to the status of Jews themselves. For Maimonides, all these things have a special status only because God stipulates them to have such a

Man, Maimonides claims, has two perfections: the first perfection, that of the body; and the second one, the perfection of the soul. Of these, the second, again, is the much more important one:

> His ultimate perfection is to become rational *in actu*, I mean to have an intellect *in actu*; this would consist in his knowing everything concerning all the beings that it is within the capacity of man to know in accordance with his ultimate perfection. It is clear that to this ultimate perfection there do not belong either actions or moral qualities and that it consists only of opinions toward which speculation has led and that investigation has rendered compulsory. It is also clear that this noble and ultimate perfection can only be achieved after the first perfection has been achieved. For a man cannot represent to himself an intelligible even when taught to understand it and all the more cannot become aware of it of his own accord, if he is in pain or is very hungry or is thirsty or is hot or is very cold. But once the first perfection has been achieved it is possible to achieve the ultimate, which is indubitably more noble and is the only cause of permanent preservation.[155]

As this passage makes clear, moral qualities or actions do not belong to the perfection of the intellect, as the fall of the intellect was precisely a fall into a consideration of material means and ends or, in other words, into a consideration of moral actions. Nevertheless, the perfection of the body and, along with it, of the moral character of the individual is a necessary if not sufficient condition for intellectual perfection.

By the same token, the religious law *restores* or *perfects* the human intellect; it does not create a new intellect in man nor make it into an ontologically different, "higher" intellect:

> There is one and the same general answer to all these three questions and to all the others that belong to the same class: Though all miracles change the nature of some individual being, God does not change at all

status. In other words, God could have stipulated that some other people in some other language could have received and expressed a divine law that could have been wholly otherwise than it is. In this way, the divine law is not unlike the laws of nature: God could have created them differently. Menachem Kellner, *Maimonides' Confrontation with Mysticism* (Oxford: The Littman Library of Jewish Civilization, 2006).

155. *Guide*, III, 27 (Pines, 511; Munk, 60b).

the nature of human individuals by means of miracles. Because of this great principle it says: "O that they had such an heart as this," and so on. It is because of this that there are commandments and prohibitions, rewards and punishments. We have already explained this fundamental principle by giving its proofs in a number of passages in our compilations. We do not say this because we believe that the changing nature of any human individual is difficult for Him, may He be exalted. Rather it is possible and fully within capacity. But according to the foundations of the Law, of the Torah, He has never willed to do it, nor shall He ever will it. For if it were His will that the nature of any human individual should be changed because of what He, may He be exalted, wills from that individual, sending of prophets and all giving of a Law would have been useless.[156]

The sending of the law and the prophets presupposes a fallen nature that can be restored by divine grace. This grace is made manifest and effective in the law; and the primary objective of the law is to purify the intellect by pulling it away from material cognition and concerns and thereby restoring the intellect to its true and primal nature. And when we imagine material things to be the only real or ultimate things, we fall into *idolatry*. The whole goal of the law, therefore, in addition to purification of the intellect, is to destroy idolatry: "In the case of most of the *statutes* whose reason is hidden from us, everything serves to keep people away from *idolatry*."[157] All the statues and commands of the law are therefore designed to inculcate in them right belief about the unity and immateriality of God: "Accordingly every commandment or prohibition of the Law whose reason is hidden from you constitutes a cure for one of these diseases, which today—thank God—we do not know any more."[158]

156. *Guide*, III, 32 (Pines, 529; Munk, 72a–b).

157. *Guide*, III, 49 (Pines, 612; Munk, 119b). Maimonides accordingly draws a contrast between a "true" belief of God, which is de-anthropomorphized and de-personalized, and the popular belief in God. For the former, "God ... is an object of pure, disinterested love and contemplation, and man's most exalted worship and piety is this kind of disinterested, contemplative love." Isaac Frank, "Maimonides and Aquinas on Man's Knowledge of God: A Twentieth-Century Perspective," in Buijs, *Maimonides: A Collection of Critical Essays*, 299.

158. *Guide*, III, 49 (Pines, 612; Munk, 120a).

Maimonides accordingly spends much of part 3 of the *Guide* giving what he believes are plausible rational explanations for the various commandments and statutes of the law in the light of this aim—to destroy idolatry. Some of the commandments and laws have obvious or straightforward explanations; others do not, although that fact does not prevent Maimonides from trying to give some. But in almost all cases, the explanation Maimonides gives is that the commandment in question is meant to purify the Jewish people from idolatry and to keep them apart from the *gentes* or "nations" as a holy people (even if, as Maimonides says in the passage cited above, the immediate historical reason for the commandment has passed away and is no longer operative).[159] But the aim (to abstain from idolatry) has the even higher aim of intellectual apprehension of God:

> "And thou, Solomon my son, know thou the God of thy father and serve Him," and so on. "If thou seek Him, He will be found of thee," and so on. The exhortation always refers to intellectual apprehensions, not to imagination; for thought concerning imaginings is not called *knowledge*, but *that which cometh into your mind*. Thus it is clear that after apprehension, total devotion to Him and the employment of intellectual thought in constantly loving Him should be aimed at.[160]

The religious law perfects the intellect and enables intellectual apprehension of God because it focuses all of the attention of the pious Jew on nothing but God and what God has ordained. Since moral and material matters are dealt with in detail by the law, the Jew who follows the laws scrupulously has an intellect that is free from such concerns and

159. Needless to say, this view of the "reasons for the law" does not sit well with Jewish orthodoxy in several respects. (1) It privileges the intellect and makes salvation attainable only by those who engage in philosophical contemplation. (2) In Maimonides's view, virtue and the religious Law have a purely instrumental value. Thus, blood sacrifice has no atonement value in itself but was a concession of God to the times where animal sacrifice was an integral part of all worship, pagan or otherwise. This raises serious objections not just from a Jewish but also Christian standpoint. (3) It implies no personal immortality but rather the survival of just one separate intellect (or *intellectus agens*). We have here neither the space nor the competence to treat this topic adequately. See Hava Tirosh-Samuelson, "Virtue and Happiness," in Nadler and Rudavsky, *Cambridge History*, 737.

160. *Guide*, III, 51 (Pines, 621; Munk, 125b).

is thus free for the love and contemplation of God. To the extent that one does not follow the law (or not follow it conscientiously and with knowledge), to that extend is the bond between the human intellect and the divine intellect weak or broken. Alternatively, to the extent one follows the law closely and with a deep knowledge of both the content and intent of the law, to that degree is the bond between the human and divine intellects strong. The choice, Maimonides emphasizes, is ours.[161]

The key, of course, is that one follow the law with knowledge and with love, and not simply obey the law mechanically or out of tradition alone:

> Know that all the practices of worship, such as reading the Torah, prayer, and the performance of the other *commandments*, have only the end of training you to occupy yourself with His commandments, may He be exalted, rather than with matters pertaining to this world; you should act as if you were occupied with Him, may He be exalted, and not with that which is other than He. If, however, you pray merely by moving your lips while facing a wall, and at the same time think about your buying and selling; or if you read the Torah with your tongue while your heart is set upon the building of your habitation and do not consider what you read; and similarly in all cases in which you perform a *commandment* merely with your limbs—as if you were digging a hole in the ground or hewing wood in the forest—without reflecting either upon the meaning of that action or upon Him from whom the commandment proceeds or upon the end of the action, you should not think that you have achieved the end. Rather you will then be similar to those of whom it is said: "Thou art near in their mouth, and far from their reins."[162]

Following the law of Moses with knowledge should transform our entire way of thinking, acting, and living. This is because by this law, we come to sit in the very presence of God, who gave it to Moses face to face on Mount Sinai. As we do not sit and conduct ourselves in the presence of a king in the same way that we sit and conduct ourselves in our home, so we should not think and act in the divine presence as we would without being aware of his presence. It is the law that not only makes us think

---

161. *Guide*, III, 51 (Pines, 621; Munk, 125b–126a).
162. *Guide*, III, 51 (Pines, 622; Munk, 126a).

and act properly in God's presence, but also makes us aware that we are *always* in God's presence, since our intellect is re-formed according to his intellect by the ordinances of the law:

> This king who cleaves to him and accompanies him is the intellect that overflows toward us and is the bond between us and Him, may He be exalted. Just as we apprehend Him by means of that light which He caused to overflow to us—as it says, "In Thy light do we see light"—so does He by means of this selfsame light examine us; and because of it, He, may he be exalted, is constantly with us, examining from on high: "Can any hide himself in secret places that I shall not see him?" Understand this well. Know that when perfect men understand this, they achieve such humility, such awe and fear of God, such reverence and such shame before Him, may He be exalted—and this in ways that pertain to true reality, not to imagination—that their secret conduct with their wives and in latrines is like their public conduct with other people.[163]

This then is the highest purpose of the religious law, which is also the highest purpose of metaphysics. For the goal of metaphysics is to unite the human intellect with the First Intellect, the First Cause of being who is existence in itself. And the law makes the one who follows it constantly conformed to the First Intellect: "This purpose to which I have drawn your attention is the purpose of all the actions prescribed by the Law."[164] So the giving of the law is a grace by which, as we saw in the passage immediately above, God unites his intellect with ours "by means of that light which He caused to overflow to us." Through the Law God unites himself to the believer not through the imagination, but through the intellect, for it is the fallen intellect that is led by imagination, but it is the redeemed intellect that is led by the light of God himself through the law, although the law uses and guides the imagination towards pure intellection. *Wisdom* [ḥokhmah] means in Scripture nothing else than the apprehension of God and that nothing in the law equals this apprehension; but everything in the law is a preparation for such apprehension and is for the sake of this end.[165]

---

163. *Guide*, III, 52 (Pines, 629; Munk, 130b).
164. *Guide*, III, 52 (Pines, 629; Munk, 130b).
165. *Guide*, III, 54 (Pines, 636; Munk, 135a).

It is by a love that is purified by the commands and inner workings of the law that the intellect of the pious believer becomes united to
God. So the law does not pit love against intellectual comprehension,
but rather shows how each is necessary for the purity of the other:

> You know to what extent the Torah lays stress upon *love*: "With all thy
> heart, and with all thy soul, and with all thy might." For these two ends,
> namely, *love* and *fear*, are achieved through two things: *love* through the
> opinions taught by the Law, which include the apprehensions of His
> being as He, may He be exalted, is in truth; while *fear* is achieved by
> means of all actions prescribed by the Law, as we have explained. Un-
> derstand this summary.[166]

By purifying the intellect from all idolatry, the law prepares it to contemplate God as the purely immaterial unity from which all things proceed.
But by being a *command* that is addressed to the believer *qua* individual,
the law is also an act of supreme love.

Maimonides notes that we can be perfected in four ways: with regard
to our possessions and material goods, with regard to our bodily form,
and with regard to our moral virtues. But it is with regard to the perfection of our intellect that we are perfected with regard to what is most
essential and individual to us, even though, paradoxically, this perfection
comes about in a unity with the one who is universal being or existence:

> This is what gives the individual true perfection, a perfection belong-
> ing to him alone; and it gives him permanent perdurance; through it
> man is man. If you consider each of the three perfections mentioned
> before, you will find that they pertain to other than you, not to you,
> even though, according to the generally accepted opinion, they inevita-
> bly pertain both to you and to others. This ultimate perfection, howev-
> er, pertains to you alone, no one else being associated in it with you in
> any way: "They shall be only thine own, and so on."[167]

The contemplation and love of God is the end and goal of every intellectual being, because it is in God that we are perfected with regard to
our intellect, and thus united with universal being; but at the same time,

---

166. *Guide*, III, 52 (Pines, 630; Munk, 131a).
167. *Guide*, III, 54 (Pines, 635; Munk, 134a–b).

we also know that we, as someone created directly by God, are willed individually by God. We are thus perfected in our individual being to the degree that our will accompanies our intellection of God with love. For, "the perfection of which one should be proud and that one should desire is knowledge of Him, may He be exalted, which is the true science."[168] Thus, to know *and* love God is to achieve, each one of us, our own *unique* perfection and end, because God is not only our cause but a cause who willed us into being not by caprice but as an integral part and even shining ornament in and of his created order.

CONCLUSION

We encounter in Maimonides an understanding of the relation between revelation and the law at once very similar to and yet radically different from Averroes. Like Averroes, Maimonides sees prophecy as an integral part of divine providence, allowing the masses to participate in some way in the reparation and perfection of the intellect, which is the goal of all philosophical reflection. But unlike Averroes, Maimonides sees the human intellect as fallen. Philosophical reflection, therefore, cannot on its own repair and perfect the intellect. The revelation of the divine law is thus providential, not just for the correct ordering of society in order to make philosophical perfection possible, as in Averroes, but for the very healing and restoration of the intellect itself. And this difference has its roots not only in the very different anthropology found in the Bible and the Quran, but also in the way revelation is conceived. For Maimonides, as for any knowledgeable Jew, revelation is covenantal: God choses to bind himself in a relationship with a people he himself chooses with promises if the covenant is obeyed and threats if the covenant is broken. This relationship mirrors God's relation to creation and also the nature of prophecy: God commits himself to a rational order in creation, an order that he binds himself to observe. Thus, while it is the law and not philosophical reflection that heals the human intellect, God's covenantal faithfulness establishes and guarantees the rational order of creation and

168. *Guide*, III, 54 (Pines, 636; Munk, 134b).

thus the goodness and power of the individual human intellect. And yet, paradoxically, he binds himself to that rational order freely, having been free to choose any other order. So, it is in prophecy and, by extension, revelation itself: prophetic knowledge is a pure intellection of divine things flowing directly from God, the First Intellect; nevertheless, God is free to choose what and to whom he reveals himself. Thus, revelation is always a dialectic of universality and particularity: God is universal being and intellection that imparts existence and intelligibility to all creatures; and yet the divine Will is utterly free, manifesting that freedom and its choices, which establish relationships with particular prophets and peoples. Hence, revelation is an intellection of God, but one that can only be completed by a total and free love of God.

CHAPTER 4

NATURA AS CREATURA

Aquinas on Nature as Implicit Revelation

Thomas Aquinas interprets the world as creation.[1] This means that the realm of *natura* is seen by Thomas as the realm of *creatura* or creature. According to Aristotle, the nature or *physis* of any thing is the intrinsic principle of its motion or rest,[2] and Aquinas follows him in this understanding. The consideration of the natures of things then leads Aristotle to an investigation of the cause of motion and organization in the *cosmos*, that is, of universal order. But Aquinas sees more at work in the natures of things, some principle that sustains natures in being and gives them intelligibility.[3] In other words, if the world is created,

---

1. One can interpret the world as mechanism, as in the modern era. But to do so is to invalidate all interpretation of the world, including the mechanistic one. For, in the mechanistic interpretation of the world, there is no inherent meaning in the world to interpret. Such an interpretation can only be about the techno-mathematical order that we *project* upon the world and not about the nature or order of the world as it is in itself. In this sense, Kant's philosophy is the great, but self-contradictory, alternative to the Thomistic interpretation of the world. The Thomistic interpretation, by contrast, is rooted in the meanings that beings themselves reveal about themselves and is, as such, a "phenomenology."

2. Aristotle, *Physics* II, 1 (192b12).

3. "God's action does not eliminate the natural action but rather He is the cause and sustainer of it. There is no incompatibility between the action of the external cause and that of the intrinsic principle, but a '*concursus*' of God and nature." Jan Aertsen, *Nature and Creature: Thomas Aquinas's Way of Thought* (Leiden: E. J. Brill, 1988), 290.

the human intellect must search not just for the cause of motion and of order, but for the cause of the very existence of things themselves. This is what it means to say that Thomas interprets the world as creation: it is not just the motion or order of things that is in question, but the very existence of things in the first place, for to be created is to come to be out of nothing (*ex nihilo*). But more than that, to see things as *creatures* is also to inquire into their fundamental *truth*: if all things are created or made, then in accordance with what measure or standard are they made? To see things as created is to see them as related to an intellect—not simply to our intellect but to an eminently creative intellect that brings things into existence.

Many prominent scholars and even general readers of Aquinas have already pointed out the centrality of the doctrine of creation to his thinking. Josef Pieper in fact refers to it as the "unspoken" first principle or *a priori* of all of Aquinas's thinking.[4] G. K. Chesterton supposedly remarks that so central to Thomas's thinking was the doctrine of creation that, just as we have come to call saints after their most distinctive spiritual trait, like "St. John of the Cross," so we should call Thomas Aquinas, "St. Thomas of Creation."[5] And as both point out, the doctrine of creation is central to Thomas's thought precisely because it is central to his task of understanding *revelation*, that is, the fact of revelation itself, why we need it, and its specific content or teaching. This is because, as both Pieper and Chesterton argue, we cannot see or understand the world as truly good and intelligible unless it be the product of a supreme intelligence creating it out of a completely freely given love or goodness.[6] And such a free intelligence could only be known fully if it should

4. Josef Pieper, *The Silence of St. Thomas* (South Bend, Ind.: St. Augustine Press, 1957).

5. I cannot find the exact place where Chesterton says this; I am working from memory. But certainly he sees creation and the Incarnation as central to Thomas's thought in his magisterial work, *Saint Thomas Aquinas: "The Dumb Ox"* (New York: Doubleday, 1956).

6. "For instance, the meaning of propositions such as 'all that exists is good,' or 'all that exists is true,' is misunderstood, as is, in my opinion, the general significance of the so-called transcendental concepts (in the traditional sense)—unless it be realized that the concepts and theses in question do not refer to a neutral Being that simply exists, not to an *ens ut sic*, not to an indeterminate world of 'objects,' but formally to Being as *creatura*." Pieper, *Silence of St. Thomas*, 48.

choose to reveal itself freely, because it could not be known otherwise.

Only if we see being as the intelligible product of that love, does the central doctrine of the Christian faith, namely the Incarnation of God in Jesus Christ, become intelligible, let alone transformative to one who understands and accepts it.[7] Understanding this aspect of Aquinas's thought will also help us see how it, and the Christian tradition to which Aquinas belongs, differs from that of Averroes and Maimonides and the Muslim and Jewish religious traditions, especially considering how central the very doctrine of creation is to both Averroes and Maimonides in thinking about the nature of revelation (as we have shown).

NATURA AS CREATURA: SUMMA THEOLOGIAE I, 44, 2

The correlation between the doctrine of creation and the fulfillment, perfection, and proper functioning of the human intellect comes to the fore in the second article of question forty-four of Thomas's *Summa theologiae*. Here, Aquinas asks, "Whether prime matter is created by God?" (*Utrum materia prima sit creata a Deo*). At first glance, this question might seem to be of only secondary importance; but it is not. "The notion of prime matter poses a special difficulty for the idea of creation," says Jan Aertsen.

> That appears from the parallel texts in the *Summa contra Gentiles* and the commentary on the *Physics*. The common supposition of the Greek philosophers was that "from nothing comes nothing" (*ex nihilo nihil fit*). On the basis of this supposition Averroes had controverted the teaching of the Christian faith about creation from nothing (*ex nihilo*). Every instance of coming-to-be requires something pre-existent, a substratum that in the final analysis is prime matter.[8]

7. "Far from being or signifying a secularization of genuine Christian teaching, the affirmation of the reality of creation in the theology of St. Thomas surges from the very depths of Christian intuition, namely, from reverence for the reality of the Incarnation of God. According to St. Thomas, the Evangelist John had deliberately said the Word was made *flesh*, in order to exclude the Manichean principle that the body is evil." Ibid., 33.

8. Jan Aertsen, *Medieval Philosophy and the Transcendentals: The Case of Thomas Aquinas* (Leiden: E. J. Brill, 1996), 151–52.

As a result, Thomas must argue that even prime matter is created by God out of nothing and thus has being only by participation. But it is *how* Thomas goes about proving this that is particularly interesting and illuminating. Thomas approaches this problem indirectly by giving us, as he is sometimes wont to do, a powerfully concise "history of philosophy." What the history of philosophical thought shows, Thomas argues, is that the notion of creation of all things, even prime matter, out of nothing is both the culmination of human thought about being *qua* being and the perfection of our very intellect.

First off, the fact that things exist not by themselves is not a given but was the result of a logically necessary, though groping, development: "The ancient philosophers little by little, as if step by step, came upon the recognition of the truth" (*Antiqui philosophi paulatim, et quasi peditentim, intraverunt in cognitionem veritatis*). At the dawn of philosophical reflection, in the thought of those whom we now call the Presocratics (Thales, Anaximander, Anaximenes, Heraclitus, etc.), human thought did not rise above what it could perceive through the senses. And so such early philosophers considered all of being to be synonymous with material nature and all change and motion to be accidental change or motion: "Those who posited movement in them [sensible beings—*entia sensibiles*] did not consider motion except according to certain accidents, as, for instance, rarefication and condensation, union and separation. And supposing the substance itself of bodies uncreated, they assigned various causes for these accidental changes, such as friendship, strife, intellect, and other such causes."[9] Thus, Thales thought of all change as mere modification to the universal material substance, water, and Heraclitus posited all change as modifications of fire, etc. All things were simply accidents or qualities of one underlying material substratum, and all change was only understood as accidental change, that is, a mere alteration of an essentially unchanging material substratum. Nor could these *antiqui* adequately explain the causes of change, using anthropomorphic abstractions such as "friendship and strife" or "mind" to explain this process of alteration.

The next stage in the progression of human thought, Thomas con-

9. Thomas Aquinas, *Summa theologica*, trans. Friars of the English Dominican Province (New York: Benzinger Bros., 1948), I, 44, 2. Henceforth, *S. Th.*

tinues, was when philosophers were able to distinguish "through the intellect" (*per intellectum*) between form and matter: "Proceeding further, they [the early philosophers] distinguished by means of the intellect [*per intellectum*] between substantial form and matter, which they posited as uncreated; and perceived that the transformation in bodies occurs according to essential forms. They posited certain universal causes of these changes, such as the oblique circle of Aristotle (*De Gener.* ii) or the ideas, according to Plato."[10] These philosophers, more specifically, Plato and Aristotle, were able to distinguish between the formal nature of the thing, the cause that makes a thing "what it is," that is, a substance, and the underlying matter, which they "posited to be uncreated." In other words, these philosophers were finally able to distinguish between formal reality that makes a thing what it is universally—the "humanness" of Socrates, for example—and the material substratum that makes Socrates "this human being" individually. Aquinas also remarks that the discovery of the formal cause of things opened up philosophical thought to "more universal causes." In this respect, he mentions the transcendent ideas of Plato, within which, especially in the Neoplatonic tradition that Plato inspired, there was a hierarchy of more universal forms, usually culminating in the "One." In Aristotle, it is the movement of the heavenly bodies, which are themselves ultimately moved by the purely active, immaterial, substantial form which he calls "God." So, Plato and Aristotle made great strides in coming to a knowledge of more universal causes of being, certainly in comparison with the Presocratics. And they were able to do this because they rose to the level of "intellect" (about which more later).

Nevertheless, great philosophers as they were, neither Plato nor Aristotle were able to raise themselves to the perfection of human intellection, mainly because they could not intuit the cause of the existence of immaterial, substantial forms of things:

> But it must be considered that matter is contracted through form to a determinate species, as the substance of some species is contracted to a determinate mode of being [*essendi*] through a supervening accident, as "man" is contracted through "white." Both, therefore considered being

10. Ibid.

from a particular point of view, or insofar as it is *this being*, or insofar
as it is *such a being*. And thus, they assigned particular causal agents to
things [*Utrique igitur consideraverunt ens particulari quadam consideratio-
ne, vel inquantum est hoc ens, vel inquantum est tale ens. Et sic rebus causas
agentes particulares assignaverunt*].[11]

That is, Plato and Aristotle inquired only into the *essential properties* of
being and not into being as such. Or to put it another way, they only
asked, what makes a being a being, *given its existence*? What makes
something *this being* rather than *that being*; and makes a being *such and
such a being* rather than a different kind of being? They did not ask the
crucial question: *why are there any beings at all?* What makes this being
or this kind of being *exist at all*, rather than remain a mere possibility or
a mental being? These sorts of questions only arose, according to Thomas, in the third stage of the development of philosophical thought:

> Others [*aliqui*] further raised themselves to considering being *qua* being
> [*ens inquantum ens*] and considered the cause of things, not only as they
> are *these*, or as *such*, but as *beings*. Therefore, that which is the cause
> of things insofar as they are beings, must be the cause of things not
> only according whether they are *such* through accidental forms, nor ac-
> cording to whether they are *these* through substantial forms, but rather
> according to all that pertains to their existence [*esse*] in any way at all.
> It is necessary therefore to posit even prime matter as created by the
> universal cause of beings.[12]

11. What the "both" (*utrique*) refers to here has been the subject of some speculation.
Mark Johnson asserts that Gilson mistranslated this word as referring to Plato and Aristotle. Gilson thus argued, mistakenly in Johnson's view, that Thomas is contrasting an
understanding of a truly creative and universal cause of being with the more limited views
of Plato and Aristotle. If Thomas were referring to Plato and Aristotle specifically, he would
have used the word *uterque*. *Utrique*, by contrast, refers to two *groups* or *schools* of philosophers. Aristotle's understanding of God as the universal *and* creative cause of being is,
therefore, not Thomas's target here. I think that this interpretation is forced: Thomas frequently refers not to Plato and Aristotle individually but to their schools of thought (thus
his many mention of the "Platonists," etc.). Even in the very article, Thomas refers to the
various philosophical positions as held by groups or schools, such as the *antiqui philosophi*
or the *aliqui* (more on whom in a note below). See Mark F. Johnson, "Did St. Thomas
Attribute a Doctrine of Creation to Aristotle?" *New Scholasticism* 63, no. 2 (1989): 144–45.

12. "Et ulterius aliqui erexerunt se ad considerandum ens inquantum est ens: et consideraverunt causam rerum, non solum secundum quod sunt *haec* vel *talia*, sed secundum

Such thinkers (*aliqui*), most likely those following in the footsteps of Avicenna,[13] were finally able to "raise themselves" up to the point where they were able to understand not simply the causes of substances as substances or of accidental change in substances, but to an intellection of existence itself and its cause. And the cause of existence as such is without doubt the most universal cause, since logically nothing can exist outside of existence. So to intuit existence as such and to think to its ultimate cause is to conclude that nothing, not even matter, is not an effect of existence itself. Thus, even prime matter is caused, that is, created.

---

quod sunt *entia*. Hic igitur quod est causa rerum inquantum sunt entia, oportet esse causam rerum, non solum secundum quod sunt *talia* per formas accidentales, nec secundum quod sunt *haec* per formas substantiales, sed etiam secundum omne illud quod pertinet ad esse illorum quocumque modo. Et sic oportet ponere etiam materiam primam ab univerali causa entium." *S. Th.* I, 44, 2.

13. The identity of these thinkers—the *aliqui*—is a matter of some dispute. Etienne Gilson had argued that the insight into a universal *and* creative cause of being belonged to Avicenna and that neither Plato nor Aristotle could rise above their "essentialism" to an intuition of the act of existence itself (see *The Christian Philosophy of St. Thomas Aquinas*, 461n6). This claim was disputed by Anton Pegis: he agreed with Gilson that, while Plato and Aristotle rose to a consideration of the universal cause of being, they did not recognize this cause as creative, that is, as giving the act of existence to formal being. Nevertheless, Pegis argues that such a creative cause is *implicit* in Plato and Aristotle's thought and that it was the genius of Thomas that brought this unstated insight into the light of day. (Anton Pegis, "A Note on St. Thomas, *Summa Theologica* I, 44, 1–2," *Medieval Studies* 8 (1946): 159–68.) More recently, scholars like Mark Johnson and Lawrence Dewan have further disputed Gilson's claim (and to a certain extent, Pegis's), arguing that the *aliqui* refer to Plato and Aristotle or their epigones and that Thomas saw them as teaching a full-blown doctrine of creation, their only mistake being that Aristotle at least saw this creation as eternal. This is not to say that they *did* teach such a doctrine, but Johnson and Dewan argue that Thomas certainly thought that they did. (Johnson, "Did St. Thomas Attribute a Doctrine of Creation to Aristotle?"; Lawrence Dewan, "Thomas Aquinas, Creation, and Two Historians" in *Laval théoligique et philosophique* 50, no. 2 [1994]: 363–87; and Dewan, "St. Albert, Creation, and the Philosophers" in *Laval théoligique et philosophique* 40, no. 3 [1984]: 295–307.) But all these objections have serious problems of their own, with most recent scholars returning to the position of Gilson, that Avicenna and his followers are the *aliqui*, though basing their assertion on reasons different from those of Gilson. As R. E. Houser argues: "the Platonic and Aristotelian arguments conclude to the existence of a creative God without proving in what sense he is creative. Aquinas seems to have realized that these arguments leave the issue of creation unresolved, and therefore added the Avicennian argument which clarifies the even stronger sense in which God is a creator, that is, the efficient cause not of essence, but of *esse*, apart from which a creature would be absolutely nothing." R. E. Houser, "Avicenna, *Aliqui*, and the Thomistic Doctrine of Creation" (2000), 18, http://t4.stthom.edu/users/houser/avicenna2000.

There are several remarkable things about this account that Thomas gives of the history of philosophy. The first is that, as Rudi te Velde observes,

> the different phases correspond to the different ways in which intellect relates to its object, according to *sensus, ratio,* and *intellectus.* Each way of relating to its object corresponds to a certain relationship internal to the relationship of substance (matter) and accident; on the level of reason being is conceived according to the essential relationship of form and matter; and finally on the level of intellect being is conceived according to the relationship of essence and *esse,* a relationship which is constitutive of being as such.[14]

Te Velde continues his observation by noting that the progression in Aquinas's account is dialectical: what is taken as given in the first stage—the material substratum—is itself resolved into material substance in the second stage. And as Plato and Aristotle analyzed the nature of material substance in the second stage, they were lead to a consideration of immaterial form or substance, which brought them to the threshold of the third stage, in which even immaterial substance is resolved into a "substratum" or, better, limiting principle for the act of existence (namely, "essence"). "The origin of being as such cannot be 'generation,' because it no longer presupposes anything in that which is caused. It is *creatio,* for to produce being absolutely pertains to the essence of creation."[15] Hence, it is reality itself, as it reveals itself more and more fully to human perception that moves and finally perfects the human intellect. So intuition into the reality of creation, as implied in

14. Rudi te Velde, *Aquinas on God: The "Divine Science" of the* Summa Theologiae (Farnham, UK: Ashgate, 2006), 137. Also, "The concept of creation is formally deduced from the concept of God. In the determination *ipsum esse subsistens,* God is thought in such a way that he is productive of every other being. But what must not be forgotten here is that this metaphysical determination of God does not spring from an intellectual intuition of his essence, but rather expresses how God must be thought 'from out of his own activity' as the First Cause of all things. The concept of God (*ipsum esse subsistens*) and the concept of Creation (*ens per participationem*) relate to each other in a circular manner." Rudi te Velde, "Schöpfung und Partizipation (S.th. I, qq. 44–47 und qq. 103–105)," in *Thomas von Aquin: Die Summa Theologiae, Wirkinterpretationen,* ed. Andreas Speer (Berlin: de Gruyter, 2005), 112.

15. Aertsen, *Medieval Philosophy and the Transcendentals,* 154.

the intellection of the problem of existence as such, corresponds also to the perfection of the human intellect, to its fullest and most authentic mode of existence.

The second notable feature of Thomas's argument for prime matter being created is related to the first: his argument for the created-ness of matter resolves all the concepts of the human intellect into the one concept that all other concepts of the human intellect presuppose, the concept of "being" (*ens*). And here, we have a clear reference to the Avicennian background to Thomas's own insights into the nature of being *qua* being. Thus, as Jan Aertsen asserts, "the distinctive feature of the way of thought in the third phase is that it is transcendental."[16] By "transcendental" medieval philosophers and theologians denote those concepts corresponding to the most basic and universal features of all things, starting with the concept "being." "Being" is most basic and universal because it applies to or "runs through" all the ten categories of being that Aristotle had enumerated in his *Categories*, such as "substance," "quantity," "quality," "place," "time," "relation," etc. The concept "being" applies to them all in some way, though these ways differ. But there are other concepts that are said to be "convertible" with "being," because they refer to the same extensive reality as the term "being," but add to our concept of "being" an understanding of the relation inherent in any being as being. These concepts are "one" (*unum*), "true" (*verum*), and "good" (*bonum*). The transcendental concept of "one" adds to the concept "being" a negative relation in being as being, namely, the insight that every being as being is "undivided"; it negates any division in itself. The concept "one," therefore, is not negative in any sort of nihilistic sense, which would be absurd applied to being as such, but actually refers to a positive attribute of the negation of any negation. Of the "true" and the "good" we shall have much more to say below, but suffice it to say here that every being is true insofar as every being, as being, is intelligible or, perhaps more accurately, is able to actualize and perfect an intellect as intellect. Every being is good insofar as every being, as being, is desirable, which is to say that every being as being is able, in proportion to its ontological reality,

16. Ibid., 155.

to satisfy the rational appetite or will. Thus, the intuition of existence in itself leads the human intellect to inquire into the "relationality" inherent in being or existence as such.

Again, the point here is not that Aquinas is producing some sort of "proof" for the truth of the doctrine of creation *ex nihilo*. He is not. In any case, as we shall develop further, the concept of "being" (*ens*) towards which such a metaphysical resolution into first concepts leads us does not refer in any special way to God. It refers to each and every being as being. Nevertheless, it does lead the human intellect to inquire into what might be the *cause* of that being as being, since, as we saw above, no finite, natural being can be the cause of its own existence. We are left, therefore, with seeing the natural being as having a *participated* being, a being whose existence is *ab alio*, from something else (a point that Thomas develops in the article just prior to q. 44, a. 2, of the first part of the *Summa*, namely in q. 44, a. 1). In other words, once the human intellect has arrived, by the very nature of things and the force of logic, to the universal cause of existence itself, it is impossible for it not to interpret the natural thing as *creature*.

Metaphysics, therefore, properly understood and applied, opens up interpretive possibilities that were not there in Aristotle or Plato, both of whom did not take their metaphysical insights far enough. It is important here that Thomas, in *Summa theologiae* I, question 44, article 2, does not refer to Scripture at all in his argument; it is a purely metaphysical argument.[17] And as a metaphysical argument, it is not intended to give us any knowledge about God: the "proper subject matter," as the medievals would have put it, of metaphysics is not God but being *qua* being; God comes into view only as the first or ultimate cause of being *qua* being. Only revelation and its systematic study in Christian theology (or *scientia divina*, "divine science") consider God as God— consider God as its proper subject matter.[18] Nevertheless, the meta-

---

17. "One of the most remarkable features of *Summa theologiae* I, 44, 2, is that the idea of creation appears as the result and the completion of the internal development of human thought. The argument does not appeal to any text from Scripture." Aertsen, *Medieval Philosophy and the Transcendentals*, 156.

18. "Thomas's conclusion makes the precise theoretical distinction between philosophical

physical argument remains crucial to Thomas as a *manuductio* of the
human intellect from being *qua* being to its transcendent cause. As te
Velde perceptively argues,

> without reason's *manuductio*, by which the subject of the revealed doc-
> trine of faith is given an intelligible determination, the Christian *reve-
> latio* cannot be understood to be what it is assumed to be: knowledge
> which is true of God. Without the *manuductio* of metaphysics, leading
> to a transcendent reality, the Christian revelation will lapse into the im-
> manence of human history, at least in the sense that its putative refer-
> ence to transcendence remains unintelligible.[19]

To sum up: metaphysical reflection leads us necessarily to the concept
of being *qua* being (*ens inquantum ens*). Thus, the cause of being as such,
or *creation*, becomes, if not the subject matter of metaphysics, then the
limiting principle of metaphysics. That is, the fact of creation becomes
the ultimate *horizon* against which any metaphysical inquiry must take
place. Just as importantly, this realization of creation *ex nihilo* as the
limiting horizon of all rational thought, not only about being as such
but about any being as being, is also paradoxically a realization of the
human intellect's own perfection (also in the sense of reaching reason's
outermost *limit*). With the fact of creation, human reason meets its limit
and, by doing so, can intuit being as such and its cause in an act of intellection.

One aspect of this metaphysical limit or horizon is that the human
intellect cannot intuit whether the world is created *de novo* or from eternity. In asserting this, Thomas follows closely the position of Maimonides: human reason in and of itself by its observation of the world as it
exists now, cannot reason to whether the world had a beginning in time

---

theology (or metaphysics) and Christian theology clear. The proper subject-matter of metaphysics is not God, but rather the being of beings. Against the theological conception of
metaphysics, that dominated among Greek commentators of Aristotle, Thomas stresses
in his commentary on the *Metaphysics* the ontological character of First Philosophy. This
science treats God only insofar as he is the cause of being. The subject-matter of Christian
theology, however, is God himself." Jan Aertsen, "Die Rede von Gott: Die Fragen, 'ob er ist'
und 'was er ist.' Wissenschaftslehre und Transzendentalienlehre (S.th. I, qq. 1–12)," in Speer,
Thomas von Aquin, 35.

19. Te Velde, *Aquinas on God*, 30.

or not. Only God is eternal in himself. Whether the world is eternal or not, however, is impossible to determine, since this depends upon the divine will: God could have willed to create the world from all eternity, or he could have willed it to have a beginning in time. Both are possible:

> Nothing except God can be eternal. And in fact to assert this is not impossible. It was shown above (I, 19, 4) that the will of God is the cause of things. Thus anything is necessary, insofar as it is necessary that God wills it to be, since the necessity of the effect depends on the necessity of the cause, as is asserted in *Metaph.* V, 6. It has been shown above (I, 19, 3), however, that, absolutely speaking, it is not necessary that God will anything other than himself. It is therefore not necessary that God will that the world to have always been. But so long as the world exists, to that extent God wills it to exist, since the existence [*esse*] of the world depends upon the will of God as its cause. It is therefore not necessary that the world to have existed always. Hence this [the eternity of the world] cannot be proved demonstratively.[20]

So, while it is indeed *possible* that God could have willed the creation of the world from all eternity, it is not at all *necessary*. Now, we can deduce some things about God's will from its effects: its efficaciousness, its goodness, its supreme wisdom and intelligence. But we cannot deduce from its effects the very mode in and by which God willed the world to come into being; this we can know only from what God chooses to reveal to us about himself in revelation. That is why Aquinas argues that the creation of the world *de novo* is precisely an article of faith:

> We hold by faith alone and cannot prove by demonstration that the world did not always exist, as was said above concerning the Trinity (I, 32, 1). And the reason for this is that the newness of the world cannot be demonstrated on the part of the world itself [*novitas mundi non potest demonstrationem recipere ex parte ipsius mundi*]. The principle of demonstration is what something is [*quod quid est*]. Now everything according to its species is abstracted from *here* and *now*, hence the saying that "universals are everywhere and always." Hence it cannot be demonstrated that man, or the sky, or a stone did not exist always. Similarly, [this cannot be demonstrated] from the part of an agent cause, which

20. *S. Th.* I, 46, 1.

acts voluntarily. For the will of God cannot be investigated by reason, unless concerning those things which it is absolutely necessary for God to will; but what he wills concerning creatures is not among these, as was said above (I, 19, 3). The divine will can, however, be made known through revelation, on which faith rests [*potest autem voluntas divina homini manifestari per revelationem, cui fides innititur*]. Hence, that the world had a beginning is something credible, but not demonstrable or knowable.[21]

The Christian must rely on the testimony of the Scriptures to what God has revealed about himself in order to know the answer to this question. This for Thomas is not at all irrational: indeed, it is eminently rational insofar as it recognizes the limits of human reason on this question. The word itself cannot give us any indication of its newness or eternity; it is rational to recognize this. What Aquinas does affirm here can, however, be easily overlooked: he unequivocally affirms the rationality of creation itself. Creation is through and through intelligible and orderly; we know this by abstracting the intelligible structure of things and the order of the world from our sensible experience of it. God's will is not capricious; his creation is eminently intelligible. But what the human intellect cannot abstract from things is the act in and by which creatures came into existence. This act is of an entirely different order, because it results from and establishes a free relationship of God to his creatures. Thus, it is only in the free relationship in and through which God reveals himself to creatures that this free creative act becomes known and the human intellect becomes, paradoxically, perfected by a relationship that lies beyond its ability to grasp rationally, yet establishes the horizon within which creation becomes rational and intelligible.

TRUTH AND INTELLECT

Basic to Thomas's insight into the correlation between being and the perfection of the intellect is actually something that was discerned at the dawn of Western philosophy. This was the insight of Parmenides

---

21. Ibid., 2.

that "being and thought belong together" or "for the same is to think as to be" (*to gar auton noein estin te kai einai*).[22] There is, at some level, an essential and necessary relation between being and thinking or intellect. This essential or necessary connection between being and thought is expressed by the Scholastic transcendental concept "true." That is, as was mentioned above, every being insofar as it exists is "knowable," or "capable of being related to an intellect," or "capable of actualizing or perfecting an intellect as intellect." This relation of being as being to the intellect is not, as the phrases above indicate, accidental to being as such; this relation is already inherent in being.[23] Or as Thomas expresses it: "being cannot be understood without the true, because being cannot be understood without the fact that it corresponds to or is adequate to an intellect."[24] We cannot understand being as being without understanding why it not only corresponds naturally or necessarily to our thought but why, as we saw above, it is *most basic* to our thought.[25] Without the concept "being," there can be no thought of anything; but by the same token, being in itself arises and *is as such and in itself* only through thought or intellect.

Now on the face of it, these assertions might strike the modern mind as rather odd, if not outlandish. Is not this just a species of discredited idealism to say that being depends upon thought? Things are whether

22. G. S. Kirk and J. E. Raven, *The Presocratic Philosophers* (Cambridge: Cambridge University Press, 1964), 269.

23. "The realm of being does not extend further than the realm of things, which are correlated to a knowing mind, and therefore it follows that there is no being to which this correlation is lacking." Josef Pieper, *Wahrheit der Dinge: Eine Untersuchung zur Anthropologie des Hochmittelalters* (Munich: Im Kösel, 1966), 39.

24. Thomas Aquinas, *Quaestiones Disputatae de Veritate*, in *Quaestiones Disputatae*, ed. P. Bazzi, M. Calcaterra, T. S. Centi, E. Odetto, and P. M. Pession (Turin: Marietti, 1953), I, 1, ad 3: "Ens non potest intelligi sine vero, quia ens non potest intelligi sine hoc, quod correspondeat vel adaequatur intellectui." *De veritate*; hereafter, *De ver.*

25. "The method Thomas uses in *De veritate* 1.1 is not to be found in either of the other two basic texts. The fascinating thing about this text is that the doctrine of the transcendentals is prepared through a reduction to that which is the foundation of knowledge and science. This approach could be called 'transcendental' in the Kantian sense, because according to Kant, in transcendental science the point is no longer to go forward but to go backward. Thomas's *resolutio* is a going back to that first which is presupposed in all knowledge." Aertsen, *Medieval Philosophy and the Transcendentals*, 79.

we know them or not; surely it is absurd to claim that being and thought go together essentially and necessarily?

It is not only the modern mind, however, that recoils from these assertions about the essential convertibility between being and truth, many medieval theologians did as well. While it was common in the early to mid-thirteenth century to argue that being and truth were convertible, most theologians tried to give a strictly "ontological" definition of this convertibility.[26] That is, they tried to define what makes every being, insofar as it is a being, true without reference to the intellect. In doing this, they seemed to find warrant in Aristotle, whose discussion of being as truth in book 7, chapter 4, of his *Metaphysics* argues that being in the intellect or being as truth belongs to being accidentally. According to Aristotle, being is in substances, not in the mind. Thus, some medieval scholastics defined truth, for example, as "that which is" (*id quod est*) and so forth. What is interesting about Thomas's position is that, in contrast to most thirteenth-century theologians, he argues quite clearly and forthrightly that we cannot define truth adequately without reference to an intellect: "The basic idea running through Thomas's discussion of truth like a scarlet thread is that relation to the intellect is essential for truth."[27] Any definition of truth without reference to the intellect simply makes no sense, Aquinas argues. And, he further argues, we can make this reference without falling into a "subjective idealism" (though he never uses this modern term).

So, what is truth according to Thomas? He deals with this question in one of the most extensive, important, and earliest of his disputed questions, his *Disputed Questions on Truth*, where the first question is, as we would except, "what is truth?" (*Quid sit veritas?*). In answering this question, Thomas takes us on a brief but dense excursus in fundamental metaphysics. As we have seen above, Thomas remarks first off that "that which the intellect first conceives as most known, and into which it resolves all concepts, is 'being,' as Avicenna says in the beginning of his

26. Jozef Van de Wiele, "Le problème de la vérité ontologique dans la philosophie de saint Thomas," *Revue philosophique de Louvain*, 52, no. 36 (1954): 521–71; Raymond J. McCall, "St. Thomas on Ontological Truth," *New Scholasticism* 12, no. 1 (1938): 9–29.

27. Aertsen, *Medieval Philosophy and the Transcendentals*, 246.

Metaphysics" (*Illud autem quod primo intellectus concipit quasi notissimum, et in quo omnes conceptiones resolvit, est ens, ut Avicenna dicit in principio* Metaphysicae *suae* [*Lib. I, c. ix*]). So the question of truth is unavoidably a question of being: the inherent goal or final cause of the intellect as intellect is to know being *qua* being, because to grasp being *qua* being is also to grasp what underlies all our other concepts.

Once we resolve all our concepts to the most basic and fundamental concept, "being," we can regard it from several angles. We can look at what follows from every being considered in itself. We can do this either affirmatively or negatively. Thus, we do so affirmatively insofar as "being" refers to *what* something is or its essence; we call it a "thing" (*res*). We do so negatively when we say being is "one," insofar as "being" refers to what is undivided from itself (*unum*). Or we can consider the concept "being" in relation to another (*Alio modo secundum convenientiam unius entis ad aliud* ...). If we regard a being in its relation to another being, we call it "something" (*aliquid*). But this is not the only relation that we can discern in the concept "being"; there is the relation of being to a knower and a desirer of being, which, on reflection, is just as fundamental to the concept "being" as is "thing," "one," or "something," for we only have access to being as such in its being thought and desired.

It is no accident, then, that Aquinas looks at the concept "being," in relation to the human soul. The human soul and, in particular, the intellect that is the highest power of that soul, is open to all being. It is through and in the human intellect that being comes to be as such—as being *qua* being and not just this or that being—at least in the flux of the natural world and human life. As Jan Aertsen puts it, "this transcendental openness of the mind is the condition for the possibility of metaphysics as the science of being-as-being."[28] Lest there be any confusion, however, we must quickly add that "being *qua* being" does not depend in any way for its own "being" on the human intellect. As we shall see,

---

28. "Man's horizon is unlimited. An intellectual substance has 'more affinity' to the whole of things than does any other substance. Through its intellect it is able to comprehend the entire being (*totius entis comprehensive*). This transcendental openness of the mind is the condition for the possibility of metaphysics as the science of being-as-being." Aertsen, *Medieval Philosophy and the Transcendentals*, 259.

realization of this "non-dependence" will actually have great implications for Aquinas's teaching on the relation of creation to revelation. What is does mean, however, is that necessarily implied in the concept of "being *qua* being" is relation to an intellect. "To be" in its purity and in itself is "to be" *for* and even, ultimately, *in* an intellect, because only in and through an intellect is being *qua* being revealed, that is, as what it *truly* is.

Thus, to unfold what is already implied in the concept of "being," we must turn to the human soul (for that is the one, in our experience, who is doing metaphysics). Thomas notes that, in the human soul, we find two powers:

> In the soul there is a cognitive and an appetitive power. The term "good" expresses the conformity [*convenientiam*] of the being to the appetite, as is said at the beginning of the *Ethics*: "the good is what all things desire" [*Bonum est quod omnia appetunt*]. The term "true" expresses the conformity [*convenientiam*] of the being to the intellect. All cognition, however, is perfected by the assimilation of the knower to the thing known, thus this assimilation is said to be the cause of cognition: as vision cognizes color through being disposed as such through the species of color.[29]

Since every being as being is desirable, that is, able to satisfy our will, every being as being is *good*. Likewise, since every being as being is knowable, that is, able to actualize itself as itself (*qua* its intelligible species) in an intellect, it is *true*. But notice the example Thomas uses: "Every cognition is perfected by assimilation of the knower to the thing known, thus such assimilation is said to be the cause of cognition, just as vision cognizes color by that which is prepared through the species of color." According to Aristotle, whom Aquinas follows here, color is in the things only potentially; it becomes actualized as color only in the act of vision (by a living thing having a soul). Thus, for Aristotle, color is not a purely "subjective" or "mental" quality, since its cause is in the colored thing. But its actualization as this particular color only exists in and through the act of vision. So it is, Thomas seems to be saying, with

29. *De ver.*, I, 1.

being: being is really in the things—otherwise they would not exist! And insofar as being is in the thing, it is the cause of whatever notion or concept of being that is formed in the human intellect. But *as* being, being comes to be *qua* being only in and through the intellect; and it exists in and through the intellect as what is *true*.

We can, therefore, define being as true in three ways:[30] "the first comparison of the being to the intellect is according to its agreement with the intellect, which correspondence is said to be an adequation of thing and intellect; and in this definition of the true is formally perfected."[31] As the formal definition of truth, this—the adequation of thing and intellect[32]—is the root definition of truth. In the act of knowing, the being in itself and its being in the intellect are one and the same thing—they are convertible. Hence, we do not have here a "correspondence theory" of truth, where truth happens when the *representation* of a thing in the intellect "corresponds" with what it represents. Despite his use of the Latin word *correspondere*, Aquinas does not understand truth in this sense at all: more fundamental to his understanding of truth is the word *adaequatio*, which indicates a "being equal" or, perhaps, being "flip sides of the same coin" (to put it colloquially). Knowing and being known are two aspects of the same act or activity. We look at the truth of being in a second way in what precedes the definition of truth, and "in what the true is grounded; and thus Augustine defines truth in his book *The Soliloquies*: 'the true is that which is.'"[33] That is, every being

30. For an extensive discussion of these three ways, see John F. Wippel, "Truth in Thomas Aquinas, Part I," *The Review of Metaphysics* 43, no. 2 (1989): 295–326; and "Truth in Thomas Aquinas, Part II," *The Review of Metaphysics* 43, no. 3 (1990): 543–67.

31. *De ver.*, I, 1: "Prima ergo comparatio entis ad intellectum est ut ens intellectui correspondeat: quae quidem correspondentia, adaequatio rei et intellectus dicitur; et in hoc formaliter ratio veri perficitur."

32. Aquinas attributes this definition to the Jewish philosopher Isaac Israeli, as he says further on in the same question: "Et *alio modo* definitur secundum id quod formaliter rationem veri perficit; et sic dicit Isaac quod 'veritas est adaequatio rei et intellectus.'" But, as had been shown, this definition appears nowhere in the works of Isaac Israeli: J. T. Muckle, "Isaak Israeli's Definition of Truth," *Archives d'histoire doctrinale et littéraire du moyen âge* 8 (1933): 5–8.

33. *De ver.*, I, 1: "Uno modo secundum id quod praecedit rationem veritatis, et in quo verum fundatur; et sic Augustinus definit in lib. Solil. [c. v]: verum est id quod est."

is true in the sense that it can *cause* truth in an intellect; it can actualize the intellect as intellect. The third way in which we can consider being as true is "according to the consequences of its effects; and thus Hilary [of Poitiers] defines that the true is what manifests and declares existence."[34] The true is being as manifest or revealed.

Truth and being, therefore, go together not accidentally but essentially: "being *qua* being" makes no sense without relation to an intellect, because only in relation to an intellect is being being. But this also creates a conundrum: relation to an intellect is essential to being *qua* being, but any being is related to any human intellect only accidentally. That is, Aquinas is committed to the realist position that things in the world exist quite independently of us knowing them or not. They emphatically do not depend upon our knowing them in order to be. Thus Aristotle did not give much attention to being insofar as it is known, since he thought this was an accidental relationship; and even scholastic theologians of the early thirteenth century, as we mentioned above, tried to define truth without relation to the intellect. So how does Thomas resolve this conundrum which holds that relation to an intellect is essential to the notion of being *qua* being, but its relation to the human intellect is only accidental? He does this in the second question of the *De veritate*.

In this question, he asks "whether truth is more principally found in the intellect than in things" (*Utrum veritas principalius inveniatur in intellectu quam in rebus*). In his answer, he states quite clearly that to think of truth apart from its relation to the intellect is impossible and self-contradictory. "Things are not said to be true except according to their adequation to an intellect; thus the true is only posteriorly found in things, but [is found] in a prior fashion in the intellect" (*Res autem non dicitur vera nisi secundum quod est intellectui adaequata; unde per posterius invenitur verum in rebus, per prius autem in intellectu*). But, Aquinas continues, we must distinguish what sort of intellect we are talking about: if it is the practical intellect (that is, the intellect as employed in making something), then it is the intellect that "measures" or determines what the thing is by making it, but if it is the speculative intellect, then it is the

---

34. Ibid.: "Et tertio modo definitur verum, secundum effectum consequentem; et sic definit Hilarius, quod verum est manifestivum et declarativum esse."

intellect that is "measured" or determined by the thing known, since in speculative knowing or contemplation it is purely receptive to the truth of the thing:

> But it must be known that a thing is compared to the practical intellect in one way and otherwise to the speculative [intellect]. For the practical intellect causes the thing; hence it is the measuring of things which come to be through it. But the speculative intellect, because it receives [its cognition] from things, is in some way moved by the things themselves, and thus things measure it. This is clear in the case of natural things, which measure our intellect and from which our intellect gets its knowledge (*scientia*), as is said in book ten of the *Metaphysics*. But those things are measured by the divine intellect, by which all things are created, as all man-made things are measured in the mind of the artisan. Thus the divine intellect measures but is not measured; the natural thing measures and is measured; while our intellect is measured measuring not natural things, but artificial beings only [*Sic ergo intellectus divinus est mensurans non mensuratus; res autem naturalis, mensurans et mensurata; sed intellectus noster est mensuratus, non mensurans quidem res naturales, sed artificiales tantum*].[35]

That the things we make through our intellect are intelligible is clear, because we make them in accordance with a form or intelligible species of the thing in our minds. Why things that we do *not* make but are nevertheless quite intelligible to us (insofar as we think them speculatively) is not clear unless we suppose that they themselves *are made* by an intellect infinitely superior to our own. In other words, that beings are intelligible is due to the fact that they are essentially related to or measured by a supreme *creative* intellect—creative, because it makes them to be out of nothing. This intellect, of course, is the divine intellect. All things, therefore, for Thomas are "constituted," as it were, "between two intellects":

> The natural thing, therefore, is constituted between two intellects and is said to be true insofar as it is adequate to both. According to its adequation to the divine intellect, it is said to be true insofar as it fulfills the end to which it is ordered through the divine intellect.... It is said to be

35. Ibid., 2.

true according to its adequation to the human intellect insofar as it is in its nature [or "born"—*nata est*] to form from itself a true judgment; as to the contrary, things are said to be false the natures of which are ["born to"—*natae sunt*] such as to appear what they are not, or seem to possess qualities they do not possess, as is said in book five of the *Metaphysics*.[36]

Created things, therefore, act as a "screen," as it were, between two intellects, the divine and the human. There is not, at least naturally and at the beginning, a direct relation of measure and being measured between the human and divine intellects. The divine intellect measures the things that it creates and is not measured by them; creatures themselves are measured by the divine intellect but, in turn, measure the human intellect, since the human intellect cannot know anything apart from sense experience of creatures. Finally, the human intellect is measured by creatures but does not measure them; it is only the measure of what it makes through art or technology. Created beings, therefore, always mediate knowledge between the created intellect and the creative intellect.

Natural things are creatures precisely because they are intelligible, that is, *created*; and because they are created they can measure the human intellect and cause truth in it. Thus, natural beings are true precisely to the extent that they are created. But since the relation of creatures to the human intellect is accidental, they are true in the sense of being able to cause truth in an intellect; they are, in their very being-ness, first related to a divine, creative intellect. Thus, if, as is perfectly possible, the human intellect did not exist, then things would still remain true or knowable, but not if the divine intellect did not exist:

> The first notion of truth inheres in the thing prior to the second, because the conformity to the divine intellect is prior to that with the human. Thus, even if the human intellect did not exist, things would still be true due to their being ordered to the divine intellect. But if we were to try to conceive both intellects not to exist ["to be taken away"— *auferri*], which is impossible, then in no way would the notion of truth remain [*nullo modo veritatis ratio remaneret*].[37]

36. Ibid.
37. Ibid.

The non-existence of the divine intellect is impossible not just because Thomas is a Christian theologian committed to the truth of the Catholic faith. It is impossible from the nature itself of things, because without the divine intellect as the measure and creator of things, there would be no truth in things to discover or "unveil."[38] "Truth" would then only denote the contents of our mind without any reference to what is beyond the mind (which describes, in essence, the modern, post-Cartesian view of truth).

What this means, of course, is that the human intellect has no direct access to the divine intellect; it can only know the divine intellect through the things it has made. That is, we know the divine intellect only insofar as its contents are "incarnated" in some way. Hence, as we shall see in detail later, Romans 1:20, runs like a leitmotif through much of Aquinas's thinking: "Ever since the creation of the world, his invisible nature, namely, the eternal power and deity, has been clearly perceived in the things that have been made." Insofar then, as we use our natural powers of reason, we can come, indirectly, to a knowledge of God's existence and nature as well as to the truths of things. Nevertheless, this knowledge of the truths of things is very imperfect, as Pieper explains: "We can of course know things; we cannot formally know their *truth*. We know the copy, but not the relation of the copy to the archetype, the correspondence between what has been designed and its first design. To repeat, we have no power of perceiving this correspondence by which the formal truth of things is constituted. Here we can notice how truth and unknowability belong together."[39] The divine "archetypes" of things remain inaccessible to us. So while Plato was correct to

---

38. "Only what is thought can be called in the strict sense 'true,' but real things *are* something thought! It is essential to their nature ([Aquinas] would continue), that they are thought. They are real precisely *because* they are thought. To put it more explicitly, they are real because they are thought *creatively*, that is, they have been fashioned by thought. The essence of things is that they are creatively thought. This is to be taken literally and not in a figurative sense. Further, because things are themselves thoughts and have the 'character of a word' (as Guardini says), they may be called—in a quite precise and legitimate usage of the term—'true,' in the same way as one ordinarily calls true thoughts and what is thought." Pieper, *Silence of St. Thomas*, 51.

39. Ibid., 59.

posit archetypal forms or ideas for all things and his followers among the Neoplatonists were even closer to the truth in positing that these ideas were in a divine mind, they erred in thinking that the human intellect was capable of knowing them directly by detaching the soul from the body. Aristotle, on the other hand, was right to argue that what the human intellect knows primarily is the formal cause inherent in the natural thing itself and made accessible to us by sense perception. But since Aristotle did not think deeply enough to the reality of creation, he could not see that all things have an eminent, transcendent, and archetypal cause. For Thomas, it is the Christian (and Jewish) revelation of creation that allows the half-truths of Plato and Aristotle to come together into a full truth about the being of things and, indeed, their very truth.

For there to be truth, therefore, intellect must be prior to being, or at least created being. As Aquinas argues in question four of the *De veritate*, "Whether there is one Truth by which all things are true" (*Utrum sit una tantum veritas qua omnia sint vera*), we must say that truth is properly found not in beings but in the intellect just as "health" is properly found in the living organism and not in urine or a diet, although we call both "healthy" in relation to the living organism: "Truth is properly found in the human and divine intellect, as health in the animal. In other things, however, it is found in relation to an intellect, just as health is said to be in some other things insofar as it produces or conserves the health of an animal."[40] Thus, properly speaking, the truths of all things are most properly found as they are known or thought in the divine intellect, where, since God is perfectly simple and one, all truths are united in the one divine Truth. Nevertheless, in a secondary or derivative sense, there are many truths insofar as the truths of all things as found in the divine intellect are multiplied, via creatures, into the many minds or intellects of rational or intellectual creatures:

> If, therefore, truth, properly speaking, is accepted according to which all are principally true, all are therefore true by means of one truth, the truth of the divine intellect. And this is what Anselm says concerning truth in his book, *On Truth* [chaps. 8 and 12]. If, however, truth prop-

40. *De ver.*, I, 4.

erly speaking is accepted according to which things are said to be true secondarily [*secundum quam res secundario verae dicuntur*], then there are many truths of many true things in diverse souls. If, however, truth is accepted *improperly* speaking, according to which all things are said to be true [*secundum quam omnia dicuntur vera*], then there are many truths of many true things; but there is only one truth of any one thing.[41]

In one sense, then, there are many truths insofar as there are many created minds (human and angelic) in which the truths of things subsist; but in another sense, there is only one truth of every thing, which is the exemplar of each thing in the divine mind. "Every being is true, because through its form it is conformed to the divine intellect and conformable to the human intellect, that is, capable of making itself known."[42] This relation to intellect in general and to the divine intellect in particular is essential to the assertion that all beings, insofar as they exist, are true.

The intellect, then, is not just an accidental feature of our world. That any particular intellect exists is, of course, accidental, but not intellect as such.[43] Indeed, from this very fact—that intellect is an essential feature of the natural world, and yet any particular (created) intellect is accidental to it—leads Aquinas to posit, in both the venerable Peripatetic and Neoplatonic traditions, a hierarchy of intellects.[44] As we shall argue throughout, this hierarchy of intellects is a key element in Aquinas's philosophical theology. Intellectual substances are, of course, an integral part of the natural order that God has created—a Cartesian dualism where mental being and material being exist in separate, parallel realities is foreign to Thomas's thought. But intellectual substances

41. Ibid.

42. Aertsen, *Medieval Philosophy and the Transcendentals*, 398.

43. Such, indeed, is the thesis of a recent and very controversial book by Thomas Nagel, *Mind and Cosmos: Why the Materialist, Neo-Darwinian Conception of Nature Is almost Certainly False* (Oxford: Oxford University Press, 2012). Nagel, however, does not infer from this that "theism" is true.

44. "The fundamental principle of intellectualist metaphysics is that every spiritual Person is an idea, that there is a perfect identity between idea and spiritual reality. 'Intelligence in act' and 'intelligible in act' are for him two convertible notions. True ideas, true '*noumena*,' as one would say today, are pure spirits, 'subsistent intelligibles.'" Rousselot, *l'Intellectualisme de Saint Thomas*, xvii.

have properties that make them interact with other natural substances in uniquely important ways. One of these ways is that an intellectual substance is able to return upon itself; it is able to be aware of its own proper operation. Thus, when Aquinas deals with the question in *De veritate*, "Whether there is truth in the senses" (*Utrum veritas sit in sensu*, I, 9), Thomas distinguishes between the "non-reflexive" nature of sense perception and the self-reflective nature of intellection or cognition. Sense organs merely sense a property adequate to it; it does not judge what it senses and, hence, cannot tell us whether what it senses is truly in the thing sensed.[45] The case is wholly otherwise with intellectual substances, who are able to "return to their essence in a complete return":

> The reason for this is that those which are most perfect among beings, namely, the intellectual substances, return to their own essence with a complete return. In knowing something that is posited outside themselves, they proceed in a certain way outside of themselves; but to the extent to which they know themselves to know, they already begin to return to themselves, because the act of knowing mediates between the knower and the thing known. But this return is completed according to the degree to which they know their proper essences. Thus it is said in the *Book of Causes* [prop. 15] that everyone knowing his own essence, returns to his essence by a complete return [*omnis sciens essentiam suam, est rediens ad essentiam suam reditione completa*].[46]

What makes an intellectual substance unique among substances is its ability "to go out" and receive the intelligible species of things and then "return to itself" with those species. And in doing so, it does not become less than what it is but more: the intellection or cognition of those intelligible species actualizes it more as a distinct substance, not less. On the one hand, intellectual substance is open to receiving within itself in their formal reality all beings as beings. Indeed, as intellectual, it is able to "read into" (*intus-legere*) the essences of all beings and even into

45. See *De ver.*, I, 9: "Quamvis enim sensus cognoscat se sentire, non tamen cognoscit naturam suam, et per consequens nec naturam sui actus, nec proportionem eius ad res, et ita nec veritatem eius."
46. Ibid.

the essence of being *qua* being. By contrast, the senses and the imagination can only remain "on the exterior" of things.[47] But on the other hand, the intellectual substance is quite distinct from other natural substances precisely because it can "go out" into things but then "return into itself" with its intellectual nature "reinforced" rather than "diluted." It is this very "relationality" to the world around it in tension with a distinct "inner world" that makes the intellectual substance what it is.

Nevertheless, crucial to understanding what Thomas asserts about the relation of the intellect to being, to creation, and to the phenomenon of revelation is an understanding of what Thomas presents as a "hierarchy" or, better, a "scale" of intellects (Thomas never uses the word "hierarchy" in this context). As the Jesuit priest Pierre Rousselot pointed out more than a century ago, "intellection is not something 'univocal,' but is intrinsically different … according to the different intelligent beings."[48] The human intellect, it is crucial to realize, is at the bottom of this hierarchy: it is an intellect that is essentially united to a body, because it needs sense perception in order to know any specific content and thus be actualized as intellect. It can, therefore, only return to itself via sense perception:

> We are the last, the lowest, in the intellectual order; we are blind before the greatest clarity of nature, like the bat is before the sun. The entire noetic of Saint Thomas is nothing other than the development of this primal idea; all of his intellectualism, when applied to man, is dependent upon it. It is therefore necessary to consider it at all times. When one forgets this capital restriction and reads Saint Thomas implicitly supposing the identity of human intelligence with intelligence as such, then his entire system becomes something childish and contradictory. When Averroes made intelligence in itself equal to what is humanly comprehensible, he had said something "very ridiculous."[49]

Contrary to what he supposed Averroes to have held, Thomas argues strenuously that the human intellect is fully individualized in a real flesh

---

47. "Sensus enim et imaginatio sola exteriora accidentia cognoscunt." Ibid., 12.

48. Rousselot, *l'Intellectualisme de Saint Thomas*, 3.

49. Ibid., 56. See also Aquinas, *Summa contra Gentiles*, ed. Ceslaus Pera (Turin: Marietti, 1961), III, 45. Hereafter, *SCG*.

and blood body. For only when we understand the human intellect's true place within the framework of creation do we understand the true nature of the world as creation and the necessity for grace and revelation for the perfection of the human intellect. Only by understanding the inherent limits of the human intellect is Thomas able both to affirm the human intellect's intellectual nature and ability to know the truth and to put into relief its need for the grace of revelation.[50] And as Josef Pieper notes, this affirmation of the "over-intelligibility" of being is what is prior and more fundamental:

> Because hope is much closer to affirmation than to denial, the "negative element" in the philosophy of St. Thomas, which we set out to formulate, must be envisaged against the background of an embracing affirmation. That the essences of things are unknowable is part of the notion of the truth of Being. But so little does this denote objective inaccessibility, the impossibility of cognition, or darkness on the part of things, that there is, on the contrary, this striking paradox: In the last resort, things are inaccessible to human knowledge precisely because they are all too knowable.[51]

Every being as being is knowable; but the truth, the exemplar or idea in the divine mind, in and through which that being was created, came to be, is not knowable (to a finite intellect, at least). And yet, as Pieper argues, the first knowability stands on or is founded on the second unknowability. Things are knowable precisely to the extent that their knowable content exceeds the power of our intellect to know that content. Thomas is not a naïve realist who thinks that our minds can correspond perfectly with the things it knows. Rather, he is a critical realist: our minds can know the truth of things, but what things are in their ultimate, creative truth, it cannot know.

For something to be *in* its truth is for it to be in the mind that made

---

50. "Thus, examining more closely its demands in the matter of certain truth, one is convinced that one of the essential pieces of philosophy is a contemptuous criticism of human understanding. His [Thomas's] intellectualism stands opposed to 'rationalism' above all. 'The human soul is the last in the series of intelligences, participating the least intellectual power.'" Rousselot, *l'Intellectualisme de Saint Thomas*, 236.

51. Pieper, *Silence of St. Thomas*, 70.

it. As the prologue to St. John's Gospel says, the essences of things, even those without life, are life in the mind of God. So all things can be seen in two ways: either with respect to the existence they have in themselves or with respect to their being in the Word of God, in the divine mind.[52] All things, therefore, find their ultimate truth not in some abstract essence or form, but in the first intellectual substance;[53] they find their truth in the life of God's Word.

In book four of his *Summa contra Gentiles*, Thomas links the order or gradation of intellects with "generation" and life of the divine Trinity.[54] In this remarkable passage, Thomas traces a continuum between the ontological structure of the lowest, most basic natural beings to the superabundant life and intelligence of the Holy Trinity. First, Thomas states as a basic principle, "the higher some nature is [in the scale of being], to that degree what emanates from it is more intimate to it" (*Quanto aliqua natura est altior, tanto id quod ex ea emanat, magis ei est intimum*). Now, "in all things, inanimate bodies hold the lowest place" (*In rebus enim omnibus inanimata copora infimum locum tenent ...*). The actions of such beings can only act "one upon another," such as when fire generates fire or consumes or alters another being by its action, while remaining in quality and species fire. This is in contrast to the lowest of animate beings, plants (*inter animata vero corpora proximum locum tenent plantae ...*). Unlike inanimate bodies, plants have a principle of motion and development within them due to their immanent form or soul. But the life of plants is still imperfect, "because, granted that the emanation in them proceeds from within, nevertheless gradually that which emanates issuing from within is found finally to be completely

52. "'Even the essences of things, that in themselves do not have life, are life in God's mind.' And in the commentary on John, he writes concerning the 'Word' of the prologue: 'What was made, was in him life': things can be seen in a twofold manner: according to the being they have in themselves and according to their being in his WORD." Pieper, *Wahrheit der Dinge*, 51.

53. "The philosophy of St. Thomas cannot be a 'panlogism,' because it places at the origin of things not axioms or an axiom, but freedom and a living mind." Rousselot, *l'Intellectualisme de Saint Thomas*, 117–18.

54. *SCG* IV, 11: "Quodmodo accipenda sit generatio in divinis, et quae de filio Dei dicuntur in scripturis."

extrinsic" (*est tamen vita plantarum imperfecta: quia emanatio in eis licet ab interiori procedat, tamen paulatim ab interioribus exiens quod emanat, finaliter omnino extrinsecum invenitur*). Thus, Aquinas says, the "humor" to be found in the tree gives rise to a flower, then a fruit, which then is separated completely from the tree to become the seed of another tree. Beyond plants, however, we find a higher grade of life:

> Which is the sensitive soul: whose proper emanation, even if it begins from the outside [that is, in sense perception], terminates in the inside [that is, in sensory experience]; and the more that the emanation advances, the more it reaches what is within [*quanto emanatio magis processerit, tanto magis ad intima devenitur*].... Still its life is not completely perfect, since its emanation always arises from some first to some second.[55]

The animal experiences sense objects, which, then, actualize and become part of its imagination and memory. The sense objects, as sense objects, become a part of the animal's inner life. Nevertheless, the animal, in both its perceptions and its actions, is still governed by those sense objects. It is wholly determined by its sense environment.

This brings Aquinas to the highest "grade" of living substance—the intellectual substance—of which it is crucial to note that, within this grade, there are various further grades of intellect.[56] As Aquinas mentions here, what characterizes an intellectual substance most of all is that it can "turn back into itself" (*in seipsum reflectitur*) and thus "be able to understand itself" (*seipsum intelligere potest*).[57] At the lowest grade of intellect is, of course, the human intellect, which has been noted before. The human intellect can only be actualized from outside, by sense experience, and can, therefore, only think by means of sense images or phantasms. The human intellect can "turn back into itself," and it can "understand itself," but only indirectly, by reflecting upon its cogni-

---

55. Ibid.

56. "In intellectuali vita diversi gradus inveniuntur." Ibid.

57. "*Omnis intelligens est rediens ad essentiam suam reditione completa.* By definition, it is necessary to know oneself in order to know the truth as such. Reflection is thus a condition of intelligence, and intellection, type of the immanent act, is postulated as the only action that can be perfectly the grasp of the other." Rousselot, *l'Intellectualisme de Saint Thomas*, 16.

tion of sense objects. This is in contrast to angelic intellects, "in whom the intellect proceeds to a cognition of itself not from anything exterior [to it], but cognizes itself through itself" (*perfectior igitur est intellectualis vita in angelis in quibus intellectus ad sui cognitionem non procedit ex aliquo exterior, sed per se cognoscit seipsum*). Since angels are pure intellects not in need of a body for their proper operation, they know things not through sense perception but by means of intelligible forms or species of all things infused in them at their creation by God. Or to put it in other words, their knowledge of things is innate to them. Thus, their knowledge of things proceeds from inside out: they know a thing by looking at the intelligible species of the thing innate in themselves. Still, angelic intellects do not constitute the highest grade of intellect for the simple reason that their intellects are finite and created; they do not exist in and of themselves but need an act of God's creative power in order to come to be. "Their understanding is not the same as their existence" (*non est idem in eis intelligere et esse*).

"The ultimate perfection of life, therefore, belongs to God, in whom to understand is not other than to be.... Thus it is necessary that in God the intention understood be the divine essence itself."[58] A word that Thomas uses here, "intention" (*intentio*), is a technical scholastic term that demands some explanation. When the human intellect understands or "cognizes," it always understands "something": that is, the human mind always "reaches out" or "intends" an object in thought. It does this by means of an "intelligible species," which is the intelligible form of the thing known insofar as it is in relation to some mind or intellect. Thus, strictly speaking, the intelligible species belongs neither to the thing as such nor to the intellect as such: it arises only insofar as it unites the intelligible (the thing) and the intelligence (the intellect) in one act. Hence, we have sciences whose objects are things themselves (such as physics) and others whose objects are the intentions in and through which we understand the intelligible forms or aspects of things (such as logic).[59] But this distinction cannot hold for God, in whom,

58. *SCG* IV, 11: "ultima igitur perfectio vitae competit Deo, in quo non est aliud intelligere et aliud esse ... ita oportet quod intentio intellecta in Deo sit ipsa divina essentia."

59. "unde et aliae scientiae sunt de rebus, et aliae de intentionibus intellectis." Ibid.

due to his utter unity and simplicity, what is understood and the intention by which it is understood are one and the same. What is known and the act by which it is known are one and the same. God does not "generate" concepts or ideas as we do. We cannot, therefore, compare any generation in God with the kinds of generation with which we are familiar in the natural world: God does not generate as inanimate things do by imprinting their species onto matter; nor does he generate as plants or even animals do by generating a thing exterior to themselves; nor does he generate like the sensitive soul or even the human intellect, by receiving and forming impressions or species from outside of himself, because God is prior to all things and sufficient in himself. "It remains therefore that divine generation must be understood as an intellectual emanation" (*reliquitur igitur quod generatio divina secundum intellectualem emanationem sit intelligenda*).

The implications of this insight for Thomas's understanding of the essential place of the intellect within creation cannot be overemphasized. For the human intellect it is of capital importance that its act of intellection is not the same as its act of existence; its knowing is contingent upon its being, which is itself contingent being. The human being as *pure intellect* (*à la* Descartes) is not a "true human being" but rather a "similitude" of one:

> It is not thus [as with the divine intellect] with the word of the human intellect. When our intellect understands itself, the being [*esse*] of its intellect is one thing while its understanding is another: the substance of the intellect was understanding in potency before it understood in act. It follows therefore that the being [*esse*] of the intention understood is one thing, while the intellect itself is another, since the being [*esse*] of the intention understood is the being itself understood. Hence it is necessary that, in the man who understands himself, the inner word that is conceived is not the true man, having the natural being [*esse*] of a man; but is *man-intellect* only, a certain similitude, as it were, of the true man apprehended by the intellect [*sed sit "homo intellectus" tantum, quasi quaedam similitudo hominis veri ab intellectu apprehensa*].[60]

60. Ibid.

The image or similitude by which the person grasps him- or herself in thought is always "less" that the flesh and blood human being. This is not the case with God whose being (*esse*) and understanding (*intelligere*) are one and the same. He can, therefore, grasp himself in a Word that is fully adequate to himself, who is indeed true God and not just a similitude or image:

> The Word of God itself, from which it is that God is intellect, is true God, having naturally the divine being [*esse divinum*]: in it the natural being of God is not one thing and his understanding another thing, as has been said. Hence it is said in John 1:1: "God was the Word." This is so because, said absolutely, it demonstrates that the Word of God ought to be understood to be true God. The word of a man cannot be said simply and absolutely to be man, but only in a derivative way, insofar as man is intellect [*Verbum enim hominis non posset dici simpliciter et absolute homo, sed secundum quid, scilicet homo intellectus*]: hence this would be false: *man is word*; but this can be true: *the man as intellect is word*. When, therefore, it is said, *God is Word*, it is shown that the divine Word is not only the intention understood, as our word [is]; but it is also a thing existing and subsisting in nature. The true God is a subsistent thing, since he is maximally being in itself [*per se*].[61]

It follows from this that the Word of God in God is not simply an image or similitude of God but God himself; but since the Word is generated eternally from God's intellection, the Word, who is true God, is called "Son" (*reliquitur igitur quod Verbum Dei non solum sit imago, sed etiam Filius*). That is to say, the Word of God is not just an intellectual reality, like an image or idea for us, but a fully subsistent being, like for us the son of a father. Only God can apprehend himself as "true God," that is, as fully what God is in himself, which is to say, in his truth. The human being cannot do this; he or she can only grasp an image or similitude of him- or herself in thought. Hence, as we shall see, the Incarnation of the Word of God in Christ will become key not only to human knowledge about God but even to human self-knowledge. For as both God and man, fully each without distinction or mixture, Christ is able to present

61. Ibid.

man with an object adequate to understanding both himself and God.[62]

We have thus, in the divine being, a qualified inversion of Aristotle's assertion that, in the categories of being, substance comes first, followed by the accidents of quantity, quality, and so on down to relation, which he argued denoted the "least" being among the categories.[63] And with regard to natural beings, Aristotle was, of course, right: relations depend on substances for them to be at all. But when we look at creation and the creative intellect that grounds creation, things are not so simple. In the divine intellect, relation expresses the fullness and perfection of substance even if, as Norris Clarke argues, substance remains the "primary mode" of reality:

> It turns out, then, that relationality and substantiality go together as two distinct but inseparable modes of reality. Substance is the primary mode, in that all else, including relations, depend on it as their ground. But since "every substance exists for the sake of its operations," as St. Thomas has just told us (*S. Th.* I, 105, 5; SCG III, 113), being as substance, as existing *in itself*, naturally flows over into being as relational, as turned *towards others* by its self-communicating action. *To be* fully is to be *substance-in-relation*.[64]

Being is not being if it is inert; "to be" is "to act" and "to act" is to communicate its being, to be, as Clarke puts it, "*substance-in-relation*."[65] Indeed, we already saw in the passage above from book four of the *Summa contra Gentiles* how even the lowest level of beings communicate themselves by impressing their species onto matter; only they do not and cannot return into themselves. The higher we move up in the scale of

---

62. *S. Th.* III, 59, 2, ad 1: "Utrum iudicaria potestas conveniat Christo secundum quod est homo."

63. *Aristotelis Metaphysica*, ed. W. Jaeger (Oxford: Oxford University Press, 1957), N, 1 (1088a30).

64. Norris Clarke, SJ, *Person and Being* (Milwaukee: Marquette University Press, 1993), 14.

65. This is not to say that "to be" or "to exist" is to be in a constant state of change or flux: the act referred to here is primarily the first act of the substance upon which all its other acts are founded and from which all its other acts flow. As long as a being is, it is in act, whatever *accidental* changes may occur to it. Thus, separate or spiritual substances are always in act although they do not "change" per se.

being, however, the more intimately substance relates to the world and to itself. Substance does this first as the human intellect in its knowing an "outside world" in relation to the "inner world" of the intellect. Already in being able to actualize an intellect as intellect (and not as what the thing is in its natural being), beings show within themselves an inherent relationality to a knowing subject as "objects" that are "already there" as objects.[66] This relationship deepens in the human being when the act of knowing becomes one of self-presence and self-possession— when we become a self-aware and self-determining person:[67] "To be a person in its own right, such a nature would have to possess or 'own' its own act of existence (*esse*).... Ordinary language indicates quite clearly the distinction by two distinct questions:'*who* am I?' (person) and '*what* am I?' (nature)."[68] But, as Father Clarke argues, in realizing himself as a person, the human being also opens himself up to being as being, which takes him beyond his own proper form to relate to the cause of being itself:

> To be a person is to be intrinsically expansive, ordered toward self-manifestation and self-communication. This is the decisive advance over the Aristotelian substance, which was indeed, as nature, ordered toward action and reception, but, as form, was oriented primarily toward self-realization, the fulfillment of its own perfection as form, rather than sharing with others. The Neoplatonic dynamism of the self-diffusiveness of the good as taken over by St. Thomas is needed to expand this orientation toward action beyond the self-centered viewpoint

66. "The doctrine of the truth of things asserts that things are in fact by their very nature 'object,' that they have thus from their very nature 'being for someone.' Truth [as knowability] is as inherent in things as being itself.... Every correlation between being and infinite spirit exists already before any actual realization of knowing takes place. The relationship of object-subject is thus not, according to the old doctrine of being, 'a creation of the mind,' as Nicholas Hartmann says; it is much more the case that it is discovered by it [the mind] already." Pieper, *Wahrheit der Dinge*, 69–71.

67. "In a word, when being is allowed to be fully itself as active *presence*, it *ipso facto* turns into luminous *self-presence* and *self-possession*, that is, self-consciousness in the order of knowledge and self-determination in the order of action. But these are precisely the essential attributes of person. To *be* fully, without restriction, therefore, is to be personal." Clarke, *Person and Being*, 25.

68. Ibid., 27.

of form towards the wider horizon of other persons and the universe as a whole.[69]

In the self-presence and self-possession of the human person, there opens up the possibility of relating as person to the cause of all there is, to the Creator himself. This possibility issues logically from the meta-physical analysis of being as being and being as true. Nevertheless, it opens up onto a uniquely Christian vision of existence and the human being's place in it.[70] Indeed, precisely because it is the lowest of intel-lects, the human intellect is capable of God: in its pure intellectual po-tency, it can be "made over" into the divine image. Hence, the realization that being as being is true, leads to the realization that true being is intellectual being and true intellectual being is personal being, which graciously draws all being into relation to itself as person and intellect. Thus, while relation does not replace substance as the highest category of being, it perfects substance in its own category.

INTELLECT AND GRACE

Aquinas not only argues that being as being is intelligible, but also that being as being is also far more intelligible than our limited minds can grasp. What things are in their ultimate truth—in the divine exemplars in and through which they are created—we cannot know in this life. But the intellect is not our only route to the divine; we also have a will, a rational appetite, that desires and seeks the ultimate good. That which is desirable, we call "good." That which actualizes us in our properly human functions is a *true* good (and hence, truth is the good of the intellect). That which fully actualizes us with respect is the ultimate or

69. Ibid., 71–72.

70. As Rousselot noted long ago, while Muslim philosophers, in order to maintain God's absolute transcendence and inaccessibility, made our beatitude consist in union with the angelic intellects (as we saw with Averroes, we only know God to the degree that our union with the separate intellects is *analogous* to the unity of God with his own intellect) and even Jewish philosophers, like Ibn Gabriol, denied any proportion between God and the "separate intellect," Aquinas, without in any way compromising the divine transcen-dence, asserted that the lowest of intellects are "capable of God." Rousselot, *l'Intellectualisme de Saint Thomas*, 38.

supreme good that is beyond any created nature to attain is the *summum bonum*. Since our desire for this supreme good takes us beyond what our intellect can know, we must consider it as an essential concept in coming to a full understanding of being and the ultimate cause of being. Hence, we must look at the transcendental, "good" (*bonum*).

In question 21, article 1, of the *De veritate*, Aquinas asks in what sense "good" "adds" something to the notion, "being" (*Utrum bonum aliquid addat supra ens*). Thomas answers by noting that something can be added to something in three ways: (1) something can be added to something else as something outside the essence of the thing added to—such as saying that a body is white; (2) something can be added as a contraction to a genus, such as adding "humanity" to "animal"; or (3) something can be added in reason only, as a man can be said to be blind, since blindness is not anything in nature but is a privation. "Good" cannot be added to being in the first two senses, since goodness is neither a "quality" accidental to being nor is it a "species" of being. That leaves the third sense of "addition." But goodness is not a privation but is something eminently positive. Hence, it adds something to being by reason in a sense different from the usual one insofar as it adds the notion of a "positive" relation of being to the will. That is, every being insofar as it exists is desirable at some level and this desirability is essential to it, not accidental. Being as being is inherently capable of satisfying an appetite or desire. So whereas being as true perfects the thing known rather than the knower (save incidentally, as knower or intellect) by bringing it into intellectual existence, as participation of its original existence as an exemplar in the divine mind, being as good perfects the one who desires it.

Between knowledge and what is knowable and between desire and what is desirable, there is an asymmetrical relationship. Human knowledge and desire depend on the things known and desired for them to come into being; it is not the other way around.[71] As such then, being as true and good adds over the concept "being" the notion of something that perfects (*Oportet igitur quod verum et bonum super intellectum entis addant respectum perfectivi*). That is to say, being as being perfects or

71. *De ver.*, XXI, 1.

fully actualizes the human soul with respect to its most salient, proper, and essential operations—that of understanding and will. But, more specifically, being as good actualizes the human soul not just as intellect but as whole human being, body and soul:

> In another way a being is perfective of another not only according to the formal reality (*ratio*) of its species, but also according to the existence which it has in the nature of things. And in this mode the *good* is perfective. The good then is in things, as the Philosopher says in book 6 of the *Metaphysics*. Insofar as one being is, according to its existence [*esse*], perfective of another and conserves it, it stands as an end with respect to that which it perfects; and that is why all who rightly define the good posit in its notion [*ratio* something which pertains to having an end. Thus the Philosopher says in book 1 of his *Ethics*, that "they define the good the best who say that the good is that which all things desire."[72]

Knowledge of the true alone, therefore, is not completely perfective of the human being as creature, at least not insofar as he or she depends completely on their natural powers of reason alone or in what they can know from nature alone. As we saw above, the ultimate truth of things is inaccessible to us in our fallen state. It is only the desire for the good, and in particular the "good that all things desire" that the whole human being, intellect included, is drawn beyond creatures to a relationship with the Creator himself that is, in turn, genuinely perfective of the human intellect as intellect.

Thus, Thomas argues that, while absolutely speaking, the true is prior to—more basic logically and ontologically—than the good, it is not that way in our fallen state, that is, insofar as we are pilgrims on this earth (*in via* or insofar as we are *homines viatores*). As Thomas argues in article 3 of question 21 of the *De veritate* (*Utrum bonum secundum rationem sit prius quam verum*), we can look at perfections in two ways: "in one way from the perspective of the perfection itself, and in another way from the thing perfected" (*uno modo ex parte ipsarum perfectionum; alio modo ex parte perfectibilium*). From the second perspective, the good is prior to the true for two reasons: "the first is because the perfection of the good extends

72. Ibid.

to more things than the perfection of the true" (*Primo, quia perfectio boni ad plura se extendit quam perfectio veri*). All things, whether intelligent or not (and even whether animate or not, since inanimate elements, such as the earth, seek or "desire" their proper place), desire the good; while only beings with intelligence can know the true. Secondly,

> because those which are capable of being [or are "born to be"—*nata sunt*] perfected by the good and the true, are perfected by the good before they are by the true. From the fact that they participate in existence [*esse*], they are perfected by the good, as was said; from the fact, however, that they know something, they are perfected by the true. Now cognition is posterior to existence [*esse*]; hence in this consideration from the standpoint of perfectible beings, the good precedes the true.[73]

While the true is prior to the good in that all things aim towards their immaterial exemplar or truth in the divine mind, nevertheless, from our standpoint, knowledge of the truth depends on our existence, and existence is a perfection of things in their natural being, which is what is meant by the "good." It follows from this that, while the intellect is, absolutely speaking, "higher" (*altior*) than the will, because its end is contemplation of God and his Truth without restriction, the will is, nevertheless, "higher" in this life, because a will that is rightly guided by love of God and the truth perfects the human being while "here below" in his or her created existence.[74] This is because it often happens that the will can have an object that is "nobler" than what the human intellect can grasp or understand in this life:

> And thus the Philosopher said in *Metaph*. VI that *good and evil*, which are objects of the will, *are in things*; but *true and false*, which are objects of the intellect, *are in the mind*. When therefore the thing in which there is good is nobler than the soul, in which the notion [*ratio*] is understood; in relation to such a thing, the will is higher than the intellect. When however, the thing in which there is good is below the soul, then in relation to such a thing, the intellect is higher than the will. Hence, love of God is better than knowledge of God; whereas to the contrary,

---

73. Ibid., 3.
74. *S. Th.* I, 82, 3: "Utrum voluntas sit altior potentia quam intellectus."

knowledge of corporeal things is better than love of them. Nevertheless, simply speaking, the intellect is nobler than the will.[75]

The love of God is better than the knowledge of God, when God as he is in his essence cannot be known by our fallen and finite intellect. By necessity, we must love what we do not fully know, even though that love yearns for its completion in full and clear knowledge of the beloved. In short, this love of God presents itself to us as a *mystery*: as a desire for an absolute Good that is yet veiled and hidden from us. It is a mystery in no way unlike the mystery of the human person, where there is someone who draws us to him- or herself in love and desire, and yet whose inner life and thought remain hidden from us, except insofar as he or she chooses to reveal aspects of that life to us. This knowledge of the other grows as intimacy in love grows, which is why Aquinas remarks that, in this life, it is better to love God than to know God: the sort of knowledge we have of God as he is in himself (as opposed to as he is as First Cause) can *only* come about through such loving intimacy. This is why creatures constitute, as we saw above, a sort of "screen" between the divine and human intellects: it is to draw the human intellect more deeply into the mystery of the Creator as *person*, as *substance-in-relation*. Material creation, therefore, is not an obstacle but a means of grace (and hence, the original *sacrament*). Pure, Christian love is not simply a defective or substitute mode of knowing but the very way to a higher mode of knowing divine truth in itself. This mode of knowing whereby someone freely reveals something about him- or herself to another that is either inaccessible to the other or accessible only with great difficulty is precisely what Thomas means by *revelation*. As such then, all revelation is the *gracious* giving of truth about God himself; revelation is a *grace*, which is consequent upon God's pure goodness and truth and which builds upon the goodness of his creation.

Now, the subject of grace in Thomas's thought is vast and complicated and we cannot do it here anywhere near the justice it deserves.[76] But what

75. Ibid.

76. For a fuller account of Thomas's understanding of grace, see Joseph Wawrykow, "Grace," in *The Theology of Thomas Aquinas*, ed. Rik van Nieuwenhove and Joseph Wawrykow (South Bend, Ind.: University of Notre Dame Press, 2005), 192–221; and John F. Wippel, "Natur und Gnade (S.th. I-II, qq. 109–14)," in Speer, *Thomas von Aquin*, 246–70.

we can say is that, because creation itself is a free and gratuitous act, we cannot reason to the essential being of the first cause through creation alone. We can reason *that* there is a cause and, given the inherent nature of a First Cause, what must be some of the necessary attributes of that cause. But we cannot know *who* that being is in himself from creation alone, any more than I can know the hidden inner life of someone from what he or she makes (though I can make guesses about his or her skill, knowledge, and sensibility from those products). In addition to the "natural light of reason" the human being needs a "light of grace" (*lumen gratiae*) in and through which God graciously reveals himself to us.[77] But as Rudi te Velde notes, the need for grace "is not a defect of creation. The work of grace is not a supplement to creation in the sense that the work of creation would otherwise remain imperfect and incomplete."[78] Grace relates us to the mystery of God's being, truth, and love in ways that would be impossible from the standpoint of purely natural being. "The point of grace is, so to speak, that God gives himself freely to be known and to be loved by raising the human creature to the level of the divine nature, which is superior to any created nature."[79] Rather than an obstacle to unity between the human and the divine, creation makes possible an even deeper, more intimate and personal unity in that it opens up the mystery of truth in love. To quote te Velde again:

> The intellectual desire for truth cannot find its ultimate satisfaction in the philosophical knowledge of the transcendent and divine causes of visible reality, as the conditions of such knowledge remain bound to its starting point in sense-perception. Perfect happiness requires that the created intellect become connected with the infinite (uncreated) essence of God, a connection that can never be realized by the finite power of created nature itself. The proper dimension of grace in the Christian promise of eternal life in unity with God can only be accounted for against the background of the notion of creation, since the idea of creation implies the free transcendence of God with respect to created (finite) nature as such. This is why, according to Thomas, true happiness

---

77. *S. Th.* I-II, 109, 1: "Utrum homo sine gratia aliquod verum cognoscere possit."
78. Te Velde, *Aquinas on God*, 151.
79. Ibid.

cannot be conceived of as part of nature (*aliquid naturae*), but only as the end of nature as such (*finis naturae*).[80]

Creation opens up a mystery that cannot be penetrated by natural reason; it also opens up the possibility of love and grace that can close the gap between Creator and creature such that the creature can share in the divinity of the Creator, because by the same freedom in and by which God created the world God can create the human being anew in a way that transcends his natural being. For while "grace" or favor shown by a human being toward someone presupposes some good in the person shown favor, God's grace actually makes good, even divine, as an "adopted son or daughter," the one shown his grace.[81] In grace, the Christian is not shown favor due to any of his or her own qualities or the merit of his or her works; but simply by relating in love and faith to the mystery of God's love and self-revelation in Christ, he or she is drawn into the divine life and related in the essence of his or her soul to the divine life, which is itself *substance-in-relation* or Trinitarian.

Of course, this participation of the Christian in the divine life is very imperfect in this life. But by the same token, grace is not simply some exterior force that moves us toward God; it transforms us from within. Or, as Thomas puts it, grace is not an efficient cause moving toward God, like a stick moving a stone, but rather it operates more like a formal cause, as "whiteness makes white and justice makes just."[82] In other words, grace is meant to transform us into what or who is its source essentially, a creative intellect who in his goodness communicates himself to himself essentially and to his creatures by participation.[83] It is through grace, then, that the mysteries of creation and participation, of truth and the super-intelligibility of the world such that it surpasses the capability of our finite intellect to know become manifest.

80. Ibid., 159.

81. *S. Th.* I-II, 110, 1: "Utrum gratia ponat aliquid in anima."

82. "Sicut albedo facit album, et iustitia iustum." Ibid., 2, ad 1: "Utrum gratia sit qualitas animae."

83. The human soul, of course, participates imperfectly in the divine goodness and thus participates in the divine goodness in a way inferior to the way in which it is its own substance. But since the divine goodness is so much nobler than the nature of the soul, it is still able to transform it. See ibid., ad 2.

CONCLUSION

For Aquinas, a philosophical analysis of the our most basic concepts leads us to the seeing of all being *qua* being as one, true, and good. And indeed, this is a basic insight that he owes in no small part to the work of the Muslim philosopher Avicenna. Being as such is undivided, knowable, and desirable. And why is this so? Because it is already united, known, and desired by a being that can only be being, oneness, intellect, and goodness in itself, and by necessity, God. But whereas for Avicenna the forms that give things their being, intelligibility, and goodness "emanate" from a separate agent intellect,[84] for Aquinas these forms and the intelligibility and desirability that follow upon them are deeply *incarnate* in creation. We know creatures, and through them God, not by being attuned to a separate intellect but in and through our embodied presence in the world. Thus, God already reveals himself in a way in the embodied things of this world and through them reveals himself to the human intellect. And to the extent that the human intellect is open to the natures of things through a properly ordered love of them, then it is conformed by grace to the divine Truth.

But this understanding of the human intellect as perfective in its incarnate individuality faced a direct challenge in the assertion by many in the thirteenth century. Following the authority of the Commentator (Averroes), certain thinkers claimed that there could only be one separate intellect for all men. To establish, therefore, what the Christian tradition claimed to be the proper relation between reason and revelation, Aquinas had to meet this challenge head-on.

84. Averroes was actually quite critical of this aspect of Avicenna's "cosmological psychology," arguing that this went decisively against the teaching of Aristotle that the forms were immanent in the material things themselves and did not emanate from a separate intellect. Nevertheless, as we saw in chapter two and will see again in the next chapter, Averroes compounded his difficulties by arguing not only that the *agent* human intellect by which we know the intelligible forms of things is ontologically separate but also the *material or potential* intellect too. That is, he only keeps the forms of things in the material world by taking the human intellect out of it.

CHAPTER 5

WHY DOES THE UNITY OF THE INTELLECT BECOME SUCH A BURNING ISSUE IN MEDIEVAL THOUGHT?

Aquinas on Human Knowing as Incarnate Knowing

It is not often that Thomas Aquinas allows passion to break through the calm dispassion of his words. Yet, the tone of Thomas's little treatise *De unitate intellectus contra Averroistas*, or *On the Unity of the Intellect against the Averroists*, shows surprising flashes of impatience and even anger at his philosophical opponents. This is not to say that Thomas loses self-command: he marshals his arguments with the same precision as ever; nevertheless, the reader gets a distinct feeling that something in the doctrine of the "Averroists" has touched a nerve. What is it precisely that has touched this nerve?

DEFINING THE PROBLEM

The immediate cause for Thomas's concern is that "He [Averroes] tries to assert that the intellect that Aristotle calls the possible intellect, but that he himself calls by the unsuitable name 'material,' is a certain substance in its being separate from the body nor in any way united to it as its form, and furthermore that this possible intellect is one for all men."[1] Now, this is clearly destructive of religion as understood by any informed Christian:

> It is not now our affair to show that this position stated above is false, for it is repugnant to the truth of the Catholic faith; this is quite obvious to whoever looks into it. If we take away from men the diversity of intellect, which alone among the parts of the soul appears to be incorruptible and immortal, it follows that after death nothing would remain of the souls of men except the single substance of the intellect; and so would be taken away the recompense of rewards and punishments and their diversity.[2]

It should be clear that such a doctrine is in conflict with the core tenets of the Christian faith as it had always been understood (just as al-Ghazali argued was the case for orthodox Islam). If there is no individual intellect, then there is no personal responsibility before God, making rewards and punishments in the hereafter meaningless.

But, as Thomas remarks from the outset in his little treatise, "we intend to show that the above-mentioned position [of the Averroists] is no less against the principles of philosophy than against the teachings of the Faith."[3] That is, the position of the Averroists is not only theologically untenable, but also philosophically untenable. If Averroes and his Latin followers are right, every act of understanding on the part of the human being would constitute *a miracle*, since, on their account, human knowing is the work, ultimately, of an extrinsic and, indeed, supernatural principle. The writings of certain Latin Averroists, like Siger de Brabant, seemed to argue for a bifurcation between natural and supernatural knowledge: philosophy deals with *rationes naturales* and, as such, cannot grasp what exists in the world due to "*miracula Dei*."[4]

---

1. Thomas Aquinas, *De unitate intellectus contra Averroistas*, proem., no. 1, in *Thomas d'Aquin contre Averroes: L'Unité de l'intellect contre les Averroistes*, ed. and trans. Alain de Libera (Paris: Flammarion, 1994), 76.

2. *DUI*, proem., no. 2.

3. Ibid.

4. Zdzislaw Kuksewicz, "Das 'Naturale' und das 'Supernaturale' in der averroistischen Philosophie," in *Mensch und Natur im Mittelalter*, ed. Albert Zimmerman and Andreas Speer, (Berlin: Walter de Gruyter, 1991), 372.

Philosophy deals with only *causae inferiores*, that is, with only the "horizontal dimension" of reality, whereby things of the same ontological status or perfection affect each other; theology or faith, on the other hand, deals with *causae superiores*, that is, the effects of God's direct action in the world (such as those worked through miracles).[5] On the Averroist account, *any act of intellection is a miracle because it is the operation of a superior cause.* If that is the case, then there would really be no such thing as revealed truth or revealed knowledge, since what we call "revelation" would simply be natural knowledge considered under a different aspect.

Thus, Thomas sees defending a purely naturalistic, philosophical account of human knowing as a defense also of the possibility of an authentic revelation, which is, of course, for Aquinas a specifically *Christian* revelation. So, while Aquinas's focus in this treatise will be on the philosophical cogency of the Averroist account of human knowing, his argument is, indirectly, a defense of a specifically Christian theology that posits as its basic datum the reality of a divine, incarnate revelation. In doing so, Aquinas will not use any particularly new arguments: most of the arguments he marshals in the *De unitate intellectus* are already present as far back as his commentary on the *Sentences* and developed in more detail in his *Summa contra Gentiles*.[6] What is new, I think, is my claim that Thomas is concerned to defend a view of the intellect that preserves what he sees as the proper relationship between the truths of reason and those of revelation and that lays the philosophical groundwork for a proper and authentic understanding of divine revelation.

To fulfill his project, Thomas must engage in exegesis: in this case, the exegesis of a secular, philosophical text, the *De anima* of Aristotle. This, for Thomas, is fitting, because it challenges the Averroists on their

---

5. "In reality Siger views in addition to the world in its '*causae inferiores*' the world also in its '*causa superior*' thanks to '*miracula*' some of which cannot be traced back to the productive effects of '*causae inferiores*.' With regard to knowledge, Siger distinguishes natural knowledge concerning this world from faith, which comes from revelation and transmits knowledge about the '*causa suprema*' and its effects in the world." Ibid., 374.

6. For a survey of Thomas's treatment of the subject over his career, see Edward P. Mahoney, "Aquinas's Critique of Averroes' Doctrine of the Unity of the Intellect," in *Thomas Aquinas and His Legacy*, ed. David M. Gallagher (Washington, D.C.: The Catholic University of America Press, 1994), 83–106.

own ground to be adherents of "pure philosophy." It is in the proper interpretation of the philosophy of Aristotle in particular that all these issues come to a head. As Anton Pegis remarks: "The problem which thus faced the thirteenth century was a fundamental one, and the positions adopted by the various thinkers marked decisively the different mentalities of the age; for in their attempt to express to themselves and to others their attitude towards the philosophy of Aristotle, the theologians of the thirteenth century were called upon to formulate in an explicit way their own philosophical decisions."[7] It was, therefore, not essential for Aquinas's purposes to distinguish carefully between the doctrines of Averroes himself and the often quite different (and "radicalized") doctrines of his Latin followers.[8] Thomas's whole objective was not to "oppose one fiction by another fiction" but to "replace the doctrine of Averroes in the entirety of the interpretive tradition of Aristotle's *De anima*."[9] The question of the unity of the intellect emerges, therefore, as more than a curiosity of intellectual history. It becomes a central issue in medieval philosophy because the whole Christian understanding of the proper relation between nature and grace, reason and revelation, philosophy and Scripture is at stake. More particularly, what is at stake is the proper differentiation of the Christian understanding of revelation from the Islamic one.[10]

7. Anton Pegis, *St. Thomas and the Problem of the Soul in the Thirteenth Century* (Toronto: Pontifical Institute of Mediaeval Studies, 1934), 12.

8. Recent research, however, seems to suggest that the Latin Averroists' understanding of their master was much more faithful and accurate than previously supposed. See Richard C. Taylor's introduction to Averroes, *Long Commentary on the "De Anima"*, xcvi–cvi.

9. De Libera, introduction to *Thomas d'Aquin contre Averroes*, 47.

10. What is at stake, also, is the very meaning of Aristotle's philosophy in the context of Christian revelation. Is Aristotle a radical rationalist essentially opposed to revelation (or, as Averroes would have it, expounding a purer and more complete version of the truth given imaginatively and rhetorically in revelation)? Or does the true understanding of the meaning and import of Aristotle's philosophy force the inquirer to make a distinction between natural knowledge and revealed knowledge, between nature and grace? For the true import of the corporeality of human thinking and acting—while certainly there *in potentia* in Aristotle's thinking, especially in his teaching on the soul—does not become evident until the very doctrine of the Incarnation and the goodness of material creation is at stake. It is with this in mind, I think, that Thomas takes up his pen against the "Averroists."

PHILOSOPHY AND INTERPRETATION

Thomas begins his argument with a few basic definitions. He starts, of course, with the definition of "soul" found in the *De anima*: "the soul is the first act of a physical organic body."[11] Thomas adds, "For he says, 'universally speaking it has been said what the soul is: it is a substance in the sense of form, that is to say that which is the essence [*quod quid erat esse*] of this type of body, that is, the substantial form of a physical, organic body.'"[12] Aristotle, according to Aquinas, clearly states that the human soul by its very essence is the form of a material body. Without the soul, there would be no organic, human body; there would be no formed matter at all. But is not the human soul a *rational* or *intellective* soul? Is not its "specific difference" "reason" or "intellect"? And if this is the case, is not reason or intellect an immaterial "thing," since it is able to know universals and contemplate immaterial substances? Does that not make it an immaterial substance? If it is an immaterial substance, then how can it be the form of a body? These are all good questions. But right from the beginning, Thomas notes that, while the intellect is included under this general definition of "soul," it does not follow that soul and intellect are coterminous.[13]

The root of the problem in thinking about the relationship of the soul to the intellect is a fallacy that, for Thomas, causes us to err not only in this question but in several others as well, the fallacy of misplaced concreteness. This fallacy is to confuse *what* we understand with that *by which* we understand. This is a fallacy as old as Plato, who, in discovering the fact that we think *by means* of immaterial concepts concluded falsely that *what* we understand exists in its own right as an immaterial and separate "form." Here, the problem is that many confuse that *by which* the human soul thinks with *that which* it thinks, a subsistent immaterial being in its own right. But, following Aristotle, Aquinas

---

11. Aristotle, *Aristotelis De anima*, ed. W. D. Ross (Oxford: Oxford University Press, 1956), II, 1 (412b5).

12. *DUI*, I, no. 3.

13. "Adhuc autem manifestius ex sequentibus apparet quod sub hac generalitate definitionis etiam intellectus includitur." Ibid., no. 5.

argues that knowledge and thinking are no more the substance of the soul than health is the substance of the body: knowledge is present in a well-functioning rational soul as health is present in a well-functioning body.[14] What is primary metaphysically is the *soul*, of which the intellect is a *power*. Now, as Aquinas argues elsewhere, the human soul is *both* the substantial form of a body *and* a spiritual substance in its own right, able to subsist in its own (even if in a truncated way).[15] The intellectual power in human beings is rooted in and flows from a certain incorporeal and subsistent principle (*quoddam principium incorporeaum et subsistens*), which is the human soul. This is important to note because crucial to Aquinas's argument, as we shall see, is that the human intellect is the lowest in the grade of intellects or self-subsistent spiritual substances. The human soul is a self-subsistent intellect; thus, it belongs to the gradation of spiritual substances; but as the lowest in that gradation, it needs a body in order for it be actualized as intellect. Hence, it is also the form of a body.

This "duality" in the soul is not strange if we view, as Thomas always does, the human soul within the ontological gradation of substances clearly visible to us in nature:

> Little by little, we see, to the degree to which forms are more noble, to that degree they have some powers that more and more go beyond matter. Whence the last of the forms, which is the human soul, has a power—namely the intellect—going totally beyond bodily matter. Therefore, the intellect is separate because it is not a power in the body; but it is a power in the soul, while the soul is the act of the body.[16]

Here Thomas becomes more precise. The intellect is "separate because it is not a power in the body, but is a power in the soul," but, at the same

---

14. "Et sic patet scientiam esse formam anime, et sanitatem corporis." Ibid., no. 10.

15. *S. Th.* I, 75, 2; *Quaestiones disputatae de anima*, in Thomas Aquinas, *S. Thomae Aquinatis Quaestiones Disputatae*, ed. P. Bazzi, M. Calcaterra, T. S. Centi, E. Odetto, and P. M. Pession (Turin: Marietti, 1953), 1. Aquinas presents his arguments for the self-subsistent nature of the human soul before he argues that it is the form of the body as well (*S. Th.* I, 76, 1). Indeed, Anton Pegis argues that the problem of how to reconcile the soul as substantial form and as self-subsistent spiritual substance was one of the central philosophical problems of the thirteenth century. See Pegis, *St. Thomas and the Problem of the Soul*.

16. *DUI*, I, no. 27.

time, "the soul is the act of the body." This intellectual power is rooted in the soul, which, as a self-subsistent intellectual substance, is a *hoc aliquid* that can exist on its own. But since the human intellect, as a power, is pure potentiality to intelligible forms, it cannot operate fully (at least in the beginning) through itself. It is necessary that the soul in-from a body, which can then actualize the soul's intellectual power by providing it with sensible species, that is, content it can work on.

Thomas does concede that Aristotle leaves at least two things unsettled about the intellect and its relation to the concretely existing human being. "First, whether the intellect is separated from the other parts of the soul only by reason, or also in location."[17] The second thing left unsettled is the precise difference between the intellect and the other parts of the soul. Aquinas clearly sees this, referring to Aristotle's use of the word "separate" to describe the intellect. But contrary to the Averroists, Aquinas argues that the intellect is not some separate substance but is a power within the human being, who has that power by means of his or her formal cause, which is the soul.[18] What makes the intellect "separate" is not that it is a separate substance but that it does not need a bodily organ in order to perform its operation. In fact, it *must* be free of any corporeal organ in order to function as intellect, as we shall see. But, for the moment, the point that Thomas wants to make is more fundamental: a form that is the formal cause of a material substance can also have an immaterial power, and this is clear to us from the gradation of forms in matter.

Formal causes or structures exist only insofar as they give essential being to concrete existents. By "concrete," however, Thomas does not just mean material or corporeal being: angels have a concrete but immaterial existence. For what makes a being "concrete" is not materiality, but its individual act of existence or *actus essendi*.[19] Be that as it may, the rational soul of the human being does not cease to exist after the death of

17. Ibid., no. 15.
18. Ibid., I, no. 26.
19. See Thomas, *In De causis librum expositio*, in *Sancti Thomae de Aquino Super Librum de Causis Expositio*, ed. H. D. Saffrey, OP (Louvain: Editions E. Nauwelaerts, 1954), prop. 4, 30.

the body. Insofar as the human rational soul has a potency or power that is in principle if not in actuality separate from any bodily organ, it can survive apart from the body. This is because the intellectual power in human beings flows from an intellectual substance or soul that must by its very nature as intellectual substance be self-subsisting.[20] Or as Aquinas puts it in the *De unitate*, not all of the rational soul exists through the composite, unlike forms and souls lower down on the ontological scale. Since there is a power in the soul that transcends its existence in matter, it follows that the form in which this power inheres will not disappear or be destroyed by the destruction of the body.[21]

While a defense of the immortality of the soul is only incidental to Aquinas's purpose here, it is nevertheless relevant. In the first place, because, as Thomas says in the very beginning of the *De unitate intellectus*, unless the soul subsists after death, *qua* individual soul, it would ultimately not be responsible to God for its thoughts and actions, and, hence, all the requirements of religion and worship would be for naught. Second, part of the attraction of the Averroist philosophy was that it seemed to guarantee both the immortality of the intellect (albeit in an impersonal way) while at the same time acknowledging the materiality of the human being. "To understand [for Aristotle] is said to be the act of the composite not *per se* but *per accidens*, inasmuch as the object of the act, that is, the phantasm, is in a bodily organ; not that that act is exercised *through* a bodily organ."[22] A big problem for his contemporaries, as Thomas sees it, is that they did not yet have the conceptual tools or understand the concepts needed to comprehend how the human being can at the same time be a spiritual creature with a self-subsistent, immortal soul and also a fully flesh and blood individual; or, to put it another way, they could not understand how the human being uniquely straddles the boundary between the gradation of material forms and that of intellects. For Thomas, understanding the proper relation between intellect and soul is the way out of this thicket.

The first and second chapters of the *De unitate*, therefore, not only

20. *S. Th.* I, 75, 6.
21. *DUI*, I, no. 35.
22. Ibid., no. 36.

try to develop a proper reading or exegesis of Aristotle, but also, in doing so, they try to clear the metaphysical ground for the arguments that
follow, especially in chapters three and four.[23] The main principle that
Aquinas wants to establish is that what is primary metaphysically is
the existent individual, not the abstracted form or universal. Now this
existent individual may be individuated by a material body, or solely by
a unique act of existence in the case of spiritual creatures. Nevertheless, what is primary is the existent individual, a doctrine that Thomas
finds latent, though not fully developed, in Aristotle. In this way, Aquinas combats the Neoplatonic tendency to "reify" or make into concrete
things that which are merely conceptual abstractions.[24]

THINKING AND THE INDIVIDUAL

With a statement of metaphysical principles in place, Aquinas can then
move onto an argument against the Averroist position proper. The Averroist position is twofold: it argues (a) that Aristotle's possible intellect
is ontologically or really separate (that is, not simply in thought) from
the human soul and that the human soul only thinks when "conjoined"
to it, and (b) that this possible intellect is one for all men.[25] These two

23. The second chapter of the *De unitate* deals very briefly with the interpretations
of Aristotle made by the Greek commentators of late antiquity, such as Themistius and
Alexander of Aphrodisias.

24. "In other words, what St. Thomas has done is to put his finger on what was
perhaps the greatest single weakness of the Neoplatonic doctrine throughout its whole
tradition, namely, the lack of any adequate metaphysical explanation to safeguard the intrinsic unity of the compositions resulting from participation. He has remedied this by
transposing the whole framework into the only adequate theory of unity in metaphysical
composition so far developed, the Aristotelian doctrine of act and potency as correlative,
incomplete metaphysical principles, intrinsically ordered one to the other so as to form a
per se unit." W. Norris Clarke, "The Meaning of Participation in St. Thomas," *Proceedings
of the American Catholic Philosophical Association* 26 (1952): 155.

25. The assertion of the separability and oneness of the agent intellect was more
common and less controversial in the thirteenth century, in part, perhaps, because it
seemed to be easily reconciled with Augustine's doctrine of divine illumination. See
R. A. Gauthier, "Notes sur les débuts (1225–1240) du premier 'Averroïsme,'" *Revue des sciences philosophiques et théologiques* 66 (1982): 321–74; "Notes sur Siger de Brabant: I. Siger
en 1265," *Revue des sciences philosophiques et théologiques* 67 (1983): 201–32; and "Notes sur
Siger de Brabant: II. Siger en 1272–1275, Aubry de Reims et la scission des Normands,"

positions are related and yet distinct: if the possible intellect is onto-logically separate and immaterial, then, upon a rigorous application of Aristotelian principles, the possible intellect must be one, since it has no matter to multiply it into individuals.[26] They deal, however, with two separate issues: (1) the relation of the individual to the intellect, and (2) the nature of the intellect itself.

If we look first at the *action* or operation proper to the human in-tellect, then we must reject the Averroist thesis that the possible intel-lect is separate for all men.[27] As W. Norris Clarke has shown, Aquinas consistently sees action and being as two sides of the same coin: "to be"

Revue des sciences philosophiques et théologiques 68 (1984): 3–49. For a more extensive ac-count of the pervasive influence of Avicenna on the attempts of Christian theologians to combine Augustine's teaching of divine illumination and the new Aristotelian ideas flood-ing into Europe, see the two classic accounts of Etienne Gilson: *Pourquoi Saint Thomas a critiqué Saint Augustin (suivi de) Avicenne et le point de départ de Duns Scot* (Paris: Vrin, 1986); and "Les sources gréco-arabe de l'augustinisme avicennant," *Archives d'histoire doctri-nale et littéraire du moyen âge* 4 (1929): 6–149.

26. This is not to say that Averroes still does not have some defenders. Deborah Black argues that Averroes's position is a perfectly legitimate and coherent reading of Aristotle that "saves all the phenomena." As Black points out, Averroes's position is consistent so long as one takes into account that he attributed to the faculty of the imagination, where phantasms are formed, a much more active and independent role in cognition than did Thomas. See Deborah Black, "Consciousness and Self-Knowledge in Aquinas's Critique of Averroes's Psychology," *Journal of the History of Philosophy* 31, no. 3 (1993): 349–85.

27. We must say a word here about the term "possible intellect," because what was distinctive and controversial about the Averroist position in Thomas's day was its assertion that not only the agent intellect but also the possible intellect is ontologically separate and one for all human beings. According to Aristotle, the metaphysical principles in the hu-man mind or intellect must be twofold, just like everything else in nature. There is always, among things that change (and the human intellect, by the very act of coming to knowledge of something, changes), an active principle and a passive principle. In all natural beings, the active principle is the form while the passive one is the matter. Now the human intellect must *receive* forms or intelligible species of the things it knows. As such, the intellect is receptive and thus, in a sense passive. This passivity is *analogous* to that of matter but, it is important to stress, the passive principle in the intellect is not the same as matter, since the intellect, in order to abstract intelligible forms from matter, must itself be free of matter (which is why Thomas claims that the terminology of some commentators who call this mode of intellect the "material intellect" is misleading). But since the human intellect can receive only things that can be sensed and thus are material, it needs another power which Aristotle called the "active" or "agent intellect." The agent intellect "lights up," as it were, the intelligible aspects of a material thing and allows its form to be abstracted from the sensible thing and received by the possible intellect.

means primarily to act and, in turn, action gives us a privileged clue to the essential being of that which acts.[28] For something to be and not to act is an absurdity, just as it would be an absurdity for something non-existent to act. To be totally inert is not to be at all. Thus, we must first look at what the human intellect *does* in order to understand its essence or ontological structure and status.

In light of these principles, therefore, Aquinas gives three reasons for his rejection of the Averroist position. First, "contact of the intellect with man would not be from the beginning of man's generation as Theophrastus says and as Aristotle implies in book 2 of the *Physics*." In other words, the intellect would not belong essentially to man. Contact with the possible intellect would not be according to generation but according to the operation of sense. "For the imagination 'is moved by sense in act,' as is said in the book *De anima*."[29] Contact of the individual human being with the possible intellect would therefore be completely accidental, not essential, to the human soul, just as contact of the senses with their proper sensible objects is accidental.

Second, if contact of the human soul with the possible intellect were something extraneous to the human soul, "this conjoining would not be according to a single principle, but according to diverse principles." On the Averroist account, any cognition that the possible intellect might have of things would be indirect, that is, it would be mediated by more than one principle. For example, one way in which we might imagine how the possible intellect knows things is that it cognizes phantasms or sensible images in the human imaginative faculty and thereby "knows" things as one might see the reflection of something in a mirror. But this explanation is unsatisfying to Aquinas, because "it is manifest then that the action of a mirror, which is to represent, cannot be attributed to man because of this; it follows that neither can the action of the possible intellect be attributed to this man, Socrates, on account of the conjoining mentioned above, in such a way that we can say that this man under-

---

28. See especially his book *The One and the Many: A Contemporary Thomistic Metaphysics* (Notre Dame, Ind.; University of Notre Dame Press, 2001).

29. *DUI*, III, no. 63.

stands."[30] It would simply be an equivocation, on this account, to say that you or I understand anything, because the human role in such an act of cognition is a mere mediation of images to an ontologically separate possible intellect, which is properly said to understand.

The third reason why Thomas rejects the Averroist thesis of a separate possible intellect follows from the second. To understand human cognition properly, we must, again, make a distinction between that *by which* we understand, the intelligible form or species, and the *power* that does the understanding. The intelligible species is not what understands, but that *by which* the intellect understands; but if that is all that is in the human being, with the power of understanding separate from him or her, then we cannot properly say that any human being understands at all. As Thomas reads the Averroist position, the phantasms in the human mind, which provide the sensible material for the possible intellect's cognition, are like colors on a wall, which the possible intellect "sees" or cognizes.[31] We human beings are the "wall" in which the phantasms are "seen" and from which the intelligible species are abstracted by the possible intellect, but who are otherwise "inert."[32] According to this conception, the human being is merely a passive object—a "wall" or "mirror"—which furnishes material for the possible intellect to think. The human being on this account thinks thoughts no more than the wall "sees" color. And since "to be" means "to act," insofar as the human being, *qua* his or her intellectual power, is inert, then to that extent does he or she not exist as a knowing being.

Nor can we counter by saying that the relationship between the possible intellect and the individual human being insofar as he or she is thinking is like that between mover and moved. On this account, insofar as you or I think, we are "moved" by the action of the possible intellect to do so; just as a sailor pilots a ship, the separate possible intellect moves and directs our thinking. The fundamental problem with this position for Aquinas is that it violates the essential unity of the human being and, therefore, its status as a true substance. On the Averroist

30. Ibid., no. 64.
31. Ibid., no. 65. See also SCG, II, 59, no. 1361.
32. SCG, II, 59, no. 1362.

account, we would have to say that this man, Socrates, is not absolutely one being, but that an essential operation of Socrates belongs to some other being "using" Socrates in order to think (*et similiter intelligere non erit actus Sortis, sed intellectus tantum utentis corpore Sortis*).[33] Thinking would only "seem," then, to be an essential property of human beings. There would be built into the fabric of nature an inherent "trick" or deception which creates more problems than it solves, for, as Aristotle always insisted, "nature does nothing in vain."

There is one more option for the defender of the Averroist position. Namely, it is to say, "It is I who understands; it is just that the separate possible intellect moves me into the act of understanding just as a fire moves something combustible into the act of burning." But Thomas finds this argument unconvincing. First and perhaps most fundamentally, it has the true state of affairs backwards: "And if you say that in this way heaven understands by means of its mover, the assumption is of something more difficult: it is necessary to come to a knowledge of higher intellects through the human intellect, not the other way around."[34] The Averroists, in brief, try to explain the obscure through the more obscure. As Aquinas puts it even more succinctly in his *Summa contra Gentiles*: it is not the case that we are united to the intellect by means of an intelligible form, but rather the reverse makes much more sense: we are united to the intelligible form by means of the intellect, because the concrete is prior to the abstract.[35] The notion that a separate intellect moves us to understand does not establish that we are intellectual substances: "So therefore, even if the intellect is asserted to be united to Socrates as mover, it does not follow from this that understanding is in Socrates nor even that Socrates understands, because understanding is an act which is only in the intellect."[36] All in all, it is still necessary to suppose that the intellect is in some way "in" the soul of the person who thinks, "just like that sense by which

---

33. *DUI*, III, no. 69.

34. Ibid., no. 68.

35. "Homo autem est intelligens per intellectum sicut per virtutem cognoscitivam. Non igitur coniungitur per formam intelligibilem intellectui, sed magis per intellectum intelligibili." *SCG*, II, 59, no. 1363.

36. *DUI*, III, no. 70.

Socrates senses, that is in potency to all sensible."[37] Just as our sense faculties could not be moved unless they were "in" us as an essential feature or
power of the soul, so must the power of intellection be "in" us as a power
of the soul for us to receive and then think anything intelligible. Common
to all three counter-arguments is the assertion that the human intellect
is the lowest within the gradation of intellects: the human intellect's instantiation in an individual, material substance is essential to its nature
as intellect in potency to all there is to know and thus is in the realm of
intellects as prime matter is in the realm of material substances. It is essential to the human intellect as the lowest in the gradation of intellects to
be actualized as intellect *within* an individual material substance.

All these investigations lead Aquinas to the conclusion that the human intellect must be a power within and flowing from the essence of
the soul, which is itself the form of a body. This does not mean, however, that the intellect itself, as power, has a bodily organ through which
it must operate, like sight needs an eye. "Therefore it is necessary that
it [the intellect] be united to the body as form, not indeed so that the
intellective power itself would be the act of some organ, but because it
is a power of the soul which is the act of a physical organic body."[38] The
human intellect, since it thinks by abstracting the intelligible forms from
matter, does not have a material operation nor does it have a corporeal
organ. As the "place of species," the human intellect is able to consider
material substances as immaterial forms.[39] But, by the same token, the
human intellective power is also an "empty" power—it is devoid of any
specific content; it is wholly indeterminate. It needs sense data; it needs
experience of material substances in order for it to know anything specific. Thus, the human soul is the form of a body not despite but because
of the nature of its intellect as akin to prime matter in the order of intellects: in-forming a body is *perfective* of the human intellect, because
the in-forming of a body allows the possible intellect to receive the sense
data that would give it specific content and make it truly the "place of
forms" and actualize it as intellect. This does not compromise the "dig-

37. Ibid., no. 73.
38. Ibid., no. 77.
39. Ibid., no. 80.

nity" of the human soul as intellective or rational.[40] Nothing in the principles of nature or of metaphysics prevents there being a form that is partially immersed in matter and partially transcending it. There is nothing in the principles of philosophy that says that forms must either be purely spiritual or purely material. In fact, the whole reason why Aristotle posited an immanent formal cause in things is because he noticed how the various properties and operations of material substances transcended more and more their constituent material elements the more complex they became.[41] It therefore stands to reason that there would be at least one material substance with an operation that transcends matter altogether. The relation, therefore, of the human being to its intellect is one that is perfectly natural and in accord with the principles of nature, even if the human intellect itself is an immaterial power. It, the human intellect, is rooted in concrete natural substance.

In the fourth chapter of the *De unitate intellectus*, Thomas is thus prepared to take aim at the second major Averroist thesis, which is that the possible intellect is one in all men. In asserting the separateness of the possible intellect, one still has not committed oneself to the oneness of the possible intellect for all. But upon Aristotelian principles, this in fact seems to follow necessarily: if the possible intellect is an immaterial substance and, if matter is the principle by which an essential form is multiplied into many different subjects, then it would follow that the possible intellect would be devoid of any principle of individuation and would therefore be one for all men. But for Thomas, this conclusion does not follow if we suppose, as he has established, that the intellect is a separate *power within the soul*.[42] To understand his position, Aquinas draws, as he is wont, an analogy between intellection and sense perception. He asks us to suppose that there is one eye for all men by which we all see. It then "remains to be asked whether all men would be one who sees or many who see."[43] Would the *power* of seeing be many or one if we all

40. Ibid., no. 81.
41. "Quanto forma est nobilior, tanto in suo esse superexcedit materiam." SCG, II, 68, no. 1454.
42. *DUI*, IV, no. 84.
43. Ibid., no. 86.

saw through one eye? To clear up this difficulty, Aquinas makes a careful distinction between what is the principle agent in the substance and what is the instrument of that principle agent. In other words, is the eye the principle agent of sight or is it simply the instrument or organ of sight?

> If the eye were the principal agent in man, which would use all the powers of the soul and parts of the body as instruments, then the many having one eye would be the one seeing; if however the eye is not the principal agent of man, but if there is something more primary which uses the eye, which is diversified in diverse subjects, then there would be many acts of seeing but by one eye.[44]

So everything hinges on what is the principal agent in the human being as opposed to what is merely the instrument or organ of that principal agent. Now, for Aquinas, "it is clear that the intellect is that which is the principal agent in man, and that it uses all the powers of the soul and the members of the body as organs."[45] It follows that if there were one intellect for all men, then there would be only one principal agent using many different men as organs or instruments for its agency. But this has the nature of things in reverse: it makes the substance, that is, the human being, into a power of a power, properly speaking, which is the intellect. It makes the power of the substance the primary agent and the primary agent the substance, which reverses the ontological order whereby a power can only subsist in a substance:

> Similarly, therefore, if the intellect were one for all men, it follows that there is only one intellectual act at the same time for all men understanding the same thing; and especially since nothing according to which men would differ from each other would have a share in the intellectual operation. For phantasms are preparations for the act of the intellect, as colors are for the act of sight. Thus, the act of the intellect is not diversified through the diversity [of the phantasms], especially with respect to one intelligible.... But in two men who know and understand the same thing, the intellectual operation itself in no way can be diversified by the diversity of phantasms.[46]

44. Ibid.
45. Ibid., no. 87.
46. Ibid., no. 88.

On the Averroists' account, there can be no way of saying that there are diverse acts of intellection with regard to the human race. We could say only that there is one act of thinking going on at any time, using the phantasms of individual men as the material for its thinking (although there are difficulties here as well). There is no way in which intellectual activity could be diversified by a diversity of phantasms, since the very essence of thought is to abstract from these material particularities.

As was hinted above, some Averroists proposed that there is diversity in human "thought" due to the diversity of phantasms. We all think through the same act of intellection, goes this argument, but since the phantasm by which this thinking occurs in the possible intellect is different in me than it is from you, it follows that I think the thought from a different "perspective," so to speak, than you do. In this way, thinking is diversified. But if we think this position through, Aquinas argues, we see that it throws up insurmountable obstacles. It is a fundamental tenet of Aristotle's doctrine of the soul that the intellect is like a blank tablet before it comes to know anything: the human intellect, as pure potentiality toward receiving intelligible forms, as the "prime matter" in the order of intellects, needs sense data in order to have any content. Knowledge and intellection, therefore, are *habits* or *dispositions* that the soul acquires as it comes into possession of sense data and receives, in its possible intellect, the intelligible forms of things. It then, in turn, uses these intelligible forms "stored" in the possible intellect to think and interpret new data as they come in. In connection with this, Thomas says three things must therefore be noted: (1) "the habit of science is the first act of the possible intellect itself, which according to this [habit] comes into act and can act through itself;" (2) "before our learning or discovering, the possible intellect itself is in potency like a tablet on which nothing is written;" (3) "by our learning or discovering, the possible intellect itself is put into act."[47] It follows from these three points that the possible intellect cannot act as intellect on its own: it can only be actualized as intellect insofar as it is a "part" or a power in a composite substance. If the possible intellect is, by definition, pure potency to intellectual activity and intelligible con-

47. Ibid., no. 90.

tent, then there is no way it could acquire the habit of intellection and thought, for the simple reason that the possible intellect does not come into being, according to Averroes, but is eternal. The activity of thinking is something that it already possesses and cannot be developed and refined as a habit (that is, virtue).

It should be noted here how much Thomas views the human intellect not as a static essence, but as a dynamic activity. As the lowest intellect in the gradation of intellects, the human intellect needs to be actualized through its body and that body's relations with the material world. If the possible intellect were an immaterial and eternal substance in its own right, then there would be no first act of understanding and the intelligible species of the possible intellect would be eternal, hence making the need for phantasms in order to think anything determinate totally superfluous: "In vain therefore did Aristotle posit an agent intellect, which would make intelligibles in potency intelligibles in act; in vain also did he posit that phantasms relate to the possible intellect as colors to sight, if the possible intellect receives nothing from phantasms."[48] As Thomas points out in other places, the whole reason that Aristotle posits the existence of an agent or active intellect is because the human intellect does not have direct access to the intelligible forms of things, as Plato believed. For Plato, intellection is the simple gazing upon the self-subsistent intelligible form; but if the human intellect is only, initially, pure potentiality to intelligible forms, and if, therefore, human thinking is essentially corporeal, then we need another power by which the intellect abstracts away the material conditions of a thing's existence and considers only its immaterial, intelligible form.[49] On the Averroist account, however, phantasms and, hence, an agent intellect, would be superfluous, since the possible intellect would have the intelligible forms or species within itself from all eternity.[50] Contact of the possible intellect with the phantasms in individual human beings would be in vain, and there would therefore be an irrationality at the very basis of human reason.

48. Ibid., no. 92.

49. *Quaestiones disputatae de anima*, 4. Here Thomas is answering the question *Utrum necesse sit ponere intellectum agentem*.

50. *DUI*, IV, no. 92.

TRUTH AND THE INDIVIDUAL

Thus, the human intellect is individuated according to the multiplica-
tion of bodies and this in-corporation or in-carnation is essential to the
very identity and individuality of the human intellect. So strong is this
connection to the body that Thomas argues that the human soul retains
its individual character, as the formal cause of *this particular body*, even
after death separates it from that body.[51] But there still remains a problem—perhaps the most difficult and fundamental problem in view of
his ultimate concern in this polemic that Thomas needs to answer: how
can we be said to know the same thing if we each have individual and
particular intellects? Indeed, no small part of the attraction of Averroes's
interpretation of Aristotle was that it seemed to resolve the problem of
how we can all know the same thing, even though human beings are
individuated, material, and numerically multiple—for does not our materiality make knowledge of the immaterial universal impossible? How
can a particular intellect, which knows particular, material things, have
knowledge of the same universal? If there is a diversity of intellects, how
can we say that when you and I understand something, we understand
the same thing? Plato's answer was easy: we all in a way "see" the same
separate intelligible form. But, as Aquinas notes,[52] this leads to some
very problematic conclusions. For one, it leads to the conclusion that
we do not understand anything "here," that is, in the material world of
lived existence. For another, if the forms subsist through themselves and
intellects are intellects only insofar as they subsist in these forms by participation, then once an intellect fully participates in the form through
knowledge, then there should be no multiplicity of intellects—not only
of human intellects, which Averroes argues, but of all intellects altogether, angelic, "celestial," "divine," and otherwise, something which Averroes
and his Latin followers were not prepared to admit.

If, however, we look at just corporeal, living creatures, we find three
grades of cognitive powers. The first is that of sense perception, which

51. Ibid., V, no. 100. See also *S. Th.* I, 76, 2, ad 2.
52. *DUI*, V, no. 105.

occurs through a corporeal organ, while spiritual creatures understand through infused intelligible species, but as Thomas says in the *Summa theologiae*:

> The human intellect, however, holds a middle place: it is not to be sure the act of any organ, but it is nevertheless a certain power [*virtus*] of the soul, which is the form of the body, which is clear from what was said above (I, 76, 1). And thus, it is proper to it to know form in a certain body individually existing, not however insofar as it is in such matter. To know then that which is in individual matter, not inasmuch as it is in such matter, is to abstract the form from the individual matter, which the phantasms represent. And thus, it is necessary to say that our intellect understands material things by abstracting from phantasms; and through material things thus considered we come to some knowledge of immaterial things, just as, to the contrary, angels know material things through the immaterial.[53]

Only angelic intellects could have the kind of intellectual knowledge that Plato claims the human philosopher has in that angelic intellects and human philosophers have infused in them the pure intelligible species of things (although even in angels, the intelligible species are not *what* the angels know, but that *by which* they know other things). But since the human intellect holds but the "lowest place" in the gradation of intellects, it is pure potentiality for knowing and thus needs sense experience for its intellect to be actualized.[54] By its very nature, the human intellect must draw all intelligible content, including the intelligible species by which it knows, from "outside" itself, through its inherent and essential connection with the human body and its powers of sense perception. That is why, fundamentally, the sciences are not ultimately about our *ideas* or *concepts* of things (*pace* Kant), but about the *things themselves*:

> It must be said that according to the opinion of Aristotle that which is understood, which is one, is the nature itself or quiddity of a thing.

53. *S. Th.* I, 85, 1. See also *Quaestiones disputatae de anima*, 2, ad 5.

54. *Quaestiones disputatae de anima*, 7, answering the question *Utrum angelus et anima differant specie*. See also *De ente et essentia, Opuscula Omnia S. Thomae Aquinatis*, vol. 1, ed. R. R. Pierre Mandonnet, OP (Paris, 1927), IV, no. 10; and SCG, II, 75, no. 1555.

But natural science and other sciences are about things, not understood species. If then what is understood is not the nature itself of the stone, which is in things, but the species which is in the intellect, it would follow that I would not understand the thing which is the stone, but only the intention which is abstracted from the stone. But rather, it is the case that the nature of the stone inasmuch as it is in singulars, is understood in potentiality; but it becomes understood in act through the fact that the species from sensible things arrive by means of the senses as far as the imagination and then, by the power of the agent intellect, intelligible species are abstracted, and these exist in the possible intellect. Now these species relate to the possible intellect not as things understood, but as the species by which the intellect understands (just as the species which are in vision are not the vision itself, but that by which vision sees) except insofar as the intellect reflects upon itself, which is not able to happen in sense perception.[55]

What grounds the unity of knowledge of the various intellects in multiple, individual acts of understanding is the intelligible form in the thing known, which is the same for all. This intelligible form is intelligible only in potency in the thing known, but it becomes actually intelligible when it is abstracted out of the material thing and received by the possible intellect. Thus, what is understood is the form in the material thing itself; the intelligible form or species in the intellect is only that *by which* the material thing is understood. The intelligible form or species becomes a direct object of knowledge only when the intellect reflects on its own act of knowing in a "second act" of cognition. Self-knowledge is thus a "third" act of the intellect whereby the intellect reflects upon its own act of reflecting upon the intelligible species within itself. For Aquinas, then, all human knowing is already immersed, as it were, in the material world; all genuinely human intellective knowledge presupposes an intimate, pre-thematic contact, even a union of sorts, with material substances.[56] We know material things even before we are aware of our own knowing; indeed, even before we are aware of ourselves. But the

---

55. *DUI*, V, no. 106. See also *Quaestiones disputatae de anima*, 2, ad 5; and S.*Th.* I, 85, 2.

56. "Species enim recepta in intellectu possibili non habet se ut quod intelligitur.... Sed tamen per eas quaecumque sunt in omnibus scientiis cognoscuntur." SCG, II, 75, no. 1550.

essential point here is that the unity of understanding among human knowers is founded upon the unity of the intentional object, the intelligible form, which is itself, as we saw in the previous chapter, founded upon or "measured" by a divine exemplar or idea in the divine intellect. It is precisely the fact that human knowing is about *reality itself*—and not about innate ideas or a priori forms of cognition—that grounds both human knowledge about the world and its own inter-subjective unity and agreement.

This does not mean that two people do not understand the same thing differently. "But because to understand is an action that stays within the knower himself, as Aristotle says in book 9 of the *Metaphysics*, it follows that to understand is according to the mode of the knower, that is, according to the requirement of the species by which the knower understands."[57] And so, for the human intellect, the diversity of intellects according to the diversity of bodies, does not hinder universal knowledge, but it ensures that each act of knowing is *my act* of knowing, while at the same time opening us to universal being:

> There is therefore one thing which is understood by me and by you, but understood in one way by me and in another way by you, that is by another intelligible species. And my understanding is one thing and yours another; and my intellect is one thing and yours another. From which Aristotle said in his *Categories* that any science is of singulars with regard to the subject: "as a certain grammatical science is in a certain subject, the soul, but it is said of no subject." Thus, also my intellect, when it understands itself to understand, understands a certain singular act; when, however, it understands "to understand" simply, it understands something universal. Singularity therefore is not repugnant to intelligibility, but materiality is. It follows then that since there exist certain immaterial beings, such as was said about separate substances above, nothing prevents such singulars from being understood.[58]

I would like here to emphasize in this passage the phase, "singularity is not opposed to intelligibility, but materiality is." The more intelligible the world becomes to us, the more we become intelligible to ourselves;

57. *DUI*, V, no. 107.
58. Ibid., no. 108.

and the more intelligible we become to ourselves, the more singular and individual we become, because the more we are actualized as an intellectual substance. In other words, Thomas argues that, in the realm of the intellect, singularity and universality are not opposed, but are mutually reinforcing. This is why, as Thomas notes, angels are immaterial, and yet they are perfectly singular or individual; it is because they know themselves through their form, which is their very substance.[59] Hence, *intellectus* has two senses in Latin, as does the word *ʿaql* in Arabic: it can mean both the act of thinking and that which thinks. Thus, there is no distinction between the essence of the intellect and its operation: "its very being is to think."[60] But the human intellect, by its very nature as pure potentiality in the gradation of intellects, cannot come to self-intellection or self-knowledge by direct introspection. It needs this particular body in order to be actualized as intellect. And so, while materiality in itself is opposed to intelligibility, materiality is necessary for the human intellect to have singularity, which is not only not opposed to intelligibility, but is, in many ways, perfective of it, since it both produces and results from self-knowledge. As Thomas repeats throughout the *De unitate intellectus*, only concrete existents truly act and therefore exist; abstract universals do not truly act or exist. Therefore, the act of understanding can exist only in a concretely existing, singular subject or intellect, whose power of intellection originates from itself and returns to itself.

INCARNATE WORD AS THE PERFECTION OF INCARNATE LIFE AND THOUGHT

With this argument we return to the original danger that Thomas saw in the Averroist position that, on its own principles, the act of understanding is not mine and that I am therefore not responsible for what I think, believe or do. This position is, for Thomas, not only theologically but philosophically untenable. It is important to note here that Aquinas does not rely primarily for his argument on the maxim *hic homo intelligit*, that is, on

59. *S. Th.* I, 56, 1.

60. Jean Jolivet, "Averroès et le décentrement du sujet," in *Le choc Averroès: Comment les philosophes arabes ont fait Europe, Internationale de l'imaginaire* 17/18 (1991): 165.

the assertion that each of us has an immediate and self-evident access to our acts of intellection. As we have seen Thomas argues that we do not have such an immediate access.[61] He relies, rather, on the argument that the nature of the human intellect, as the lowest in the hierarchy of intellects, needs by necessity a body for its actualization and perfection.

But—and here is the main concern of Thomas—these arguments have very profound and far-ranging consequences for our understanding of the relation of divine grace to human knowing. Two things concern Thomas, the first explicitly, the second implicitly: one is that the doctrine of the unity of the intellect destroys individual responsibility for our choices before God. But the second is the *way* in which this doctrine is formulated by some—and here he seems to have in mind the scholar of the arts' faculty, Siger de Brabant—in which they say that philosophical reasoning leads them to conclude that there is one intellect for all men, but that the Christian faith reveals a "higher" truth which states that the intellect is individual for all men and that the choices we make with that intellect determine our eternal destiny. This argument is the focus of the fifth and final chapter of the *De unitate intellectus*:

> And here it is even more serious what he [presumably, Siger] says: "I conclude by necessity through reason that the intellect is one in number, but I hold firmly the opposite by faith." Therefore, he thinks that the faith is about certain things of which the contrary could be concluded by necessity. Since, however, we cannot conclude by necessity

---

61. *S. Th.* I, 87, 1; *De ver.*, 8, 6; 10, 8; *SCG* II, 75; III, 46; *Quaestiones disputatae de anima*, 16, ad 8. Deborah Black, in "Consciousness and Self-Knowledge," argues that Aquinas contradicts himself—or nearly does—in his attack upon Averroes by basing his polemic on the argument that access to our individual self-consciousness is immediate and self-evident, whereas almost everywhere else in his writings, he emphasizes how this awareness is mediate and indirect. As is clear from my analysis of the texts, however, Aquinas's argument does not rest on this assertion nor does he make much of it. Black does make a strong case for Averroes insofar as she points out that, for Averroes, the imagination is not like a "wall"— inanimate and inert—in which phantasms are cognized, but an active organ much more akin to the eye, which is illumined and activated by the light of the sun. Nevertheless, I think that Aquinas's main argument still stands, that for Averroes the primary agent of human thinking still remains an agent external to the human being. Ockham's Razor, whereby *ontological entities* are not to be multiplied beyond necessity, clearly favors Aquinas's own "saving of the phenomena."

anything unless a necessary truth, whose opposite is a false impossibility, it follows according to what he says that the faith is about false impossibilities, which even God cannot do—this faithful ears cannot bear to hear.[62]

For Thomas, to assert that a higher truth would conflict with the best use of human reason is an absurdity: a higher truth should enlighten and strengthen human reason, not contradict it, if it is to be truth at all, for the intellect is a created good and is by its essence directed toward truth. Thus, the doctrine of the unity of the intellect is not some obscure debate concerning philosophical and theological arcana.[63] It goes to the heart of how we are to conceive of the relationship between faith and human reason. Is the human being the source of his or her own intellectual activity or not? If not, then in what sense can human knowledge be *natural* or in what sense can we deny that, in essence, all scientific knowledge is a sort of revealed knowledge, since it comes from an ontologically separate and higher power? On the Averroist account, every act of knowing would be a miracle or, which amounts to the same thing, a *revelation*,[64] as Thomas notes in his *Summa contra Gentiles*:

> If the agent intellect is a separate substance, it is evident that it is above the nature of man. The operation then which man exercises solely by the power of some supernatural substance is a supernatural operation, such as performing miracles or prophesying, or anything else which men perform through divine favor [*Operatio autem quam homo exercet sola virtute alicuius supernaturalis substantiae, est operatio supernaturalis:*

62. *DUI*, V, no. 119.

63. "And yet, the first formulation of the doctrine of the double truth—in other words, the one that Thomas forges in order to trap his adversary—was not a general formulation bearing on the relation between faith and reason: rather it was a precise statement bearing on the problem of the intellect. It is in the context of monopsychism and concerning it alone and—to go even farther—on the exact ground of the submission of God to the principle of contradiction that the pseudo-doctrine of the double truth was born." De Libera, introduction to *Thomas d'Aquin contre Averroes*, 54.

64. And in this, Averroes's position is indistinguishable from that of al-Ghazali, as the latter argues that *any* genuinely metaphysical knowledge of God can only be revealed knowledge. The only difference is how and by what this "revelation" occurs and whether it is part of the natural order or whether there is *no* natural order but all happens by divine fiat, that is, miraculously.

ut miracula facere et prophetare et alia huiusmodi quae divino numere ho-mines operantur]. Since, therefore, man is not able to understand except by virtue of the agent intellect, if the agent intellect were some separate substance, it would follow that understanding would not be a natural operation for man. And thus, man would not be defined as being *intel-lectual* or *rational*.[65]

If the human intellect were really separate and one for all men, then any act of knowledge would be an act of prophecy, since it would literally be a reception of intellectual activity from a superior cause. This not only contradicts our own experience, but it also cheapens the act of prophecy as well. If every act of thinking is indistinguishable from a prophetic act, then there really is no such thing as prophecy. So, not only does Thomas's account of the nature of the human intellect and its relationship to the individual human being naturalize human thinking, it does so with a view to preserving the special character of divine revelation as not contrary to the operation of the intellect but as perfective of it. Revelation is precisely of that which is not contrary to human reason, but of that which human reason cannot know from its own natural resources.

Now, there are a couple of possible objections that can be made against Thomas's critique of Averroes—objections that go beyond the question, which is not our concern here, of whether Thomas understood Averroes or even the Averroists properly. One is that Averroes himself thought of his own interpretation of Aristotle to be not only faithful to the Stagirite, but also a perfectly naturalistic accounting of all the phenomena of human knowing.[66] To accuse Averroes, therefore, of resorting to "supernatural causes" is unwarranted. But his is precisely the confusion that Aquinas sees as being at the root of the problem. In refusing to "naturalize" fully the human intellect within the embodied, individual human being, Averroes and the Averroists utterly confuse the exact standing and place of the human intellect within the gradation of

---

65. SCG, II, 76, no. 1576.

66. See Deborah Black, "Conjunction and the Identity of Knower and Known in Aver-roes," *American Catholic Philosophical Quarterly* 73, no. 2 (1999): 159–84. Marc Geoffroy explores Averroes's attempt to defend against al-Farabi the possibility of the conjunction of the acquired human intellect with the agent intellect as both a natural and essential

intellects. If the act of knowing comes from or is initiated from "outside" the individual human being, that is, from an intellect of an order higher than the human soul, then there is no basis for asserting that intellectual thought is "natural," which is to say, inherent in the individual human being. As we saw in our chapters on Averroes, this confusion has a foundation in the Averroist understanding of the relation of intellection to revelation: they are essentially two aspects of the same reality and activity. The revealed book in Averroes is assimilated or "digested" into the separate intellect and, in that fashion at least, completely "naturalized." But one can, as al-Ghazali did, simply look at this relationship inversely, that is, assimilate the separate intellect into the revealed book, making all intellectual activity essentially miraculous in nature. It is no wonder, therefore, that Christian thinkers, when receiving Averroes's works, would compound this confusion with a doctrine of the "double truth."

A second objection is that Thomas himself is inconsistent: he himself used, even in his earliest writings, the Averroist account of human knowing to explain how the beatific vision is possible. Thomas argued that, since the divine essence is beyond the capacity of the human intellect to know adequately, God "in-forms" the human intellect in a manner analogous to how Averroes argues that the separate agent and material intellects "in-form" the acquired human intellect whenever it knows scientific truth. But the beatific vision lies precisely within the realm of grace. Aquinas does indeed use Averroes's argument of a separate "agent" intellect as a model for how our intellects will be strengthened by divine grace in the beatific vision. But, of course, this argument appears in a totally different context. We see this especially in his *Commentary on the Sentences* of Peter Lombard, where he writes, "Whatever is the case for other separate substances, nevertheless, we must accept that mode in the vision of God in his

---

precondition for all knowing as well as a perfectly natural consummation of all human intellectual activity. See Geoffroy, "Averroès sur l'intellect comme cause agente et cause formelle et la question de la junction," in *Averroès et les averroismes juif et latin: actes du colloque international, Paris, 16–17 juin, 2005* (Turnhout: Brepols, 2007), 77–110. Richard Taylor points out the debt that Aquinas owed to Averroes in properly understanding the process of abstraction in human cognition, even though Aquinas criticizes Averroes for making the agent of that process ontologically separate from the human being. See Taylor, "Aquinas's Naturalized Epistemology," *Proceedings of the American Catholic Philosophical Association* 79 (2006): 85–102.

essence" (*Et quidquid sit de aliis substantiis separatis, tamen istum modum oportet nos accipere in visione Dei per essentiam*), adding:

> Because the relation of the divine essence to our intellect is as the re-
> lation of form to matter. For whenever there are some two things of
> which one is more perfect than the other and these are received in the
> same recipient, there is a relation of one of the two to the other, namely
> of the more perfect to the less perfect, as is the relation of form to mat-
> ter. [This is] just as when light and color are received in the diaphanous
> [medium] for which light is related to color as form to matter. Similarly,
> when the intellective power is received in the soul and the divine essence
> itself is present although not in the same mode, the divine essence will
> be related to the intellect as form to matter [*essentia divina se habebit ad
> intellectum sicut forma ad materiam*].[67]

Indeed, Averroes would agree with Thomas against the so-called Averroists in insisting that the agent intellect actualizes knowledge in us not
as an extrinsic moving or efficient cause but as an intrinsic formal cause
or "form for us" (*al-ṣura la-na*):

> For because that in virtue of which something carries out its proper ac-
> tivity is the form, while we carry out our proper activity in virtue of the
> agent intellect, it is necessary that the agent intellect be form in us....
> For assurance of the possibility of the conjoining of the [agent] intellect
> with us lies in explaining its relation to a human being in a relation of
> form and agent, not a relation of agent alone.[68]

Nevertheless, Aquinas sees a difficulty in understanding how an agent
that is ontologically separate and higher than the human soul can be
both "intrinsic" to the soul as well as be a form that is not only "for
us" but also our perfection and final form *qua* a natural being. Hence,
throughout the *De unitate intellectus*, Thomas argues that the ultimate
formal agent of the human being is in *this* human being. If there is to be
any "in-forming" of the human being by a higher intellect, it cannot occur on the level of nature, but on the level of grace. In fact, Aquinas does
talk about the workings of grace in terms of formal causality, as "white-

---

67. S. *Thomas Aquinatis Scriptum Super Libros Sententiarum Magistri Petri Lombardi*,
ed. P. Mandonnet and M. F. Moos, vol. 4 (Paris: 1929–47), *In 4 Sent.*, d. 49, q. 2, a. 1.

68. Averroes, *Long Commentary on the "De Anima,"* 399, 401.

ness makes white or justice makes just."[69] The "in-forming" of the human intellect by the divine intellect is perfective of natural knowing and does not replace it, because the object of knowledge in the beatific vision lies beyond the natural powers of the human intellect to know unaided by the light of glory. One can argue here, again, on Thomistic grounds that Averroes and the Averroists confuse the realm of nature with that of grace and natural knowledge with divine revelation.[70]

CONCLUSION

Averroes, as we saw earlier, reduced revelation to a merely poetic and imaginative "cousin" or "relation" of philosophical cognition, which alone gives genuine knowledge, so that it might be accessible to the masses.[71] There is a good deal of evidence that the "Latin Averroists" followed Averroes in this attitude.[72] But this is not a "double truth" theory; if anything, it is actually the opposite in that it establishes a sort of "mono-truth" or univocal account of natural and revealed truth; the difference lies only in the mode in which it is presented. Again, this exemplifies an *episteme* of digestion. For Averroes, truth is predicated univocally; revealed "truth" presents in imaginative and poetic, sensual form for the masses, the same truth that is grasped more perfectly through demonstrative reasoning by the philosophical elite. Essential to Thomas's account, however, is an "analogical" account of truth: revealed truths and those truths known by natural reason indeed refer to the same truth,

69. "Gratia, secundum quod est qualitas, dicitur agere in animam non per modum causae efficientis, sed per modum causae formalis: sicut albedo facit album, et iustitia iustum." *S. Th.* I-II, 110, 2, ad 1.

70. See J. B. Brenet, "Vision béatifique et séparation de l'intellect au début du XVIe siècle: Pour Averroès et contre Thomas d'Aquin?" *Freiburger Zeitschrift für Philosophie und Theologie* 53, no. 1/2 (2006): 310–42; and Richard Taylor, "Intellect as Intrinsic Formal Cause in the Soul according to Aquinas and Averroes," in *The Afterlife of the Platonic Soul: Reflections of Platonic Psychology in the Monotheistic Religions,* ed. Maha Elkiasy-Friermtuh and John M. Dillon (Leiden: Brill, 2009), 206.

71. Richard Taylor, "Averroes' Epistemology and Its Critique by Aquinas," in *Medieval Masters: Essays in Memory of Msgr. E. A. Synan* (Houston: University of St. Thomas Press, 1999), 174.

72. See, in particular, Alain de Libera, *Penser au moyen âge.*

but the former is perfective of the latter in that it raises the believer into a lived and personal relationship with the Truth. If, however, this relationship to the Truth or Word is to be a lived and personal one for the human being, it must be one lived in and through the body; any genuine understanding of God by "this man" must come from "this man." In like manner, if God is to establish in human beings this lived and personal relationship with the Truth, which is himself, then he must himself become embodied Word in order to do so.

"Everything that is received, is received in the mode of the receiver." When we know an object, it incarnates itself in us, which is why, according to biblical usage, for a man to "know" his wife is to be united to her in one flesh. So, in Christ, human and divine knowing are united "in one flesh":[73] this, in turn, forms the basis of union with Christ in the "flesh" of the Eucharist and the "flesh" of his "body," the Church. This means that if revelation is to perfect—and not supersede—the human intellect, it must be given in an incarnate mode, not just in material images and symbols, but as an individual material substance of a rational nature, to whom we can relate as mind to mind and not simply as mind to object. For only in this way is material creation itself *redeemed* as the mediation between the human intellect and the divine intellect (as we saw in the last chapter). Indeed, if divine revelation is to perfect the human intellect, it must incarnate itself in us by taking upon itself our human nature in all its materiality and vulnerability. Then to the degree that we, as substances-in-relation relate to this incarnate revelation or Word in love, to that degree does our intellect come to participate in this incarnate revelation. To preserve this understanding of a specifically Christian revelation, I contend, is what is at the basis of Thomas's vigorous polemic against the Averroists.

---

73. "One can think that, for a scholastic, this formula would lead us back to the Incarnation, for in Christ, 'true man and true God,' there is a union without mixture of two natures, the divine and the human, in a single person, following the definition of Nicaea. Using this parallelism, one could say that whenever we know an object, it incarnates itself in us. In the same way, in the language of the Bible, whenever a man 'knows' a woman, they constitute 'one flesh' all the while remaining two. The Thomist dictum of Claudel is thus justified: if knowledge [*connaissance*] is incarnation, then even more is it a 'co-birth' [*co-naissance*]." Jean-Luc Solère, "La notion d'intentenionalité chez Thomas d'Aquin," *Philosophie* 24 (1989): 18n15.

CHAPTER 6

AQUINAS ON REVELATION
AS INCARNATE DIVINE
INTELLECT

We have seen in the two previous chapters that, though intelligible in itself, nature is also eminently *mysterious* in that its intelligibility exceeds the power of our intellect to grasp it fully. We also saw how the human intellect is essentially individual and *incarnate*. What implications do these two insights have for how Aquinas (and Christians) understand the nature and mode of revelation? It is this question that the present chapter will attempt to address.

We should also pause here to repeat something that we have already seen but which needs to made even clearer: in contrast to some contemporary notions of what constitutes "revelation," "St. Thomas holds that revelation is primarily something taking place in the human intellect and not a visible historical event or an ontological structure such as the person of Jesus Christ. According to St. Thomas it consists formally in the illumination of the mind by God."[1] The unique and overwhelming

1. Leo Elders, "Aquinas on Holy Scripture as the Medium of Divine Revelation," in *La doctrine de la révélation divine de saint Thomas d'Aquin*, ed. Leo Elders (Vatican City: Libreria Editrice Vaticana, 1990), 132. Fr. Elders continues: "The events as such, recorded in the Bible, and in particular the gospels, are not yet revelation in the strict sense of the term: the *insight* into their significance, given by God to the apostles and evangelists, constitutes revelation. In fact, revelation is the impression of God's knowledge on the mind of the apostle or prophet. This communication as such takes place in a passing way, although the knowledge communicated remains present in the apostles and in the Church."

importance of Christ, therefore, is that Christ is the Wisdom or Word in Itself that not only illumines the human intellect, but also transforms the whole human person, body, soul, and intellect, to be conformed to divine Wisdom. Whereas in the Old Testament, all revelation was mediated by angels (though the case of Moses is the subject of some dispute), with the coming of Christ such mediation ceases and the divine Word comes to "dwell among us." "Thanks to the hypostatic union, the human mind of the Word incarnate is immediately open to influxes from the divine mind, for it is the human mind of one who is personally God. The revelation from which the Christian religion takes its rise is, in the first place, a vision in the inspired intellect of Jesus, in the human soul of Christ."[2] It is through Christ, therefore, that the self-subsistent Word is made adequate to be received by the human intellect, not simply because the mode of the Word is in the mode of the receiver, but also because the mode of the Word transforms the nature of the receiver itself in such a way that human nature, by the grace of Christ, can be raised by love or *caritas* to receive and thus know and, more importantly, know the divine world because he or she *loves* the divine Word.

IS PHILOSOPHY SUFFICIENT UNTO ITSELF? AQUINAS ON THE NEED FOR DIVINE REVELATION

Thomas Aquinas begins the *Summa theologiae* with the question: "Whether it is necessary to have another doctrine other than the philosophical disciplines" (*Utrum sit necessarium, praeter philosophicas disciplinas, aliam doctrinam haberi*). To the contemporary reader, the first question of the *Summa* may seem surprising: is not Thomas, as a medieval theologian, keen to justify the existence of *philosophy* not theology? After all, as we have seen, Averroes proceeds in precisely this fashion. It is Islamic law which legitimizes and sits in judgment of philosophy, not the other way around. But here we encounter precisely where the great

2. Aidan Nichols, *Discovering Aquinas: An Introduction to His Life, Works, and Influence* (Grand Rapids, Mich.: William B. Eerdmans, 2002), 26.

chasm opens up between the ways of understanding the relation of faith and reason, of theology (or "religious law") and philosophy in the Christian and Islamic traditions. For a Christian theologian like Aquinas, it is not a question of what is *legitimate* (one, the other, or both), but of what completes or perfects the other in its proper nature and how.

In posing such a question at the outset, Aquinas is doing nothing unusual for medieval scholastic theology: for such theologians the first question in the order of inquiry is whether it is necessary to study the subject matter under discussion.[3] This question for theology, or "sacred doctrine,"[4] is all the more pressing in that the philosophical sciences (that is, metaphysics as well as physics and the "science of the soul," psychology) seem to treat universally of everything that can be known by human reason. But in his answer to question 1, Aquinas states simply that a "doctrine" or teaching other than philosophy or philosophical disciplines (like physics, natural history, psychology, or study of the soul, etc.), is necessary for two reasons: the first is because "the human being is ordered to God as to a certain end which exceeds the comprehension of reason."[5] Already, as we have seen in previous chapters, Thomas notes the limited nature of human reason; there is something in the nature of reality itself that exceeds—is "more than"—what human reason

3. See Andreas Speer, "*Sapientia Nostra*. Zum Verhältnis von philosophischer und theologischer Weisheit in den Pariser Debatten am Ende des 13. Jahrhunderts," in Aertsen, Emery, and Speer, *Nach der Verurteilung von 1277*, 248–75; Zimmermann, *Ontologie oder Metaphysik?*; and Honnefelder, "Die zweite Anfang der Metaphysik."

4. Thomas's use of the term "sacred doctrine" rather than, in his time, the newer term "theology" is significant here. As Gilles Mongeau remarks: "We should not be misled by our current understanding of the term 'revelation' into thinking that there are two bodies of knowledge, on the one hand *sacra doctrina* and on the other hand divine revelation in our sense, such that the distinction becomes one between theology and Scripture, or theology and the Church's teaching, or some similar dichotomy. Henri Donneaud points out that for Aquinas, the phrase *revelationem divinam* preserves a more 'verbal' meaning, namely God's act of revealing. Thus, 'revelatio points directly to the divine act … the act itself of revealing, of unveiling, of causing to know … *Scriptura* or *doctrina*, on the one hand, signify the result of this revelation on the side of human beings.' We can say, then, that *sacra doctrina* is human participation, in all its forms, in God's act of revealing." Mongeau, *Embracing Wisdom: The "Summa theologiae" as Spiritual Pedagogy* (Toronto: Pontifical Institute of Mediaeval Studies, 2015), 12.

5. *S. Th.* I, 1, 1: "Primo quidem, quia homo ordinatur ad Deum sicut ad quendam finem qui comprehensionem rationis excedit."

can know. There is something about the very contingency of the world that transcends human reason. Human reason cannot grasp *why* the world *is* from the world itself.

This leads Thomas to the second reason for the necessity of divine revelation: that "the truth concerning God that is investigated through reason, would come to man only by a very few, privileged people through a long time, and mixed with many errors."[6] Philosophy is for the few. Its rigorous reasoning and arcane terminology can only be but for the few. And the ancient philosophers not only admitted this fact but even boasted of it. The ancient philosophical ideal was for an intellectual and moral elite, who had the education and leisure to understand and contemplate the necessary causal structure of reality and its inner providential harmony.[7] The ideal was to understand why the cosmos *had* to be such as it was. There is nothing, therefore, that the philosopher could not in principle know. But once the world is seen and interpreted as radically contingent, that is, as freely created, this philosophical ideal breaks down and proves itself utterly inadequate. So not only is philosophical "salvation" for the few, but it turns out that it is not really "salvation" at all, but is itself an inadequate understanding of the world and is, therefore, "mixed with many errors." Hence, in order that all men might be saved, a divine revelation was necessary that oriented men beyond what reason could investigate.[8] If the human being is to know the first cause of all that exists, and the existence of all things besides the first cause is contingent, while the first cause is utterly free, then philosophy cannot know this cause. The first cause must give itself to be known through revelation.

This leads Aquinas to the second question of the *Summa*: "Whether sacred doctrine is a science" (*Utrum sacra doctrina sit scientia*). For if the world is the product of a free creation and knowledge of God the result

6. Ibid.: "Quia veritas de Deo, per rationem investigata, a paucis, et per longum tempus, et cum admixione multorum errorum, homini proveniret."

7. For an account of this philosophical ideal both ancient and medieval, see the books by Pierre Hadot, *Qu'est que la philosophie antique?* (Paris: Editions Gallimard, 1995); and de Libera, *Penser au moyen âge*.

8. *S. Th.* I, 1, 1: "quod necessarium fuit ad humanam salutem, esse doctrinam quandam secundum revelationem divinam praeter philosophicas disciplinas quae ratione humana investigantur."

of a free self-revelation, then how can we call theology a "science"? Or another way of putting it would be: does sacred doctrine exhibit a logical order in its treatment of God and how creatures relate to God? For it is of the essence of a science to show the inner logic of things; and the very structure of the *Summa* is meant to show this inner logic.[9] And yet, is there not an inherent illogic at the center of the theological enterprise? As the first of the objections to this article states, every science must proceed from principles known in themselves, but theology does not and cannot proceed from such principles, since these are known only to God. Therefore, theological reasoning and discourse must be based not on rational principles known in themselves, but on faith.[10] But this is, in fact, precisely the reason why theology is a science, indeed, a preeminent science: "And in this way, sacred doctrine is a science, because it proceeds from principles known by the light of a superior science, which is evidently the science of God and the blessed. Thus as the musicologist puts faith in [*credit*] the principles handed down to him by the arithmetician, so sacred doctrine puts faith in [*credit*] the principles revealed to it by God."[11] Or to use examples perhaps more familiar to us: just as an engineer uses the principles of physics, or a biologist the principles of chemistry, in order to build a bridge or understand metabolism, so the theologian uses principles of a "higher" or more basic or comprehensive science, namely, that which is identical with God's self-knowledge made known to us through revelation.

9. For a quick overview of the debates surrounding the structure of the *Summa theologiae*, see Brian Johnstone, "The Debate on the Structure of the *Summa Theologiae* of Saint Thomas Aquinas," in *Aquinas as Authority: A Collection of Studies Presented at the Second Conference of the Thomas Instituut te Utrecht, December 14–16, 2000* (Leuven: Peeters, 2002), 187–200. Many scholars covered in this survey are reacting to the theory put forth many years ago by Dom Chenu that the structure of the *Summa* conforms to a Neoplatonic scheme of *exitus* and *reditus* or of "emanation" and "return": cf., M.-D. Chenu, *Introduction à l'étude de saint Thomas d'Aquin* (Paris: J. Vrin, 1950). There are, however, problems with this proposal, especially since the third part of the *Summa* does not seem to fit well into this scheme. For good alternative explanations, see te Velde, *Aquinas on God*, chap. 1; and Jean-Pierre Torrell, *Aquinas's "Summa": Background, Structure, and Reception*, trans. Benedict M. Guevin (Washington, D.C.: The Catholic University of America Press, 2005).

10. Though it should be noted that Thomas does not deny that discourse about God cannot proceed from any rational principles other than God himself.

11. *S. Th.* I, 1, 2.

Now this account of the "scientific nature" of theology is open to criticism. For one thing, all other human sciences depend on "higher" sciences whose principles are, all the same, still self-evident and knowable by at least a few. The principles as they are in God's knowledge of himself are not self-evident with respect to us nor accessible to us at all (at least in this life). But while Aquinas wants to show that the status of theology as a science is not unreasonable, he does not want to argue that it is therefore reducible to or like the philosophical sciences. To the contrary, as Rudi te Velde points out:

> Thomas proceeds from a basic theological assumption, consisting in the claim that God has made known his truth to man through revelation and that, consequently, the truth claim of Christian faith—the "system of revealed truth"—is warranted by God himself. This basic assumption is nowhere formally demonstrated. And how could it be? One cannot step outside revelation in order to prove its truth from a logically independent standpoint. On the other hand: Thomas's whole work can be seen as one persistent attempt to argue for its plausibility and intelligibility by showing how its alleged truth can be made understandable.[12]

And as Bruce Marshall adds: "Aquinas apparently just rejects any attempt to root certainty about the contents of the Christian faith in certainty about their status. We cannot *infer* that the articles of faith must be true because miracles, or other naturally available signs, establish their revealed status."[13] There is no way that the human mind can judge the validity or truth of revelation using a logical standard higher than or independent of God, since God is, by definition, the first cause and therefore the principle of all rational thought. We are left, therefore, in the position where revelation must validate itself, because it is God who reveals it; and it can only do this when we accept its principles and work out their implications using the tools of philosophy. Philosophy, howev-

---

12. Te Velde, *Aquinas on God*, 3.

13. Marshall continues: "On Aquinas's account, this would be to base what is more certain on what is less certain. The faith which assents to the teaching of scripture and creed deliberately clings to the God who makes himself known through them as the source and measure of all truth—the first truth (*prima veritas*), in Aquinas's phrase." Bruce Marshall, "*Quod Scit Una Uetula*: Aquinas on the Nature of Theology," in van Nieuwenhove and Wawrykow, *The Theology of Thomas Aquinas*, 12.

er, can ultimately only prove *that* there is a first cause and, perhaps, some of its basic attributes. But *what* or *who* that first cause is, philosophy cannot tell us.[14] The First Cause must reveal himself to us, if he is to be known as he is. And this self-revelation implies a creative freedom that the principles of philosophy cannot capture. In this way the principles of sacred doctrine are higher than any human science and are, at the same time, inaccessible to human reason or science.

If the validity and authenticity of divine revelation has no independent logical verification, but relies simply on the fact that it is God himself who authenticates it, then what certainty do we have that it is real or true revelation? It would seem that Thomas's initial answer would satisfy few today:

> In both these respects [greater certitude and greater worth] this science [divine science] exceeds the other speculative sciences. With respect to greater certitude, because other sciences have certitude from the natural light of human reason, which is able to err; but this science [divine science] has certitude from the light of a divine science, which is unable to be mistaken. With respect to greater dignity of its subject matter, because this science is principally about those things which by their loftiness transcend reason, while the other sciences consider only those things which submit to reason.[15]

Thus, divine science is more certain because it comes from God himself, who cannot err, unlike merely human reason. Moreover, it is greater in worth, because divine science treats of things that are above and beyond what reason can understand. These replies may strike many as circular: divine revelation is more certain and of greater dignity because it is, well, divine. But there is, as is often the case, hints of a deeper answer in Aquinas's replies to objections to this question. He notes in his rely to objection one:

> Nothing prevents that that which is more certain according to nature be less certain to us due to the weakness of our intellect, which "relates

14. For the debates over the place of theology vis-à-vis philosophy and science in the thirteenth century, see Albert Zimmermann, "Glaube und Wissen (S.th. II-II, qq. 1–9)," in Speer, *Thomas von Aquin*, 271–97; and Speer, "*Sapientia Nostra.*"
15. *S.Th.* I, 1, 5: "Utrum sacra doctrina sit dignior aliis scientiis."

to the most evident things of nature as the eye of the owl does to the light of the sun" (*Metaph.* ii. lect. i). Whence the doubt which happens concerning certain articles of faith is not due to the uncertainty of the thing [itself], but due to the weakness of the human intellect. Yet the least which can be had by cognition of the highest things is more desirable that what could be had concerning the least things, as is said in *De animalibus*, xi.[16]

So indeed, the subject matter of divine science of theology strikes us as uncertain, but not because it is uncertain in itself, but because our intellects are in need of much help in order to grasp this divine subject matter. That help may come in the form of "subsidiary sciences" like philosophy and logic;[17] but more importantly, it must come through the grace of Jesus Christ. "As the Father's Word become our flesh, the human being Jesus Christ is in his own distinctive way the *prima veritas*. As such we have to believe his teaching simply because it is his, and not because of any evidence we might have for its divine status."[18] Since all that is known is known in the mode of the knower, the human intellect can know God as he is in himself only in and through the mode of human knowing as redeemed in the God-Man, who is Jesus Christ.

Thus, it is as man in the flesh that God has spoken to us, as man to man, that is the basis of all divine science—which is not a study of first causes but of God as he is in himself.[19] Thomas repeats this point a little later in raising the question "whether this doctrine [sacred doctrine] is argumentative" (*Utrum haec doctrina sit argumentiva*), for it would seem that, since if something is revealed by God himself, then any discussion about it is ended. But, Aquinas argues, this is not the case:

> To argue from authority is eminently appropriate for this doctrine [sacred doctrine], inasmuch as the principles of this doctrine are obtained

16. Ibid., ad 1.

17. Ibid., ad 2.

18. Marshall, "*Quod Scit Una Uetula*," 13.

19. "'What is known is in the knower in the mode of the knower' ([*S. Th.*] q. 1, a. 2, c.). Jesus Christ had spoken as a man to man; he took men seriously as a partner and taught them insofar as he bound himself to their mode of knowing and understanding and, using their own speech, exchanged thoughts and not seldom got into heated debates with them." Zimmermann "Glaube und Wissen," 277.

through revelation. And thus it is necessary that it be believed on the authority of those by whom the revelation has been made. Nor does this fact take away from the dignity of this doctrine, for granted that an argument from authority grounded on human reason is the weakest, an argument from authority grounded on divine revelation is the strongest. Nevertheless, sacred doctrine uses human reason not in order to prove faith (for that we take away from faith all merit), but in order to make evident other things which are handed down in this doctrine. Since therefore grace does not abolish nature, but perfects it, so should natural reason submit to faith as the natural inclination of the will submits to charity [*Cum enim gratia non tollat naturam, sed perficiat, oportet quod naturalis ratio subserviat fidei; sicut et naturalis inclinatio voluntatis obsequitur caritati*].... Hence it is that sacred doctrine uses even the authority of philosophers where they were able through natural reason to know the truth.[20]

There are two things that Thomas points out here. First, we should not confuse appeals to any human authority, or even human reason itself, with an appeal to divine authority, which is rooted in God's perfect knowledge of himself and of his creatures. Second, even if we grant that divine authority is much more "efficacious" than human authority, the point is not that we are able to prove the articles of faith in the same way that a mathematician proves a theorem. Rather, the point of sacred doctrine is to clarify and make transparent to reason a relationship to the divine authority that is always already there. As Thomas famously says here, "grace does not destroy nature, but perfects it." Just as charity perfects the natural bent of our will by fulfilling all that our will truly and deeply desires, so does divine revelation and our faith in that revelation perfect our natural reason by revealing who the first cause of the philosophers truly is and thereby making our reasoning more sure and clear. And just as the natural bent of our will does not find its perfection in charity until it actually falls in love, so natural reason cannot know the truth of things until it encounters that truth through faith in the authority and testimony of those who did so directly. The verification of revelation is in the perfection of the intellect itself through faith in Christ.

20. *S. Th.* I, 1, 8, ad 2.

Thus, sacred doctrine is not just a science, but it is *wisdom* (*sapientia*). Like the nature of science, it is the nature of wisdom to order things according to their essential causes showing, for example, how the essence or nature of such-and-such an animal is the cause of such-and-such properties and accidents in it. But it is of the nature of wisdom to know how all causes relate to a (or the) first cause.[21] Insofar, therefore, as sacred doctrine treats of the highest cause, it is also the essence of wisdom. But in this question, Aquinas makes an interesting distinction: ancient pagan philosophers such as Aristotle also studied all causes in relation to a first cause, which they called "god." How is their doctrine any different from the one we find in Christian revelation? The difference, Thomas asserts, is that the ancient philosophers contemplated the first and highest cause insofar as they came to know him (or it) through their investigations of sensible creatures. But sacred doctrine studies the first cause not only in this sense but also as made known "by himself alone and from himself, and to others as communicated through revelation".[22] In other words, sacred doctrine is supreme wisdom—higher than even philosophical wisdom—because its content comes not only from human reasoning but from the first cause himself as disclosed by himself. Thus, Christian wisdom distinguishes itself from philosophical wisdom in that the former both proceeds from and leads to a living and direct *relationship* with the first cause himself that is more than a relation of mind to object but a relation of mind to mind. In that sense, Christian wisdom *presumes* faith; it does not establish faith.[23]

For Aquinas, it is this direct disclosure of the first cause to the human intellect in a living relationship that makes it wisdom and thus perfective of human reason, not contrary to it. As we saw previously, the human person as person is essentially substance-in-relation. Thus, to be in relation to God, who is substance-in-relation in itself (self-subsistent

21. Ibid., 6: "Utrum haec doctrina sit sapientia."
22. Ibid.: "sibi soli de seipso, et aliis per revelationem communicatum."
23. See Mark D. Jordan, "The Protreptic Structure of the 'Summa Contra Gentiles,'" *The Thomist* 50, no. 2 (1986): 194. Jordan argues in this article that the *gentiles* of the title represent pre-Christian or extra-Christian philosophy. Thus, the whole of *Summa contra Gentiles* is an attempt to show that such philosophy without Christ is not really wisdom.

substance-in-relation or Trinity) is to be perfected in our personhood, which is our essential being. For it is in the very *claim* to self-disclosure by the first cause that human reason comes up against its own limits and conditions, for in this claim, human reason confronts the possibility that the First Cause is not just object for it but also infinite subject for itself. Human reason becomes aware that it is in no way absolute.[24] Reason becomes aware of its own limits only when confronted with the truth about God—a truth that, by definition, exceeds any ability to know it.[25] Awareness of the ineffable mystery of even the claim to self-disclosure by the first cause, whom we call "God," in itself awakes reason insofar as reason becomes aware of what is in principle beyond it. As te Velde remarks: "The mystery of God is not a mystery because it defeats the attempts of reason to understand, but because its truth attracts reason beyond its comprehension."[26] The whole notion of revelation, of the self-disclosure of the first cause to human reason, is itself a logical consequence of the *super-intelligibility* of reality. What is mysterious about reality is that *its truth is more than we can comprehend*—not that it is fundamentally irrational, for that would make the use of reason itself irrational. And if reality is more intelligible than what our intellect can understand, then it follows that the super-intelligibility of reality would have to disclose itself to us in such a way that it may be properly understood, because by its own resources the human intellect is unequipped to comprehend such a super-intelligibility.

This leads Thomas to discuss the *mode* in which the self-disclosure of the first cause of being comes to us in revelation. First, revelation seems to come to us primarily in the mode of figures and metaphors. This creates a problem: is the use of metaphors really appropriate for a doctrine that presumes to constitute not only a science but the highest

24. "Not reason as such, but the presumption of reason to have an absolute hold on truth prevents a reasonable understanding of the truth of faith. So the issue is not a defense of the 'reasonableness' of Christian faith before reason. Aquinas's objective is to confront natural reason with its own condition, to make reason aware of its own limits on the search for truth. We need more truth than our reason can grasp." Rudi te Velde, "Natural Reason in the *Summa Contra Gentiles*," *Medieval Philosophy and Theology* 4 (1994): 58.

25. Ibid., 60.

26. Ibid., 64.

wisdom? Does not the use of metaphors and figures indicate a purely "poetic" mode of thought, lacking in the clarity and rigor of rational
thought and genuine science? Aquinas confronts these questions in article 9 of question 1 of the *Summa theologiae*, "Whether sacred Scripture
ought to use metaphors" (*Utrum sacra Scriptura debeat uti metaphoris*).
In his answer, Thomas again reminds us of the peculiar position of the
human intellect at the bottom of the "hierarchy" of intellects—the human intellect is not the only kind of intellect, but one mode of intellect
among many:

> It is fitting [*conveniens est*] for Sacred Scripture that it tell of divine and
> spiritual things under the guise of corporeal things. Now God provides
> for all things according to what is suitable to their nature [*Deus enim
> omnibus providet secundum quod competit eorum naturae*]. It is, howev-
> er, natural to man that he come to intelligible truths through sensible
> things, because all of our knowledge has its beginning in sense [percep-
> tion]. Whence in Sacred Scripture spiritual realties are fittingly related
> to us under the likeness of bodily things. And this is what Dionysius
> says (*Cael. Hier.* i): "it is impossible for us to be enlightened by the di-
> vine rays unless by a variety of many sacred veils."[27]

Aquinas then adds that communicating truths through sensible images
is also necessary so that even the simple might understand the highest
truths about God, which he had also discussed in relation to the necessity of revelation itself in article 1. But the first reason is, I think, the
more fundamental one for Aquinas. If all that is known is received in the
mode of the knower, then it is necessary that divine truths be communicated through sensible images, because the human being, as a material
substance and incarnate soul, is the lowest in the gradation of intellects
and can, therefore, only understand in and through sense perception.
Hence, Thomas appeals to Dionysius the Areopagite,[28] who says that
the "divine rays" that illumine the human intellect in truth must themselves be "hidden" and "covered" with many "sacred veils." This appeal
to Dionysius is rather ironic in a double sense: in one sense, Thomas is

27. *S. Th.* I, 1, 9.

28. As Cornelius Ernst notes, this article is "pervasively Dionysian." See his, "Metaphor
and Ontology in Sacra Doctrina," *The Thomist* 37, no. 3 (1974): 405.

appealing to an authority known for his thoroughly Neoplatonic epistemology, which is most remarkable for its disregard for the importance of
the senses. Nonetheless, Thomas sees a necessary relationship between
the "blinding brightness" of divine truth and our need for sense images.
In the second sense, there is a paradox in the very words of Dionysius
themselves, insofar as they assert that a necessary condition for divine
revelation is that they be *concealed* in sense images. The condition of divine unveiling is veiling. As Thomas explains in his reply to objection
2, this has the function of drawing the believer deeper *into* the divine
mysteries and the light of truth:

> The ray of divine revelation is not destroyed because of the sensible
> likenesses by which it is covered, as Dionysius says (*Cael. Hier.* i), but
> remains in its truth so that minds to whom revelation has been made do
> not rest in the likenesses. Rather it raises them to a knowledge of intelli-
> gible things and, through them to whom revelation has been made, oth-
> ers also can be instructed in these matters. Whence those things which
> in one place in Scripture are related metaphorically, in other places are
> expounded more directly [*expressius*]. Moreover, the very hiding itself in
> likenesses is useful for the exercise of those most desirous of knowledge
> and as a defense against the ridicule of unbelievers, about whom it is
> said: "Give not holy things to the dogs" (Mt vii. 6).[29]

At the end of his reply, Thomas mentions the *usefulness* of hiding the
deeper meaning of Scripture under sensible "veils": that is, that it "exercis-
es the mind" and keeps divine truths from being ridiculed by non-believers
(*infideles*). But the bulk of his reply is taken up with the more fundamental
reason, which is to prevent the mind of the believer from "resting" in metaphors, but to pull him or her, so to speak, into an intimate knowledge
of divine truth. When the mind of such a believer has become *personally
acquainted* with such truths, he or she may then transmit them to others.
The whole point of using material figures and sense images in Scripture
is to draw the mind of the believer not into an abstract, objective knowledge of divine truths but into an intimate, inter-subjective relationship to
divine truth, which is then passed on inter-subjectively to others through

29. *S. Th.* I, 1, 9, ad 2.

intimate personal relations. In this sense, metaphors or poetic images are more than useful in "persuading the masses," as in Averroes, but serve an essential function especially for the *wise*, drawing them more deeply into truths and, more fundamentally, a *personal relationship of and to truth* that cannot be "objectified" or "impersonalized" by philosophic reason.

From this it follows that Sacred Scripture can have many senses and ever deeper layers of meaning. And in article 10 of the first question of the *Summa*, Aquinas gives us an extremely condensed exposition of these multiple senses as informed by centuries of medieval and patristic thought on the matter.[30] The issue at hand is "whether sacred Scripture may have many senses under one letter" (*Utrum sacra Scriptura sub una littera habeat plures sensus*). Thomas responds:

> It is in the power of the author Sacred Scripture, who is God, not only to signify his meaning with words [*voces*], which even man is able to do, but also with the things themselves [*sed etiam res ipsas*]. Thus, whereas in all other sciences words do the signifying, this science has the property that the things, which are signified by words, also signify something themselves. Hence the first signification, by which words signify things, pertains to the first sense, which is the historical or literal sense. That signification whereby things are signified by words, but signify in turn other things, is said to be the spiritual sense, which is based on the literal and supports it.[31]

This is a most interesting passage. According to Thomas, the multiple senses of Scripture stem from two sets of signification. In the first, you have the text of Scripture itself referring to things (God himself or creatures or events insofar as they relate something about God). This, as Thomas says, human beings can do: all our sciences are words "about" things *in rerum natura*. But in sacred Scripture, it is not just the *words* that signify things, but the *things themselves* that signify something about God. Unlike humans, God can, so to speak, "write" or communicate

---

30. In particular, see *A History of Biblical Interpretation: Volume 2, The Medieval through the Reformation Periods*, ed. Alan Hauser and Duane Watson (Grand Rapids, Mich.: William B. Eerdmans, 2009); P. C. Spicq, *Esquisse d'une histoire de l'exégèse latine au moyen âge* (Paris: J. Vrin, 1944).
31. *S. Th.* I, 1, 10.

with creatures, with things and events themselves, which fact, in turn, opens up other meanings.[32] So there are, in a sense, two texts: the actual written text of the Bible, and additionally the "text" of creation itself, which also speaks of God. Hence, you have in the medieval tradition the teaching on the "two texts" of Scripture and creation. The realization, then, that creatures come "between" the divine and human intellects is not, as we saw in our discussion of Aquinas on truth, a defect of creation but rather an essential property of its perfection; it is a condition of God's self-communication to humanity. The implications of this for the Christian understanding of revelation are significant.

Creation is a text itself. God "writes" with the things and events of the natural and historical world. Creatures and events are as much the language of God as the biblical text. Indeed, as Nicholas Healy points out, Scripture, in Aquinas, "cannot be identified with revelation":

> It is the closest possible thing we have to revelation, since it is the apostolic witness to that revealed knowledge, brought about in the minds of the prophets and the apostles, of matters otherwise unknowable to us. But it is a human document.... With Augustine, Thomas insists that it is Christ alone who is the door. It is revelation as such, the event of God's Word, which is the truth that leads us to God. Scripture is not that perfect, divine truth. But is the sure and sufficient witness to that truth, and it is on that account true.[33]

Scripture is, strictly speaking, not revelation but a *witness* to revelation, because God "writes" with things and events even more than he writes with words. Or, more accurately, the Word of God is not a written or even spoken text but a *real being*. He is a *person* or an "individual substance of a rational nature." Thus, the Word of God is not a text, properly speaking, nor a thing, but is, in a sense, *both*: the eternal and divine Word become real, created, incarnate intellect, while remaining wholly infinite, uncreated, and perfect intellect. Therefore, only the uncreated

---

32. "Sensus isti non multiplicantur propter hoc quod una vox multa significet; sed quia ipsae res significatae per voces, aliarum rerum possunt esse signa." Ibid., ad 1.

33. Nicholas Healy, introduction to *Aquinas on Scripture: An Introduction to His Biblical Commentaries* ed. Thomas Weinandy, Daniel Keating, and John Yocum (London: Continuum, 2006), 15.

Word of God as incarnate man can unite into one both the signification of words and the signification of things, so that that self-disclosure, the divine Word, may be revealed to us in a mode adequate to the human intellect. For it is the person of Christ that holds far greater mysteries than any text could capture, and yet it is in encountering this mystery of the person of Christ that we are perfect as persons, as substances-in-relation, and are thus revealed to ourselves, and the texts of both creation and of revelation (as written down in the books of the Jewish prophets) become intelligible.[34] It is in encountering Christ that the mystery of the intelligibility of the universe comes into focus as the super-intelligibility characteristic of incarnate personhood.

KNOWING AND NAMING GOD

Knowledge of God as he is in himself (and not merely as the first cause of creatures) is the end or goal of "sacred doctrine." But this statement, at first glance, is problematic: how can the human intellect reach this end, if it is naturally incapable of reaching it? How can we say that knowing God is the end of sacred doctrine when that end, according to that same doctrine, is beyond the capacity of human reason to know? Aquinas seeks to answer this question by first noting a paradox in the human condition: on the one hand, if we could never see the essence of God, then not only ultimate beatitude but also the fulfillment of the natural capacity of our intellect for knowing truth would be impossible. The first is against all the teachings of the Christian faith; the second is contrary to reason (that is, philosophy). And yet, there is a natural desire (or a *desiderium naturae*) for an intellectual being such as the human being to know the first cause of things (*primam causam rerum*). Therefore, we must say that the human being must, ultimately and in some way, be able to see God in his essence.[35] Aquinas thus begins by considering, in the first ten articles of question 12, this problem from the

34. Thus, Saint John the evangelist can say: "But there are also many other things which Jesus did; were every one of them to be written, I suppose that the world itself could not contain the books that would be written." Jn 21: 25.
35. *S. Th.* I, 12, 1.

standpoint of the ultimate perfection of our intellect: the beatific vision. In other words, we need to answer, he seems to be saying, the question of whether this ultimate end—the beatific vision—is possible before we can address how we can know God in this life (*in via*), which he addresses in articles 11, 12, and 13.

Aquinas takes as axiomatic that seeing God through any created image or similitude is impossible: any such image would by definition limit and confine God within its own created and finite boundaries. What is necessary is a new "light," the light of glory (*lumen gloriae*), which will strengthen (*confortans*) our minds for seeing God.[36] But this still does not get us very far. More illuminating is what he says a little later about what this "light of glory" does, "Whether it is possible that the essence of God be seen by bodily eyes" (*Utrum essentia Dei videri possit oculis corporalibus*). Thomas answers that we cannot, of course, ever see God with the bodily eye, but neither can we, strictly speaking, "see" the life of another with the bodily eye either:

> From this it is clear in what way he [Augustine] understands how the glorified eyes will see God, namely, as our eyes now see the life of someone else. For life is not seen by the bodily eye, as something visible in itself, but rather as something sensible by accident; which is something not known by sense but rather at once together with sense by some other cognitive power. That the divine presence is known immediately through the intellect on the sight of bodily things follows from two causes: from the perspicuity of the intellect, and from the refulgence of divine glory in the renewed bodies.[37]

In this life we already in a sense "see" the life of an animal and the rational nature of another person, although, strictly speaking, both life and the rational soul are invisible to our senses. We look to the movements and features of the body, particularly the face, in order to infer indirectly the presence of thought and life in the thing sensed. But, again, strictly speaking, thought and life are invisible to us. We therefore rely on the other to speak to us, to use *words*, in order to make known what is

36. Ibid., 2: "Utrum essentia Dei ab intellectu creato per aliquam similitudinem videatur." 37. Ibid., 3, ad 2.

invisible to our senses in the case of other intellectual beings. So, it is, Thomas argues, with the vision of God for the blessed: they shall "see" God in creation as we see another through their face. They shall see him through the visible signs of creation; but they shall also see him by means of God's own Word addressing them directly in and through the incarnate Christ. And, as Thomas says, two things are needed for this to occur: our own end as creatures with a specific nature, that is, our intellectual capacity to "see" and understand what is beyond matter and, from God's end, the light of glory "infused" into our resurrected body, so that this vision is united to and in the body. Thus, through the light of glory we come to "see" God in and through creatures, and even more, *in our bodies*, and, most eminently, God's "rational" and personal nature in and through the human face of Christ.

While the human soul remains, therefore, *capax dei* due to its intellectual nature,[38] the human intellect needs the light of grace in order to know and see God as he is. "For the known is in the knower according to the mode of the knower. Hence, the cognition of any knower is according to the mode of its nature" (*Cognitum autem est in cognoscente secundum modum cognoscentis. Unde cuiuslibet cognoscentis cognitio est secundum modum suae naturae*). If the mode of being of the object, therefore, exceeds the nature of the knower, then knowledge of that object will be beyond the reach of that nature.[39] It follows that only God has a "nature," so to speak, that is adequate to understanding himself. Only God is able to understand himself fully through his own self-subsistent Word. The human being, by contrast, needs the help of God's grace in order to know God.[40] And for this to happen, this light of grace must come to the knower in the mode of the knower if it is to be effective. This light of grace cannot be dispensed through any similitude or created image; rather it must be given "as a certain perfection of the intellect,

38. Indeed, even more so, due to its position as pure potency in the gradation of intellects and therefore more receptive to being "re-formed" by God into an intellect capable of knowing God.

39. Ibid., 4: "Utrum aliqua intellectus creatus per sua naturalia divinam essentiam videre possit."

40. "Non igitur potest intellectus creatus Deum per essentiam videre, nisi inquantum Deus per suam gratiam se intellectui creato coniungit, ut intelligibile ab ipso." Ibid.

strengthening it for seeing God. And thus it can be said that it [the *lumen gratiae*] is not the medium *in which* God is seen, but *under which* he is seen [*Et ideo potest dici quod non est medium in quo Deus videatur: sed sub quo videtur*]."[41] The light of grace is not something we can "see" in the manner of an object or even in the manner of a medium (as air is for light); rather, it alters what we already see by putting it in a "new light," that is, in a new frame of reference. Just as the natural light of our intellect enables us to distinguish between living and non-living things and rational from non-rational beings, although life and reason are, strictly speaking, invisible to the bodily eye, so the light of grace makes the natural world "come alive" as a meaningful divine creation with every creature a sign that testifies to God's wisdom and providential purpose. We come to see the inherent intelligibility or truth of creatures as marks of a personal presence in, "behind," and beyond the created order.

In other words, the natural world becomes a "mystery" in the sense that it both reveals and hides a meaning greater than what we can perceive or understand. Just as the face of a person both reveals and conceals what is in his or her soul, so does creation, in the light of grace, reveal God's attributes; but at the same time, creation hides God, for it is not God. Given this paradox, what leads the human intellect to knowledge of God is not the human intellect itself, which is incapable of knowing what is beyond its nature to know. In the beatific vision, one intellect will see God more perfectly than another not because it has a more perfect image or similitude of God—for all similitudes are created and thus fall short of being adequate for comprehending God. Rather, "it will take place because one intellect will have a greater power or faculty to see God than another." But this faculty is lacking in the created nature of the human intellect. It is, therefore, through the "light of glory" that "establishes the intellect in a kind of *deiformity*." And what prepares the intellect to receive this light is not the intellect itself, but love or *caritas*:

41. Ibid., 5, ad 2: "Utrum intellectus creatus ad videndum Dei essentiam aliquo creato lumine indigeat." See also ibid., 9: "Utrum ea quae videntur in Deo a videntibus divinam essentiam per aliquas similitudines videantur."

Hence the more the intellect participates in the light of glory, the more perfectly it will see God. Moreover, it will participate all the more in the light of glory the more charity it has, because where there is more charity, there is more desire; and to a certain extent desire makes the one desiring apt and prepared for taking on what is desired. Whence he who has more charity will see God more perfectly and will be more blessed.[42]

It is love or charity that makes the human being, intellect and soul, apt to receiving the divine light, because it is the desire inherent in love that opens up the human intellect to receive what is beyond its nature to receive.

For, as Thomas argues in the last three articles of question 12, we cannot know God in his essence in this life. This is because in this life, all human knowing is embodied and therefore "does not naturally know anything except those things which have a form in matter or those things which can be known through such a form" (*unde naturaliter non cognoscit aliqua nisi quae habent formam in materia, vel quae per huiusmodi cognosci possunt*). The divine essence cannot be known in itself since there is no created similitude that could be adequate to it in and through which we could know the divine essence. This does not mean that we cannot know anything about God: we can know that he exists and that he must have certain attributes; but we cannot know what God is in his essence short of the beatific vision in the next life.[43] This is why Thomas asserts that in this life knowledge through grace is higher than natural knowledge of God. For natural knowledge of God, two things are required: (1) sensible images or phantasms gotten from sensible objects, and (2) the natural light of reason that abstracts universals from sensible particulars. But the light of grace strengthens the human mind in both respects: it reinforces the natural light of reason by giving it the supernatural light of faith, which gives a new meaning and orientation to the things of sense in the word, and by also, in visions and prophecy, directly giving phantasms and images more adequate to comprehend-

---

42. Ibid., 6: "Utrum videntium essentiam Dei unus alio perfectius videat."
43. Ibid., 12.

ing or seeing divine truths.[44] Thus, in the last article of question 12, Thomas finishes by noting the ultimate inadequacy of natural reason in coming to know God as he is in himself and insists on the necessity of prophecy and revelation in general to come to any adequate knowledge of what and, more importantly, *who* God is.

Prophecy, then, is a sort of preparation for God's self-disclosure through grace.[45] Aquinas quite firmly argues that prophecy constitutes a cognitive act: it yields real knowledge of things or events beyond the ability of human reason to know, either by virtue of their remoteness in the future or by virtue of their being ontologically beyond our grasp.[46] Prophecy, therefore, is not a mere "mystical experience" in which the main result or end is "self-transformation." Neither is prophecy, however, a mere natural power of the human mind or intellect that can be "accessed" given the right training or conditions (a problem we saw discussed extensively by Maimonides).[47] It is a supernatural gift that gives the prophet real knowledge of divine things or future events ordained by God. As such, prophecy constitutes a real strengthening of the natural powers of the human intellect and does not negate them.

Aquinas, nevertheless, argues that prophecy is "something imperfect within the genus of divine revelation."[48] This is because, once we are in "our homeland" (*in patria*), prophecy will pass away in the light of the beatific vision. But prophecy is imperfect in another sense. A prophet can know in one of three ways: by receiving special images or visions from God that reveal divine things; by receiving the light of prophecy over and above such special or extraordinary images (thus prophets like

44. Ibid., 13: "Utrum per gratiam habeatur altior cognitio Dei quam ea quae habetur per rationem naturalem."

45. For a thorough discussion of this little "treatise" on prophecy—among many in the *Summa*—see Paul Synave and Pierre Benoit, *Prophecy and Inspiration: A Commentary on the Summa Theologica II-II, Questions 171–178* (New York: Desclee Company, 1961); and J.-H. Nicolas, "Aspects épistémologiques de la révélation," in Elders, *La doctrine de la révélation divine de saint Thomas d'Aquin*, 153–70.

46. "Quaedam quae sunt procul remota ab hominum cognitione." S. Th. II-II, 171, 1: "Utrum prophetia pertineat ad cognitionem."

47. Ibid., 172, 1.

48. "Quiddam imperfectum in genere divinae revelationis." Ibid., 171, 4, ad 2: "Utrum propheta per divinam inspirationem cognoscat omnia quae possunt prophetice cognosci."

Joseph and Daniel were prophets by virtue of interpreting by the light of prophecy the dreams and images of others—indeed, of non-believers); or a prophet may have both: special images, visions, or phantasms and the light in which to judge them.[49] The light of grace helps a prophet see or understand the divine message—giving him a "symbolic perception"—that allows a perception of divine realities in natural things themselves. It allows him to interpret both the meaning of Scripture and the meaning of the things.[50] Nevertheless, what is revealed to a prophet is still imperfect within the "genus" of revelation. The prophetic revelation is always mediated through human judgment and/or divinely created phantasms. These two media are, to be sure, illuminated or strengthened by divine grace; but it is a grace that only enlightens and strengthens the mind of the prophet, who then transmits it to others. Prophecy does not illumine the mind of every believer as such nor does it establish a direct relationship of illuminating grace with the believer. Thus, prophecy is a gift that can enlighten other believers in divine things, but only in a provisional and pedagogical way. The ultimate goal of the believer is and should be to be illumined by the mind of God himself.

Hence, in the structure of the *Summa theologiae*, the question on knowing God is followed by the question on naming God (q. 13), after a brief interlude on the mediating role of prophecy between the two (in *S. Th.* I, 12, 13). For, as was mentioned above, Aquinas asserts that prophecy is only an imperfect mode of knowing God; it is only in naming God that we have a fuller and more direct cognitive relationship with God. For, as he argues at the end of question 12, faith is indeed a type of knowledge or cognition, but it is one whose basis is "not from a vision of the believer but by the vision of the One who is believed."[51] Thus, Aquinas is moving from considerations of how we know God in a rather

---

49. Ibid., 173, 2: "Utrum in prophetica revelatione imprimantur divinitus menti prophetae novae rerum species, vel solum novum lumen."

50. Ibid.. See Jean-Pierre Torrell, "Le traité de la prophetie de S. Thomas d'Aquin et la théologie de la révélation," in Elders, *La doctrine de la révélation divine de saint Thomas d'Aquin*, 190.

51. *S. Th.* I, 12, 13, ad 3: "non procedit ex visione credentis, sed a visione eius cui creditur."

general and abstract manner—the existence and essence of God—to knowing God in a concrete, individual, and, indeed, personal manner, which is implied in the whole process of naming God. And within question 13, the logical movement is from considering the name "god" itself and whether it is adequate as applied to the first cause, to the most particular and, indeed, unutterable names of God, such "He who is" and the Tetragrammaton.[52] The problem, as Thomas sees it, is that human beings know things through the abstraction of universal forms from sensible particulars. But God cannot "have" a universal form in the sense that horses or trees have a universal form. This is because God, as the self-subsistent cause and principle of existence, cannot be merely one being among other beings; but neither can he be a universal that exists as such only in a mental abstraction. Or to put it perhaps more plainly: to name God is to try to grasp God in his utter particularity as first cause, but also in his universality as the cause *of everything*.

Therefore, affixing names to God is in no way like affixing names to a sensible substance or object of our sense-experience. As the cause of all creatures outside of whom nothing would exist, one cannot take up a position "outside" of the relationship between cause and effect, Creator and creature. This has important implications for human knowledge of God, whether natural or revealed.[53] We cannot know God as we know an object in the world. Since our very existence depends on God's causal activity, the human intellect can take up no pure, "objective" position

52. Rudi te Velde, "Die Gottesnamen. Thomas' Analyse des Sprechens über Gott unter besonderer Berücksichtung der Analogie (S.th. I, qq. 13)," in Speer, *Thomas von Aquin*, 51–76.

53. Even the fact that God is goodness itself, affects the mode in which human beings can come to knowledge of God. As Fran O'Rourke remarks: "Aquinas is even more emphatic in explaining why a knowledge of the hidden God is bestowed: 'It would indeed be against the nature of divine goodness that God should retain for himself all his knowledge and not communicate it to anyone else in any way whatsoever, since it belongs to the nature of the good that it should communicate itself to others.' Dionysius can therefore, according to Aquinas, reconcile the reserved nature of divine knowledge with the possibility of man's participation in the knowledge of God: 'He says, therefore, that although the supersubstantial knowledge of God may be attributed to God alone, nevertheless, since God is Goodness itself, it cannot be that he should not communicate himself to some existing beings.'" Fran O'Rourke, *Pseudo-Dionysius and the Metaphysics of Aquinas* (South Bend, Ind.: University of Notre Dame Press, 1992), 25.

(Thomas Nagel's "view from nowhere"). Rather, the human intellect can know anything about God only by *participation* "in the intellectual power and light of divine wisdom, and in contemplating God becomes in a manner one with him, is assimilated to him, being 'informed' by him."[54] And the human intellect can only be informed by the light of divine wisdom only insofar as the divine itself takes the initiative and informs the knower in a manner adequate to the knower.

It is in this context that we can understand the much vexed and certainly over-wrought issue of predication by analogy in Aquinas's thought, a concept that we cannot nor need not develop in detail here. "There is," as the core insight in Thomas's development of the doctrine of analogy, Rudi te Velde perceptively observes, "no way of isolating a core of commonness, to be expressed in a univocal concept, which would be neutral in both and precede their causal relationship. It is in view of this problem that Thomas introduces the notion of analogy."[55] All names that we direct to God must be understood in relation to God's creative causality. We apply univocal names, names that have one, universal meaning, to univocal causes. So, we call a man and his son "human" by virtue of the fact that a man univocally causes or generates another man (presupposing all the time the existence of a material substrate that underlies both cause and effect). Two names are used equivocally when there is no causal relationship, such as when I talk about the account in my bank while sitting on the bank of a river. We must use analogical names, however, when there is a causal relationship, but a causal relationship in which the effect falls short in many respects from the cause—as when, say, the photo falls short of the person photographed or, to use Thomas's example, the sun causes the generation of man.[56] Thus, between the limited and finite existence of creatures and the infinite per se and self-subsistent existence of God, there can

54. "In a brief parenthesis Aquinas also expresses this intimate cognitive union in terms of his own noetic, applying the fundamental principle that the intellect in act (*intellectus in actu*) is somehow identical with the object of knowledge as it is actually known (*intellectum in actu*)." Ibid., 25–26.

55. Te Velde, *Aquinas on God*, 102.

56. *S.Th.* I, 13, 5, ad 1: "Utrum ea quae de Deo dicuntur et creaturis, univoce dicantur de ipsis."

only be a relation of analogy expressed in analogical terms. The creature depends utterly on God for any existence it might have; but it is not the other way around. The relationship between God and creature is utterly non-reciprocal. That is to say, the creature cannot not be really related to God, which to say that it is utterly dependent on God's causative power not only for its operations, but also for its very existence. God, however, does not depend on[57] the creature in any way at all: his relation to the creature is not a real relation but one of reason. This means that God's presence to creatures is of a closeness and intimacy that the relation of the creature to God does not have. While we creatures cannot help but think about God, to the degree that we think about him at all, as an object "out there," God can only consider us, and every one of his creatures, as one would consider a word in their mind. Now, of course, given the nature of God, these "words" in the divine mind are creative in that they cause real beings to exist. Nevertheless, all creatures relate to God in God as word; it shall follow, then, that God would most truly and perfectly relates to creatures as creatures *and* to himself as Word. The creature, in turn, can only know God through the Word that God has of himself.

Given, therefore, the peculiar relationship of the creature to the Creator and of finite or derived existence to infinite or per se existence, Thomas concludes his question on naming God with the argument that "He who is" is the highest and most proper name for God.[58] The phrase, "He who is" or, simply, "Qui est," comes directly from Scripture (Ex 3:14). In this verse, God speaks directly to Moses in the first person. When Moses asks God what he shall tell the Israelites when they ask him who or what god has sent him, God answers Moses by saying, "'I AM WHO I AM.' And he said, 'Say this to the people of Israel, 'I AM has sent me to you.'" As Etienne Gilson argued long ago, Aquinas sees in the verse from Scripture a statement that is at once revealed and metaphysical. In this verse, Greek metaphysics and biblical revelation meet and even coincide: it is God himself who discloses the deepest truth of

57. Ibid., 7: "Utrum nomina quae important relationem ad creaturas, dicantur de Deo ex tempore."
58. Ibid., 11: "Utrum hoc nomen 'Qui est' sit maxime nomen Dei proprium."

Greek metaphysics.[59] And what is that truth? It is that more primary than immaterial being or eternal being or any essential being is the act of existence itself that brings all beings into existence. And this primal act of existence is a *someone* who reveals himself to us directly in and through his own Word.

So, what are the reasons that Thomas gives for "Qui est" as the most proper name of God? The first reason is its own signification: "it does not signify any form, but rather existence itself."[60] As such, "Qui est" signifies God not as thing or object but as the inner, yet transcendent act that actualizes all things as existents. As Fran O'Rourke quite poetically describes the significance of *esse* or the act of existence in Aquinas's thought:

> *Esse* is as the very illumination through which things first emerge and become manifest that they may appear and stand out in their own dimension and relief but which remains itself concealed; the universal and ubiquitous light which illumines all beings but cannot itself be seen. It is the silent and unceasing energy which nourishes and maintains the endless ferment of the universe. *Esse* is the quiet leaven (*aliquod fixum et quietum*) within the world of beings which, unobserved, perfects and harmonizes each and every one within the ensemble and which lies at the origin of the whole. It is the unseen interior of things which reaches outwards towards their utmost bounds, but is never enveloped by them.[61]

Secondly, *esse* or *Qui est* is the most *universal* name we can apply to God. "Now by any other name some mode of substance is determined, whereas this name *HE WHO IS*, determines no mode of being, but is indeterminate to all; and therefore, it denominates the *infinite ocean*

59. Gilson, *Christian Philosophy of St. Thomas Aquinas*, 84–95. Aquinas's (and Gilson's) reading of Exodus 3:14 has come under much criticism in recent years. The main contention is that Aquinas reads too much metaphysics into the verse, partially as a result of not knowing the subtle nuances of the original Hebrew. But, according to Aidan Nichols, the argument that the statement "he who is" contains metaphysical implications is highly justified even by the original Hebrew text. See Nichols, *Discovering Aquinas*, 43.

60. *S.Th.* I, 13, 11: "Primo quidem, propter sui significationem. Non enim significat formam aliquam, sed ipsum esse."

61. O'Rourke, *Pseudo-Dionysius and the Metaphysics of Aquinas*, 177–78.

of substance [et ideo nominat ipsum 'pelagus substantiae infinitum']."[62]
We should not, however, misunderstand Aquinas here. As te Velde explains, "'Being' signifies reality in its uttermost concreteness. It is not a
matter of a continuous movement of increasing logical indeterminacy
from species via genus to, ultimately, being. 'Being' is not what is finally
left over—like a logical substrate—when, on the level of *what* things
are, one removes their determinate content."[63] Rather, "'Being' signifies each particular thing as related to being, which is common to all
things."[64] Thus, the name *He who is* is most universal in the sense that
it names most appropriately the universal cause of all that is.[65] Third,
the name *He who is* is most proper to its "consignification" (*terto vero,
ex eius consignificatione*), which is that it signifies existence insofar as it
is "present" and not "past" or "future," since, as Aquinas argues earlier,
the various tenses of time do not and cannot be applied to God. As *esse
ipsum subsistens* or the self-subsistent act of existence, nothing is lacking
to God, which means that God is "present" at all "times" (*significat enim
esse in praesenti: et hoc maxime proprie de Deo dicitur, cuius esse non novit
praeteritum vel futurum, ut dicit Augustinus in V "De Trin"*). As with
God's relation to all creatures being a relation of reason, it follows that
God's "presence" to all creatures does not exist within a temporal flow
but is always the same. *He who is* expresses this divine relationship with
time most appropriately, for "at no time" is an existent "lacking" to God.

Indeed, for Thomas, the name *He who is* is, in a certain respect, more
fitting than the name "God":

> The name *He who is* is a more appropriate name for God than the name
> *God* as regards that to which it is assigned, namely, *existence* [*esse*] and
> as regards the mode of signification and consignification, as was said

62. *S. Th.* I, 13, 11.
63. Te Velde, *Aquinas on God*, 115.
64. Ibid., 117.
65. Thus article 11 of question 13 of the *Summa theologiae* must be read in conjunction with Romans 1:20 ("Ever since the creation of the world his invisible nature, namely, his
eternal power and deity, has been clearly perceived in the things that have been made"),
which is as central to Thomas's thought as Exodus 3:14. Emile Zum Brunn, "La 'métaphysique de l'Exode' selon Thomas d'Aquin," in *Dieu et l'être: Exégèses d'Exode 3:14 et de Coran
20, 11–24* (Paris: Etudes Augustiniennes, 1978), 261–62.

above. But as regards that to which the name is assigned by signification the more appropriate name is *God*, because it is imposed to signify the divine nature. And even more appropriate is the name Tetragrammaton, because it is imposed to signify the incommunicable and, if we may so speak, singular substance itself of God.[66]

Insofar as we wish to signify God as the end or object of our knowledge, then the name *God* is more appropriate. But most appropriate of all, Thomas remarks, is the Tetragrammaton or the four Hebrew letters (YHWH) which signify the holy and incommunicable name of God, namely, God as he is in himself apart from creation.[67] Among the three names of God: "He who is," "God," and "Tetragrammaton," the first is the most appropriate from the point of view of the origin of the name, that is, as the universal cause of existence, the second is the more suitable from the perspective of that which the name has been given to signify, that is, as the end or goal of every creature, and from this same viewpoint the third is even more fitting, that is, as the origin in whom our will and intellect find fulfillment and rest.[68] The name, "Tetragrammaton," signifies God in his impenetrable and incommunicable mystery. This mystery is completely inaccessible to human reason; and it is incommunicable *except as mystery*.

Aquinas, in short, is doing much more that bringing in Exodus 3:14 as a "proof-text" in order to confirm a metaphysical principle. Yes, Scripture confirms a metaphysical principle of the first and highest order—that God is the self-subsistent act of existence and is therefore the cause of the act of existence in all creatures. Yet, it is highly significant that *it is God himself who communicates this principle*. In other words, self-subsistent existence has *in itself* the nature of self-disclosure or revelation signified by the fact that the biblical statement is in the first person—indeed, doubly so, as if to emphasize this: "I am Who I am." Existence in itself

66. *S. Th.* I, 13, 11, ad 1.

67. The *Summa theologiae* is the only work of Thomas that recognizes a divine name that is more suitable than "he who is." Nevertheless, the *Summa* does not deny anything said in earlier writings about the appropriateness of the name. Armand Maurer, "St. Thomas on the Sacred Name 'Tetragrammaton,'" *Medieval Studies* 34 (1972): 278. Maurer notes the particular influence of Moses Maimonides on Aquinas's treatment of God's names.

68. Ibid., 281.

is luminous self-disclosure; but given the limited, embodied nature of the human intellect, this principle is so luminous that it appears dark to us, as the bat is blind in the rays of the sun. The name, "Tetragrammaton," signifies this darkness in God from the perspective of the created intellect. Hence, God's metaphysical self-disclosure necessitates a metaphysical self-concealing, which draws the creature into an ever-closer participation in the mystery of divine life. Yet, God in himself is absolutely clear and luminous, which is why God is also called by Christians, *Word*. As coterminous with God, his Word is also subsistent; God's Word is both signifier and signified. So how does God communicate his Word to his creatures, while maintaining the ineffable mystery of the very subsistence of the Word itself? How does God's Word not only communicate the incommunicable life and knowledge of God to the creature, but also transform the nature and, in particular, the intellect of that creature so that he or she is able to receive, accept, and understand that Word? These are the most crucial questions with which Thomas must grapple, and it is to his *Commentary on the Gospel of John* to which we will turn in order to see how he answers them.

WORD, FLESH AND REVELATION IN
AQUINAS'S "COMMENTARY ON JOHN"

There is no better place to explore the centrality of Christ to Aquinas's understanding of the essence of God's self-disclosure in both creation and in human history that his *Commentary on John*. The Thomistic scholar, Gilles Emery, even asserts that the *Commentary on John* gives us an even better entry into Thomas's "theological intelligence" than either of the *Summas*.[69] This relatively brief concluding section of the present chapter cannot, of course, do anywhere near full justice to the depth,

---

69. Gilles Emery, *Trinity in Aquinas* (Ave Maria, Fla.: Sapientia Press, 2006), 271. Emery also points out that Thomas's *Commentary on John* follows very closely the content and structure of the *Treatise on the Trinity* in the *Summa theologiae* (I, 27–43). For the place and nature of Aquinas's commentary, see also C. Clifton Black II, "St. Thomas's Commentary on the Johannine Prologue: Some Reflections on Its Character and Implications," *Catholic Biblical Quarterly* 48, no. 4 (1986): 681–98.

richness, and complexity of Thomas's commentary on this key Gospel. Nevertheless, we do hope to show how Thomas's *Commentary on John* brings out quite explicitly many of the themes and ideas that we have seen developed more latently in the *Summa theologiae* and elsewhere. The most important of these themes is that, as self-subsistent Word and Wisdom incarnate, Jesus is the perfection of the human intellect. As such, Christ directs the human intellect to divine realities beyond what it can know by nature. But in order to perfect the human intellect, the divine Word, as Christ, had to perfect human nature, which is not pure but embodied intellect. Hence, *the Word became flesh*. This perfection of the whole of human nature through Christ is the essence of divine *grace*, which makes possible both divine revelation and its proper reception. Hence, as Thomas argues in *Summa theologiae* I, question 1, article 10, God's Word comes most appropriately into our lives and intellects not as written or even spoken words, but in and *through the things themselves*, which is to say, through the God-Man, Jesus Christ.

Since the Gospel of John deals most clearly and explicitly of the four Gospels with the divinity of Christ, Thomas sees this Gospel as constituting the perfection of divine wisdom in written form. Quoting Augustine, Thomas explains that the Gospel of John instructs us on the contemplative life, not just the active life as do the other Gospels. It is, therefore, not only the most "metaphysical" of the Gospels but it is also the height, summation, and perfection of metaphysics itself, since it discloses the self-subsistent Word in and through which all beings have their being. Hence, Aquinas begins his commentary with a brief, customary, prologue in which he comments on a verse from the prophet Isaiah: "I saw the Lord seated on a high and lofty throne, and the whole house was full of his majesty; and the things that were under him filled the temple" (Is 6:1). In this verse, Thomas reads a description of what he calls the "fourfold height" in which the Gospel of John excels in the excellence with which it presents divine wisdom. This fourfold height is: a height of authority ("I saw the Lord"); a height of eternity ("seated"); one of dignity or nobility of nature ("on a high throne"); and a height of incomprehensible truth ("lofty"). In his exegesis of this verse, Aquinas alludes to some of the reasons that he enumerates in the first article of the first question of the *Summa* as to why we need revelation.[70] The Gospel of John presents the "height of authority" insofar as we find Christ proclaiming his divinity with the utmost authority, leading the human intellect to divine truths to which it cannot but submit on an authority which surpasses its reason. Second, John points to the "height of eternity" by showing the eternity of the divine Word made incarnate in time in Christ. Third, there is in the fourth Gospel the "height of dignity." As Thomas explains:

> Certain others however came to a knowledge of God from the very dignity of God; these were the Platonists. They considered that everything which is according to participation is reducible to something which is that thing through its own essence, as to something first and highest. Thus, all that are fiery through participation are reduced to fire, which is such through its own essence. Since therefore all things that exist participate in existence [*esse*] and are beings through participation, it is necessary that there be something at the summit of all things, which is existence itself [*ipsum esse*] through its own essence, that is that whose essence is its existence—and this is God, who is the most sufficient, most eminent, and most perfect cause of all things, from whom all that is participates in existence.... And John shows us this dignity when he says below [1:1], "the Word was God," so that "Word" is posited as subject and God as predicate.[71]

As the Platonists had argued, all "which is something by participation is reduced to what is the same thing by essence." It follows from this, that all wisdom and every divine word must be reduced to that which is the divine Wisdom and divine Word by its essence. This is the eternal Word of God, which subsists in God and proceeds from God. This Word is Truth and, as Truth in itself, it cannot be comprehended by the finite human intellect:

> Yet others came to a knowledge of God from the incomprehensibility of truth. For every truth which our intellect is able to comprehend

70. Roger Guindon, "La théologie de saint Thomas d'Aquin dans le rayonnement du 'Prologue' de saint Jean," *Revue de l'Université Ottawa* 29, special section (1959): 18–20.

71. *S. Thomae Aquinatis Super Evangelium S. Ioannis Lectura*, ed. P. Raphael Cai, OP (Turin: Marietti, 1952), prol., no. 5. Hereafter, *In Ioan.*

is finite, since according to Augustine, "everything which is known is limited by the comprehension of the knower," and if limited, it is something determinate and particular. Thus, it is necessary that the first and highest truth, which surpasses every intellect, be incomprehensible and infinite—and this is God....John implies this incomprehensibility to us when he says below (1:18), "No one has ever seen God."[72]

Finally, John's contemplation of the "height of incomprehensible Truth" was perfect insofar as the "one contemplating is led and raised to the height of the thing contemplated."[73] This is because the Word revealed in and by John draws us up and into the Word "adhering and assenting by affection and understanding to the truth contemplated," which would otherwise remain incomprehensible. In this way, the Gospel of John contains all the sciences, first and foremost, metaphysics, in a most perfect and pre-eminent way, which is by participation in the Truth or Word of God himself.[74]

Only in submission to Christ, therefore, can "the impure motives of philosophy—vanity, contentiousness, arrogance—be transformed into the motives of the Christian believer." Thus, when properly done, biblical exegetes who use philosophical concepts and tools, "by subjugating them to faith, do not mix water with wine, but turn water into wine."[75] That is to say, such exegetes do not try to fit Scripture into a Procrustean bed of some predetermined philosophical doctrine, but allow Scripture to illuminate and indeed "reveal" the "true" inner meaning of philosophical thought. But even more fundamentally, knowledge in Christ is knowledge of God by participation—the only mode in which knowledge of God is possible.[76] As we saw in our discussion of Thomas's doctrine of analogy in the previous section, it is impossible for any

72. *In Ioan.*, prol., no. 6 (Lacher and Weisheipl, 1:3).

73. Ibid., no. 8 (Lacher and Weisheipl, 1:4).

74. Ibid., no. 9 (Lacher and Weisheipl, 1:4).

75. Mark D. Jordan, "Theology and Philosophy," in *The Cambridge Companion to Aquinas*, ed. Norman Kretzmann and Eleonore Stump (Cambridge: Cambridge University Press, 1994), 235–36.

76. Matthew Levering, "Reading John with Saint Thomas," in *Aquinas on Scripture: An Introduction to His Biblical Commentaries*, ed. Thomas Weinandy, Daniel Keating, and John Yocum (London: Continuum, 2006), 102. See also Matthew Levering, *Scripture and Metaphysics: Aquinas and the Renewal of Trinitarian Theology* (London: Blackwell, 2004).

created intellect to take a purely objective, position "outside" the relation of creatures to Creator in coming to know God. As an effect of God's creative power, the human intellect can know God and the relation of the creature to its Creator only from *within* that relation. Hence, it is only by participation in those truths that the human intellect can come to know them; and it can participate in the divine Truth or Word only insofar as our human nature participates in the Word or Person of Christ.[77]

One of the goals, therefore, of Thomas's commentary on the opening verse of John, "In the beginning was the Word" (*in principio erat Verbum*), is to try to show how the divine Word is the fulfillment and perfection of the human intellect not, of course, by nature but by grace. Thomas first notes that the formation of a word is absolutely essential to any act of intellection: "wordless understanding" is a contradiction in terms.[78] At first glance, this assertion appears problematic: do we human beings not have moments of "wordless insight" or flashes of "inspiration" that we struggle or even find impossible to put into words? Indeed, we do; but this would be missing an important part of Thomas's thought on the intellect and its nature. Human words are imperfect, since the extent of their signification is limited, whereas the divine Word is perfect insofar as "he understands both himself and everything else through his essence, by one act, the single divine Word is expressive of all that is in God, not only of the Persons but also of creatures; otherwise it would be imperfect."[79] Hence, "our word is not of the same nature as we; but the divine Word is of the same nature as God.... Thus it must be subsistent, because whatever is in the nature of God is God."[80] Thus, if the human intellect cannot form a word adequate to its insight or intuition, it is not because thinking can occur without a word

---

77. This indeed is the thrust of Aquinas's analysis of the hypostatic union in Christ of two natures in one Person as developed in his disputed question, *De unione Verbi incarnati*. See the new edition of this work: Thomas Aquinas, *De unione Verbi incarnati*, trans. Roger W. Nutt (Leuven: Peeters, 2015).

78. *In Ioan.*, 1:1, no. 25.

79. Ibid., no. 27.

80. Ibid., no. 28. "Verbum nostrum non est eiusdem naturae nobiscum, sed Verbum divinum est eiusdem naturae cum Deo.... et ideo aliquid subsistens in natura divina."

but rather because it points to a higher intellection which does think through a Word perfectly adequate to its thinking. It follows that if the human intellect is to understand or, better, "intuit" through a unitative act of intellection what is beyond human reason, it must do so through a Word that proceeds from an intellect that is higher than the human intellect. This is the divine Word in the divine intellect. And the human intellect can do this only by *participating*, to the degree that is possible to it, in this divine Word.

This is why, according to Aquinas, John begins his Gospel by saying that Christ is *Word* of God, rather than the "son" or the "notion" (*ratio*) of God: he wanted to specify that Christ, as the eternally only-begotten[81] of God, is not *only* a flesh-and-blood product of a "material and changeable generation."[82] But neither does he say that Christ is the "notion" or *ratio* of God, because he wants the reader or listener to understand that Christ is not just a "mental being," a figment of the mind, but a self-subsistent reality.[83] So Christ, as divine Word, is more than a material, generated being, but is also more than a mere idea or concept: he is a self-subsistent intelligence that is, however, generable into matter and time. And this is what makes participation on the part of the human intellect in the divine Word possible:

> Order is found in learning, and this is twofold: according to nature and in relation to us, and in both ways we speak about a principle.... According to nature, in Christian teaching, the beginning and principle of our wisdom is Christ insofar as he is the wisdom and Word of God, that is, according to his divinity. In relation to us, the principle is Christ insofar as the Word was made flesh, that is, according to his Incarnation.[84]

In the ontological order, Christ as eternal Word is prior, since as Word-in-itself he is the end of all intellection, but *with regard to us*—the mode in which we come to know that order—Christ as Word made flesh is

---

81. Aquinas rarely uses the word *persona* or "person" in his exposition. "It is not easy to evaluate the motives of this discretion." Emery, *Trinity in Aquinas*, 280.

82. *In Ioan.*, 1:1, no. 31.

83. Ibid., no. 32.

84. Ibid., no. 34.

prior, since it as a sensible, historical man that we first encounter him through the testimony of the Gospels. This dual but converging order is made possible by the very nature of the Word as both more than a generable thing and more than an idea, but as a self-subsistent Word that is able to speak *into* human nature and transform it from within.

Another key attribute of the Word, then, is *life*. "All things were made through him, and without him nothing was made. What was made in him was life" (Jn 1:3–4a). The Word of God then, is neither a mere physically generated being nor a mere idea, but it is a self-subsistent, *living* Word. Drawing on Augustine, Aquinas explains that things can be considered in two ways: in themselves, many things, indeed most things, are not living. Yet, when considered in their archetypes in the divine Word, they have life, since "there" they "exist spiritually in the wisdom of God." Indeed, "they are not merely living, but also life":

> Just as a chest made by the artisan is neither in itself alive nor life, yet the notion of the chest, which proceeds within the mind of the artisan, does in some way live insofar as it has an intelligible being [*esse intelligibile*] in the mind of the artisan; not, however, that it is life, because it is not in his essence nor is it his existence through the act of understanding of the artisan. In God, by contrast, his understanding is his life and his essence and thus whatever is in God not only lives but is life itself, because whatever is in God is his essence. Whence in God the creature is the creating essence [*creatrix essentia*]. If therefore things are considered according to as they exist in the Word, they are life.[85]

As living Word that is life in itself, Christ *enlivens* all those who hear and receive him and, in turn, he or she becomes the very life of God by this grace. If the Word of God is to be heard and received by the human being and if the human being is to *live* in God and not just submit to God, that very Word must itself not only be living but incarnate, because it is only as incarnate knowing that the believer can come to participate in it and come to live in God as fully what he or she is, a human being who is body and soul. In other words, it is only in Christ that the human being becomes him- or herself a living word in the divine life.

---

85. Ibid., 1:3–4a, no. 91.

Hence, in his exegesis of John 1:9–10, "He [the Word] was the true light, which enlightens every man coming into this world. He was in the world, and through him the world was made, and the world did not know him," Aquinas explains in what ways Christ was the "true light." In Scripture, Aquinas argues, the "true" can be understood in three ways: (1) in contrast with the false, that is, to tell the truth; (2) in contrast with what is figurative, as when the types and figures of the law of Moses become fulfilled historical realities in Christ; and (3) when something that is by participation is contrasted with what it is by its essence, as the "whiteness" by which white things are white is the true "whiteness" compared to white things.[86] Christ is the "true light" in all three senses: he, of course, tells us the truth about God and about ourselves; but he also *is in the flesh and in historical time*, which was only communicated by types of figures in the law of Moses. Most importantly, Christ is the "true light" insofar as he is essentially what we are only by participation—the divine Word through whom and in whom all intellection has its perfection: "Then, since the Word is the true light by his very essence, everything that shines must do so through him, insofar as it participates in him. And so he enlightens every man coming into this world.'"[87]

Being God's Word and being the very essence of "true light" are bound up intimately with the Incarnation. In continuing his exegesis of John 1:9–10, Thomas gives three reasons for why God willed to become incarnate. The first "is because of the perversity of human nature which, because of its own malice, had been darkened by vices and the obscurity of its own ignorance." The human being, therefore, needed a concrete exemplar to follow if he or she was to be saved from sin and death. But even more profoundly, God willed to become incarnate because the testimony of the prophets and prophecy in general is insufficient to bring humanity into participation with the divine life and truth:

The prophets came and John came, but they were not able to illumine sufficiently, because "he was not the light." Hence it was necessary that

---

86. Ibid., 1:9–10, no. 125.

87. Ibid., no. 127. "Quia ergo Verbum est lux vera per suam naturam, oportet quod omne lucens luceat per ipsum, inquantum ipsum participat. Ipse ergo illuminat omnem hominem venientem in hunc mundum."

after the prophecies of the prophets and after the coming of John, the light itself should come and hand down to the world knowledge of itself. And this is what the Apostle says [Heb. 1:1]: "multifariously and in many ways God once spoke to our fathers in the prophets, but most recently he has spoken to us in the Son." And: "We have the prophetic message to which you do well to give attention, until the day dawns" (2 Pt 1:19).[88]

Prophecy as a mode of communication between human beings and God is ultimately insufficient: it has its place as a way of preparing for God's revelation of himself, but it cannot give the light of truth itself. Prophecy can offer only a reflected light. This is something that Moses Maimonides himself intuited, as we have seen, needing to resort to a notion of "super-prophecy" in order to explain why Moses, as the giver of the Torah, is unique. The reason for this is because prophecy always is removed by a degree or more from God's self-communication through creatures: prophetic utterances and writings are always in reference to creatures that are themselves "words" of God himself.

But, as Aquinas argues in the very first question of the *Summa*, which we looked at earlier in this chapter, God writes not just with words or even images but with the *things themselves*—with creatures and with the historical events in which their creation unfolds. As the Word of God made flesh, Christ unites in himself, sharing both the human and divine natures, revelation as creature and revelation as intelligible and eternal Word. In Christ, God "writes" in and with creation and historical time by becoming incarnate in human nature, which is the epitome or, as both body and spirit, the microcosm of creation itself. By thus assuming flesh and taking up human nature, God also enabled the human being to participate in the divine life and truth. For revelation is in vain if the human intellect and the human heart cannot receive nor understand it. But since human nature is afflicted with many shortcomings—indeed, since it is *fallen*—by assuming human flesh, God in Christ raises human nature to participate in the divine life and mind. This is, for Aquinas, the third reason why God willed to become incarnate.

88. Ibid., no. 141.

The reason why Christ enables this full participation in the divine life and truth is precisely because of the inter-personal nature of the relationship of the believer to Christ. Just as through love and self-giving we come to participate in the life and mind of another human being whom we love, so we come to share in the life and divine mind of Christ through love of him and giving ourselves to him. This is an intimate and personal relationship that is quite literally "face to face" with the Other who is at the same time the Same, God. Just as our access to the other is the face of the other, through which, in a way, the mind and thought of the other becomes "incarnate," so Christ is the "face" of God. Thomas compares Christ to a cloud or some "opaque" body through which we can see the light of the sun, which would otherwise be too bright for us to see in all its blinding splendor:

> For weak and infirm eyes are not able to see the light of the sun, but are able to see it when it shines in a cloud or some opaque body. Thus, before the incarnation of the Word human minds were incapable of seeing in itself the divine light, which illuminates every rational nature. And so, in order for it to be more easily discerned and contemplated by us he clothed himself in the cloud of our flesh [*nube nostrae carnis se texit*]: "they looked toward the wilderness and there saw the glory of the Lord in a cloud" (Ex 16:10), which is the Word of God in the flesh.[89]

Just as the invisible soul of the other is made manifest through the face of the other, so the invisible things of God are made visible through the face of Christ, who is, so to speak, God's "face" within creation.[90] Thus, the "blindness" of the human intellect, limited and finite in itself and damaged and corrupted through the Fall by sin, is able to see and be united to God in the incarnate Word. Just as truth properly speaking refers to truth known in the intellect, so intellect, properly speaking, refers to Christ, who, as the Word of the divine intellect, is not a mere mental abstraction or even mere mental activity, but the concrete and fully existent instantiation of Word, intellect, and therefore, of divine life:

89. Ibid., 1: 14b, no. 181.
90. *S. Th.* I, 12, 3, ad 2.

It must be noted that these two [truth and life] belong to Christ properly and per se. Truth is proper to him per se because he is Word itself. For truth is nothing other than the adequation of thing to the intellect, which happens when the intellect conceives a thing as it is. The truth, therefore, of our intellect pertains to our word, which is its concept. But granted that our word is true, it is nevertheless not truth itself, since it is not true from itself, but because it is adequate to the thing conceived. The Truth of the divine Intellect, then, pertains to the Word of God. But because the Word of God is true in itself, since it is not measured by things, but rather things are true insofar as they are similar to the Word, it follows that the Word of God is truth itself. And because no one is able to know the truth unless he adhere to the truth, it is necessary that whoever desires to know the truth should adhere to this Word [*Et quia nullus potest veritatem cognoscere nisi adhaereat veritati, oportet omnem qui veritatem cognoscere, huic Verbo adhaerere*].[91]

The human intellect grasps the truth of things through mental words or *verba*; but, as Aquinas notes, these *verba* are not the truths of things themselves. They are only true to the extent that they are conformed to what things are in themselves. But the divine Word is the truth of things themselves, because it is that according to which all things are made and have their being and nature. Christ, however, is the Word of God; hence, to adhere to Christ and to the mind of Christ is to adhere to the Truth of all things. For in Christ the Word of God comes itself to adhere in human nature and take it up into its own Truth. Christ redeems and thus enables human nature to know and to adhere to the divine Word and Truth. As Aquinas emphasizes in this passage, knowing the truth in itself, knowing the Truth from, in, and by which all truths are true, demands *adherence*: that is, not just an intellectual act but an in-formation of the whole person into and by that Truth itself. It demands a personal participation.

Christ's pre-eminence for Aquinas is, therefore, twofold. As Thomas Weinandy points out, he is, first, unique as to origin as the only and eternally begotten Son of God the Father; but, second, Christ also establishes or, better, restores a relationship of sonship between God the

91. *In Ioan.*, 14: 4–7, no. 1869.

Father and all who share in human nature.[92] And such a relationship of son to father implies a relationship of great inter-personal intimacy, whereby the son comes to know the mind of the father and the father communicates all that he knows to his son. Thomas makes the implications of such a relationship brought about by Christ in the relationship between the divine and human intellects as he continues his exegesis of John 14:4–7:[93]

> As the Apostle says: "No one knows what thoughts are in a man, unless the spirit of him who is in himself" (1 Cor 2:11), except, it must be understood, insofar as a man wishes to reveal himself. He reveals what is hidden through words, and thus no one is able to come to what is hidden in a man unless by the word of a man. Because, therefore, "those things that are in God no one knows except the spirit of God" (1 Cor 2:11), no one is able to come to a knowledge of the Father unless through his Word, which is his Son: "Nor does anyone know the Father except the Son" (Mt 11:27). And just as a man wishing to reveal himself by the word of the heart, which he then brings out of his mouth and clothes in some way in letters or speech, so does God, wishing to reveal himself to men, clothes his Word, conceived from eternity, with flesh in time. And thus no one can come to a knowledge of the Father unless through the Son, as was said above (10:9): "I am the door; if anyone should enter through me, he will be saved."[94]

We can understand the Spirit of God only by the Spirit of God; and the Spirit of God can measure the human intellect only insofar as it redeems and restores the human intellect. This can only be done, then, to the extent that the Spirit of God comes to dwell in the human intellect *qua* human intellect, which means that it must come to dwell in

---

92. Thomas G. Weinandy, "The Supremacy of Christ: Aquinas' *Commentary on the Hebrews*," in *Aquinas on Scripture: An Introduction to His Biblical Commentaries* ed. Thomas Weinandy, Daniel Keating and John Yocum (London: Continuum, 2006), 227.

93. John 14:4–7: "'And you know the way where I am going.' Thomas said to him, 'Lord, we do not know where you are going; how can we know the way?' Jesus said to him, 'I am the way, and the truth, and the life; no one comes to the Father, but by me. If you had known me, you would have known my Father also; henceforth you know him and have seen him.'"

94. *In Ioan.*, 14: 4–7, no. 1874.

the embodied intellect, that is, the Word of God must become incarnate. Hence, again, as Aquinas argues in *S. Th.* I, question 1, article 10, the Spirit of God reveals itself most properly not by spoken or written words but through the Word becoming an embodied intellect itself. Most importantly for Thomas, John's Gospel makes clear that knowledge of what is in God can only pass from *person to person*: eminently and per se in God from Father to Son and the Persons of the Trinity, by participation and *secundum quid* through our union with Christ, the Son, effected by his Incarnation.

CONCLUSION

Hence, Christ, as the divine Word become embodied intellect, reveals to us the wisdom of God not by a transfer of divine "information" nor merely by annunciating a set of "commands," but by moving the human intellect by affection to be drawn deeper into the divine life and wisdom where God's commands become understood and thus efficacious: "The world did not know God by an affective knowledge, because it did not love him, 'like heathen who do not know God' (1 Th 4:5). So, he says, 'the world has not known you,' that is, without error, and as a Father, through love."[95] What the Word incarnate gives us is an "experiential knowledge" through which we "taste" and, more importantly, "suffer divine things," as Bruce Marshall puts it:

> The indwelling of Christ gives us "a kind of instruction by which the intellect bursts out in love's affection," a taste of himself which is "a certain experiential knowledge," so that we might hold fast to what he says, to a truth we do not see. The name for this sort of knowledge is "wisdom, a kind of knowledge by taste"—a wisdom which comes not first from learning, but from "suffering divine things" (*patiens divina*). In the end, it seems, we believe the teaching of scripture and creed not because reason gives us compelling grounds to do so, still less because we merely wish that it were true, but because we have already suffered the things of which it speaks. For this reason, faith's assent to what God teaches amounts to a "certain participation in ... and assimilation to God's own

95. Ibid., 17: 24–26, no. 2265.

knowledge, in that by the faith infused in us we cling to the first truth for its own sake." And so "*sacra doctrina* is like an impression of God's own *scientia*" in us.[96]

So, the committed Christian, like the Sufi, "tastes" divine things, but not *qua* pure intellect in which all embodied individuation has been annihilated. Rather the Christian comes to know Christ though the very fragility and contingency of the flesh, precisely because Christ has taken up that flesh in the divine Word and redeemed it as a fitting vehicle for the intellect. And so, in Christ, God's revelation does not erase or annihilate the embodied individual, created in God's image, but rather completes and perfects that embodied individual as a unique and yet full image of God. And not only that, the Christian already participates in the divine life through the perfected humanity of Christ, realizing the truth of his or her being as substance-in-relation, and then, in the beatific vision, the Christian hopes to participate fully in the perfected humanity of Christ, which is nothing other than the divine perfection itself, lived in perfect relation with the three Persons of the Trinity.

96. Marshall, "*Quod Scit Una Uetula*," 14.

THE RATIONALITY OF REVELATION IN THREE TRADITIONS

At first glance, a reconciliation or "harmonization" of religious faith and human reason, of philosophy and the "revealed book," seems easiest and most straightforward in Islam. This is not just because Islam and its holy book, the Quran, eschew and even reject such mysteries as the Incarnation or the Trinity, which seem so absurd to human reason. Nor is it because Islam, unlike Judaism and like philosophy, is universal in its claims. It is mostly because the notion of revelation as consisting of a holy book "sent down" to inform and guide humanity toward God seems to replicate very closely the late antique, Neoplatonic doctrine of a separate, transcendent intellect that "emanates from above" down into a more or less passive "material" human intellect. Moreover, in this scheme, the figure of the "prophet" is easily assimilated to that of the philosopher, one who is characterized by the fact that he is uniquely receptive to the emanation of the transcendent intellect. Thus, Islamic tradition emphasizes the claim that Muhammad was *ummi*, or "illiterate," that is to say, devoid of any worldly learning that would impede such an emanation of the "intellect."

In other words, what seems to make Islam so amendable to philosophical reflection is not the assertion (or rejection) of any particular doctrines so much as the *mode* in which Islam claims divine revelation comes to us: revelation comes to us as a book "sent down" to a humanity that is not in any sense "fallen," but simply in need of guidance. In this, Islam seems like an eminently "philosophical" religion, repeating the So-cratic dictum that it is ignorance, not sin, that makes us bad and the cure for humanity's errors is intellectual guidance.

But, as has been shown, this affinity between Islam and philosoph-ical reflection is not so straightforward as it would at first seem. This should be evident from what we have seen by looking in some detail at the thought of probably the most rationalist of Muslim thinkers, Aver-roes. In his attempt to adjudicate the proper relation between philoso-phy and the religious law, Averroes cannot but assimilate the religious law and the holy book to the separate, unitary intellect of the Neopla-tonizing, peripatetic philosophers of late antiquity and the Islamic tradi-tion. For Averroes, there is indeed revelation, but revelation is grasped as *truth* only in philosophical reflection, which culminates in a conjunction with the separate intellect. This conjunction is the essence of what "rev-elation" means. What the masses and even the religious scholars (the *'ulema* and the *mutakallimun*) mean by "revelation" is nothing but a *mode* by which the highest philosophical truths are made known to believers through poetic and rhetorical language. In a sense, then, revelation in Averroes has nothing to do with any specific *content* let alone any dif-ferent *relationship* with truth, but rather, again, with the *mode* in which philosophical truths are made known. In Averroes's writings on the relation of revelation to reason, therefore, revelation and the revealed book are assimilated to philosophy and its primary organ, the separate, unitary intellect. In short, Averroes's thought exemplifies perfectly the *episteme* of digestion that, as we saw in the introduction, Brague claims is the hallmark of Islamic thought and culture. And yet this is ironically a "digestion" that eliminates revelation (at least as a source of *truth*) in favor of philosophical thought.

A side glance that we took at the thought of Averroes's prime op-ponent, al-Ghazali, only confirms this. Al-Ghazali, of course, is tradi-tionally seen as the prime foil against which Averroes worked out his own position on the relation between reason and the religious law. And yet, if we look at what al-Ghazali wrote, we see the same drive toward assimilation and "digestion"—only in the opposite direction. Instead of the separate intellect functioning as the revealed book as in Averroes (at least with regard to its inner meaning and truth, and not with respect to the persuasion of the masses), in al-Ghazali it is the revealed book that serves in every way the function of the separate and unitary intellect for all believers. Nor, as in Averroes, is salvation or redemption necessary for believers: since the individual human intellect as such is absorbed or "digested" into the revealed book/separate intellect (for Averroes as well as for al-Ghazali), there is no need for the finite human intellect to be saved or restored in its created finitude. All that is necessary is a "purification" of the individual human intellect *from* that created finitude so that it may unite with the one, separate intellect.[1]

One cannot think of a more "philosophical"—"Platonic" even—conception of revelation than the Islamic one. But precisely for this reason, in weighing the relation between faith and reason, philosophical reflection and the religious law, Islamic thought quickly reached an impasse that, I submit, has not been surmounted to this day: that is, the conception of philosophy and revelation are so identical that one must absorb or "digest" the other. It becomes impossible, on this understanding of revelation, for both to stand relatively free and independent of the other (though Averroes tried to work out a solution, as we have seen—a solution that was unsuccessful precisely because he denied inherent truth to revelation independent of philosophy). This impasse comes about as a direct result of understanding revelation as a "book" that is "sent down" in a sort of emanation.

Nevertheless, the mode of revelation *does* affect the content of revelation. What follows from the understanding of revelation as a book that is "sent down" is that it becomes difficult to give a philosophical defense of key doctrines of that revealed book: if revelation is an emana-

---

1. To be sure, al-Ghazali argues in his *tahāfut al-falāsifa*, that there is, on the strength of what is revealed in the Quran, a bodily resurrection and thus individual rewards and punishments. But he cannot explain how this bodily resurrection contributes in any way to our knowledge of God, because the very Islamic understanding of revelation rejects such a role to the body. Nor can it explain how there can be any participation in the divine, especially since the same understanding of revelation rejects such a participation of the individual *qua* individual in the divine life.

tion on the model of the separate, transcendent intellect, then how can we explain that anything can have a beginning in time, that is, creation *de novo*? The ancient Neoplatonic model to which such an understanding of revelation bears so many similarities asserted that the activity of emanation is by its very nature eternal. A rejection of the Fall is consistent with this understanding of revelation as emanated book; but with the rejection of the Fall it is impossible to conceive how any personal choices or decisions could interrupt what is essentially an impersonal emanation. But, then again, it is also impossible to conceive of how human beings have any free will at all to follow or not follow this divine guidance. Averroes avoids the problem by arguing that the function of revelation is a social or general one: it is to bring as many people as possible into some sort of participation, however remote, in the activity of philosophical contemplation. Choice has nothing to do with it. For al-Ghazali, the revealed book is the very organ of philosophical contemplation itself. To think that philosophical contemplation is mediated by anything other than the revealed book is to commit *shirk* or "associating something created" with God. It is therefore to put oneself out of any relation with the intellect and thus with that which pre-eminently makes us human. Thus, to talk of human "choice" or "free will" outside of any absorption of the intellect into the holy book makes no sense.

Al-Ghazali, to be sure, was committed to the teaching of a bodily resurrection, as traditionally taught in Islam. But on his account of how the intellect of the Sufi is united with God and is "annihilated" in God, he cannot give a reason for our bodily nature and the individuality that flows from that corporeal nature. As we saw above, what al-Ghazali means by "annihilation" or *fana'* must be understood very carefully: it can be understood not as the complete extinction of the individual *qua* his or her essential being, but simply as the extinction of the individual act of existence in the divine necessary existence. In other words, given the strong influence of Avicenna on al-Ghazali, one can understand this mystical doctrine in rational, Avicennian terms. But as a consequence of this, it becomes impossible to explain why there should be a bodily resurrection, if the body is not an essential mode in which God reveals himself; nor can he explain how the soul who is united to God as es-

sence can share in the divine life as *person*, that is, as a substance of a
rational nature individuated by the body.

The thought of Moses Maimonides, in this context, serves to high-
light the essential differences between Islam on the one side, and Judaism and Christianity on the other. His thought performs this service
precisely because, in most respects, Maimonides's thought belongs very
firmly to the cultural and intellectual world of Islamic civilization. So,
when he departs from this intellectual tradition it is because he senses,
consciously or unconsciously, that it is fundamentally inadequate for
explaining and defending the essential truths of Judaism and, more particularly, the Jewish understanding of what constitutes revelation.

Judaism cannot find its proper expression on the usual terms and
arguments of the Arabo-Islamic peripatetic philosophy not only because
Judaism's revelation is to a particular, "chosen" people and not to all people as is Islam's. In other words, the issue is not just that Judaism's claims
are particular and those of Islam are universal. Much more importantly,
it is the nature of the Jewish law itself as the result and witness to a
covenant and covenantal relationship that decisively marks off Judaism
from Islam. To repeat what was said in the introduction, revelation for
Judaism is essentially and fundamentally the covenantal self-disclosure
of God to the Jewish people, and in particular to Moses, on Mt. Sinai;
the Torah and the writings of the prophets are but witnesses and a calling back to this fundamental self-disclosure and covenant. Thus, strictly
speaking, the "books" of Moses are secondary to the covenant itself between God and the Jewish people.

This covenantal relationship that is at the heart of the relation between God and the Jewish people is seen in Maimonides's understanding of the nature of creation and the relation of the Creator to the creature. For Maimonides, creation is rational and orderly only *relatively*; it
is not so *absolutely*. That is, while God created the world to be a perfectly intelligible whole with a rational order that could be understood by
human reason, he established this order in perfect *freedom*. God could
have, if he so wished, created a completely different yet equally rational
world. In arguing this, Maimonides seeks to avoid the extremes of, on
the one hand, the *mutakallimun* (such as al-Ghazali), who argued that

any seeming "order" in creation is due to the completely arbitrary will of Allah and, on the other hand, that of the *falasifa* (such as Averroes), who argued that the present order of creation is absolutely necessary, that is, it is the only possible rational order for the world. But it is not just that Maimonides sought to avoid an impasse: he finds the solution in the very nature of revelation as understood by the Jewish people as covenant. Just as God freely binds himself in covenant with a particular people, which establishes a rational order in the lives of that people (as expressed in and maintained by the religious law or *halakha*), so does God freely establish a particular rational order in creation. And just as God could have created another equally rational world, so God could establish another equally right and just covenant with another people if he so wished. This is not a case of "reading into" philosophy or metaphysics a particular tradition's understanding of revelation. Maimonides is quite explicit on this point: it is not this Jewish understanding of the covenantal nature of revelation that drives his understanding of creation; rather, it is the nature of creation as understood by pure reason that testifies to the necessarily covenantal nature of revelation. If there is a God and God is necessarily intellectual yet free, then any self-disclosure of God to human beings will have to be both rational *and* free; that is, it must be covenantal.

Hence, Maimonides's own understanding of the phenomenon of prophecy, though in almost all respects identical with the Arabo-Islamic peripatetic accounts of an emanation of a separate, unitary intellect into an individual human being prepared by natural gifts to receive that emanation (thus making prophecy identical to philosophical intellection), nevertheless departs in significant ways from this account. The emanation characteristic of prophetic intellection is always subject to the divine Will in Maimonides's thought; God can "veto," so to speak, any emanation of the divine intellect just as he can freely choose some other rational order to create. Maimonides's argument seems rather awkward and *ad hoc*. And yet, Maimonides cannot find any other way to express the peculiar nature of the Jewish understanding of revelation. In the Jewish tradition, there cannot be between God and his prophet a purely impersonal relationship of emanation and passive reception, but the contact of one will with another in which not just knowledge and intellection are operative but also desire and love.

This quasi-personal relationship[2] between God and his prophet has further implications in Maimonides's thought. As the order of creation is the result of a supremely free choice and not a matter of logical or ontological necessity, we, believers and non-believers, prophets and philosophers, cannot know God by natural reason. We can only know God to the degree that it is God himself who wills to reveal himself to the prophet and, through the prophet, to his people. The fact that we can know nothing of God by our naturally given reason infers that the human intellect is *fallen*, that is, it cannot know God by natural reason precisely because God's relation to creation is one of a supremely free will, whose choices and the reasons for those choices can only be known by a relationship of lover to beloved and not by an intellectual relation of knower to impersonal object. Hence, the final goal of revelation for Maimonides is an *intellectual love* of God, in which the believer comes to share or participate in God's intellectual nature not by knowing God as object but by being purified of all worldly attachments through a complete love of God's rational will.

Second, in light of the peculiar relationship between God and creation that the doctrine of creation in Scripture implies, the particularity of the Jewish law begins to make more sense rationally. A covenantal relationship in which one binds oneself exclusively to an Other demands a relationship with a particular person or people. A purely universal covenant, at least at the beginning, would not be understood by human beings as a covenant at all, since it would be indistinguishable from the universal rational order of creation itself (an order, as ancient philosophers like Aristotle attest, could well be understood without a need to refer to a Creator, let alone a free Creator, or to revealed knowledge).

---

2. I say "quasi-personal," because Maimonides clearly does not conceive of God in personal terms or as a personal being. And yet, it is clear from the *Guide* that God is not just the impersonal First Cause of the philosophers nor the arbitrary Will of the *mutakallimun*. God establishes a relationship through the prophet with the Jewish people (and through the Jewish people with all people). Thus love is as essential as intellection to a proper relationship with the divine.

For, again, such a relationship is not purely intellectual but one of will to will, in which the intelligibility of the world is understood as a freely given gift, and thus unfused with a quai-personal meaning. Or, perhaps more precisely, such a relationship is purely intellectual *only* to the degree that one relates to God as a free yet rational creator by entering into covenant with him. Thus, the supremacy of the divine Will along with the rationality of the Jewish law become manifest in his giving of a law to a particular people. And this understanding of revelation as covenant is what makes Judaism in Brague's terms "inclusive"—at least *in potentia*. As dependent on the divine Will, God's covenant can always be expanded to include others, indeed, it may be expanded to become universal. This universality is not contrary to the covenantal nature of revelation but is rooted in the very rational nature of the law so revealed. But it is always a revelation rooted in a particular relationship forged in particular and contingent historical events. Thus, revelation comes to us as eternal universal truths intersecting into temporary and contingent history.

Hence, for Maimonides the role of the greatest of the Hebrew prophets, Moses, cannot be the same or even analogous to that of Muhammad in Islam. As we saw above, scholars of Maimonides have resorted to the term "superprophecy" in order to describe Moses's role in revelation as Maimonides sees it. Moses, to be sure, possessed, for Maimonides, the capacities of both intellect and imagination in order to receive the divine revelation, which is eminently intellectual in mode and content. And yet Moses saw God "face to face"; he communicated with God and even argued with God; Moses was an actor in what were, for the Jews, real historical events—events in which Moses played an integral part and which were themselves an integral part of revelation. Moses was no passive recipient of revelation but an active participant in that revelation. This does not, for Maimonides, take away from the power and purity of that revelation but, to the contrary, reinforces it, for it shows how the Jewish law brings the believer into an active participation in the divine life itself.

In many ways, Thomas Aquinas only makes more explicit what is implicit in Maimonides. God's relationship to the world is one of a free, yet rational Creator who reveals himself not just in creation itself but reveals himself directly in a relationship of intellection and love. But in Aquinas, this relationship is understood quite clearly and explicitly in personal terms. These insights on creation and its relation to revelation are, of course, determined by the new data of Christian revelation in which, similar to the Torah, eternal truths becomes manifest in temporal events.

This is seen at the very beginning of the *Summa theologiae* where Thomas argues that a doctrine—*sacra doctrina*—other than philosophy is needed if human beings are to know God and be saved. Aquinas takes up the arguments we have seen in Maimonides: knowledge of God and of what is necessary for our salvation go beyond our natural powers to know, because their "object" is beyond nature itself; it is God, who as the Creator of all, stands above and outside all (while remaining present in the most intimate way in every creature). The world is the product of a free act of a reality whose essence cannot be deduced rationally from that creation itself. Nevertheless, this creation presents us with a rational order that itself hides within its very intelligibility a "super-intelligibility" that manifests itself as *mystery*, a mystery akin to the mysterious presence of the human person. How does such a personal presence disclose itself? He or she cannot do so as a mere intellectual "object" for thought. He or she can only do so through the uttering of their inner *word*, which is given freely in an act of *grace*, that itself establishes and flows from a relation of both mind to mind and will to will. Such a disclosure cannot be the work or achievement of the hearer of the word but can only be that of the speaker of the word, because God as free Creator, is both object and subject, both pure intelligible Truth and free and active Will.

Hence, following the Gospels and Christian tradition, Aquinas asserts that divine revelation can only come to us as *self-subsistent Word*—as a pure super-intelligible intellect that is clothed in the mystery of the flesh. This self-subsistent Word is a pure "individual substance of a rational nature," to use Boethius's definition of a person. And yet, as Word addressed to humanity, revelation comes to us as in the mystery of personhood, as divine intellect incarnate. Aquinas asserts, as a fundamental metaphysical principle known self-evidently to reason, that "whatever is received is received according to the mode of the receiver." And this is why the Incarnation is the most fitting (*conveniens*) mode of divine revelation: it allows for the reception of the divine Word itself in the mode of the receiver, the incarnate human intellect or person:

> To each and every thing what is fitting is what belongs to it according to its proper nature. So, it is fitting for a human being to reason, because it belongs to him insofar as he is rational according to his nature. Now the very nature of God is goodness, as is clear from what Dionysius says (*Div. Nom.*, i). Hence, whatever pertains to the essence of goodness is fitting for God. It pertains to the essence of goodness that it communicate itself to others [*ad rationem boni ut se aliis communicet*], as is clear from Dionysius (*Div. Nom.*, iv). Hence, it pertains to the essence of the highest good that it communicate itself to the creature in the highest way. This is done chiefly through "his so joining himself to a created nature such that one person results from three things: Word, soul, and flesh," as Augustine says (*De Trin.*, xiii). Whence it is clear that it was fitting [*conveniens fuit*] that God become incarnate.[3]

It is the very nature or essence of goodness to be self-communicative, and it is the nature of pure goodness to be purely self-communicative. This means that pure goodness must be self-communicative in itself (hence, as a purely unitative self-communication of Persons—that is, as Trinity); it also means that this pure goodness communicates itself in a way and mode most intimate, fitting and transforming to and of the receiver. As Thomas implies in the passage cited above, perfect self-communication not only communicates itself in a mode most fitting for the receiver, but it transforms and raises (by grace) the nature of the receiver to receive fully this self-communication. Thomas makes this point explicitly a couple of questions later in the *tertia pars* of the *Summa*:

> Now there is a common agreement of the Person of the Son, who is the Word of God, with all creatures [*communis convenientia ad totam creaturam*], because the word of the artisan, that is his concept, is an exemplary likeness of those things which are made by the artisan. Hence, the Word of God, which is his eternal concept, is an exemplary likeness

---

3. *S. Th.*, III, 1, 1.

of every creature. And thus, just as creatures are established in their proper species by a participation in this likeness, though moveably, so it was fitting by the union of the Word with the creature not by participation but personally that the creature be restored in order to its eternal and immovable perfection; even as the artisan through the intelligible form of his art by which he brings about his handiwork restores it if it has fallen into ruin. In another way, he has a special agreement with human nature: since the Word is a concept of the eternal wisdom, from whom all of man's wisdom is derived. And thus, man makes progress in wisdom (which is his proper perfection insofar as he is rational) insofar as he participates in the Word of God, just as the pupil is instructed by receiving the word of his master.[4]

Through the Incarnation, in other words, the fallen human being is restored and reoriented in his or her whole created being, body and soul, to his or her perfect end and final completion. Most importantly, the Christian, who through the Incarnation receives Christ into his or her very nature as a human being, comes to *participate*, again fully in his or her created being, soul, flesh and all, in the divine Wisdom, which is also life. And a Wisdom that is living and self-subsistent is what we mean by Person. Thus, we participate in the divine Life and Wisdom only to the degree that the divine Life and Wisdom participate in our fallen created being (though without sin).

We can see from the foregoing why a key "subordinate" thesis of this book is that the problem of whether the human intellect is separate and one for all human beings is much more than a curiosity of intellectual history or even simply a debate about the narrower theological problem of the rationality of divine rewards and punishments for individual souls. The problem touches upon the most fundamental problem of all for medieval thinkers: how are we to understand the mode of revelation itself and therefore its truth and rationality. As we saw earlier in this book, Aquinas argues quite vigorously against the notion of a single and separate intellect for all human beings. What is most important for us is that he makes his arguments against this doctrine and for the individuation—indeed, "incarnation"—of the human intellect on purely

4. Ibid., 3, 8.

rational, philosophical grounds. The aim of this is not just to show that the Averroists are wrong; its other (unstated) purpose is to demonstrate that the incarnation of the human intellect is not only possible but also more rational than any other alternative. That is, it is the truth of the Christian understanding of what revelation is and how we receive it that is stake. The mode of revelation whereby the divine Word comes to the incarnate intellect must be incarnate as well. And this is shown to be the case by philosophy itself, which demonstrates that the human intellect must be individuated according to the flesh. Thus, for Thomas, the mode of revelation that honors the nature of the human intellect and human being as established by sound philosophical reasoning is far more rational than that mode in which divine revelation is supposed to "come down" to us in a "book," very much like a separate and single intellect. And like with Maimonides and the doctrine of creation, it is philosophical reflection that testifies to the pre-eminent rationality of this mode of revelation, although this revelation has no need in itself of this testimony, since it is the personal encounter of the human being with the fullness of his or her own personhood in the Person of Christ that this revelation validates itself.

So, far from being irrational and inscrutable doctrines, Aquinas argues that the Christian mysteries of the Incarnation and, following upon it, of the Trinity, once properly penetrated and understood, emerge as eminently rational or, at least, much more rational than the alternatives. For the Incarnation illustrates how in Christianity the mode of revelation, the God-Man, Jesus Christ, *is* the revelation itself. This, of course, is also the case in Islam and Judaism, where the mode of revelation is, in a sense, the revelation itself: for a Muslim, the "book" *is* the revelation; for a Jew, the covenant *is* the revelation. But only in the Jewish and Christian revelation does God *give himself* to be encountered, known, and participated in in that revelation. In Islam, the revelation is *not* himself and cannot be himself, since the revelation is a book and not Allah, and thus the believer can never come to participate in the divine life *qua* embodied individual.[5]

5. It is, of course, a central tenet of orthodox Islam that the Quran is eternal. But it also a central tenet that the Quran is not Allah. How something can be eternal, express the will

As a result, implicitly for the Jew and explicitly for the Christian, the mode in which we know God through revelation cannot be identical with the mode in which we known things through reasoning or the senses. We can know God only in the way we can know persons: through a relationship of love and trust, or in what Maimonides calls "intellectual love," but one that can only be mediated by the divine Word. Such a relationship for Aquinas does not negate philosophical reasoning—far from it. Rather, it illumines natural human reason by inserting the believer back into the primal, free and loving relationship in, by, and through which God created the world itself.

Thus, the Christian and Jew can make a distinction between, on the one hand, knowledge in which the thing known participates in our intellect by reason and, on the other hand, knowledge by faith, where we come to participate, as creatures in all our integrity, in the divine intellect itself. In Islam, there is no such distinction and there cannot be such a distinction, since revelation is understood as an impersonal "book," which can affect no *personal* and *integral* participation of the human being in the divine Life and Wisdom. Indeed, as we saw earlier, al-Ghazali claims that "faith" is the lowest mode of knowing for the Muslim, because "faith" is understood as blind imitation of traditions and not as that which leads to and results from a relationship of love and trust. The highest mode of divine knowledge is that subsequent upon the absorption of the knower, *qua* essence, in God, whereby all that remains is the divine, solitary being and knowing. The Jewish and Christian understanding of revelation, by contrast, leads to an *episteme* of inclusion (but here in a sense that goes beyond what Brague gives it), insofar as the higher mode of knowledge (faith), does not negate the lower (reason), but relates and inserts it into a supreme fellowship of luminous love with its Creator. On this understanding of revelation, human reason and all the sciences that flow from its activity have an independent integrity all of their own. The rationality of the world that these sciences describe is, of course, from the standpoint of Maimonides and Aquinas contin-

_____

of Allah, and not be God, and yet not commit *shirk* (associating something else with Allah) is a conundrum that tested the minds of even the best of the *mutakallimun*.

gent; but it is a contingency rooted in super-rational or intellectual love of the Creator, who cannot be known by reason alone but by an act of faith and love. In other words, for Aquinas and the Christian tradition at least, the validity of human reason can only be rooted in a *personal knowledge* of the Creator that can only be effectual insofar as God reveals himself in the mode of the receiver.

BIBLIOGRAPHY

AVERROES

Al-Kashf 'an Mānahij al-'Adilla fi 'Aqā'id al-Milla. Edited by Muhammad Abd
Al-Jabri. Beirut: Markāz Dirasāt al-Waḥda al-'Arabī, 1998. Translated by
Ibrahim Najjar as *Faith and Reason in Islam: Averroes' Exposition of Religious
Arguments.* Oxford: Oneworld Press, 2001.

Averroes Cordubensis Commentarium Magnum in Aristotelis De Anima Libros.
Edited by F. Stuart Crawford. Cambridge, Mass.: Medieval Academy of
America, 1953. Translated by Richard C. Taylor as *Averroes (Ibn Rushd) of
Cordoba: Long Commentary on the "De Anima" of Aristotle.* Introduction
and notes by Richard C. Taylor, with Thérèse-Anne Druart, subeditor.
New Haven, Conn.: Yale University Press, 2009.

La Béatitude de l'âme. Latin text edited and introduced by Marc Geoffroy and
Carlos Steel. Paris: Vrin, 2001.

Decisive Treatise and Epistle Dedicatory. Facing Arabic text, translated and introduced by Charles E. Butterworth. Provo, Utah: Brigham Young University
Press, 2001.

L'Islam et la raison: Anthologie de textes juridiques, théologiques et polémiques.
Facing Arabic text, translated by Marc Geoffroy, introduction by Alain de
Libera. Paris: Flammarion, 2000.

Le Livre du discours décisif. Facing Arabic text, translated by Marc Geoffory and
introduced by Alain de Libera. Paris: Flammarion, 1996.

On Aristotle's "Metaphysics": An Annotated Translation of the So-called "Epitome."
Edited by Rütiger Arnzen. Berlin: De Gruyter, 2010.

Tafsīr ma ba'd at-tabi'āt. Edited by Maurice Bouyges, SJ. Beirut: Imprimerie
catholique, 1948. Book 12 of Averroes's *Commentary on the by Metaphysics.*
Translated by Charles Genequand as *Ibn Rushd's Metaphysics: A Translation
with Introduction of Ibn Rushd's Commentary on Aristotle's Metaphysics, Book
Lamda.* Leiden: E. J. Brill, 1986.

Tahāfot At-Tahāfot. Edited by Maurice Bouyges, SJ. Beirut: Imprimerie Catholique, 1930. Translated by Simon Van Den Bergh as *Tahāfot At-Tahāfot (The Incoherence of the Incoherence)*. 2 vols. Cambridge: Gibb Memorial Trust, 1978.

MOSES MAIMONIDES

Dalalāt al ḥa'irīn. Judeo-Arabic text established by S. Munk and edited with variant readings by Isshachar Joel. Jerusalem: J. Junovitch, 1930–31. Translated by Shlomo Pines as *The Guide of the Perplexed*. 2 vols. Chicago: University of Chicago Press, 1963.

THOMAS AQUINAS

De Ente et Essentia, Opuscula Omnia S. Thomae Aquinatis. Vol. 1. Edited by R. R. Pierre Mandonnet, OP. Paris, 1927.

De unione Verbi incarnati. Latin text with introduction, translation, and notes by Roger W. Nutt. Leuven: Peeters, 2015.

In Librum Beati Dionysii de Divinibus Nominibus Expositio. Edited by Ceslaus Pera, OP. Turin: Marietti, 1950.

Sancti Thomae Aquinatis in Aristotelis Librum de Anima Commentarium. 4th ed. Edited by P. F. Angelo M. Pirotta, OP. Turin: Marietti, 1959.

Sancti Thomae de Aquino Expositio Super Librum Boethii De Trinitate: Ad Fidem Codicis Autographi nec non Ceterorum Codicum Manu Scriptorum. Edited by Bruno Decker. Leiden: E. J. Brill, 1955.

Sancti Thomae de Aquino Super Librum de Causis Expositio. Edited by H. D. Saffrey, OP. Louvain: Editions E. Nauwelaerts, 1954. Translated by Vincent A. Guagliardo, OP, Charles R. Hess, OP, and Richard C. Taylor as *Commentary on the Book of Causes*. Washington, D.C.: The Catholic University of America Press, 1996.

S. Thomae Aquinatis Liber de Veritate Catholicae Fidei contra errores Infidelium seu "Summa Contra Gentiles." Edited by Ceslaus Pera after the Leonine edition. 3 vols. Turin: Marietti, 1961. Translated by Anton Pegis, F.R.S.C., as *Summa Contra Gentiles*. Introduced and annotated by Anton Pegis, F.R.S.C. 4 vols. Notre Dame, Ind.: University of Notre Dame, 1955.

S. Thomae Aquinatis Quaestiones Disputatae. Edited by P. Bazzi, M. Calcaterra, T. S. Centi, E. Odetto, and P. M. Pession. 2 vols. Turin: Marietti, 1953. *De veritate*, translated from the definitive Leonine text by Robert W. Mulligan, SJ, as *Truth*. 2 vols. Chicago: Regnery, 1952.

S. Thomae Aquinatis Scriptum Super Libros Sententiarum Magistri Petri Lombardi. Edited by P. Mandonnet and M. F. Moos. 4 vols. Paris: 1929–47.

S. *Thomae Aquinatis Summa Theologiae.* 5 vols. Edited by Peter Caramello after
the Leonine edition. Turin: Marietti, 1962. Translated by the Friars of the
English Dominican Province as *Summa Theologica.* 5 vols. New York: Benzinger Bros., 1948.

S. *Thomae Aquinatis Super Evangelium S. Ioannis Lectura.* Edited by P. Raphael
Cai, OP. Turin: Marietti, 1952. Translated by Fabian Lacher, OP, and James
A. Weisheipl, OP, as *Commentary on the Gospel of John.* Introduction and
notes by Daniel Keating and Matthew Levering. 3 vols. Washington, D.C.:
The Catholic University of America Press, 2010.

Thomas d'Aquin contre Averroes: L'Unité de l'intellect contre les Averroistes. Latin
text edited with a facing French translation by Alain de Libera. Paris:
Flammarion, 1994. Translated by Beatrice H. Zedler as *On the Unity of the
Intellect against the Averroists.* Milwaukee: Marquette University Press, 1968.

SECONDARY AND OTHER ANCIENT
AND MEDIEVAL SOURCES

Abelard, Peter. *Dialogus inter Philosophum, Iudeaum et Christianum.* Edited by
Rudolf Thomas. Stuttgart: Friedrich Frommann Verlag, 1970. Translated
by Paul Vincent Spade as *Ethical Writings: Ethics and Dialogue between a
Philosopher, a Jew, and a Christian.* introduced by Marilyn McCord Adams.
Indianapolis: Hackett, 1995.

Adamson, Peter, ed. *The Cambridge Companion to Arabic Philosophy.* Cambridge: Cambridge University Press, 2005.

Aertsen, Jan. *Medieval Philosophy and the Transcendentals: The Case of Thomas
Aquinas.* Leiden: E. J. Brill, 1996.

———. "Die Rede von Gott: Die Fragen, 'ob er ist' und 'was er ist.' Wissen-
schaftslehre und Transzendentalienlehre (S.th. I, qq. 1–12)." In *Thomas von
Aquin: Die Summa Theologiae, Werkinterpretationen,* edited by Andreas
Speer, 29–50. Berlin: De Gruyter, 2005.

Aertsen, Jan, K. Emery Jr., and A. Speer, eds. *Nach der Verurteilung von 1277.
Philosophie und Theologie an der Universität von Paris im letzten Viertel des 13.
Jahrhunderts.* Miscellanea Mediaevalia 28. Berlin: Walter de Gruyter, 2000.

Altmann, Alexander. *Essays in Jewish Intellectual History.* Hanover, N.H.: University Press of New England, 1981.

———. "Essence and Existence in Maimonides." In *Maimonides: A Collection
of Critical Essays,* edited by Joseph A. Buijs, 148–165. Notre Dame, Ind.:
University of Notre Dame Press, 1988.

Arberry, A. J. *Revelation and Reason in Islam (The Forwood Lectures for 1956 Delivered in the University of Liverpool)*. London: George Allen and Unwin, 1957.

Aristotle. *Aristotelis De Anima*. Edited by W. D. Ross. Oxford: Oxford University Press, 1956.

———. *Aristotelis Metaphysica*. Edited by W. Jaeger. Oxford: Oxford University Press, 1957.

———. *Aristotelis Physica*. Edited by W. D. Ross. Oxford: Oxford University Press, 1950.

Arnaldez, Roger. "La doctrine de la création dans le 'Tahafut.'" *Studia Islamica* 7 (1957): 99–114.

———. "La théorie de Dieu dans le 'Tahafut.'" *Studia Islamica* 8 (1957): 15–28.

———. *Averroes: A Rationalist in Islam*. Translated by David Streight. Notre Dame, Ind.: University of Notre Dame Press, 2000.

Attali, Jacques. *Raison et foi: Averroès, Maïmonide, Thomas d'Aquin*. Paris: Bibliothèque nationale de France, 2004.

Benmakhlouf, Ali. *Averroès*. Paris: Les Belles Lettres, 2000.

Benor, Ehud Z. "Meaning and Reference in Maimonides' Negative Theology." *Harvard Theological Review* 88, no. 3 (1995): 339–360.

Berman, Lawrence V. "Maimonides on the Fall of Man." *AJS Review* 5 (1980): 1–15.

Berstein, Jeffrey A. "Righteousness and Divine Love: Maimonides and Thomas on Charity." In *Questions on Love and Charity: "Summa Theologiae, Secunda Secundae," Questions 23–46*. Edited, translated, and introduced by Robert Miner, 336–54. New Haven: Yale University Press, 2016.

Black, C. Clifton, II. "St. Thomas's Commentary on the Johannine Prologue: Some Reflections on Its Character and Implications." *Catholic Biblical Quarterly* 48, no. 4 (1986): 681–98.

Black, Deborah. "Consciousness and Self-Knowledge in Aquinas's Critique of Averroes's Psychology." *Journal of the History of Philosophy* 31, no. 3 (1993): 349–85.

———. "Conjunction and the Identity of Knower and Known in Averroes." *American Catholic Philosophical Quarterly* 73, no. 2 (1999): 159–84.

Brenet, J. B. "Vision béatifique et séparation de l'intellect au début du XVIe siècle: Pour Averroès et contre Thomas d'Aquin?" *Freiburger Zeitschrift für Philosophie und Theologie* 53, no. 1/2 (2006): 310–42.

Brague, Remi. *Au moyen du moyen âge: Philosophies médiévales en chrétienté, judaïsme et islam*. Paris: Flammarion, 2006.

———. *Du dieu des chrétiens et d'un ou deux autres*. Paris: Flammarion, 2008.

Buijs, Joseph A., ed. *Maimonides: A Collection of Critical Essays*. Notre Dame, Ind.: University of Notre Dame Press, 1988.

———. "The Philosophical Character of Maimonides' *Guide*: A Critique of Strauss' Interpretation." In *Maimonides: A Collection of Critical Essays*, edited by Joseph A. Buijs, 59–70. Notre Dame, Ind.: University of Notre Dame Press, 1988.

Burrell, David. *Knowing the Unknowable God: Ibn Sina, Maimonides, Aquinas.* Notre Dame, Ind.: University of Notre Dame Press, 1986.

———. "The Unknowability of God in al-Ghazali." *Religious Studies* 23, no. 2 (1987): 171–82.

———. *Freedom and Creation in Three Traditions*. Notre Dame, Ind.: University of Notre Dame Press, 1993.

Chenu, M.-D. *Introduction à l'étude de saint Thomas d'Aquin*. Paris: J. Vrin, 1950.

Chesterton, G. K. *Saint Thomas Aquinas: "The Dumb Ox."* New York: Doubleday, 1956.

Clarke, W. Norris. "The Meaning of Participation in St. Thomas." *Proceedings of the American Catholic Philosophical Association* 26 (1952): 147–57.

———. *Person and Being*. Milwaukee: Marquette University Press, 1993.

———. *The One and the Many: A Contemporary Thomistic Metaphysics*. Notre Dame, Ind.: University of Notre Dame Press, 2001.

Corbin, Henry. *Histoire de la philosophie islamique*. Paris: Gallimard, 1986.

Davidson, Herbert A. "Maimonides' Secret Position on Creation." In *Studies in Medieval Jewish History and Literature*, edited by I. Twersky, 16–40. Cambridge, Mass.: Harvard University Press, 1979.

———. *Alfarabi, Avicenna, and Averroes on Intellect: Their Cosmologies, Theories of the Active Intellect, and Theories of Human Intellect*. Oxford: Oxford University Press, 1992.

———. *Moses Maimonides: The Man and His Works*. Oxford: Oxford University Press, 2005.

Dewan, Lawrence. "St. Albert, Creation, and the Philosophers." *Laval théologique et philosophique* 40, no. 3 (1984): 295–307.

———. "Thomas Aquinas, Creation, and Two Historians." *Laval théologique et philosophique* 50, no. 2 (1994): 363–87.

Dobbs-Weinstein, Idit. "Medieval Biblical Commentary and Philosophical Inquiry as Exemplified in the Thought of Moses Maimonides and St. Thomas Aquinas." In *Moses Maimonides and His Time*, edited by Eric L. Ormsby, 101–120. Washington, D.C.: The Catholic University of America Press, 1989.

———. *Maimonides and St. Thomas on the Limits of Reason*. Albany, N.Y.: State University of New York Press, 1995.

Dobie, Robert J. *Logos and Revelation: Ibn 'Arabi, Meister Eckhart and Mystical Hermeneutics*. Washington, D.C.: The Catholic University of America Press, 2010.

———. "The Phenomenology of *Wujud* in the Thought of Ibn al-'Arabi." In *Timing and Temporality in Islamic Philosophy and Phenomenology of Life*, edited by A-T. Tymieniecka, 313–22. Dordrecht, The Netherlands: Springer, 2007.

———. "Incarnate Knowing: Theology and the Corporeality of Thinking in Thomas Aquinas' *De unitate intellectus contra Averroistas*." *The Thomist* 77, no. 4 (2013): 497–529.

———. "Jesus in the Muslim and Christian Mystical Traditions: Ibn 'Arabi and Meister Eckhart." In *Nicolas of Cusa and Islam: Polemic and Dialogue in the Late Middle Ages*, edited by Ian Christopher Levy, Rita George-Tvrtkovic, and Donald F. Duclow, 235–51. Leiden: E. J. Brill, 2014.

Dunphy, William. "Maimonides and Aquinas on Creation: A Critique of Their Historians." In *Graceful Reason: Essays in Ancient and Medieval Philosophy Presented to Joseph Owens, CSsR*, edited by Lloyd P. Gerson, 361–79. Toronto: Pontifical Institute for Mediaeval Studies, 1983.

———. "Maimonides' Not-So-Secret Position on Creation." In *Moses Maimonides and His Time*, edited by Eric L. Ormsby, 151–72. Washington, D.C.: The Catholic University of America Press, 1989.

Elders, Leo. "Aquinas on Holy Scripture as the Medium of Divine Revelation." In *La doctrine de la révélation divine de saint Thomas d'Aquin*, edited by Leo Elders, 132–52. Vatican City: Libreria Editrice Vaticana, 1990.

———, ed. *La doctrine de la révélation divine de saint Thomas d'Aquin*. Vatican City: Libreria Editrice Vaticana, 1990.

Emery, Gilles. *Trinity in Aquinas*. Ave Maria, Fla.: Sapientia Press, 2006.

Ernst, Cornelius. "Metaphor and Ontology in Sacra Doctrina." *The Thomist* 37, no. 3 (1974): 403–25.

Fakhry, Majid. *Islamic Occasionalism and Its Critique by Averroes and Aquinas*. London: George Allen and Unwin, 1958.

———. *Averroes (Ibn Rushd): His Life, Works and Influence*. Oxford: One World Publications, 2001.

Feldman, Seymour. "A Scholastic Misinterpretation of Maimonides' Doctrine of Divine Attributes." In *Maimonides: A Collection of Critical Essays*, edited by Joseph A. Buijs, 267–83. Notre Dame, Ind.: University of Notre Dame Press, 1988.

Fraenkel, Carlos. "God's Existence and Attributes." In *The Cambridge History of Jewish Philosophy: From Antiquity through the Seventeenth Century*, edited by

Steven Nadler and T. M. Rudavsky, 561–98. New York: Cambridge University Press, 2009.

Frank, Daniel H. "Divine Law and Human Practices." In *The Cambridge History of Jewish Philosophy: From Antiquity through the Seventeenth Century*, edited by Steven Nadler and T. M. Rudavsky, 790–807. New York: Cambridge University Press, 2009.

Frank, Isaac. "Maimonides and Aquinas on Man's Knowledge of God: A Twentieth-Century Perspective." In *Maimonides: A Collection of Critical Essays*, edited by Joseph A. Buijs, 284–305. Notre Dame, Ind.: University of Notre Dame Press, 1988.

Frank, Richard. "Al-Ghazali's Use of Avicenna's Philosophy." *Revue des études islamiques* 55–57 (1987–89): 271–84.

Fox, Marvin. *Interpreting Maimonides: Studies in Methodology, Metaphysics, and Moral Philosophy*. Chicago: University of Chicago Press, 1990.

Gauthier, R. A. "Notes sur les débuts (1225–1240) du premier 'Averroïsme.'" *Revue des sciences philosophiques et théologiques* 66 (1982): 321–74.

———. "Notes sur Siger de Brabant: I. Siger en 1265." *Revue des sciences philosophiques et théologiques* 67 (1983): 201–32.

———. "Notes sur Siger de Brabant: II. Siger en 1272–1275, Aubry de Reims et la scission des Normands." *Revue des sciences philosophiques et théologiques* 68 (1984): 3–49.

Geoffroy, Marc. "L'Almohadisme théologique d'Averroès (Ibn Rushd)." *Archives d'histoire doctrinale et littéraire du moyen âge* 66, no. 1 (1999): 9–47.

———. "Averroès sur l'intellect comme cause agente et cause formelle et la question de la junction." In *Averroès et les averroismes juif et latin: actes du colloque international, Paris, 16–17 juin, 2005*, edited by Jean Jolivet, 77–110. Turnhout: Brepols, 2007.

Al-Ghazali, Abu Hamid. *Ihya' 'ulūm al-dīn*. 5 vols. Dar al-afāk al-'arabīyya: Cairo, 2004. Book 21 translated by Walter James Skellie as *Kitāb sharḥ 'ajā'ib al-qalb: The Marvels of the Heart, Book 21 of the Ihya' 'ulūm al-dīn: The Revival of the Religious Sciences*. Introduced by Walter James Skellie. Louisville, Ky.: Fons Vitae, 2010.

———. *The Incoherence of the Philosophers*. Facing Arabic text, introduced, translated, and annotated by Michael E. Marmura. Provo, Utah: Brigham Young University Press, 2000.

———. *The Niche of Lights (mishkāt al-anwār)*. Facing Arabic text, translated, introduced, and annotated by David Buchman. Provo, Utah: Brigham Young University Press, 1998.

Gianotti, Timothy J. *Al-Ghazali's Unspeakable Doctrine of the Soul: Unveiling the*

Esoteric Psychology and Eschatology of the "Ihya." Leiden: E. J. Brill, 2001.

Gilson, Etienne. "Les sources gréco-arabes de l'augustinisme avicennant." *Archives d'histoire doctrinale et littéraire du moyen âge* 4 (1929): 6–149.

———. *Reason and Revelation in the Middle Ages.* New York: Charles Scribner's Sons, 1948.

———. *The Christian Philosophy of St. Thomas Aquinas.* Translated by L. K. Shook, CSB. New York: Random House, 1956.

———. *Pourquoi Saint Thomas a critiqué Saint Augustin (suivi de) Avicenne et le point de départ de Duns Scot.* Paris: Vrin, 1986.

Goodman, Lenn E. "Ghazali's Argument from Creation." *International Journal of Middle East Studies* 2, no. 1 (1971): 67–85.

———. "Did Al-Ghazali Deny Causality?" *Studia Islamica* 47 (1978): 83–120.

———. "Creation and Emanation." In *The Cambridge History of Jewish Philosophy: From Antiquity through the Seventeenth Century,* edited by Steven Nadler and T. M. Rudavsky, 599–618. New York: Cambridge University Press, 2009.

Gottlieb, Michah. "Mysticism and Philosophy." In *The Cambridge History of Jewish Philosophy: From Antiquity to the Seventeenth Century,* edited by Steven Nadler and T. M. Rudavsky, 121–64. New York: Cambridge University Press, 2009.

Griffel, Frank. *Al-Ghazali's Philosophical Theology.* Oxford: Oxford University Press, 2009.

Gruenwald, Ithamar. "Maimonides' Quest beyond Philosophy and Prophecy." In *Perspectives on Maimonides: Philosophical and Historical Studies,* edited by Joel L. Kraemer, 141–57. Oxford: Oxford University Press, 1991.

Guindon, Roger. "La théologie de saint Thomas d'Aquin dans le rayonnement du 'Prologue' de saint Jean," part 1. *Revue de l'Université Ottawa* 29, special section (1959): 5–23.

———. "La théologie de saint Thomas d'Aquin dans le rayonnement du 'Prologue' de saint Jean," part 2. *Revue de l'Université Ottawa* 29, special section (1959): 121–42.

Haberman, Jacob. *Maimonides and Aquinas: A Contemporary Appraisal.* New York: Ktav Publishing House, 1979.

Hadot, Pierre. *Qu'est que la philosophie antique?* Paris: Editions Gallimard, 1995.

Hartman, David. *Maimonides: Torah and Philosophic Quest.* Philadelphia: Jewish Publication Society, 1976.

Harvey, Warren Zev. "A Third Approach to Maimonides' Cosmogony-Prophetology Puzzle." *Harvard Theological Review* 74, no. 3 (1981): 287–301.

Hauser, Alan, and Watson, Duane, eds. *A History of Biblical Interpretation,* vol. 2, *The Medieval through the Reformation Periods*. Grand Rapids, Mich.: William B. Eerdmans, 2009.

Hayoun, Maurice-Ruben, and de Libera, Alain. *Averroès et l'averroisme*. Paris: Presses Universitaires de France, 1991.

Healy, Nicholas. Introduction to *Aquinas on Scripture: An Introduction to His Biblical Commentaries*, edited by Thomas Weinandy, Daniel Keating, and John Yocum, 1–20. London: Continuum, 2006.

Honnefelder, L. "Die zweite Anfang der Metaphysik. Voraussetzungen, Ansätze und Folgen der Widerbegründung der Metaphysik im 13./14. Jahrhundert." In *Philosophie im Mittelalter, Entwicklungslinien und Paradigmen*. Hamburg: Felix Meiner, 1987.

Hourani, George F. "Averroès Musulman." In *Multiple Averroès: Actes du colloque international organisé à l'occasion du 850e anniversaire de la naissance d'Averroès, Paris 20–23 septembre 1976*, edited by Jean Jolivet, 21–30. Paris: Les Belles Lettres, 1978.

Houser, R. E. "Avicenna, *Aliqui*, and the Thomistic Doctrine of Creation." http://t4.stthom.edu/users/houser/avicenna2000, accessed on March 7, 2017.

Hyman, Arthur. "Maimonides on Religious Language." In *Perspectives on Maimonides: Philosophical and Historical Studies*, edited by Joel L. Kraemer, 175–91. Oxford: Oxford University Press, 1991.

———. "Les types d'arguments dans les écrits théologico-politiques et polémiques d'Averroès." In *Penser avec Aristote*, edited by Muhammad Allal Sinaceaur, 653–665. Toulouse: Erès, 1991.

Ivry, Alfred L. "Maimonides on Creation." In *Creation and the End of Days: Judaism and Scientific Cosmology*, edited by David Novack and Norbert Samuelson, 185–213. Lanham, Md.: University Press of America, 1986.

Jacobs, Jonathan. "Aristotle and Maimonides: The Ethics of Perfection and the Perfection of Ethics." *American Catholic Philosophical Quarterly* 76, no. 1 (2002): 145–163.

Janssens, Jules. "Al-Ghazzali's *Tahafut*: Is It Really a Rejection of Ibn Sina's Philosophy?" *Journal of Islamic Studies* 12, no. 1 (2001): 1–17.

Jeffery, Arthur. *The Qur'an as Scripture*. New York: Russel F. Moore Co., 1952.

Johnson, Mark F. "Did St. Thomas Attribute a Doctrine of Creation to Aristotle?" *New Scholasticism* 63, no. 2 (1989): 129–55.

Johnstone, Brian. "The Debate on the Structure of the *Summa Theologiae* of Saint Thomas Aquinas." In *Aquinas as Authority: A Collection of Studies Presented at the Second Conference of the Thomas Instituut te Utrecht, December 14–16, 2000*, 187–200. Leuven: Peeters, 2002.

Jolivet, Jean. "Divergences entre les métaphysiques d'Ibn Rushd et d'Aristote." *Arabica* 29, no. 3 (1982): 225–245.

———. "Averroès et le décentrement du sujet." In *Le choc Averroès: Comment les philosophes arabes ont fait Europe. Internationale de l'imaginaire* 17/18 (1991): 161–69.

———, ed. *Multiple Averroès: Actes du colloque international organisé à l'occasion du 850e anniversaire de la naissance d'Averroès, Paris 20–23 septembre 1976*. Paris: Les Belles Lettres, 1978.

Jordan, Mark D. "The Protreptic Structure of the '*Summa Contra Gentiles*.'" *The Thomist* 50, no. 2 (1986): 173–209.

———. "Theology and Philosophy." In *The Cambridge Companion to Aquinas*, edited by Norman Kretzmann and Eleonore Stump, 232–51. Cambridge: Cambridge University Press, 1994.

Kaplan, Lawrence. "Maimonides on the Miraculous Element in Prophecy." *Harvard Theological Review* 70, no. 3/4 (1977): 233–56.

Kasher, Hannah. "Self-Cognizing Intellect and Negative Attributes in Maimonides' Theology." *Harvard Theological Review* 87, no. 4 (1994): 461–72.

Kellner, Menachem. *Maimonides' Confrontation with Mysticism*. Oxford: The Littman Library of Jewish Civilization, 2006.

Kemal, Salim. *The Philosophical Poetics of Alfarabi, Avicenna and Averroes: The Aristotelian Reception*. London: Routledge, 2003.

Kirk, G. S., and J. E. Raven. *The Presocratic Philosophers*. Cambridge: Cambridge University Press, 1964.

Klima, Gyula. "Aquinas on the Materiality of the Human Soul and the Immateriality of the Human Intellect." *Philosophical Investigations* 32:2 (2009): 163–81.

Kogan, Barry S. "Averroes and the Theory of Emanation." *Medieval Studies* 43 (1981): 384–404.

———. "Eternity and Origination: Averroes' *Discourse on the Manner of the World's Existence*." In *Islamic Theology and Philosophy: Studies in Honor of George F. Hourani*, edited by Michael E. Marmura, 203–35. Albany, N.Y.: State University of New York Press, 1984.

———. *Averroes and the Metaphysics of Causation*. Albany, N.Y.: State University of New York Press, 1985.

———. "'What Can We Know and When Can We Know It?' Maimonides on the Active Intelligence and Human Cognition." In *Moses Maimonides and His Time*, edited by Eric L. Ormsby, 121–137. Washington, D.C.: The Catholic University of America Press, 1989.

———. "Understanding Prophecy: Four Traditions." In *The Cambridge History of Jewish Philosophy: From Antiquity through the Seventeenth Century*, edited by Steven Nadler and T. M. Rudavsky, 481–523. New York: Cambridge University Press, 2009.

Koterski, Joseph W. *An Introduction to Medieval Philosophy: Basic Concepts.* Chichester, UK: Wiley-Blackwell, 2009.

Kramer, Joel L. *Maimonides: The Life and World of One of Civilization's Greatest Minds.* New York: Doubleday, 2008.

Kreisel, Howard. "Philosophical Interpretations of the Bible." In *The Cambridge History of Jewish Philosophy: From Antiquity to the Seventeenth Century*, edited by Steven Nadler and T. M. Rudavsky, 88–120. New York: Cambridge University Press, 2009.

Kuksewicz, Zdzislaw. "Das "Naturale" und das "Supernaturale" in der averroistischen Philosophie." In *Mensch und Natur im Mittelalter*, edited by Albert Zimmerman and Andreas Speer, 371–82. Miscellanea Medievalia 21/1. Berlin: Walter de Gruyter, 1991.

Leaman, Oliver. *Averroes and His Philosophy.* Oxford: Oxford University Press, 1988.

Levering, Matthew. *Scripture and Metaphysics: Aquinas and the Renewal of Trinitarian Theology.* London: Blackwell, 2004.

———. "Reading John with Saint Thomas." In *Aquinas on Scripture: An Introduction to His Biblical Commentaries*, edited by Thomas Weinandy, Daniel Keating, and John Yocum, 99–126. London: Continuum, 2006.

Libera, Alain de. *Penser au moyen âge.* Paris: Editions du Seuil, 1991.

Lobel, Diana. "'Silence Is to Praise to You': Maimonides on Negative Theology, Looseness of Expression, and Religious Experience." *American Catholic Philosophical Quarterly* 76, no. 1 (2002): 25–49.

Luxenberg, Christoph. *The Syro-Aramaic Reading of the Koran: A Contribution to the Decoding of the Language of the Koran.* Berlin: Verlag Schiler, 2007.

Madkour, I. *L'Organon d'Aristote dans le monde arabe.* 2nd ed. Paris: Vrin, 1969.

Mahdi, Muhsin. "Remarks on Averroes' *Decisive Treatise*." In *Islamic Theology and Philosophy: Studies in Honor of George F. Hourani*, edited by Michael E. Marmura, 188–202. Albany, N.Y.: State University of New York Press, 1984.

Mahoney, Edward P. "Aquinas's Critique of Averroes' Doctrine of the Unity of the Intellect." In *Thomas Aquinas and His Legacy*, edited by David M. Gallagher, 83–106. Washington, D.C.: The Catholic University of America Press, 1994.

Malino, Jonathan. "Aristotle on Eternity: Does Maimonides Have a Reply?" In *Maimonides and Philosophy*, edited by S. Pines and Y. Yovel, 52–64. Dordrecht: Martinus Nijhoff, 1986.

Marmura, Michael E. "Al-Ghazali." In *The Cambridge Companion to Arabic Philosophy*, edited by Peter Adamson, 137–54. Cambridge: Cambridge University Press, 2005.

Marshall, Bruce. "*Quod Scit Una Uetula*: Aquinas on the Nature of Theology." In *The Theology of Thomas Aquinas*, edited by Rik van Nieuwenhove and Joseph Wawrykow, 1–35. South Bend, Ind.: University of Notre Dame Press, 2005.

Maurer, Armand. "St. Thomas on the Sacred Name 'Tetragrammaton.'" *Medieval Studies* 34 (1972): 275–86.

———. "Maimonides and Aquinas on the Study of Metaphysics." In *A Straight Path: Studies in Medieval Philosophy and Culture; Essays in Honor of Arthur Hyman*, edited by Ruth Link-Salinger (editor-in-chief), Jeremiah Hackett, Michael Samuel Hyman, R. James Long, and Charles H. Manekin, 206–15. Washington, D.C.: The Catholic University of America Press, 1988.

McCall, Raymond J. "St. Thomas on Ontological Truth." *The New Scholasticism* 12, no. 1 (1938): 9–29.

Mongeau, Gilles. *Embracing Wisdom: The "Summa theologiae" as Spiritual Pedagogy*. Toronto: Pontifical Institute of Mediaeval Studies, 2015.

Muckle, J. T. "Isaak Israeli's Definition of Truth." *Archives d'histoire doctrinale et littéraire du moyen âge* 8 (1933): 5–8.

Nadler, Steven, and T. M. Rudavsky, eds. *The Cambridge History of Jewish Philosophy: From Antiquity through the Seventeenth Century*. New York: Cambridge University Press, 2009.

Nagel, Thomas. *Mind and Cosmos: Why the Materialist, Neo-Darwinian Conception of Nature Is Almost Certainly False*. Oxford: Oxford University Press, 2012.

Nicolas, J.-H. "Aspects épistémologiques de la révélation." In *La doctrine de la révélation divine de saint Thomas d'Aquin*, edited by Leo Elders, 153–170. Vatican City: Libreria Editrice Vaticana, 1990.

Nichols, Aidan. *Discovering Aquinas: An Introduction to his Life, Works, and Influence*. Grand Rapids, Mich.: William B. Eerdmans, 2002.

Niewöhner, Friedrich. "Zum Ursprung der Lehre von der doppelten Wahrheit: eine Koran-Interpretation des Averroes." In *Averroismus im Mittelalter und in der Renaissance*, edited by Friedrich Niewöhner and Loris Sturlese, 23–41. Zurich: Spur Verlag, 1994.

Ormsby, Eric L., ed. *Moses Maimonides and His Time*. Washington, D.C.: The Catholic University of America Press, 1989.

O'Rourke, Fran. *Pseudo-Dionysius and the Metaphysics of Aquinas*. South Bend, Ind.: University of Notre Dame Press, 1992.

Pegis, Anton. *St. Thomas and the Problem of the Soul in the Thirteenth Century.* Toronto: Pontifical Institute of Mediaeval Studies, 1934.

———. "A Note on St. Thomas, *Summa Theologica* I, 44, 1–2." *Medieval Studies* 8 (1946): 159–68.

Pessin, Sarah. "Matter, Form, and the Corporeal World." In *The Cambridge History of Jewish Philosophy: From Antiquity to the Seventeenth Century*, edited by Steven Nadler and T. M. Rudavsky, 269–301. New York: Cambridge University Press, 2009.

Pieper, Josef. *The Silence of St. Thomas.* South Bend, Ind.: St. Augustine Press, 1957.

———. *Wahrheit der Dinge: Eine Untersuchung zur Anthropologie des Hochmittelalters.* Munich: Im Kösel, 1966.

Pines, Shlomo. "Truth and Falsehood versus Good and Evil: A Study in Jewish and General Philosophy in Connection with the Guide of the Perplexed." In *Studies in Maimonides*, edited by Isadore Twersky, 95–157. Cambridge, Mass.: Harvard University Press, 1990.

Prémare, Alfred-Louis de. *Aux Origines du Coran: questions d'hier, approches d'aujourd'hui.* Paris: Téraèdre, 2004.

The Qur'an. Translated by M. A. S. Abdel Haleem. Oxford: Oxford University Press, 2004.

Ravitzky, Aviezar. *History and Faith: Studies in Jewish Philosophy.* Amsterdam: J. C. Gieben, 1996.

Rousselot, Pierre. *L'Intellectualisme de Saint Thomas.* Paris: Félix Arcan, 1908.

Rubio, Mercedes. "Maimonides' Proofs for the Existence of God and Their Aristotelian Background in the 'Guide of the Perplexed.'" In *Was ist Philosophie im Mittelalter: Akten des X. Internationalen Kongresses für mittelalterische Philosophie der Societé Internationale pour l'étude de la Philosophie Médiévale 25. Bis 30. August 1997 in Erfurt*, edited by Jan A. Aertsen and Andreas Speer, 914–21. Berlin: Walter de Gruyter, 1998.

Rynhold, Daniel. *An Introduction to Medieval Jewish Philosophy.* London: I. B. Taurus, 2009.

Seeskin, Kenneth. "Sanctity and Silence: The Religious Significance of Maimonides' Negative Theology." *American Catholic Philosophical Quarterly* 76, no. 1 (2002): 7–24.

———. *Maimonides on the Origin of the World.* New York: Cambridge University Press, 2005.

Shanab, R. E. A. "Ghazali and Aquinas on Causation." *Monist: An International Quarterly Journal of General Philosophical Inquiry* 58, no. 1 (1974): 140–150.

Smith, Gerard, SJ. "Avicenna and the Possibles." *New Scholasticism* 17, no. 4 (1943): 340–57.

Solère, Jean-Luc. "La notion d'intentenionalité chez Thomas d'Aquin." *Philosophie* 24 (1989): 13–36.

Speer, Andreas. "*Sapientia Nostra.* Zum Verhältnis von philosophischer und theologischer Weisheit in den Pariser Debatten am Ende des 13. Jahrhunderts." In *Nach der Verurteilung von 1277. Philosophie und Theologie an der Universität von Paris im letzten Viertel des 13. Jahrhunderts,* edited by J. Aertsen, K. Emery Jr., and A. Speer, 248–75. Miscellanea Mediaevalia 28. Berlin: Walter de Gruyter, 2000.

———, ed. *Thomas von Aquin: Die Summa Theologiae, Werkinterpretationen.* Berlin: De Gruyter, 2005.

Spicq, P. C. *Esquisse d'une histoire de l'exégèse latine au moyen âge.* Paris: J. Vrin, 1944.

Stern, Josef. "Meaning and Language." In *The Cambridge History of Jewish Philosophy: From Antiquity through the Seventeenth Century,* edited by Steven Nadler and T. M. Rudavsky, 230–66. New York: Cambridge University Press, 2009.

Strauss, Leo. "How to Begin to Study the Guide of the Perplexed." In Maimonides, *The Guide of the Perplexed,* translated by Shlomo Pines, vol. 1, xi–lvi. Chicago: University of Chicago Press, 1963.

Synave, Paul, and Pierre Benoit. *Prophecy and Inspiration: A Commentary on the Summa Theologica II-II, Questions 171–178.* New York: Desclee Company, 1961.

Talmage, Frank. "Apples of Gold: The Inner Meaning of Sacred Texts in Medieval Judaism." In *Jewish Spirituality: From the Bible through the Middle Ages,* edited by Arthur Green, 313–355. New York: Crossroad, 1986.

Taylor, Richard. "Averroes on Psychology and the Principles of Metaphysics." *Journal of the History of Philosophy* 36, no. 4 (1998): 507–523.

———. "Averroes' Epistemology and Its Critique by Aquinas." In *Medieval Masters: Essays in Memory of Msgr. E.A. Synan,* 147–77. Thomistic Papers 7. Houston: University of St. Thomas Press, 1999.

———. "'Truth Does Not Contradict Truth': Averroes and the Unity of Truth." *Topoi* 19, no. 1 (2000): 3–15.

———. "Averroes." In *A Companion to Philosophy in the Middle Ages,* edited by Jorge Gracia and Timothy Noone, 182–195. London: Blackwell, 2003.

———. "Averroes." In *The Cambridge Companion to Arabic Philosophy,* edited by Peter Adamson, 180–200. Cambridge: Cambridge University Press, 2005.

———. "Aquinas's Naturalized Epistemology." *Proceedings of the American Catholic Philosophical Association* 79 (2006): 85–102.

————. "Intellect as Intrinsic Formal Cause in the Soul according to Aquinas and Averroes." In *The Afterlife of the Platonic Soul: Reflections of Platonic Psychology in the Monotheistic Religions*, edited by Maha Elkiasy-Friemuth and John M. Dillon, 187–220. Leiden: Brill, 2009.

te Velde, Rudi. "Natural Reason in the *Summa Contra Gentiles*." *Medieval Philosophy and Theology* 4 (1994): 42–70.

————. "Die Gottesnamen. Thomas' Analyse des Sprechens über Gott unter besonderer Berücksichtung der Analogie (S.th. I, qq. 13)." In *Thomas von Aquin: "Die Summa theologiae": Werkinterprationen*, edited by Andreas Speer, 51–76. Berlin: Walter de Gruyter, 2005.

————. "Schöpfung und Partizipation (S.th. I, qq. 44–47 und qq. 103–105)." In *Thomas von Aquin: Die Summa Theologiae, Wirkinterpretationen*, edited by Andreas Speer, 100–124. Berlin: De Gruyter, 2005.

————. *Aquinas on God: The "Divine Science" of the* Summa Theologiae. Farnham, UK: Ashgate, 2006.

Tirosh-Samuelson, Hava. "Virtue and Happiness." In *The Cambridge History of Jewish Philosophy: From Antiquity through the Seventeenth Century*, edited by Steven Nadler and T. M. Rudavsky, 707–67. New York: Cambridge University Press, 2009.

Torrell, Jean-Pierre. "Le traité de la prophetie de S. Thomas d'Aquin et la théologie de la révélation." In *La doctrine de la révélation divine de saint Thomas d'Aquin*, edited by Leo Elders, 171–95. Vatican City: Libreria Editrice Vaticana, 1990.

————. *Aquinas's "Summa": Background, Structure, and Reception*. Translated by Benedict M. Guevin. Washington, D.C.: The Catholic University of America Press, 2005.

Touati, Charles. "Les Problèmes de la génération et le rôle de l'intellect agent chez Averroès." In *Multiple Averroès: Actes du Colloque International organisé à l'occasion du 850e anniversaire de la naissance d'Averroès, Paris 20–23 septembre 1976*, edited by Jean Jolivet, 157–64. Paris: Les Belles Lettres, 1978.

Treiger, Alexander. "Monism and Monotheism in al-Ghazali's *Mishkat al-anwar*." *Journal of Qur'anic Studies* 9, no. 1 (2007): 1–27.

————. *Inspired Knowledge in Islamic Thought: Al-Ghazali's Theory of Mystical Cognition and Its Avicennian Foundation*. London: Routledge, 2012.

Tsakiridou, Cornelia. "Theophany and Humanity in St. Symeon the New Theologian and in Abu Hamid Al-Ghazali." *International Journal of Orthodox Theology* 2, no. 3 (2011): 167–187.

Turki, Abdel Magid. "La Place d'Averroès juriste dans l'histoire du Malikisme et de l'Espagne musulmane." In *Multiple Averroès: Actes du colloque interna-*

tional organisé à l'occasion du 850e anniversaire de la naissance d'Averroès, Paris
20–23 septembre 1976, edited by Jean Jolivet, 33–43. Paris: Les Belles Lettres,
1978.

Urvoy, Dominque. Ibn Rushd (Averroes). Translated by Olivia Stewart. London:
Routledge, 1991.

Vajda, Georges. "La pensée religieuse de Moise Maimonide: unité ou dualité?"
Cahiers de civilisation médiévale 33, no. 1 (1966): 29–49.

Van de Wiele, Jozef. "Le problème de la vérité ontologique dans la philosophie
de saint Thomas." Revue philosophique de Louvain, 52, no. 36 (1954): 521–71.

Van Nieuwenhove, Rik, and Joseph Wawrykow, eds. The Theology of Thomas
Aquinas. South Bend, Ind.: University of Notre Dame Press, 2005.

Wahlberg, Matts. Revelation as Testimony: A Philosophical-Theological Study.
Grand Rapids, Mich.: Eerdmans, 2014.

Wawrykow, Joseph. "Grace." In The Theology of Thomas Aquinas, edited by Rik
van Nieuwenhove and Joseph Wawrykow, 192–221. South Bend, Ind.: University of Notre Dame Press, 2005.

Weinandy, Thomas G. "The Supremacy of Christ: Aquinas' Commentary on the
Hebrews." In Aquinas on Scripture: An Introduction to His Biblical Commentaries, edited by Thomas Weinandy, Daniel Keating, and John Yocum,
223–44. London: Continuum, 2006.

Weisheipl, James A. Friar Thomas d'Aquino: His Life, Thought and Works. Washington, D.C.: The Catholic University of America Press, 1974.

Wensinck, Arent Jan. "On the Relationship between al-Ghazali's Cosmology
and His Mysticism." Mededeelingen der Koninkijke Akademie van Wettenschappen, Afdeeling Letterkunde, Deel 75, Serie A (1933): 183–209.

Wippel, John F. "Truth in Thomas Aquinas, Part I." Review of Metaphysics 43,
no. 2 (1989): 295–326.

———. "Truth in Thomas Aquinas, Part II." Review of Metaphysics 43, no. 3
(1990): 543–67.

———. "Natur und Gnade (S.th. I-II, qq. 109–114)." In Thomas von Aquin: Die
Summa Theologiae, Wirkinterpretationen, edited by Andreas Speer, 246–70.
Berlin: De Gruyter, 2005.

Wohlman, Avital. Al-Ghazali, Averroes and the Interpretation of the Qur'an: Common Sense and Philosophy in Islam. London: Routledge, 2010.

Wolfson, Harry A. "Maimonides on Negative Attributes." In Studies in the History of Philosophy and Religion, vol. 2, edited by Isadore Twersky and George H.
Williams, 195–230. Cambridge, Mass.: Harvard University Press, 1977.

Zimmermann, Albert. Ontologie oder Metaphysik? Die Diskussion über den

Gegendstand der Metaphysik im 13. Und 14. Jahrhundert. Leiden: E. J. Brill, 1965.

————. "Glaube und Wissen (S.th. II-II, qq. 1–9)." In *Thomas von Aquin: "Die Summa Theologiae": Werkinterpretationen,* edited by A. Speer, 271–97. Berlin: Walter de Gruyter, 2005.

Zine, Mohammed Chaouki. "L'interprétation symbolique du verset de la lumière chez Ibn Sina, Ghazali et Ibn 'Arabi et ses implications doctrinales." *Arabica* 56, no. 6 (2009): 543–595.

Zum Brunn, Emile. "La 'métaphysique de l'Exode' selon Thomas d'Aquin." In *Dieu et l'être: Exégèses d'Exode 3:14 et de Coran 20, 11–24,* 245–69. Paris: Etudes Augustiniennes, 1978.

INDEX

Abelard, Peter, 8n24

Abraham, 128, 133, 141

"Account of the Beginning" (Maimonides), 125–26

"Account of the Chariot" (Maimonides), 125–26, 143–44

adaequatio, 177

Adam: and Eve, 99, 106, 107; sin of, 67n20

Aertsen, J., 17n42, 160n3, 162, 167n15, 168, 169n17, 169n18, 173n25, 174n27, 175, 183n42

afterlife, 45

agency: human and divine, 93n70

Alexander of Aphrodisias, 142n125, 210n23

allegory, 105

Almarovids, 19n3

Almohads, 19n3, 31n31, 54

analogy: doctrine of, 255–56

Anaximander, 163

Anaximenes, 163

Andalusia, 54

annihilation. *See fana'*

Anselm, 31n31, 182

'aql, 224. *See also* intellect

Aquinas, Thomas, 12–13, 14, 15n38, 15n39, 16–17, 18, 20, 46, 57, 75n39, 116n54, 127n89, 142n125, 143, 160, 161, 162, 163, 167, 169, 171, 172, 174, 175, 176, 177, 178, 179, 181, 182, 183, 184, 185, 186, 187, 188, 191, 192, 193, 194, 195, 196, 198, 199, 200, 201, 202, 203, 204, 205, 206, 207, 208, 210, 212, 213, 214, 215, 216, 217, 218, 219, 220, 221, 222, 224, 225, 226, 227, 228, 229, 230, 231, 232, 233, 234, 235, 236, 237, 238, 239, 240, 241, 242, 243, 244, 245,

246, 247, 248, 249, 251, 252, 253, 254, 255, 256, 257, 258, 259, 260, 261, 262, 263, 264, 265, 266, 267, 268, 269, 270, 271, 272, 281–87

Arabic language, 29

Arberry, A. J., 4n5

Aristotle ("the Philosopher"), 7, 13, 17, 19, 23, 29, 34, 37n42, 38n43, 39, 46, 59n1, 72, 73, 74, 77n44, 88, 90, 94, 99, 100, 105, 108, 119, 120, 124, 127n89, 129–30, 132, 133, 135, 136, 143n127, 144n129, 145, 147, 148, 150n147, 160, 164–65, 166n13, 167, 168, 169n18, 174, 176, 177, 182, 192, 193, 196, 197, 202, 205, 206, 207, 208, 209, 210, 211, 212, 214, 216, 218, 220, 221, 223, 227, 241, 280; on God, 40

Arnaldez, R., 19n3, 31n31, 33n35, 47, 53n77, 76n42, 82n50

Arnzen, R., 79n47

Ash'arites, 19n3, 23, 30n29, 33, 36, 37, 45, 53, 54n79, 62n5, 82–83, 88–89

atheism, 89

Attali, J., 56n85

Augustine/Augustinianism, 142n125, 177, 210n25, 246, 248, 258, 261, 263, 266, 283

Avempace, 76n42

Averroes, 5n11, 7, 8, 9, 16, 17, 18, 19n3, 20, 21, 22, 23, 24, 25, 27, 28, 29, 30, 31, 32, 33, 35, 36, 37, 38, 40, 42, 43, 44, 45, 46, 48, 50, 51, 52, 53, 54, 55, 56, 57, 58, 59, 60, 61, 71, 72, 73, 74, 75, 76, 77n43, 78, 79, 80, 81, 82, 83, 84, 85, 86, 87, 89, 90, 91, 92, 93, 94, 95, 96, 97, 98, 120, 121, 123, 126, 131, 135, 142n125, 143, 149n142, 151, 158, 162, 185, 186, 194n70, 201, 202, 203, 205, 211n26, 225n61, 226n64, 227, 228,

Haberman, J., 133n104
Hartmann, N., 193n66
hadith, 27, 31n33, 34, 67
Hadot, P., 235n7
Hallaj, 67n18
Hanbalites, 30n29, 87
happiness: as knowledge of God, 27
Hartman, D., 99n4
Harvey, W. Z., 103n13
Hauser, A., 245n30
Hayoun, M. R., 74n37
ḥayy ibn yaqdhān, 44n35
Healy, N., 246
heart: of the Sufi, 68, 70
Hebrew language, 111, 151n154
Heraclitus, 163
heresy, 32, 50
hikma, 49n68
Hilary of Poitiers, 178
Honnefelder, L., 17n42, 234n3
Hourani, G., 19n3
Houser, R. E., 166n13
Hyman, A., 27n21, 109n32

Ibn al-'Arabi, 7n19, 49n68, 76
Ibn Gabriol, 194n70
Ibn Hazm, 81
Ibn Rushd. *See* Averroes
Ibn Sina. *See* Avicenna
Ibn Tibbon, 103n13
Ibn Tufayl, 44
Ibn Tumart, 19n3
idolatry, 111, 153–54
ijtihād, 43
illumination: divine, 210n25; inner, 64, 71, 76n42
image/likeness, 106
imaginative faculty, 140
imitation. *See* taqlīd
Incarnation, 108, 162, 191, 205n10, 231, 265, 267–69, 272, 274, 283–84, 285
Incoherence of the Incoherence (Averroes), 81, 83n53, 85n55, 86
Incoherence of the Philosophers (al-Ghazali), 22n8, 42, 49, 62, 65, 84, 276n1
innovation. *See* bida'

intellect, 9–10; agent intellect, 72, 73–76, 77, 78–80, 83, 87, 94, 139, 140, 149, 154n159, 201, 202, 219, 222, 229; in al-Ghazali, 61–71; angelic, 221; in Aristotle, 211n27; as creative, 179–80; as fallen, 10, 16, 99–100, 105–111, 121, 139–40, 149–50, 280; gradations of, 183, 185–86, 188–89, 215, 221–24, 227–28; and human knowledge, 221–24; as image of God, 121; material, passive, or potential intellect, 73–76, 83, 87, 94, 201n84, 202–3, 210, 212–15; and metaphysics, 156–57; as mirror, 67–69; nature of, 119–20, 184–85, 190; and negative theology, 118; as one in all men, 216–19, 222, 284–85; practical and speculative, 178–79; and prophecy, 142–43; and reason (*ratio*), 11–12, 15; and revelation, 26, 274–75; and the soul, 208, 209, 215–19; in the universe, 43. *See also* 'aql
intentio, 189–90
interpretation. *See* ta'wil
interpretive effort. *See* ijtihād
Isaac, 141
Isaac Abrabanel, 123n78
Isaiah, 261
Islam, 1, 3, 5, 97, 98, 274–75, 278, 285, 286; as *episteme* of digestion, 6
itiṣāl, 73–78, 84, 92, 95, 275
Ivry, A., 124n81

Jacob, 141
Jacobs, J., 150n147
Janssens, J., 61
Jeffrey, A., 4, 5,n11
Jesus. *See* Christ
Johnson, M., 165n11, 166, n13
Johnstone, B., 236n9
John (evangelist), 247n34, 263, 265
John, Gospel of, 187, 191, 261, 262, 263, 271; Aquinas's commentary on, 260, 261
John the Baptist, 267–68
Jolivet, J., 73n34, 76n40, 224n60
Jordan, M., 241n23, 263n75
Joseph (prophet), 253

Thinking through Revelation: Islamic, Jewish, and Christian Philosophy in the Middle Ages was designed in Jensen Pro, with Mr Eaves Sans Light display type, and composed by Kachergis Book Design of Pittsboro, North Carolina. It was printed on 60# House Natural Smooth Web and bound by Sheridan Books of Chelsea, Michigan.